The Jewish People and Jesus Christ After Auschwitz

A Study in the Controversy Between Church and Synagogue

Jakob Jocz

BAKER BOOK HOUSE

Grand Rapids, Michigan 49506

This volume is dedicated to
my colleagues and students
at Wycliffe College,
University of Toronto,
in gratitude for happy years
of friendship.

Contents

Introduction 7
1. Auschwitz 13
2. Where Was God? 23
3. Where Was the Church? 35
4. The Church and the Jews 52
5. The Way to Reconciliation 63
6. Quest for a New Image of Jews and Judaism 79
7. Who Is Jesus? 102
8. What Is Judaism? 116
9. Who Is a Jew? 127
10. Jews and Jewish Christians 140
11. Conversion and Missions 152
12. The Dialogue 168
13. Persistent Issues 186
Epilogue 211
Notes 218
Bibliography 249
Index of Subjects 259
Index of Names 265

The author wants to express his gratitude to his friend and colleague, the Rev. Norman Green, formerly of the McLaughlin Planetarium, Toronto, for his invaluable help in proofreading; to his wife Joan Alice and his daughter Elisabeth Anne for preparing the indices; and last but not least to Mr. Ray Wiersma, project editor of Baker Book House, for his painstaking care in the production of the book—*todah rabbah*—many thanks.

Introduction

The intended purpose of the present work is to bring the convoluted story of Jewish-Christian relationships after World War II up-to-date. It is meant to serve as a sequel to an earlier book published in 1949—*The Jewish People and Jesus Christ.*

"After Auschwitz" is deliberately chosen as part of the title to indicate the end of a period in history. Auschwitz is a landmark ranking high in the scale of tragic events in the history of the Jewish people, equal to, if not surpassing, the tragedy of the Fall of Jerusalem in A.D. 70. But Auschwitz is not only a tragedy for Jews; it is a tragedy for mankind.

Hitler's political victory in 1933 brought to an end the dream of German Romanticism. The intellectual life of nineteenth-century Germany had been dominated by the Romantic movement, which was founded upon the premise of man's basic incorruptibility. The glorification of man was the dominating theme of the arts and sciences. Swinburne spelled it out with touching naiveté: "Glory to Man in the highest: for Man is master of all things."

After Auschwitz Swinburne's "Hymn to Man" reads like mockery. The German extermination camps are a visible demonstration of the hollowness of the idealistic dream and of the brittleness of pseudo-Christianity. Between Goethe and Hitler stands the cynical mirage of Nietzsche's superman with his contempt for the weak and the humble. It was Nietzsche's achievement to provide the justification for a transition from Romanticism to the philosophy of power. The descent from the mastery of nature to the mastery of man reached its ultimate fulfilment in the gas ovens of the extermination camps. The process of the degradation was mightily accelerated by the domineering role of the physical sciences and technology. By being chained to the machine

7

man was reduced to an animated tool and thus became dispensable. C. G. Jung's warning came too late: "It is dangerous to tell man of his low nature, without telling him of his greatness at the same time."

The problem for contemporary man is the recovery of his God-intended dignity. The moral crisis of our age stems largely from a misinterpretation of man's position in the world. We either over-estimate ourselves and become tyrants, or we underestimate ourselves and wallow in the gutter. Auschwitz became possible only when man was reduced to animal status. As one slaughters cattle so one slaughters man. Blaise Pascal showed remarkable insight when he placed man under the law of contradiction—man is always two things: "the offscouring of the universe" and the image of God. At Auschwitz he revealed himself as a spectre and a monstrosity.

After Auschwitz the world can never be the same. It marks the collapse of all facile idealism. It is not good enough for Goethe to sing, *"Edel sei der Mensch, hilfreich und gut"* ("Man should be noble, helpful and good"), without telling us how to achieve this. The characteristic mark of humanistic philosophy is to camouflage the demonic forces which tear at the human psyche. Godless man is a danger to himself and to society. Godlessness is a destructive force and ultimately self-defeating. Man cannot survive nor can he recover his dignity without faith in God. Auschwitz stands as an ominous warning we cannot afford to neglect.

"After Auschwitz" marks the possibility of a new beginning for the Jewish people, for the Church, for the world. In regard to Jewish-Christian relationships two events are of outstanding importance: the creation of the State of Israel and Vatican II. Both these events will have far-reaching consequences for the future.

In the annals of Jewish history the date May 14, 1948, is of momentous significance: Israel became a sovereign nation. Though the struggle for survival is far from over, the cry *"Yisrael hai!"* ("Israel lives!") has brought new hope and a new dignity to millions of Jews the world over. But as is usual in human affairs, new solutions bring new problems. A political answer to the Jewish problem can never satisfy Israel's aspirations. Many Jews now realize that a political solution is insufficient to solve human needs. National renaissance cannot be separated from spiritual revival. The problem is that traditional Diaspora Judaism is ill-equipped to cope with the demands of an independent State under modern conditions.[1] The political compromise achieved by the inclusion of the orthodox minority in the Israeli Knesset can be only a tentative measure. The majority of the population will not permanently accept the straitjacket of rabbinic rule. Jews, both in Israel and in the Diaspora, are in search of a new spirituality more in tune with the requirements of democracy and freedom. There is gradually evolving a new kind of Judaism, more tolerant, better adjusted to modern life and less introverted.

The question of what is "normative" for Jewish faith is repeatedly raised both in Israel and in the Diaspora. An increasing number of Jewish writers object to making Zionism the quintessence of Jewish faith. Men of the stature of Yehezkel Kaufman, Hans Kohn, David Riesmun, Simon Dubnow, and Philip Roth have come to question the political interpretation of the Jewish destiny.[2] Arthur A. Cohen refuses to regard the political rebirth of Israel as "theologically significant."[3] He interprets the exile as the God-given opportunity for the Jewish mission to the world. Cohen sees Jewish life in the Diaspora as a necessary condition for Israel's calling as the People of God. It would seem that the present *Kulturkampf* involving world Jewry is turning on the question of whether the Israeli State is a cultural or a spiritual solution, or both. Traditionally, culture and religion were never separable in Jewish experience, but under modern conditions of secularized society the shift of emphasis becomes important. In the quest for spiritual values a person may decide against Judaism without ceasing to be a Jew. This is the prevailing situation both in and outside Israel today.[4] Under such conditions the Hebrew Christian has a chance to follow his conscience without compromising his loyalty to his people.

The most remarkable development in Jewish culture is the increasing acceptance of Jesus the Jew. There is a genuine effort made to incorporate the Nazarene into the history of Jewish spirituality, not as the Christ of the Church but as a teacher in Israel. Therefore, the question, "Who is Jesus?" is repeatedly asked and answered in a variety of ways. The question regarding Jesus raises the problem of the "normalcy" of rabbinic Judaism. The discovery of the Qumran literature in the Dead Sea caves opened new insights into the structure of religious life at the time of Jesus. Until that discovery it was taken for granted that Pharisaic Judaism was the normative religion in Israel. The Church therefore was seen as an offspring of the Synagogue. Jewish (and even Christian) writers frequently speak of Christianity as the daughter of Judaism, meaning rabbinic Judaism. But the recently recovered facts contradict such a position. Judaism at the time of Jesus was by no means a homogeneous entity. There were many sects in competition with each other, none normative. This is an important point in assessing the status of ancient Hebrew Christianity. The claim to "Jewishness" cannot be sustained anymore as a prerogative of rabbinism. On historic grounds it will be difficult to substantiate the claim that Hebrew Christians have abandoned Judaism. Rather, they have opposed rabbinic Judaism with their own brand, as did the monks at Qumran.

The other important event which bears upon Jewish-Christian relationships is Vatican II. The Council's conciliatory pronouncement on the Jews initiated a rapprochement between the two faiths which is unique in the history of the Church. Partly, this is due to a new concept of ecumenism which has strong syncretistic overtones, but it is also the expression of a shocked conscience for wrongs committed against the Jewish people.

The churches have renounced proselytism and accepted the principle of dialogue. Such dialogical endeavour is not new in Jewish-Christian relationships. But it was never pursued with such zeal and consistency as it is at present. It involves clergy and laity and there is an ever-growing literature on the subject produced by both sides. It is inevitable that Christian encounter with Jews should raise theological issues such as the Covenant, the question of election, the meaning of Messiahship, etc. Such discussions are important for the clarification of old differences and the dispelling of prejudice. However, Jewish defensiveness and Christian ignorance of Judaism are obstacles to discussion in depth. Much of the dialogue moves on the surface and concerns itself with social issues such as anti-Semitism. There is the additional difficulty that partners in dialogue frequently lack religious conviction and thus become involved in discussion of cultural differences without touching upon matters of faith. On the Jewish side there is a definite reluctance to engage in discussions of a theological nature.

Both Church and Synagogue suffer from the spiritual malaise prevailing in the Western world. Old values are deemed obsolete and new values are not available. Moral disintegration, the prevalence of violence, the breakdown of family life, social unrest and economic uncertainty, make Jews and Christians natural partners in the quest for a better world. These mundane issues tend to take precedence over the more abstract matters of faith. There are yet other reasons why Jewish-Christian dialogue is not conducive to a creative encounter between Church and Synagogue. But in spite of the difficulties, Jews and Christians are discovering each other in a new and civilized way. This fact must not be underestimated and augurs well for the future.

Christians can never give up the vision of a united humanity in Christ when "in the fullness of time" the one new man will appear —messianic man, uniting in his person divided humanity. This is the specific witness of the Christian to Jew and Gentile alike: that Jesus is our peace who has made both "one new man in place of the two" and has "broken down the dividing wall of hostility" (Eph. 2:14–18), so that we may grow together into a "holy temple" to the glory of God the Father. To this end the present work is dedicated.

"After Auschwitz" presents the Church with a singular challenge to repentance. In some strange and demonic way Christianity has been involved in Jewish martyrdom. It is argued on many sides that Christian contempt for Jews throughout history prepared the way for Hitler's success in exterminating one-third of world Jewry. The indictment cannot be treated lightly. A heavy burden of guilt rests upon the Christian conscience. It is this fact, if no other, which demands of the Church the rethinking of its attitude towards the Jewish people not only sociologically but from a theological point of view. These two aspects are closely related and cannot be treated separately.

As to the Jewish attitude towards Jesus, it is closely related to their experience of the historic Church. The Church intrudes at every point in the encounter between the Jewish people and Jesus Christ. Such an encounter is both historically and psychologically conditioned. It cannot be otherwise. It is therefore impossible to deal with our subject without constant reference to the Church, its attitude and its theology regarding the Jewish people. This treatise therefore deals to a large extent with past and present Christian attitudes towards Jews.

The Jew sees Jesus in and through the Church. This is an unfortunate identification but it is one dictated by history. The promising feature of the present is that Church and Jews face each other in a new and chastened spirit. It is the hope and prayer of the author that this treatise will contribute towards a deeper understanding of the issues separating both sides.

There is, however, yet another entity which bears upon the relationship of the Jewish people to Jesus Christ. There have always been Jewish Christians in the Church. Of late, their numbers have greatly increased, especially in the United States. They are known under several names, such as Hebrew Christians, Messianic Jews, B'nai Yeshua, etc. Their relationship with the Gentile Churches is not always clearly defined but their commitment to Jesus as Messiah is beyond question. To the Jewish community they are both a puzzlement and an offence. The greater their emphasis upon their Jewishness the greater the offence.[5] No work on the Jewish people and Jesus Christ is complete without accounting for the presence of Jewish Christians wedged in between the Church and their own people. The present treatise differs from most other works on the same subject in that it pays special attention to the Jewish Christian position in the ongoing dialogue between the Church and the Jewish people.

Unless indicated otherwise, all Scripture quotations are from the Revised Standard Version.

Chapter 1

Auschwitz

The small Polish town of Oswiecim, about halfway between Krakow and Katowice, can be located only on a detailed map. Except for the fact that the camp near the town became one of the most notorious of all extermination camps in Europe during the Second World War, no one outside Poland would have ever heard of the name. Under the German name of Auschwitz it has become a by-word for untold cruelty and human degradation. From statistical records it has been estimated that about four million human beings of different nationalities, but mostly Jews, were put to death behind its barbed wires "mainly by gas, but also by phenol injections, shooting, hanging, malnutrition, and disease."[1]

As a result of this outrage, "Auschwitz" has acquired the meaning of "Holocaust." Jews use "Holocaust" and "Auschwitz" as synonyms. The name *Auschwitz* has thus lost its geographical confinement and stands for genocide pure and simple. "Genocide" is a term which came into heavy use in the mid-forties as the grisly news of the "Final Solution" became known outside Germany.

Rumours of brutality against the Jewish population of occupied Europe began to circulate early in the war. But Nazi propaganda emanating from Germany described these rumours as calumny invented by the enemy. The stories told of such cruelty as to make them unbelievable. Even Jews in Germany were slow to believe that the rumours were true—until they themselves became victims of the Final Solution.

Auschwitz did not happen all at once and without preparation. In *Mein Kampf,* written years before he came to power, Hitler had plainly stated what he intended to do with the Jews. The Final Solution decided upon at the Gross Wannsee Conference (January 20, 1943)[2] was the last act in the process of extermination predetermined long before.[3] While Hitler was engaged in the struggle for power, his anti-Semitic policy, frightening as it was, was so extreme that few people took him seriously. No one could believe that the threats would be acted upon once power passed into Nazi hands, even though *Der Stürmer,* a Nüremberg weekly edited by Julius Streicher, spewed unbounded violence and hatred against the Jews. Its motto was, "The Jews are our misfortune," and its war cry, "Germany awake, Judah perish!"[4] With Hitler's assuming power on January 30, 1933, twelve years of agony began for the Jewish people, which ended only with Germany's unconditional surrender on May 8, 1945. During those dark and bitter years the Jews underwent a martyrdom unequalled in history.

The so-called Nüremberg Laws (Sept. 15, 1935), promulgated "for the protection of German blood and German honour," reduced the Jewish citizens to pariahs. By a decree in 1938 they ceased to be citizens altogether. A further order of August 7, 1938, compelled every Jewish woman to add to her identification card the name *Sarah* and every man the name *Israel.* This was followed by an additional order (Oct. 8, 1938) which provided for every Jewish passport to be stamped with the letter "J," standing for *Jude* (Jew). With the invasion of Poland on September 1, 1939, the physical destruction of the Jews began in earnest.

It is an irony of history that German Jewry, which was destined to be the first to experience the brutal hand of Nazism, was totally committed to the Vaterland. There were no more loyal subjects than the German Jews. A poem by Gustav Levinstein in celebration of the tenth anniversary of the German-Jewish Alliance (1903) well expresses Jewish feeling for their native land. The second stanza reads:

> For Germans we are, to serve the Vaterland
> With all our heart and blood;
> For this we are united with bonds of love.
> What once was dear to us upon this earth
> Of Zion's songs lives on in German tongue.
> The sound of harp wafts through the German land,
> In the poorest hut it can be heard—
> The hope of the Universe—Israel's prayer.[5]

The heart-rending diary of Alice Randt relating her experiences at Theresienstadt concentration camp conveys something of the bitter anguish of a German Jewess who is suddenly made to understand that her pride in Vaterland counts for nothing. In the eyes of her Aryan masters she was not even human, let alone German.[6]

The difficulty in believing that educated people, many with university training, could stoop to such beastly acts of cruelty was utilized by the Nazi war propaganda to dispel the rumours concerning the camps. "The very monstrosity of the crime," writes a Jewish scholar regarding the Final Solution, "made it unbelievable." Of course, Jews were not the only victims of Hitler's tyranny. His political enemies, especially Communists, as well as Poles, Russians, Roman Catholic priests, Protestant ministers, Jehovah's Witnesses, and many others, suffered bitter persecution, and in many instances death. But only Jews and Gypsies "were gassed as a matter of policy."[7]

Henry Friedländer, a specialist in documentation of the Holocaust, writes: "The Nazis persecuted their political and ideological opponents—Marxists, liberals, or Churchmen—for what they believed, said or did; only Jews suffered for just existing."[8] Because of this attitude Jews were by far the largest group in all the labour and extermination camps scattered over occupied Europe. Until the end of the war, new victims were constantly brought into the camps by the never-ceasing transports, where they were subjected to overwork, starvation, disease, or direct massacre. No distinction was made between the young and the old, between men, women, and children. No one received reprieve, not even the dying. Alice Randt's mother, at the age of eighty, was brought to Theresienstadt in a wheelchair.[9] Rudolf Vrba, who became an inmate at Auschwitz at the age of seventeen, gives an eyewitness account of the gassing of a group of four thousand Jews, among them a large number of children. They were all lured into believing that they were on the way to a holiday camp. The youngest child was only about two years old. Vrba writes: "The SS men treated them with consideration, joking with them, playing with the children."[10] This was all part of the ruse. Within a few days they all went up in smoke—literally.[11]

Whatever Auschwitz may mean to the world, for Jews it stands as the symbol of the Holocaust of approximately six million of their people.[12] A disaster of such proportions required a new term to express the magnitude of the loss. The traditional term *ḥurban*, usually associated with the destruction of the Second Temple, was felt to be inadequate to describe the tragedy of European Jewry. "The scandalous uniqueness" of the Holocaust, in Prof. Emil L. Fackenheim's words,[13] could be expressed only by a new nomenclature. The phrase now used among Jews is *yom ha-shoah* ("The Day of the Tempest").[14] "Holocaust"—the burnt-offering or wholesale destruction—and Auschwitz are twin expressions of the terrible and terrifying fact that man is to man a wolf. A letter written by Prof. Fackenheim's wife to a Christian minister well expresses the outer limits of language necessary to give voice to the devastating fact of which Auschwitz is the symbol: "overwhelming in scope, shattering in fury, inexplicable in its demonism."[15]

Mrs. Fackenheim does not exaggerate. The demonic aspect of Auschwitz becomes apparent when it is realized that Hitler's determination to liquidate the Jewish people took precedence over winning the war. To the very end, even when transporting troops was a dire necessity, Eichmann's trains, packed with Jews, were moving towards Poland, without a break. "Hitler's war against the Jews," writes Jacob Robinson, "had priority over his war against all other enemies." He goes on to say: "Himmler and Eichmann indefatigably insisted that despite urgent requirements by the armed forces, priority should be given to the deportations."[16]

The sheer physical extent of the operation must have been staggering. Every country occupied by the Germans had a network of camps. These stretched from Norway in the north to Greece in the south, from the Ukraine in the east to France in the west. In Germany alone there were about twenty-five major camps with several hundred auxiliary camps attached to them. But the most notorious were the extermination camps located in Poland. It was there that the mass murders were initiated in May, 1941, and continued with increasing fury until January, 1945. Chelmno, Belzec, Sobibor, Treblinka, Lublin-Majdanek, Trawniki, Poniatowa, are names written in streams of Jewish blood and sorrow. Above all, there was Auschwitz. As the number of deportees grew, so grew the size of the camp. When it reached its utmost limits an additional camp was established—Birkenau or Auschwitz II. There was even an Auschwitz III. Officially, it was represented as being a labour camp, but in fact it was used for mass destruction. Gerald Reitlinger records: "Throughout the twenty-eight months of selections at Auschwitz the procedure was by rule of thumb. Children under fifteen, men over fifty, and women over forty-five went to the gas chambers. To save the SS difficulties all mothers who accompanied young children went to the gas chambers, irrespective of their age."[17]

The systematic hounding of Jews extended even beyond Europe. Under German influence it spread to Libya and even reached Japan. The tortures were not only physical but also mental. Many of the hapless victims committed suicide both inside and outside the camps. Others faced their death with dignity, especially those sustained by religious faith. Elie Wiesel, himself an inmate at Birkenau, who miraculously survived, tells the ways in which many Jews retained their humanity even under the most depraving circumstances. They pitied their executioners and "went to their deaths without anger, without hate, without sadness and without shame." A number of orthodox Jews even persisted in observing some of the religious precepts, to the point of fasting on the Day of Atonement.[18]

In addition to the extermination camps, where death was administered scientifically, mainly by gassing, executions were taking place all over occupied Poland and Russia: in small towns and villages, in woods and open fields, in prisons, etc. Men, women, and children, even babies in their mothers' arms, were shot like wild animals. There was a ritual for this: first, the victims were made to undress; then the men were put to digging graves; finally all were placed in a position so that they would fall into the mass grave when shot. At the Nüremberg Trials there was sworn testimony by an eyewitness, Hermann Friedrich Graebe, of such an execution outside Dubno in the Ukraine.[19] Others have borne similar witness at the many war trials in Germany and elsewhere. The large collection of photographs taken by German officers as "mementoes" provides authentic evidence of such executions of innocent people. There are also the many memoirs of survivors and the mass of documents which fell into Allied hands at the end of the war.[20] It is not edifying reading. What happened at the camps will not only affect Jews for generations to come, but the whole framework of Western society as the truth about Auschwitz percolates into the subconscious of humanity. The fact of Auschwitz puts under a question mark the whole European enterprise with its culture, isms, and aspirations. In fact, it casts doubt upon the very foundation of Western society. Prof. Fackenheim asked the pertinent question: "Can we confront the Holocaust, and yet not despair?"[21]

The demonic nature of Auschwitz is revealed in the scientific, cold-blooded organization of the enterprise. There was even a rationale behind it: to justify the extermination of people because of their race, Jews were presented as subhuman creatures. This was done with a fanaticism and a conviction based upon pseudo-scientific evidence. For this purpose the racial theory of German or Nordic superiority was adopted as orthodox Nazi doctrine. But even so, this would not yet justify the extermination of an "inferior" race. It had to be shown that Jews were not only subhuman, but a pest worthy of extermination; they were described as "vermin, carriers of germs and diseases."[22] Himmler is quoted as having referred to "the extermination of the Jewish people" as "this most glorious chapter in our history . . . ." He is supposed to have admitted that such an extreme solution was disagreeable both to himself and the rest of Germany, but that as devoted followers of Hitler, they "made this great sacrifice, thus doing their patriotic duty for the sake of Germany's future."[23]

When the events which led up to the Holocaust and the Holocaust itself are not considered as impersonal statistics but as involving real people of flesh and blood, people with aspirations, dignities, and achievements in every sphere of life, the story of Auschwitz acquires dimensions beyond human grasp. Gerd Korman, in the Preface to *Hunter and Hunted,* has put it in these words: "Everything about the Holocaust was extraordinary because the systematic destruction of European Jewry eludes the mind of all understanding."[24] How "extraordinary" the whole matter was becomes evident from the carefully documented presentation of detail provided by H. G. Adler in his book *Der verwaltete Mensch.* Adler's concern is that of a historian who seeks to understand the mind-set of those who were actively engaged in aiding and abetting the grisly enterprise. It could not have been accomplished without the cooperation of hundreds of thousands of otherwise ordinary Germans who were husbands, fathers, and honourable citizens.

Adler's book, which runs to more than a thousand pages, documents the treatment meted out to individual Jews and whole families in the carefully structured system of the "sluice," the conveyor belt, which led to destruction. He does not write as a mere onlooker for he was an inmate, first, at Theresienstadt, and, after thirty-two months there, at Auschwitz. His parents perished in different camps in Poland. Considering his personal involvement, he shows remarkable detachment in his treatment of the subject from a sociological and political perspective.

Adler examines what it meant to take a human being, against his will, from the place of his origin, to deprive him of all means of subsistence, to rob him of everything he possessed, to turn him into a nonperson and to have him killed twice over, first administratively and then physically, and to do all this in a pseudo-legitimate manner.[25]

Der verwaltete Mensch is an unusual title: Verwaltung in German means "administration." The book is an effort at analyzing the history of administration in Germany, before and after Hitler. Der verwaltete Mensch is a human being, a man or woman, who ceases to be a person in his own right and is totally managed by the State, card-indexed, a "statistical factor" with a given number.[26] To accomplish the feat of depersonalization it was not enough to promulgate anti-Jewish laws. It was necessary to create an administrative apparatus for supervising and controlling every single movement of every individual. This task fell to the German police.

Whereas in the past the police force had served as the executor of the law, under Hitler it became the executor of the party—"an instrument of the Führer."[27] But the police were not murderers. They acted as go-betweens by "managing" (verwalten) the system. Their involvement in murder was indirect; their part was bureaucratic murder. Adler calls it Schreibtischmord (desk-murder). The actual management of the slaughterhouse was in the hands of a specially organized party elite known as the SS (Schutzstaffel—security brigade).

The top party hierarchy realized that the grisly work of killing required a special corps totally dedicated to the cause. According to Himmler, the execution of Nazi policy could not be left in the hands of the police for they were under oath as civil servants. What was needed was a specially trained brigade in total obedience to the Führer and inspired by a fanatical faith in National Socialism.[28] To the police was left the administration of the racial laws, which they carried out with proverbial German efficiency. Not a stone was left unturned where Jews were concerned. Not only Jews—men, women, children, and infants—but even half-Jews and the German spouses of Jews, unless they agreed to separation. Among those singled out for victimization were not only

famous scholars, scientists, actors, and artists, but high-ranking officers and highly decorated soldiers, many of them still bearing
the scars of wounds from the First World War for the sake of the
Vaterland.

The "administration" of the racial laws knew no limits and the
addiction to bureaucratic scrupulosity left nothing to chance. The
law was executed to the last letter. Before deportation to the East
Jews were to surrender all they possessed to the State. Nothing escaped the eagle eye of the bureaucrats: a small silver chain removed from a woman's neck, eighteen postal stamps, sixty-nine
Reichspfennige (pennies) from a purse, one pencil, three silver
bracelets, two silver rings, one silver brooch, one pair of silver ear-
rings—all taken from one person. The smallest item was carefully
indexed, and there was a file for every single Jew in Germany.[29]

Here is another instance: four hot-water bottles, a pair of spec-
tacles, sunglasses, two toothbrushes, shoe polish—all confiscated
as property belonging to the Reich. The picayune mind of the
typical German official is nowhere more apparent than in the official lists of items confiscated from the unfortunate deportees:
three pairs of stockings, one blouse, one woollen skirt, one winter
coat, six handkerchiefs.[30]

The restrictions placed upon the Jews were so fantastic as to be
unbelievable. The documents listed by Adler read like a nightmare or the antics of the inmates of a madhouse, with the difference that they were enacted by apparently sane people and in all
earnestness. They performed their task without humour and with
a perverse sense of duty: "Der Jude Sternfeld" was found in possession of a pound of butter and some bread—these were confiscated and distributed among the poor of Steinach. Those who
sold him the food were to be prosecuted. The fact that "the Jew
Sternfeld" was responsible for feeding a family of five made no
difference—Jews must not eat. But this is not all; the same Jew
dared to buy his three-year-old daughter a balloon while attend-
ing a German folk festival. He was accused of "provocative
behaviour."[31]

What bureaucracy, German-style, can achieve is best illustrated
by the case of a certain Simon Ansbacher: he was put on trial for
maltreating seven German geese by confining them in too con-
stricted an area. His punishment: three months in prison twice
over. After this incarceration he was sent to Dachau, where he
died. Simon Ansbacher was a farmer in a small village near Karl-

stadt, a war invalid under constant medical treatment. Mrs. Ansbacher was dutifully informed of her husband's demise, and then sent off to Theresienstadt. And in the meantime there had gone on an endless process of investigation, house-searches, correspondence, etc.—even in abbreviated form the Ansbacher case covers ten pages in Adler's text.[32] The case must have required a whole army of officials buzzing round the poor Jewish farmer's homestead and his seven geese. The Ansbacher crime was that the family was Jewish.

The most brazen brigandage covered by pseudo-legality concerned Jewish property. Nothing, literally nothing, that Jews possessed were they allowed to call their own. Even such personal items as watches, alarm clocks, fountain pens, pencils, razors, pocket knives, scissors, wallets, etc., were confiscated from the deportees. All gold was appropriated by the Treasury of the Reich; other articles were distributed to the soldiers at the front. To add insult to injury, every householder destined for deportation was forced to prepare a list of every item left behind, lock up the house, and surrender the key to the Gestapo. It was a major and severely punishable crime to sell or give away anything in the family's possession. This was regarded as robbing the State.[33]

There were almost no exemptions from being deported. Even those who were privileged to go to Theresienstadt were ultimately destined for extermination in the East. What Theresienstadt was like is vividly described by H. D. Dietrich in *Die Schleuse:* dysentery, typhoid, lice, hunger and humiliation at every step. Here is an example: a certain Dr. Beck was caught smoking a cigarette —he was beaten for the crime and incarcerated for three months. But worse than all the tortures put together was the constant threat of being selected for deportation to the East. Somehow, the inmates knew that from the Polish camps there was no return, in spite of every subterfuge the Germans used to deceive them.

In German eyes, a Jew was a Jew, no matter what his merits. A case in point, taken at random, is that of *Geheimrat* (Privy Councillor) Arthur von Weinberg, a well-known industrialist, highly decorated, related to members of high society in both Germany and Italy, a former officer of the German army—he died at Theresienstadt at the age of eighty-one. There was no escape from the clutches of the police. Except for a small number who managed to cross the frontier illegally and those who were able to hide, every Jew was liable to deportation. Evasion was a capital offence and even sickness was no excuse.[34] Extreme age provided no immunity. *Staatssekretär* (high state-official) von Weizsäcker asked for a Gestapo ruling about a non-Aryan woman aged eighty-seven. She was half-Jewish and living in Berlin: must she be deported? He received the following answer: "In the case of Jews no difference is to be made in respect to age."[35]

In order to camouflage the real purpose for deporting Jews the bureaucrats evolved a jargon of their own. The verb they used for deportation was *abschieben*, which means "to remove," "to push aside"; it can also mean "to transfer," "to move to another place," but is usually applied to objects and only derisively to people. In spite of all the pretense and efforts at deception it soon became known to the general public what were the dire consequences of being *abgeschoben*—"being pushed away" to death.[36] Yet people found it difficult to believe that the rumours about the extermination camps were true. Even German Jews, with few exceptions, failed to grasp the import of the Final Solution.[37] Officially these rumours were impugned as deliberate lies to besmirch the good German name before the world: they were called *Greuelmärchen* —horror tales.[38]

In the task of hunting down Jews, it was not only the police who cooperated to the hilt. Many civilians, especially young people, were constantly on the lookout for hidden Jews. There were, however, exceptions. Adler cites an incident in which a group of working women, witnessing the usual maltreatment of several old Jewesses, protested to the Gestapo with the cry: "Leave the old women in peace. Go to the front where you ought to be!" Not that it made any difference. The police allowed no interference, and the women were soon dispersed.[39] No organized resistance on the part of the public was possible, mainly for two reasons: (1) it became a punishable offence to offer any help whatsoever to Jews; (2) the Nazis made clever use of the German antipathy towards Jews which had built up over the centuries.

The story symbolized by Auschwitz is gruesome and dreadful. Auschwitz was irrational, sinister, and totally inhuman. Behind it was an alliance with the demonic powers of evil whereby men sold their souls to the devil in return for power and greed. The bitter irony of the situation was that the *Untermenschen*—the subhumans —were not the Jews but their executioners, and they did not know it.[40]

Chapter 2

Where Was God?

A uschwitz casts a black pall upon the civilized world. Not only
is man's humanity put under a question mark, but God himself stands accused. Jews are asking insistently: Where was God
when our brothers and sisters were dragged to the gas ovens?

Elie Wiesel relates the gruesome death of a small boy on the
gallows. He was sentenced to die with two men for some trifle
which displeased the Auschwitz hangmen. The boy was so ema-
ciated that his body was too light for the noose to break his neck.
He was thus suspended between heaven and earth with his tongue
out, neither dead nor alive. This was a public hanging which all
the inmates were forced to watch. Wiesel overheard someone in
the crowd groan: "Where is God now?" Inwardly, Elie said to
himself: "Here he is—he is hanging on the gallows." Wiesel has
never rid himself of the sight, nor of the question: Where was the
God of Israel, the God of the Covenant, when his people were led
like sheep to the slaughter?[1]

In confrontation with evil, man has always asked the question,
but for Jews it is a question of life and death. Auschwitz stands between the Jewish people and their traditional faith in God. Loss of
faith in God is also loss of faith in man. In Judaism these two entities are never separated. Trust in God leads to trust in man and
vice versa.

Alexander Donat well describes the effect the Holocaust exerts
upon the Jewish people. Since the days of Moses Mendelssohn
(1729–86) Germany had occupied a special place of dignity for
the Jews of Eastern Europe. It was looked upon as the well of culture, philosophy, and idealism. The Holocaust completely and for
all time shattered that illusion. Donat writes: "What defeated us,
was Jewry's indestructible optimism, our eternal faith in the goodness of man—or rather—in the limits of his degradation." Jews

23

have always looked upon Berlin as the very cradle of lawfulness, enlightenment, and culture: "We just could not believe that a German, even disguised as a Nazi, would so far renounce his humanity as to murder women and children—coldly and systematically." Donat says that Jews paid a terrible price for the delusion, "the delusion that the nation of Kant, Goethe, Mozart and Beethoven cannot be a nation of murderers."[2]

But worse than loss of faith in man is despair about God. Auschwitz has inevitably raised the question whether God exists. And if he exists, does he care? Foremost among those asking the question publicly is Rabbi Richard L. Rubenstein. The Holocaust forced Rubenstein to reconsider his position both as a Jew and as a human being. The result is a radical departure from traditional Judaism and the Covenant relationship between Israel and God. Jews, he writes, can no longer hold on to "the myth of an omnipotent God of History, nor can they maintain the corollary, the election of Israel." All this has been totally changed since Auschwitz. After Auschwitz Jews must be prepared to accept the unpalatable truth that "as children of the Earth, we are undeceived concerning our destiny. We have lost all hope, consolation and illusion."[3]

Disillusionment with God and man has led Rubenstein to deny that there is any meaning to life and existence. He now views himself as placed in an empty universe and is prepared to draw the consequences from this discovery. He writes: "I have elected to accept what Camus has rightly called the courage of the absurd, the courage to live in a meaningless, purposeless cosmos rather than believe in a God who inflicts Auschwitz on his people."[4] The logic behind Rubenstein's position is dictated to him by the meaning of the Covenant: the God of Israel is the God of history. If this is the case, Hitler must be viewed as an instrument of God's wrath, in the same way as Nebuchadnezzar was viewed by Jeremiah (Jer. 27:6–7). But how is one to connect the God of Israel to Auschwitz and still make sense? Either God is a sadist who inflicts suffering for his own pleasure, or else he measures out chastisement for moral ends. In either case Auschwitz does not fit into the scheme, for the gas ovens where thousands perished served no purpose to God or man. Rubenstein continues: "If the God of the Covenant exists, at Auschwitz my people stood under the most fearsome curse that God ever inflicted. If the God of history does not exist, then the Cosmos is ultimately absurd in origin and meaningless in purpose." There is an undeniable pious streak in Rubenstein's reasoning: he feels that connecting God to Auschwitz would be obscene. He prefers, therefore, to deny God's existence rather than to assume his involvement in the Holocaust. But denial of God leads to the fearful sequence: "We have been thrust into a world in which naked amorphous life proliferates, has its hour, only to disappear amidst further proliferation of life .... We simply are there but for a moment only to disappear into the midnight silence of Eternal Chaos."[5]

This mood of total defeat, Chaos spelled with a capital *C*, well conveys the climate of thought as a result of Auschwitz not only among Jews. But Jews are more intimately involved in the story of Auschwitz than is anyone else. There is an undeniable consistency in Rubenstein's expression of nihilism: "My position is not a-theism," he explains, "it is paganism." What concerns him vitally "is the character of religious existence *after* Auschwitz." Once faith in the traditional God of history has become impossible, what does one put in his place?[6]

This does not mean the end of religion for Rubenstein. Other Jewish leaders, like Rabbi Sherman Wine of Birmingham, Michigan, still pursue religious ends. But it is a religion without God. This trend has gained intellectual respectability since Julian Huxley lent his authority for atheistic religion.[7] Mordecai M. Kaplan's *Judaism Without Supernaturalism* (1958) and Rabbi Jack J. Cohen's *Case for Religious Naturalism* (1958) move in the same direction. The religious principle underlying Kaplan's "Reconstructionism" is "the centrality of the peoplehood of Israel." If not outright atheism, it is a form of agnosticism with the Jewish people at its core. In Cohen's scheme of things faith in a personal God is no longer possible in a scientific age.[8]

For Rubenstein, turning to neopaganism is the only way out of spiritual chaos. "To be a pagan," he writes, "means to find once again one's roots as a child of the Earth and to see one's own existence as wholly and totally an earthly existence."[9] Except for mother Earth there is nothing left for man to hold on to anymore. Not only Jewish bodies went up in smoke at Auschwitz, but the Covenant as well: "the Covenant died there."[10] This sentiment is echoed by Rabbi Marc E. Samuels: "The Holocaust has, indeed, made it very difficult to believe in a God of love, a God of justice and goodness. It has also made it difficult to believe sincerely in a God of history."[11]

The supreme demonstration of God's failure is seen by many

Jews in the fact that in history brutal force prevails over justice. There seem to be no human rights, except the right of the strong. But not all writers are prepared to take the extreme position of God-denial. Elie Wiesel, himself a survivor of Auschwitz, distinguishes between rebellion against God and a quarrel with God. He finds it curious that most of the rebels are men who have never been in a concentration camp. Those who have been inmates and have survived the agony do not rebel; they simply keep silent. Wiesel reserves for himself the right to question God. This is in keeping with biblical tradition. He dramatizes the Jewish quarrel with God in a story about a Synagogue beadle in a small Polish town. The beadle, a half-crazed Jew by the name of Reb Bunem, returns to the Synagogue each time a transport of Jews is removed from the town. He wants God to know that he is still there. In the end, all Jews have gone, except Bunem. He enters the Synagogue, opens the ark of the Torah, and cries: "Master of the Universe, I want you to know that I am still here—but where are you?"

Elie Wiesel refuses to yield to despair.[12] God is still the God of Israel. But as a former inmate of Birkenau, Wiesel confesses: "I have my problems with God, believe me. I have my anger and I have my quarrels and I have my nightmares. But my dispute, my bewilderment, my astonishment is with men." This means that Wiesel refuses to put the whole burden of blame upon God's shoulders; at least a major part of the blame is with men.

Other writers are not so generous. In Bernard Malamud's novel *The Fixer*, Yakov is in prison, accused of the "blood libel," namely, that Jews use Christian blood, chiefly of innocent children, for making the unleavened Passover bread. In his bitterness he says to his father-in-law who visits him: "I blame him [God] for not existing." He then refers to Job's experience: "To win a lousy bet with the devil he [God] killed off all the servants and the innocent children of Job. For that alone I hate him, not to mention the ten thousand pogroms . . . ." We have here an interesting dichotomy between outright denial and reproach. Yakov is saying two things: God does not exist and God is unjust. This quarrel with God is not unknown to biblical man. We find it in the Psalms, in the prophetic writings, and elsewhere. Worse than reproaching God is utter indifference. The bulk of American Jewry is suffering not from irreligion but nonreligion. Frequently God plays no part in the Synagogue. Norton Mezvinsky, in his review of *Jews of Subur-*

bia (1959) by Albert I. Gordon, shows surprise "that there is nearly no mention of God" in the responses to a questionnaire attempting to discover why Jews join a synagogue: "There was a conspicuous absence of answers suggesting prayer and/or worship."[13] Faith in the living God is largely replaced by a desire to preserve Jewish identity, and Jewishness is reduced to sociology.[14]

Wiesel found that the weakest resistance in concentration camps came from the irreligious Jews; they easily yielded to torture and were quick to cooperate with their torturers. These were "the intellectuals, the liberals, the humanists, the professors of sociology, and the like." On the other hand, God-fearing men (Roman Catholic priests, Protestant ministers, Hasidic rabbis, orthodox Jews) remained firm; "they were the resisters." Yet the problem about God remains. It is not a problem for the atheist but a problem for the believer. Addressing himself to Rubenstein, Wiesel asks: "Can you compare the tragedy of the believer to that of the unbeliever?" Wiesel continues: "The real tragedy, the real drama is the drama of the believer," who chooses in spite of all the suffering "to believe in God."[15] We understand him to say that the atheist's answer is too easy a solution. It is the suffering saint who has the problem: Where is God? Wiesel, who is himself a sufferer, expresses astonishment at man's capacity to inflict suffering upon others, while his unbounded admiration goes to those who are able to endure suffering with dignity and courage. The Jewish inmates who retained their humanity in the face of greatest provocation thereby gave testimony to the power of faith. They are the real heroes. Though it is more difficult to live with God than without him, the true believer, betrayed by man and abandoned by God, must not yield. He must retain his *Jewishness* and continue in prayer as a man of faith, even though he has a quarrel with God. Such is Elie Wiesel's answer to the question: Where was God when Israel was being martyred?[16]

The problem of God's silence is for Wiesel the greatest trial of faith. He sees it as the central dilemma in the story of the Holocaust (cf. his play "The Trial of God," 1979). In all his writings there is an unresolved tension between his faith and his rebellion. André Neher discusses the problem of God's silence both in the Old Testament and in Wiesel's works. The question is raised: Is God playing hide-and-seek with man? Both Job and Wiesel face the same problem. But for both of them there is hope—for there is always a tomorrow. In the end neither God nor his people can be defeated. Neher quotes Margarete Sussmann: *"Nie ist Liebe anders als Heimsuchung. Indem Gott sein Volk sucht, wie er Hiob sucht, sucht er es heim, zu sich"* ("Never is love other than a search and trial. God in seeking his people, as he seeks Job, seeks it for himself" —there is a play on the word *Heimsuchung,* which means both "visitation" [cf. Exod. 34:7] and "home-seeking").[17]

There is a difference between blaming God and blaming man. Believers may be quarreling with God but know that man is the real culprit. Man's capacity for evil seems beyond limit. If God is guilty, he is guilty only for creating man. Eugene B. Borowitz feels sheer horror at "man's talent for creating evil." What is even more frightening to him is the fact that so much evil comes to us in the guise of good. Borowitz quotes the Jewish scholar, Prof. Irving Kristol, who expresses his doubts about the moral structure of the universe: "The spiritual distress of the modern world does not arise merely because man perversely chooses evil rather than good. If it were as uncomplicated as all that, present day Judaism . . . would have an answer right at hand. The horror that breathes into our faces is the realization that evil may come by doing good—not merely intending to do good, but doing it."[18] This extreme pessimism so characteristic of our age has made devastating inroads into Jewish thinking as a result of the Holocaust. It questions not only human evil, but even human good. This is what is meant by the "crisis of faith."[19] The step from pessimism to nihilism is a short one. The gap between traditional Jewish optimism and philosophical nihilism as embodied in the writings of Jean-Paul Sartre is in danger of disappearing. Sartre's play "The Devil and the Good Lord" presents Kristol's theme in dramatized form. The legendary Götz von Berlichingen, the hero of the Peasant War in Germany (sixteenth century), is inspired by high idealism, but his best intentions only bring additional suffering to those whom he wants to help. The philosophical implication of Sartre's play is that this is an irrational and empty universe and that only chaos rules in the affairs of men.

Human behaviour is certainly a puzzle in its utter irrationality. Elie Wiesel asks: "Is it possible to be born into the upper or middle-class, receive a first-rate education, respect parents and neighbours, visit museums and attend literary gatherings, play a role in public life, and begin one day to massacre men, women and children, without hesitation and without guilt . . . ?" He wants to know how "one may torture the son before his father's eyes and still consider oneself a man of culture and religion. And dream of a peaceful sunset over the sea."[20]

Prof. L. Rubinoff echoes Wiesel's puzzlement at the contradiction. For him Auschwitz "demonstrates that culture and cold-blooded murder do not necessarily exclude each other." Rubinoff is forced to conclude "that culture and the indifference to the spectacle of evil" are able to coexist without much difficulty. The discovery of the demonic dimension of evil has opened a gap in traditional Jewish thinking regarding man. Perhaps it is more than a gap; it is a precipice. Rubinoff writes: "The Jew was the victim not only of demonic evil but of the indifference of mankind to what was happening. God's failure was matched by man's."[21]

The crisis is therefore not only religious. As a result of the Holocaust, Jews are being forced to reassess man's humanity in a technological age. The Holocaust casts a deep shadow upon the whole endeavour of modern man. Rabbi Rubenstein sees Auschwitz not as an accident but as a triumph of our technology: "Auschwitz was in reality the first triumph of technological civilization in dealing with what may become a persistent human problem, the problem of the waste disposal of superfluous human beings in an overpopulated world."[22] What has come to the surface is the frightening discrepancy between being human and being "civilized." Civilization as comprehended in technological terms has the capacity to dehumanize man and to make a parody of his better self. "The most awful figure of this century," writes Prof. Franklin H. Littell, "is the technologically competent barbarian—especially when he claims the sanction of religion for his politics of pride."[23] The precariousness of the human condition appears most clearly whenever man has been entrusted with power, whether it be physical or spiritual. It is at this point that the vulnerability of man becomes the testing ground of his humanity. In the well-chosen words of Father Bertram Hessler: "God's majesty is nowhere so vulnerable as in man, His unprotected image."[24] Man is capable of great and heroic sacrifice and of abysmal villainy. The most puzzling fact of all is that the selfsame person is capable of both.

The ambiguity of the human condition becomes apparent in the inward struggle between good and evil. There is a conflict in the human soul which even the worst cannot escape. We are told that Himmler, while watching an execution, suddenly "turned giddy and almost fell to the ground."[25] Himmler was not totally devoid of human feeling. Even Rubenstein, in spite of his pessimism, acknowledges the awesome interaction between "Promethean self-assertion and penitent submission" in the human soul.[26] Hans Frank, the notorious Governor-General of occupied Poland, shed tears while watching a film of German atrocities. At the Nüremberg Trials he acknowledged his part of the blame for the extermination of Polish Jewry, though he placed the main responsibility upon others.[27]

Those who blame God for Auschwitz are apt to overlook the main culprits. The Nazi death machine could not have functioned with such efficiency without the cooperation of thousands of Germans and others, in some cases even Jews. A multitude of men and women had a hand in the wholesale murder, either directly or indirectly. Emmanuel Ringelbaum's bitter indictment of the Jewish police in the Warsaw ghetto is evidence of the fact that there is no radical difference between men.[28] There is a fearful truth in the saying that each man is a potential criminal. The ghetto police, all Jews, to ingratiate themselves with their German masters, rounded up men and women for deportation even above the assigned quota. That there were orgies and frivolities in the ghetto is shown by the fact that sixty-one night clubs carried on a flourishing business in 1941. The Warsaw *Judenrat*, which was composed of the leading Jews in the community, has been accused of many injustices against fellow Jews. The image of God in man is indeed awesomely unprotected. As one Jewish writer put it: "We are all hooked on crime . . . in our innermost being most of us partly wish to be gangsters ourselves."[29]

The spiritual disarray resulting from the Holocaust affects every aspect of Jewish life. "The Absence of God" is a theme which recurs in literature and art. Harold Fish describes the extent to which Hebrew poetry is affected by "the two poles of messianic hope and metaphysical despair."[30] "Messianic hope" stands for Israel; "metaphysical despair" has reference to God, man, and the world. The bitterness of despair finds personal expression in Erwin Blumenfeld's book *Durch tausendjährige Zeit*. Blumenfeld's response to his frustration with mankind is unmitigated hate.[31] But man cannot successfully continue in hate without harm to his own human self. In order to live he has to come to terms with himself and with the world. This means coming to terms with God either by total rejection or total submission to his unsearchable ways.

There are degrees of doubt and degrees of faith. Rabbi Bruce S. Warshal regards it as a special challenge to Jews of today to spell out in particulars what they expect of God and what is to be expected of themselves in order to live up to the Covenant. The concept of the Covenant with Israel, the rabbi suggests, is a kind of *chutzpah* ("presumption"), and reveals something of the high view ancient Jews took of the worth of man. Warshal argues: "An inherently evil man could in no way gain the stature needed to write a contract with God." It is obvious that for Rabbi Warshal the Covenant is not a gift but a pact binding both parties—Israel and God.[32] If this is the case, something has gone wrong with the pact, as is evident from the fact of Auschwitz. But such an argument puts faith in peril. Rabbi Ignaz Maybaum, himself a refugee from Hitler's Germany, seeks to give to Auschwitz a positive connotation. He compares God's use of Hitler to his use of Nebuchadnezzar (Jer. 27:6). Hitler in God's purpose performed the role of a surgeon with the result that a new Israel was born: "*Am Yisrael ḥai*" ("The people of Israel live") is the cry.[33]

A somewhat similar position is taken by Prof. Emil Fackenheim. He regards Auschwitz as a challenge, a commandment to active fidelity: those who believe in the voice of the Prophets will know that their voices speak louder than the voice of Hitler. God's promise of salvation reaches beyond the crematoria and the silences of Auschwitz.[34] Eliezer Berkovits, an orthodox rabbi, had the courage to exercise his faith and exonerate God for Auschwitz.[35] "This is the first time to my knowledge," says a reviewer of Rabbi Berkovits's book, "that an orthodox rabbi has undertaken to write a Holocaust theodicy." Other writers find it more difficult to explain God's goodness in relation to his power. Elliot N. Dorff writes: "If we are going to be able to make any sense of the relationship of God to the Holocaust, we are going to have to sort out once again the two elements of power and goodness." Dorff suspects that there must be some sort of evil element involved in God's reign: "There is evil in this world, and to leave God out of it would," he thinks, "make him a very pallid God, a mere personification of our desires and moral conceptions."[36] Such a positive declaration of the assimilation of evil in the Godhead is regarded by S. Levin, a Johannesburg physician, as a special trait of Judaism. Levin explains that a God with limits "is not found in Christianity or Islam but is a unique Jewish concept." It is typical for Judaism, according to him, to "excuse God's culpability for evil on the grounds that He is somehow uninvolved in its perpetration, and this within the paradox of omnipotence and omnipresence."[37]

But in spite of these gallant efforts on the part of those who acknowledge the evil but refuse to surrender to despair, the problem remains. Rubenstein continues to point an accusing finger heavenwards: "A God who tolerates the suffering of even one innocent child is either infinitely cruel or hopelessly indifferent." He agrees with Rabbi Cohen that it is not possible for contemporary man to believe in a personal God.[38] Rubenstein's surrender of faith is reflected in his assessment that man "has proven capable of irredeemable evil." He sees man as "essentially a tragic, ironic figure of extremely limited possibilities."[39] The demonic side of man is part and parcel of a "demonic cosmos" in which man finds himself trapped "without hope of exit."[40]

Only those who still hold to the God of Israel are able to come to terms with the Jewish past in the context of the Covenant. This constitutes a major trial of faith. Prof. Seymour Siegel of the Jewish Theological Seminary of America acknowledges that "the most poignant challenge to the doctrine of Israel's uniqueness in our time comes from the experience of the Holocaust." But unlike Rubenstein, Siegel refuses to accept the extreme position that the Covenant is an illusion. On the contrary, like Berkovits, he sees the Holocaust as a sign of the Covenant's affirmation of Israel's uniqueness, though "perhaps in a perverse" way. "The Jew stands for something which tyrants cannot abide." And thus, according to Siegel, the Holocaust must be seen in the light of the very fury and irrationalism of Israel's persecutors.[41]

The result of a more positive perception of the Holocaust is a renewed determination for survival as Jews. Hitler must not be allowed the posthumous victory which would be his if Jewry were to surrender to despair. To this end Rubinoff agrees with Fackenheim that there must be added an additional commandment to the 613 rabbinic precepts which govern Jewish life, the commandment for survival: "Midrashic stubbornness begins with a refusal to be terrorized by Auschwitz into adopting a posture of apocalyptic despair."[42] This, however, does not mean that the quarrel with God is over. The search for a metaphysical rationale for the Holocaust still continues. The Holocaust remains a puzzle and a mystery even to the God-fearing Jew. Some try to rationalize by connecting the Holocaust to the national renaissance. They see, as it were, in the establishment of the Israeli State a compensation for the suffering in Europe. Rubenstein is one of those who reject the argument. The puzzle remains. In the words of Rabbi Reuben Slonim: "One cannot approach this terrible time [of the Holocaust] without a sense of dreadful mystery."[43]

This is also the sentiment expressed by Prof. Uriel Tal of Tel Aviv, who recognizes in the Holocaust a strange element of metaphysical significance which reaches "beyond the limitations of time, of space, of causality, or any category of reason."[44] Other writers feel the same way. Gerd Korman of Cornell University, who provided the Preface for the collection of essays *Hunter and Hunted*, writes: "Everything about the Holocaust was extraordinary because the systematic destruction of European Jewry eludes the mind of all human understanding." What puzzles him is the totality of the death verdict: "Each and every Jew, even if he considered himself a non-Jew or a convert to Christianity, was marked for annihilation."[45] Even more puzzling to him is the fact that this was perpetrated by one of the West's most enlightened nations, while other nations acquiesced in this extraordinary attempt at mass murder.

No human being is able to live successfully with the burden of meaninglessness. The quest for meaning in human affairs is a psychological necessity. The difficulty of understanding what happened at Auschwitz lies in its "radical uniqueness," as Prof. Rubinoff puts it. The fact that it was "pure demonic evil, for evil's sake," is difficult (if not impossible) to grasp "in terms of normal categories of scientific inquiry." It contradicts all the accepted standards of reason and moral values. Auschwitz can be considered only at the level of the absurd and the perverse. But Jewish tradition allows no room for absolute chaos in the order of things. Such a world would contradict the purposefulness of a good and intelligent God. Behind even the most grotesque events in history is some purpose; otherwise life ceases to make sense. The questions about Auschwitz are, therefore, in the last analysis, questions about God. In what sense is he still the *ribono shel olam* ("the Lord of the Universe")?[46]

In the Yiddish weekly of Buenos Aires there appeared a piece by Zvi Kolitz which has since been copied by many writers. Entitled "Yossel Rackover Speaks with God," it was mistakenly regarded as an authentic document from the Warsaw ghetto, dated April 28, 1943. What Zvi Kolitz is saying is felt by a multitude of Jews in this post-Auschwitz era.

The fictional Yossel Rackover of Tarnopol, a follower of the Hasidic Rabbi of Ger and a descendant of a long line of devout Jews, is addressing himself directly to God, as is the custom among Hasidim. He tells God: "I am ashamed of being a man and not a dog." He complains to the Master of the Universe that life for Jews has become a "disaster, death a release, man a torment, the beast a model, the sun a terror and the night a comfort." After pouring out his heart to God he bangs with his fists on the table of the Almighty and demands an explanation. These are his words: "Something extraordinary is taking place in the world —ours is the time when the Almighty turns His face away from those who pray to Him."

Yet Yossel Rackover's quarrel with God is not that of a stranger but of a son. He says: "I believe in the God of Israel, even though He has done everything to destroy my faith in Him. I believe in His laws, even though I cannot justify His ways . . . . Earlier in my life I often wished to draw a dividing line between what He says and what He does. Now, I see that our greatest test as the chosen people is to do what we know He says in spite of everything that He seems to be doing."[47]

Faith in the God of Israel, in the God of the Covenant, in the God of history, is always a test and a challenge, but after Auschwitz it is an agonizing venture for every thinking Jew.[48]

Chapter 3

Where Was the Church?

Not only European Jews, but Jews the world over, emerged from the shock of the Holocaust reeling and stunned. The first reaction was despondency but this soon gave way to the determination not to yield. Jewish resilience asserted itself and the will for survival was only strengthened by the calamity. Defiance of Hitler and his Final Solution became a matter of honour. The cry "*am Yisrael ḥai*" ("the people of Israel live!") became the motto of world Jewry. The late H. D. Leuner, a Jewish Christian and a fervent Zionist, raised the question whether Auschwitz may not be regarded as the end of an era and a new beginning for the Jewish people. He answered the question in the affirmative. The Holocaust as the watershed of evil's triumph "in a so-called Christian world" was not the end of the story.[1] After Auschwitz a new chapter in Jewish history must begin, inspired by a new faith and a new hope in the Jewish destiny.

But Auschwitz not only left the Jews decimated and bleeding; the Christian Church was equally stunned. How was such a crime possible in the heart of Christian Europe? Where were Christians when Jews were hunted like animals and sent to the slaughter? Where was the Church?

The sense of guilt, both among Christians and non-Christians, which quickened in the wake of Hitler's massacres was instrumental in the appearance of the Israeli State in 1948. It was widely felt that there could be no real security for a homeless people except a haven which they might call their own. In addition to the tremendous flood of Jewish refugees, it was world opinion, as expressed at the United Nations, which made Jewish national renaissance possible. The Western nations, especially Great Britain and the United States, had a nagging conscience with respect to the Jews in occupied Europe. But more particularly, the Christian churches knew themselves guilty of both acts of commission and acts of omission. This raised one of the most complex questions in Jewish-Christian relationships, namely, the question of anti-Semitism. Christians were stung by the Jewish accusation that Hitler's massacres were the fruits of age-long Christian anti-Jewishness. Hitler, Jews maintained, was the direct heir of Christian anti-Semitism. This initiated a process of research and examination which is still going on. An important landmark in the process was the pronouncement of Vatican Council II regarding the Jewish people.

It is only natural that the process of reexamination began in Germany. Both the Protestant and the Roman Catholic churches emerged from the war with a crushing sense of guilt. Blind submissiveness to Hitler, fanatical nationalism, a willingness to compromise in doctrine and morals, and, above all, ordinary human cowardice, made the bulk of German Christians indifferent to Jewish suffering. The most obvious culprits in this respect were the Church leaders. This was especially the case in the Protestant camp, where loyalty to Hitler ran deeper than among Roman Catholics. It is therefore not surprising that immediately after the war, as early as October, 1945, the Lutheran Church of Germany made a public confession of guilt for its shameful failure to act more courageously in defence of the persecuted Jews.

Germany at large, and the German Church in particular, have a long history of anti-Jewishness. Therefore, resistance to racial discrimination against Jews introduced by the Hitler regime was only minimal. Failure of nerve became apparent in 1938 after the pogrom which the Nazis called *Kristall Nacht* (the night of broken glass). This was the night when rampaging Nazi youths assaulted Jewish men and women, broke windows, looted shops, and burnt synagogues. The reaction on the part of the churches to this shameful display of savagery was almost nil. Except for a few protesting voices, chiefly that of Dietrich Bonhoeffer, nothing was said by leading churchmen. Not even the Confessional Church, which was at variance with the State on some important issues, had much to say in defence of the Jews. Karl Barth summed up the situation: "Many of the best men in the Confessional Church still close their eyes to the insight that the Jewish problem [has] today become a question of faith."[2] He accused himself for failing to include the Jewish question as a matter of prime Christian concern when the two Barmen Declarations were formulated in 1934.[3] Only Bonhoeffer reacted vigourously to what happened on November 9, 1938. He is reported to have said: "Only he who cries in protest on behalf of the Jews has a right to sing the Gregorian chant."[4]

On the Roman Catholic front the performance was not much better, though the bishops were well aware of the tragedy that was being played out before their eyes. This is readily admitted by the Roman Catholic sociologist, Prof. Gordon C. Zahn. He attributes their poor performance to a failure of nerve. The only justification he can think of is that others in less tense circumstances have done the same. Zahn asks: "Was the silence of the German hierarchy over the war atrocities committed by the Nazi forces that much more complete than the silence of the American Catholic hierarchy over My Lai . . . the widespread use of napalm and chemical warfare against a predominantly peasant population? I am afraid not."[5] But this hardly exonerates the German Church leaders; it only shows up the pusillanimity of Christians in time of crisis.

But not all Christians were silent, though it was difficult, even dangerous within the Reich, to protest with any measure of success. When the law demanded that all Jews appear in public with the Star of David upon them, the wife of a pastor in Breslau published a petition on behalf of the *Sternträger* (star-bearers). The result was that she was immediately arrested.[6] But in spite of the danger, voices were raised and clandestine rescues were carried out both in Germany and throughout occupied Europe. The official voice of the Church may have been muted, even silent, but Christian institutions, groups, and an untold number of individuals, were actively engaged in helping persecuted Jews, wherever and whenever possible. It is a heartening experience to read Kurt R. Grossmann's book *Die unbesungenen Helden (The Unsung Heroes)*[7] and discover that the spirit of humanity was not entirely dead during those bitter years of tragedy. Philip Friedman's *Their Brothers' Keeper* (1957) well augments the story of heroic courage and self-sacrifice of noble men and women in all walks of life who took every risk in their effort to help the persecuted. These records show that not all Germans, and certainly not all Christians, betrayed their humanity in order to save their own skin. Though the main rescue work took place outside the Reich, rescue work was performed by Germans, sometimes even with the help of the police. In this, clergy and laymen combined forces to outwit the Nazi executioners wherever possible.

There has been much controversy regarding the silence of Pope Pius XII.[8] He is accused of failing to condemn Hitler and his henchmen publicly. His motives have been scrutinized by both his defenders and detractors. The depiction of the Pope in Rolf Hochhuth's play *Der Stellvertreter* ("The Deputy"), which was first performed in West Berlin in February, 1963, released a flood of letters to the press both in defence and criticism.[9] The central issue in Hochhuth's play is the silence of the Pope, who refrained from any open condemnation of the Nazi inhumanities while he knew that millions were being put to death. But Pinchas Lapide has been able to provide evidence that the Pope's reticence was not the result of personal fear of Hitler nor of political expediency. Lapide quotes sources to prove that any public pronouncement would only have resulted in greater loss of life for Jews and others. Lapide expresses the conviction that the Pope's method of quiet diplomacy proved by far a more effective way, and he credits the Pope's efforts with the saving of some 860,000 Jewish lives. Another Jewish writer, himself a deportee from Rumania to the Ukraine, supports the contention that the Pope beneficially intervened during the time of bitter trial. The Pope's nuncios in Portugal, Spain, France, Italy, Rumania, Hungary, and Slovakia, were all exerting their influence on behalf of the persecuted Jews.[10]

Opinion is divided on this issue. Carlo Falconi, a Roman Catholic, admits the culpability of Pope Pius XII, though he has no doubt about his piety and sincerity. Falconi rejects the idea that silence was the best method to adopt. He maintains that a Church worthy of its Christian name cannot afford to remain silent in the face of such provocation.[11] The fact remains, however, that the Pope, with the help of his many emissaries, was able to exert a moderating influence in many lands of occupied Europe. This applies preeminently to Italy, where the Pope made it possible for numbers of Jews to find shelter in monasteries, nunneries, and other Catholic institutions. This has been acknowledged by the former chief Rabbi of Rome, Eugenio Zolli, who was taken under the protection of the Vatican and employed as a librarian.[12]

In Germany itself, in spite of the stranglehold of the Gestapo on the population, not all Church leaders were intimidated to the same degree. Monsignor Lichtenberg, Dean of the Roman Catholic Cathedral Church in Berlin, spoke out openly from the pulpit against Jewish persecution with the result that he spent two years and died at Dachau.[13] Philip Friedman writes that the Roman Catholic Bishop of Münster was "a lone strong voice in a land where silent obedience had become the accepted way of life." There were others. Friedman writes with appreciation of three Cardinals: Clemens August von Galen, Michael Faulhaber, and Count von Preysing. As a result of the Pope's Christmas broadcast in 1942, he himself was accused by Heydrich of defending the Jews.[14] Dr. Gertrud Luckner, one of the originators of the *Freiburger Rundbrief*, a Roman Catholic publication dedicated to the defence of the Jewish people, spent some hard years in a concentration camp for her work among Jews.[15]

The most dramatic resistance came from outside the Reich. In countries like Denmark, Finland, and Holland the Christian effort on behalf of Jews was both courageous and sacrificial. Friedman writes about Denmark: "The story of the survival of Danish Jewry is the story of Denmark's Christian free men, who defied all the might of Germany to carry out one of the most miraculous sea rescues in history."[16] In this dramatic venture, the Danish King, a committed Christian, played a key role. Except for fifty-two Jews who were deported prior to the rescue operation, the whole Jewish community of Denmark was clandestinely removed to Sweden by small ships.

When the occupying Germans demanded from the Finnish Government the surrender of the Jewish inhabitants, the Finnish Foreign Minister bluntly declared: "Finland is a decent nation. We will rather perish together with the Jews . . . . We will not surrender the Jews!"[17] Of Finland's two thousand Jews only four were deported.

There is the moving story of a Lithuanian priest in charge of thirty Jewish children whose parents were executed by the Germans. When a German officer arrived to remove the children from the church where they were in hiding, the priest blocked the entrance with the words: "If you kill the children, you will have to kill me first!" The Germans killed both him and the children.[18]

In Mława (Poland) the Gestapo arranged a public execution of fifty Jews and forced the local population to witness the grisly spectacle in the interests of "racial education." One of the Poles was so outraged by the gruesome sight that he started shouting:

"Down with Hitler! Innocent blood is being shed!" He was instantly arrested and executed.[19]

It was a capital offence to shelter Jews in those fearful days. "People found guilty of sheltering or helping a Jew were usually executed on the spot without trial, beaten to death in jail, or hanged publicly."[20] There were cases when men and women paid with their lives for the mere selling of bread to a Jew. This gives some indication of what was involved in the work of rescue. It was not only a matter of personal safety but of exposing members of one's family to suffering and even death. Eduardo Focherini, the editor of a Bologna Catholic daily, raised his voice in defence of Jews. In punishment, all his seven children were murdered by the Nazis.

Joan Bel Geddes, in the course of reviewing Friedman's book, adds some important details of her own concerning Roman Catholic involvement in resisting Hitler's racial policy. "In August 1941, the Dutch hierarchy came into open conflict with the German authorities over a decree that Jewish children were to be taught only by Jewish teachers." On other issues concerning Jews, "when private protests did not produce any but minor concessions, the Archbishop of Utrecht issued a magnificent pastoral letter." This letter was read in all the Catholic churches of Holland on Sunday, July 26, 1942, and aroused much excitement.[21] The other Dutch denominations were equally defiant and many Christians were actively involved in rescuing Jews.

Père Marie-Benoit's daring exploits in France on behalf of Jews have become legendary. Archbishop Gerlier took an active part in the clandestine activities of an anti-Nazi Christian group, *l'Amitié Chrétienne*, which was directed by the Jesuit priest Pierre Chaillet. This group was chiefly concerned with the rescue of children. A Carmelite priest, Abbé Bunel, known in the resistance movement as "Jacques," was ultimately deported to a concentration camp for his rescue work among Jews. Together with Chaillet, the priest Deveaux specialized in the rescue of infants. Fr. Chaillet stood up to the Vichy Government and defiantly refused to surrender his charges to the Germans. It is estimated that about twelve thousand Jewish children were saved thanks to the courage and ingenuity of these men. Of this number some four thousand were smuggled across the frontier to Switzerland. Unfortunately, about fifteen thousand Jewish children were captured by the Germans and deported to the East.

Similar deeds of heroism were performed in Poland, where anti-Semitism is endemic among the population. Poland has a reputation for anti-Semitism, chiefly within the Church. It is recorded that Poles encouraged the Gestapo in their ruthless destruction of the Warsaw ghetto on Easter Sunday of 1943. The "deplorable record of Polish Catholic anti-Semitism" was not conducive to widespread sympathy for Jewish suffering.[22] But there were always individuals—priests, nuns, and laymen—who risked their lives to help the persecuted. Adults were supplied with Aryan papers and baptismal certificates; children were hidden away on farms and in other remote places. Some men found refuge in monasteries and women in convents. Many Polish names deserve to be written in golden letters in Jewish annals. Foremost among them is Archbishop Andreas Sheptycky, of Lwów, the titular head of the Uniate Catholic Church. Joan Bel Geddes says of him: "This seventy-seven-year-old prelate was an active fighter against the Nazis; he hid many Jews in his palace and in churches, convents and monasteries under his jurisdiction."[23] There were many others who performed similar deeds of mercy. To mention a few of the outstanding heroes: Janina Stankiewicz, Marian Melicki, Engineer Kalinowski, Mrs. Chomicz, Mrs. Choms, known among Jews as the "angel of Lemberg" (Lwów) for the risks she took on their behalf. Brave Mr. and Mrs. Malicki, both deported to Treblinka for helping Jews. His hands and feet were broken to make him divulge the names and whereabouts of hidden Jews, but he never yielded.

There is the heartwarming story of Maria Kielbasa, described as "a blunt-featured peasant woman from Poland who can neither read nor write," who rescued a Jewish baby girl from certain death. The child's mother had been shot by the Germans. A woman who discovered the baby intended to kill her. Maria became the child's foster mother and brought her up in the knowledge of her Jewish origin. The child became deeply attached to the Polish family; and after she emigrated to Israel, Maria would come to visit her.[24] There are many similar stories.

Even within Germany itself there were some remarkable feats of daring. Several hundred Jews survived the persecution and the war in the heart of the Reich—in the capital city of Berlin— thanks to the help and cooperation of German friends and neighbours.[25]

One of the most remarkable accomplishments was that of Oskar

Schindler, who managed a ceramics factory for the Germans. This brave man, with the help of friends in the German army, was able to employ more than one thousand Jewish workers right through the war and thus save their lives. Although the police supposedly suspected what was going on, they did not interfere.[26] Another man who was reportedly instrumental in saving Jewish lives was none other than the Baltic German, Felix Kersten, Himmler's masseur and confidant.

Charlotte Hoffmann of Berlin, a civil servant whose Christian conscience forbade her to take the oath of allegiance to Hitler, displayed remarkable courage and determination. In a letter to the President of the Court, dated December 13, 1934, she declared: "The oath of loyalty to the person of Hitler constitutes an obvious blasphemy."[27]

There were countless others all over Europe who did their utmost to help, such as Raoul Wallenberg, the kindly attaché at the Swedish Embassy in Budapest to whom many Jews owe their lives. The Pope, archbishops, bishops, priests, pastors, laymen, were all involved in the dangerous task of helping Jews. In spite of the obvious failures, the rescue work attempted by Christians stands out as a testimony to faith and courage. Ignaz Maybaum recognized the importance of the Christian influence upon a pagan world: "There is room for us [Jews] in the Christian history of the nations of the world. Here our love for humanity can develop and there is scope for our co-operation in the aims of mankind. But where the history of the nations of the world loses its Christian character and becomes pagan history we are cast out. Our alienation becomes acute, and there results Jewish martyrdom which before God is our Jewish justification, and before the nations of the world our glory."[28]

This does not mean that Christians have cause for boasting. For every Christian who risked his life on behalf of Jews, there were thousands who lent themselves as willing or unwilling instruments in the gruesome business of the destruction of Jews. Nevertheless, Albert Einstein's words in a letter to the Episcopal Bishop Edward R. Welles, which was made public in 1945, come as a comfort to our burdened conscience: "Being a lover of freedom . . . I looked to the universities to defend it, knowing that they had always boasted of their devotion to the cause of truth; but, no, the universities immediately were silenced. Then I looked to the great editors of the newspapers whose flaming editorials in days gone by had proclaimed their love of freedom; but they, like the universities, were silenced in a few short weeks. Only the church stood squarely across the path of Hitler's campaign for suppressing the truth. I never had any special interest in the church before, but now I feel a great affection and admiration because the church alone has had the courage and persistence to stand for intellectual truth and moral freedom. I am forced to confess that what I once despised I now praise unreservedly."[29]

Unfortunately, there is another side to the story of Jewish-Christian relationships which bears upon the events in Europe during the war. It shows that the Church was indirectly responsible for the Holocaust at Auschwitz. We now have to turn to that darker side of the tale.

The Christian faith began, grew, and developed upon Jewish soil. Except for short trips beyond Judea and Galilee, Jesus never left Israel. Almost all the events recorded in the Gospels took place among Jews. The acts of Jesus and the life of the early Church were infused with the spirit and hopes of the Old Testament. Jesus' mission was primarily to Jews and they were the first to respond to and follow him. A split between conservative Judaism and the new "heresy" initiated by Jesus of Nazareth was inevitable. It always happen like that; the masses are never prepared for change.

Because the name of Jesus was identified with Israel's messianic hope by those who believed in him, they persevered in his mission "to the Jew first" (Rom. 1:16; cf. Acts 1:4, 8). It was only natural that the early disciples should be concerned first and foremost with their own people. To pray for the conversion of the Jewish people was a matter of loyalty both to the Messiah and to the messianic hope. Paul the Apostle confesses a deep sorrow and unceasing anguish on behalf of his kinsmen. He declares himself prepared to be cut off from Christ for their sake, if this were a means of winning them for the Gospel (Rom. 9:1–5). It is his heart's desire and prayer that Israel might be saved (Rom. 10:1), and salvation for him meant faith in Jesus as Messiah. From the early Jewish Church the Gentile Church inherited the tradition of praying for Israel's conversion. Justin Martyr (c. 100–165) tells Trypho the Jew that Christians pray for the Jewish people and do so in spite of the persecution which they suffer at their hands. Christians, he explains, are commanded to pray for their enemies (*Dia-*

logue with Trypho the Jew 96). The *Didascalia Apostolorum,* a third-century work purporting to be the original "Teaching of the Twelve Apostles," probably composed by a Jewish Christian, exhorts Gentile believers to persevere in prayer for the Jews, most particularly during Passover week. It prescribes prayer on behalf of the Jewish people on all festivals as well as on the fourth and sixth days of the week. The anonymous writer reminds his readers that the Jews are their brothers, even though they are hostile to Christians.[30]

Thus, praying for the salvation of Israel became an established custom within the Church, especially during Holy Week. In the historic churches this custom continues to this day. But gradually the concern for the Jewish people diminished as the rift between Church and Synagogue grew. In the end, prayer for the Jews became a mere formality and was continued only because it was built into the liturgy. In the Latin rite, the Solemn Prayers for Good Friday include prayer for the Jews as part of the peculiar Office of the day. The rubric prescribes that a prayer be offered on behalf of all humanity, Christian and pagan—"even the Jews are not excluded." Such prayers are generally offered while kneeling, and the congregation responds with the Amen. But it has become the custom not to kneel when the Jews are prayed for, and no Amen is prescribed in the liturgy. The rubric explains: "Here there is no invitation to the faithful to kneel because the Jews used this act of adoration as a further means of outraging Jesus during His passion." This odd bit of apocryphal calumny has no foundation in the New Testament, nor does it make any sense, except to those who are reared in prejudice towards Jews. The text of the prayer in the English version reads as follows: "Let us pray for the faithless Jews: that our Lord and God would draw aside the veil from their hearts, that they also may acknowledge Jesus Christ our Lord."[31] In the Latin text the phrase *pro perfidis Judaeis* carries a greater ambiguity than the expression "for the faithless Jews." But none of the connotations of the Latin word *perfidus* is complimentary. Even when taken at its least offensive, it is bound to arouse antipathy towards Jews. The faithful are thus left to interpret the prayer in accordance with their acquired prejudices and animosities. No wonder that Holy Week was for Jews a time of dread and pogroms in so-called Christian Europe.

Change in the Roman liturgy came about by the intervention of the "Jewish Pope," John XXIII, in 1959. Pope John directed that the phrase *pro perfidis Judaeis* be expunged. Several different prayers were substituted.[32] Instead of the warning to the faithful ("In horror, turn away from Jewish unbelief, and reject Jewish superstition"), the new prayers convey a positive image of the Jews and of Judaism. Thanks to Pope John a long-established tradition which perpetuated antipathy and prejudice is now on the wane. Friedrich Heer may be right that nothing would have changed except for the benevolence of this remarkable Pope. Heer writes: "John XXIII dared to leap across these centuries."[33] Pope John made history and created a stir in the world press when he greeted a Jewish delegation with the words from Genesis 45:4: "I am Joseph, your brother!" Those well-chosen words were to indicate not only his personal goodwill but also the historic connection between Israel and the Church. The Pope knew only too well the differences which divided Judaism from Christianity, but it was his conviction that they must "not repress the brotherhood that springs from their common origin."[34]

That there was no such sense of brotherhood is the tragedy of Jewish-Christian relations through history. It was Pope John's example and influence that prepared the way for the "Declaration on the Jewish People" of Vatican II. The other man who must be mentioned in this connection is Cardinal Bea, whom Msgr. Oesterreicher regards as the father of the "Declaration on Jews."[35] Jewish critics have objected to the Declaration on the grounds that Judaism was singled out from among the other non-Christian religions for special attention. Cardinal Bea has assured the critics that the singling out of the Jews should by no means be taken as *captatio benevolentiae*—a subtle attempt to trap them with feigned kindness. Rather, it was an acknowledgement on the part of the Council of "all that the Church has received from God through the Jewish people." In this way the Church fathers gave expression to the fact that Israel was God's first choice. Cardinal Bea goes out of his way to stress that Christianity is closer to Judaism than to any other religion by reason of "the common spiritual patrimony which determines the specific nature of the relationship of the two faiths to each other."[36]

The documents of Vatican II contain several references to ancient Israel and to contemporary Jewry. In the schema "On the People of God" the Council refers to Israel's election: "God chose the race of Israel as a people unto Himself." A comparison is made between Israel's wandering through the desert and the "new Israel" on its pilgrimage to the City of God. The Council acknowledges the historic connection between the People of God and the Church of Christ: "On account of their fathers, this people remains most dear to God, for God does not repent of the gifts He makes nor of the call He issues." This is a reference to Romans 11:28–29. Again, in the schema "On Revelation," the Council speaks of Abraham, Moses, the Prophets, and the nation of God, who were taught to acknowledge him as the only true God. In the same spirit, in the short "Document on the Old Testament" reference is made to the people of Israel to whom God made himself known in words and deeds. But it is chiefly in the "Declaration on the Non-Christian Religions" that we find the Jews singled out for special attention.

Here the Synod affirms "the special bond linking the people of the New Covenant with the stock of Israel." The document proceeds to note that Jesus, Mary, and the Apostles were all Jews. It stresses the "spiritual common patrimony" between Christians and Jews and then proceeds to make the following statement: "This sacred Synod wishes to foster and recommend that mutual understanding and respect which is the fruit above all of biblical and theological studies, and brotherly dialogue." By declaring the Jewish people guiltless of the death of Jesus the Council broke away from one of the most entrenched notions in Christendom, a notion which put Jews under a perpetual curse. Though Jews were involved in the trial of Jesus, "still what happened in His passion cannot be blamed upon all the Jews then living, without distinction, nor upon the Jews today." The Church, therefore, the Council announces, disapproves *(reprobat)* of all persecution. Jews "should not be presented as repudiated or cursed by God, as if such views followed from holy Scripture." It is this statement, more than anything else, which lays a new foundation for Jewish-Christian coexistence.

The "Declaration on the Non-Christian Religions" goes on to recommend that all those engaged in catechetical teaching and in preaching God's Word should take care not to say anything that would contradict the truth of the Gospel and the spirit of Christ. By way of warning, the document states that this Synod "deplores the hatred, persecutions, and displays of anti-Semitism directed against the Jews at any time and from any source."[37]

Behind these affirmations is a long history of conflict and calumny which the Council is desperately trying to correct. It all originated with the age-old accusation that the Jews are guilty of deicide. Jews regard this accusation as the source of Christian anti-Semitism, which in turn prepared the way for Hitler's Holocaust. Cardinal Bea, in an Appendix to his book *The Church and the Jewish People*, deals with the question of deicide. He denies that there is any connection between modern anti-Semitism and the Jewish involvement in the Crucifixion of Jesus. He sees in anti-Semitism political, nationalist, psychological, and economic causes.[38] It must be admitted, however, that the weight of opinion is against him. Though it is true that the accusation of deicide was never part of official Church doctrine, it is also undeniably true that this was a prevailing view in Christendom. Whatever the case may be, the Council's repudiation of both the deicide libel and anti-Semitism is of great significance to the Jewish people. Prof. David Flüsser regards the repudiation of the latter of even greater importance than repudiation of the idea of collective Jewish guilt.[39]

There is truth in Cardinal Bea's contention that anti-Semitism is a complex phenomenon compacted of many causes. But this does not dispose of the fact that traditional Christian attitudes have helped to tarnish the image of the Jewish people and have preconditioned the populace to use them as scapegoats for all their ills. A living example is the endemic anti-Semitism in the essentially Catholic country of Poland. Lucy S. Davidowicz, in her review of a book on Jewish life in Poland between the two world wars, well sums up the situation: "The conventional anti-Semitism which the Catholic Church had preached for generations to the illiterate and superstitious peasantry was fanned by the Polish nationalists into a relentless and violent hatred of the Jews."[40] There was here an easy transition from religious prejudice to racial hatred. This is the argument of Jewish writers and also of many Christians. Hitler found the soil well-prepared by the Church for his ruthless racial policy.

Charles Y. Glock and Rodney Stark, who have devoted much time to the study of anti-Semitism and its origins, have shown how orthodox Christianity with its literalist interpretation of Christian dogma is still the main source of anti-Jewish prejudice.[41] This is borne out by several national surveys in the United States. About 15 percent of the Catholics and 23 percent of the Protestants attribute Jewish suffering to the fact that they rejected Jesus. Gertrude Selznick and Stephen Steinberg are convinced that only changes in religious dogma can make a difference in this attitude.

They quote one Catholic respondent as remarking: "I used to believe that the Jews killed Christ, but they are changing the law in Rome." It is not so much religious affiliation as "acceptance of certain tenets of religious ideology" which affects people's attitude towards others.[42]

The discoveries by Glock and Stark stirred the Christian denominations in the United States either to respond in their own defence or to acknowledge the truth of the findings. Rabbi Solomon Bernards, surveying the reaction to the book, writes: "Meetings and consultations that might have taken years to mature have been set up with relative speed. Within Christian leadership has been implanted a new sense of urgency of doing something concrete and substantial about anti-Semitism and the stereotypes which predispose to it."[43]

A survey over a period of five years by the Anti-Defamation League of B'nai B'rith reports that 69 percent of adult Church members believe that Jews bear the responsibility for crucifying Jesus. This belief the League holds to be "a cruel, critical factor in perpetuating anti-Semitic prejudice."[44] On this point there is universal consent. Though there is a distinction between social and religious prejudice, as Hannah Arendt points out, the characterization of the Jew as an inferior person, lacking in innate qualities of nobility, is common to both. In Russia, Germany, Austria, and France, political anti-Semitism enjoyed the support of large sections of the Church.[45] The Nazis went only a step further and reduced the Jews to nonpersons. Hitler is reported to have told Bishop Berning and Msgr. Steinmann in an interview on April 26, 1933, that he merely intended to do, and do more effectively, what the Church had been doing for centuries in regard to the Jews.[46] To accomplish the Nazi intention, Jews were reduced to the status of vermin—*Ungeziefer*. Under the Nazi regime animals were better off than Jews. Hitler was a lover of dogs and canaries. According to Himmler's personal physician, Himmler never took part in hunting, which he regarded as a brutal act of destroying innocent animals. Walter Sulzbach, who records these traits, is at a loss to understand how these two men could act with such cruelty where Jews were concerned. The only explanation he can think of is the twin source of hatred—xenophobia and the Christian doctrine of salvation.[47] Unlike some other Jewish writers, Sulzbach is not totally negative about Christianity. He appreciates all that Christians did to help Jews at the time of persecution. He even goes so far as to admit that the Church cannot afford to surrender her theological position in respect to mission. To do this would be betrayal of her trust *(sich selbst verleugnen)*, yet the Church must realize the danger of her theological stance when she identifies the Jews with the devil.[48]

It is this kind of pleading which has met with sympathetic response on the part of many scholars and resulted in a renewed effort to examine Christian attitudes towards Judaism. This has required a new appreciation of the Jewish faith and the Jewish people. How desperately this new appreciation is needed becomes clear when we consider, for example, Arnold Toynbee's negative and deprecating characterization of Pharisaic Judaism as "a fossil of Syriac civilization."[49] Oddly enough, Prof. Toynbee's excuse for misrepresenting Judaism was that Christianity had preconditioned him to such an attitude. These are his words: "It is difficult for anyone brought up in the Christian tradition to shake himself free from the official Christian ideology. He may have discarded Christian doctrine on every point; yet on this particular point he may find that he is still influenced, subconsciously, by the traditional Christian view in his outlook on Jewish history . . . . I am conscious that my own outlook has been affected in this way."[50] If this can happen to a man of Toynbee's stature, it is easy to see the negative influence the Church can exert upon the minds of simple people regarding Jews and Judaism. There may be justification in Rabbi Tanenbaum's remark that "the Jew will never be entirely understood to the satisfaction of Christians," though the reasons he gives are rather philosophical and scholastic.[51]

The misunderstanding, no doubt, is on both sides, but the Church is by far the greater culprit. Eugene Fisher, writing as a Christian, cites a number of typical Jewish misinterpretations of Christian faith and doctrine. He attributes them chiefly to the all-too-human addiction to generalize, with the result that Jews frequently "manhandle" Christian attempts at apologia.[52] Fisher would like Jews to understand that "Christianity speaks with many voices" and that it is a mistake to treat such a multi-faceted phenomenon as a homogeneous whole. Naturally, the same can be said about contemporary Judaism. Judaism is no longer an undivided faith. Jews also speak with several voices, though in respect to Christianity they are more or less agreed on basic issues. Their efforts at apologia arise from the constant Jewish need to maintain a defensive position in a hostile world. Because of the secularization of Jewish life, a distinction must be made between Judaism and the Jewish people. In this respect E. H. Flannery's point is well taken: the Church must in no way acquiesce to anti-Semitism, but at the same time it cannot accept Judaism as a way of salvation.[53] This is a basic issue for which there seems to be no easy solution. Fr. Flannery, who is deeply involved in the field of Jewish-Catholic relations, is only too well aware of Christian coresponsibility for Jewish suffering. This gives some indication of the dilemma in which Christians find themselves with respect to Judaism. One of the major problems is that on both sides Judaism and the Jewish people are treated as identical entities, which they are not.

Unfortunately, rejection of Judaism easily leads to depreciation of Jews. A symposium of German Protestant theologians dating back to the year 1913 is a good example of the ambiguity which adheres to the subject under discussion. Here is a typical statement by the President of the Protestant *Oberkonsistorium* of Munich, Hermann von Bezzel: "It is a tragic sight to observe Israel sold out to false values, holding on to stiff-neckedness, to what is anachronistic and lifeless." He characterizes orthodox Judaism as rigid, lifeless, and addicted to a literalistic frame of mind, and liberal Judaism as atheistic and given over to gross materialism.[54] This kind of wholesale rejection of Judaism in every form is simultaneously a rejection of Jews no matter what views they hold. This kind of attitude on the part of a leading churchman is typical of the abysmal ignorance of otherwise intelligent and well-educated men.

The whole symposium breathed a spirit of rejection and judgemental haughtiness. Prof. Ludwig Lemme, a well-known theologian, Privy Church Councillor of Heidelberg, averred: "Judaism is an anachronism." In his view, Israel had crucified its Messiah and still continues to do so by its hatred of Christianity *(in dem starken Christentumhass)*. Lemme expressed the hope that Zionism would fail, for it could only contribute to continued anti-Christian obduracy *(Verstockung)*. However, Prof. Lemme tried to soften the blow with the advice that "Anti-Semitism must be directed against the thing, such as the corrupt Jewish press and Jewish usury, but never against the race, against the people." How to differentiate between the usurer and the usury he did not explain. It is a proven fact that by belittling Judaism the Jew is belittled and vice versa.

"Christian influence" is a very elastic phrase which can be pulled in all directions. According to one source, a Roman Catholic scholar who taught moral theology at the Paderborn Seminary was consulted by Hitler on the question of euthanasia for the mentally sick and deformed. Prof. Josef Mayer is supposed to have confirmed the State's right to kill off unwanted people. The Jesuit historian, Fr. Robert A. Graham, sees in this pronouncement a prelude to the gas ovens of Auschwitz.[55] The testimony of Karl Hartl, a former Nazi official, at a war-crimes trial at Limburg is good evidence for Fr. Graham's theory. We do not know whether Hitler had any scruples concerning the killing of German mental patients, but it is doubtful whether he needed any encouragement with regard to Jews.

We have asked the question, "Where was the Church when Jews were being massacred?" The answer is that she was and she was not there to help and to succour. In cases of individual believers, high and low, clergy and laity, brave men and women who risked their lives for the sake of conscience, the Church was there. In respect to organized resistance, to a mighty voice of protest, to prohibiting any Christian participation (whether direct or indirect) in the dirty work of human slaughter, the Church was absent. She just was not there when the need was greatest.

Chapter **4**

The Church and the Jews

The question of the Jewish future is essentially a matter of Jewish concern and in the final analysis a matter of faith. Prof. Emil Fackenheim poses the question dialectically: "Dare we *morally* raise Jewish children, exposing our offspring to a possible second Auschwitz decades or centuries hence?" This is followed by a second question: "And dare we *religiously not* raise Jewish children, completing Satan's work on his behalf?" These two questions sum up the dilemma of present-day Jewish existence. Behind these two questions are both disillusionment with contemporary civilization and the challenge not to yield to despair. Fackenheim's affirmation of Jewish life and history is directly opposed to the viewpoint of Rabbi Richard Rubenstein. For Rubenstein Jews have no special claim to favour. Israel is no different from any other people; Jewish survival is not essential to the world; Jews have no God-given destiny; the Covenant is a myth. Hamlet's question, "To be or not to be?" has received a political answer with the establishment of the State of Israel. But for nonbelieving Jews this can be only a temporary answer. The troublesome question still remains: If there is no longer (or never was) a God of the Covenant, what point is there in being Jews? To survive in the Diaspora, Jews need the conviction that they are the People of the Covenant. But, on the other hand, if God is still the God of the Covenant, how can Jews live with him after Auschwitz?

Prof. Fackenheim has grasped the problem in all its complexity but refuses to abandon faith in the God of Israel. In true biblical tradition, his quarrel with God continues, but it is a quarrel within the family: "Contend with God we must, as did Abraham, Jacob, Job. And we cannot let him go."[1]

For centuries Christians have believed they possess the key to the Jewish problem—Jews suffer in perpetuity for rejecting and crucifying their Messiah. Though not written in the Canons, this has been and still is the conviction within the churches. Ignatius (died c. 107) in his letter to the Magnesians in Asia Minor tells them that Jesus "underwent the passion and endured the cross at the hands of the Christ-killing Jews" (ch. 11). Justin Martyr in his *First Apology* (c. 155) already implies that Israel's exile is in punishment for the Crucifixion. Justin makes it quite plain to Trypho that what happened to Judea, namely, the fall of Jerusalem and the Jewish Captivity, is "in fairness and justice, for you have slain the Just One and his prophets before him" (*Dialogue with Trypho the Jew* 16). What Justin was doing was interpreting history in biblical style; by doing so he set an example for others to follow.

The Latin father Tertullian (died c. 220) indiscriminately declares the whole Jewish people guilty of the Crucifixion: "All the Synagogue of Israel did slay him, saying to Pilate, 'His blood be upon us and upon our children' " (*Answer to the Jews* 9). He seems to have forgotten that Jesus prayed for those who assigned him to death, asking that God forgive them (Luke 23:34). For Tertullian Jews labour under a curse; therefore God has introduced another people to take their place (ch. 10). To prove his point, Tertullian produces a plethora of Old Testament texts, in most cases tearing them from their context and disregarding the original meaning.[2] Commodianus (probably fifth century), a Latin poet, describes the Jews as always evil, recalcitrant and stiff-necked. He says: "There is not an unbelieving people such as yours, O evil men!"[3]

Some tension between Church and Synagogue is already indicated in the New Testament, but hostility to the Jews as a people is completely lacking. The term *Jews* in John's Gospel refers to the hierarchy and the spiritual leaders of the Pharisaic party who opposed Jesus. The phrase "Synagogue of Satan" (Rev. 2:9) is an indictment of Jews who do not live up to their high calling. But it is an indictment of Jews by a Jew, and that is a crucial point. When Gentiles entered upon the scene and took over the criticism of God's people, it was no longer self-criticism but criticism of others. We have here a reenactment of the parable about the Pharisee in the Temple who knew himself to be better than the publican (Luke 18:9ff.). But this time the Pharisee is the Christian and not the Jew.

This brings us to the contested text of Matthew 23:38–39 (cf. Luke 13:35) in which Jesus predicts the fall of the Temple: "Your house is left deserted . . . until you say, 'Blessed be he who comes

in the name of the Lord.' " It is to be noted that the text is a con-
traction of at least two Old Testament passages—Psalm 118:26
and Jeremiah 22:5 (cf. I Kings 9:7). What was originally meant as
a warning became in the course of translating from Hebrew to
Greek, to Latin, etc., an act of vengeance on the part of God: the
Jews rejected the Messiah; therefore they went into exile. A careful study of Matthew 23:38–39 reveals quite a different situation.
What Jesus is saying is that this is his last visit to the Temple and
he will not be seen there again until he is greeted with the words
of Psalm 118:26; that is, until he is welcomed as the legitimate
messenger from God.[4] It is interesting to note the transition from
the Latin Vulgate *(ecce relinquitur vobis domus vestra deserta)* to
English. The King James has for *deserta* "desolate." In our understanding of the text these words are addressed to the Temple
hierarchy and not to the whole "house" of Israel. The New English Bible, for no justifiable reason, goes one step further by adding the phrase "forsaken by God"!

In order to justify their judgemental attitude, the Church
fathers had to go beyond the Gospel text to the Old Testament
imprecations of Israel. The "Letter of Barnabas" is a classic example. This old text, probably written by an Alexandrian Christian
between A.D. 70 and 100, abounds in Old Testament quotations
to prove the annulment of God's Covenant with the Jews.

Naturally enough, there was animosity on both sides. Justin
complains of Bar Kokhba's hostility towards Christians *(First Apology* 31) and accuses Jews of deliberately spreading calumnies
against them *(Dialogue with Trypho the Jew* 17).[5] But when Christians became a power in the Empire, they paid back in kind many
times over. Jews were soon reduced from Roman citizenship to, in
effect, the status of barely tolerated immigrants. In the end they
lost all legal rights to protection.[6] Allowance must be made, however, for the fact that religion dominated society and that the
Church tolerated no rival faith. The Jews, only a small minority,
scattered among the hostile and frequently barbarian nations, had
to pay the price for being different. This attitude was entirely religious and not racial. It is therefore inaccurate to speak of anti-
Semitism prior to the nineteenth century. Even Luther with all his
venom against Jews was not an anti-Semite in the modern sense.
In fact he extolled Jews: "We Gentiles are in no way equal to the
Jews," he said. "Paul therefore makes an excellent distinction between Sarai and Hagar, and their two sons" (cf. Gal. 4:24–31).[7]

Luther stressed the link between the Jewish people and the Christian Church. What he resisted, and resisted fiercely, was rabbinic Judaism, which to him appeared full of superstition and hostile to the Christian faith.[8]

Unfortunately, the transition from anti-Judaism to anti-Semitism occurs almost imperceptibly, for "Jews" and "Judaism" are regarded as synonyms by most people, including scholars. Very few people (among them are Nicolas Berdyaev and Edward Flannery) are able to see the difference between the two utterly distinct concepts: Judaism is a faith; Jews are a people. There was a time when the two were inseparable but this is no longer the case. Christians have inherited a polemic against Judaism; this goes back to the very inception of the Christian Church. But they cannot afford to have prejudices against Jews as Jews. Berdyaev sees this very clearly: "The Christian religion actually is opposed to the Jewish religion . . . . Judaism which preceded Christ's coming, and that which succeeded it, are two distinct spiritual manifestations." But no Christian can be an anti-Semite without denying the Christian faith. Berdyaev regards Christian anti-Semitism as even worse than racial anti-Semitism, for logically it leads to anti-Christianity.[9] He would prefer people to renounce Christ openly rather than to use his name for selfish and unworthy ends. But Christian anti-Semitism is a fact in history, and the distinction between a religious controversy and racial contempt for Jews has virtually been ignored. Not only laymen, but scholars and theologians have fallen into the trap of treating Jews and Judaism as identical.

The French Jewish historian, Prof. Jules Isaac, justifiably traces anti-Semitism to the particular Christian teaching which encourages contempt for the Jewish people.[10] He, and many others, regard the myth that Jews are guilty of deicide as the root cause of all the trouble—"this capital accusation, to which is tied the theme of capital punishment, the terrifying curse weighing down Israel's shoulders explaining (and justifying in advance) its wretched destiny, its cruel trials, the worst violences committed against it, the rivers of blood from its constantly re-opened and inflamed wounds."[11] This may sound like exaggeration to modern ears, but in the context of history it is a fair description. Berdyaev puts it more succinctly: "Those who rejected the Cross have to carry it, while those who welcomed it are so often engaged in crucifying others."[12]

The idea that the whole Jewish race, both past and present, is under the curse of God has prevailed in Christendom for centuries. The utter cruelty of this view lies in its all-inclusiveness for all time. The accusation of deicide is "hurled at the whole Jewish people, without exception, without any kind of distinction . . . ." Included among those with this attitude are not only the blind Christian masses, but also the cold, reasoning theologians, "who taught, and even now teach, that every Jew of every age is under the curse of God." Jewish scholars accuse the Gospel of John of being the most hostile document, for in it Jews are made out to be in league with the devil (cf. John 8:44). Given the human addiction to generalization, the already prejudiced reader will fail to distinguish between the Jews who followed Christ and those who opposed him, and will acquire "an overwhelming feeling of aversion to the Jewish people in toto . . . ."[13]

Prof. Isaac writes in a spirit of pleading gentleness, calling upon Christian theologians to amend their ways and to desist from exploiting the New Testament text for immoral ends. Other Jewish writers are less restrained and more bellicose. Chief amongst them is Dagobert D. Runes, who calls for a complete revision of the New Testament text. He wants all references to the Cross eliminated: "Christianity is the only religion that has made the gallows a symbol of love." He is puzzled as to how a Christian can ever love a Jew "if he forever lives in the sight of the gallows." The solution, he suggests, is to change Christian symbolism; instead of the Cross let Christians adopt the fish, which will serve as a reminder of "the great fisherman of souls."[14] A somewhat similar position is taken by Prof. Blu Greenberg, who sees in the Gospel tradition negative forces which are (even for an intelligent believing Christian) "virtually impossible to overcome." Were he a Christian, Greenberg says, and were the Gospels the chief authority for his faith, he would certainly hate Jews. Like Runes, Greenberg therefore suggests that parts of the Gospels have to be "altered or amended" on the principle that "only the Gospels can 'undo' what the Gospels have done."[15]

Dagobert Runes has in fact been working on a revision of the Fourth Gospel, deleting the term *Jews* wherever it appears in a negative light, and substituting "people" or "crowd" (e.g., John 7:13; 19:38; 20:19). He has elicited the sympathy of at least one Christian scholar in the person of Prof. Krister Stendahl of Harvard Theological School, who writes: "Many of us would prefer a New Testament without the marks of bitter feelings between

Church and Synagogue." Yet Stendahl doubts whether "the production of a fraudulent text can help anyone. There is no manu-
script basis whatsoever for these deletions and changes."[16]

Runes is convinced that the anti-Jewish references in the Gospels are later interpolations. This view is widely held among Jewish scholars. Ernest L. Abel notes that the Passion narratives "were
not originally intended to denounce the Jews as Christ-killers." At
first, at a time of persecution, these narratives strengthened and
encouraged believers; but at a later age they were misused as hate
propaganda. Unfortunately, "the metaphor became distorted and
misused as the historical milieu changed."[17] That these texts were
misused, misinterpreted, and misapplied, no one can deny. But
many will contend that the fault is not with the text but with those
who use it unworthily and for the wrong ends; that is, with those
who use it as a pretext for rationalizing deep-seated prejudices.
Alan A. Spears, commenting on Berdyaev's book on anti-Semitism, aptly explains that anti-Semitism is "a malady which is hidden in the depths of the human soul." It lays "bare the evil incli-
nation of man himself and the degradation of his divine image."[18]

Cardinal Bea rejects the idea that the New Testament requires
alteration. What is needed, he thinks, is a better understanding of
Judaism and a more Christian attitude towards Jews. Bea, after
examining the supposedly offending texts, sums up his conclusions: (1) Jews are not marked out as deicides; (2) the New Testament blames only those who were directly involved in the Crucifixion; (3) there can be no collective guilt attributed to the rest of
the Jewish people.[19] Similarly, Kurt Schubert finds no fault with
the Gospel account: "The historical facts were accurately reported
in the gospel narrative, but were put to polemical use . . . ."[20]

The Crucifixion account has received much scrutiny from Jewish scholars. Not only do they question the authenticity of the narrative, but also the legal assumptions behind it. They see the anti-
Jewish bias particularly in the characterization of Pontius Pilatus.
In history he is known as an utterly unscrupulous man of great
cruelty. The vacillating governor of the Gospels ill fits the man as
known from other sources.[21] Other inconsistencies in the story
have to do with rabbinic law and legal custom. The Sanhedrin
could not have been called on the spur of the moment. The trial
could not have taken place on the eve of a major feast, etc. On
these, and similar grounds, some writers even deny any involvement on the part of the hierarchy in the trial of Jesus. Solomon

Zeitlin, on the other hand, allows that there was priestly involvement, but excludes the Pharisees.[22] Joseph Hager, in a more conciliatory mood, looks upon the question of Jesus' trial as an inter-Jewish quarrel similar to the one between the schools of Hillel and Shammai, which ought to be of no consequence to the Gentile world.[23] Haim H. Cohn, an Israeli High Court judge, has subjected the record of Jesus' trial to minute investigation and has found it unreliable on many counts. He questions the idea that the Jews demanded Jesus' death. The whole trial was a Roman affair. Judge Cohn shows that, in view of Roman law, Pilate was left with no option. He had to proceed against the Nazarene because of his claim to Messiahship, which always carried political implications. In fact, the story "would have been simple and straightforward were it not for the fact that the evangelists, for theological and political purposes, had to shift the guilt for the death of Jesus to the Jews."[24] Jesus, says Cohn, was tried for sedition, which was an offence within the exclusive jurisdiction of the Roman governor—it had nothing to do with Jewish law. Pilate could not possibly have been swayed by the clamouring crowd; this would have been contrary to the Roman code, which laid down that "the vain voices of the people must not be listened to."[25] Moreover, if the Jews had wanted to destroy Jesus, they could have done so without the help of Pilate.[26] Judge Cohn is able to detect other inconsistencies; for instance, because of the imminent Passover, Jews could not have entered the courtroom. His conclusion is that the Jews had no part whatsoever in the trial and death of Jesus.[27]

The findings of the late Paul Winter's study on the trial of Jesus are very similar to those of Judge Cohn.[28] Jewish scholars admit that there may have been some cooperation on the part of the Jewish hierarchy for political and selfish reasons. But the Jewish people had no part in it. Nor was there any real reason for a trial as far as Jewish law was concerned. Jesus was not guilty of apostasy or blasphemy. But Messiahship meant kingship and it was as the King of the Jews that Jesus died at the hands of the Romans. In Zeitlin's words, Jesus died "*as a political offender against the Roman state.*"[29]

The Jewish concern with the trial of Jesus is not historical but chiefly apologetic. It is motivated by an effort to clear the Jewish name from any complicity in the Crucifixion. The necessity of making this effort was imposed upon Jewry by the accusation of deicide. More than a century ago a French Jewish writer by the name of Jacques Cohen wrote a book noting that many Christians have affirmed that "the sufferings of the Jewish people . . . are the expiation for their crime: they closed their eyes to the light, they killed a God, they rejected salvation . . . they have endured chastisement for their sin." Cohen makes the point that this kind of reasoning contradicts all that Christians and Jews know about the God of Israel.[30]

A more recent trial before the District Court of Troyes (France) on the subject of Jesus' death attracted world attention. A French lawyer, Jacques Isorni, an expert on legal history, had requested the Court "to fix the blame for the crucifixion of Jesus on Pontius Pilate, the Roman governor of Judea, and thereby absolve the Jewish people of collective guilt." The case was in the form of a libel suit against Abbé Georges de Nantes, a fanatical priest who attacked Isorni "for falsifying the New Testament" in his book *The Trial of Jesus* (1967). Isorni's contention in his book is that Jesus was a guerilla leader and that his trial was entirely political; hence the trial before the Roman governor.[31] Isorni, a non-Jew, on his part accused his adversary of justifying all the Nazi crimes on the grounds that "the Jews supposedly killed Christ." The case created a stir in the world press and contributed to awakening the Christian conscience about the Jews.[32]

The idea that the Jews are under divine judgment for the death of Jesus is widely held among Christians. Even men of the stature of the late Heinrich Grüber, Dean of the Cathedral Church of Berlin, and a proven friend of the Jewish people, have adhered to this view. Grüber could never be accused of anti-Semitism; he suffered in a concentration camp for his defence of non-Aryans and did everything in his power to help Jews during their time of trial. He was the only German called to testify against Eichmann at his trial in Jerusalem. Yet Grüber's theology was in part responsible for Richard Rubenstein's rejection of God and the Covenant. In Rabbi Rubenstein's words: "I recognize that Grüber is not an anti-Semite and that his assertion that the God of the Covenant was and is, in the ultimate, Author of the great events in Israel's history, was no different from the faith of any traditional Jew. Grüber was applying the logic of Covenant Theology to the events of the twentieth century . . . . Adolf Hitler is no more nor less an instrument of God's wrath than Nebuchadnezzar." But, Rubenstein reasoned, if the Covenant means that God is justified in visiting Auschwitz upon Jews, then there is something radically wrong with God and with the Covenant. By this course of reasoning Rubenstein was led to reject both. He concludes: "I would rather be rejected by my people than affirm their guilt at Auschwitz."[33]

The problem is not easily solved except by an exercise of goodwill on both sides. There is truth in the contention that "the Crucifixion story as preached and taught by the majority of Christians" has a detrimental effect upon the young which prevents them thereafter "from looking upon Jews in a normal light." Alan A. Spears is convinced that here lies the source of anti-Jewish prejudice. It is tragically ironic that "such teaching disseminates the very seeds of the negation of Christ and the objects of his teachings."[34] But on the other hand, there is the biblical record, which to Christians is a sacred text and cannot be amended. Reinhold Niebuhr, some years ago, in quite a different connection, put down these words: "The record is pretty plain and the fact that the Jewish leaders rather than the Roman soldiers were the real crucifiers is supported not only by evidence but by logic."[35] No one would ever accuse Niebuhr of anti-Semitism; he certainly would have been the last to accuse the Jewish people of deicide. The problem is not the record but the use of it.

But there is an additional issue which complicates the problem, namely, the universality of the Christian claim. Some critics hold that as long as Jesus is presented as the sole Saviour of man, all other religions, including Judaism, stand condemned as inauthentic. This makes Judaism an inferior faith. Radicals therefore advocate a total reconstruction of Christian theology in order to legitimize the non-Christian religions. Their voice was strongly heard at a symposium of Christians and Jews held at the Church of St. John the Divine in New York City in June, 1974. It is noteworthy that the most revolutionary trend was represented by Roman Catholics — Rosemary Ruether, Gregory Baum, John Pawlikowski—all known for their scholarship and literary output. The unanimity of their theological orientation allows us to speak of a radical school in close association with Judaism. The most militant of the three is Rosemary Ruether. She has no doubt that "at its roots, anti-Semitism in Christian civilization springs directly from Christian theological anti-Judaism." Behind this evil, she holds, is an all-inclusive Christology which makes Jesus the only Saviour of mankind. This means that those who reject him are *ipso facto* outside God's Kingdom. John Pawlikowski uses the term *fulfilment theology* to describe that line of Christian thought which leaves no

room for other religions and no room for Jewish existence. Gregory Baum points to the inconsistency contained in the Vatican
Declaration which, on the one hand, holds on to the absolute
uniqueness of Jesus Christ and, on the other, affirms the authenticity of Judaism. These scholars are all agreed that in order to
solve the contradiction "a rethinking of the Church's Christological position" is necessary.[36]

This does not mean that all participants in the symposium were
in unanimous agreement. Even on the question of anti-Semitism
there was a difference of opinion. Ruether's simplistic view was
corrected by a Jewish scholar, Prof. Yosef Yerushalmi of Harvard,
who stressed the difference between Christian anti-Judaism and
racial anti-Semitism. Baum, in a more conciliatory mood, suggested a compromise: there is no need for a dramatic either-or;
we must allow for a process of adjustment. The fact that the
Church now has become reconciled to religious pluralism will ultimately reduce the claim to uniqueness. There are other ways to
salvation, all equally valid. Ecumenism, once set in motion, will
work itself out to its logical conclusion.

Apart from the moral issue of collective guilt, there is, of
course, a theological inconsistency in the Christian attitude which
claims the benefit of the Cross while putting under perpetual
curse the progeny of those who enacted the drama. Even the law
of Moses limits the sins of the fathers to the third and fourth generation (Exod. 34:6–7), but in the mind of many Christians all
Jews stand equally condemned. It took the horrors of the Holocaust to alert Christian writers and leaders to the implications of
such an attitude. But does recognition of the implications of this
attitude necessitate a revision of the New Testament record and a
radical change in Christological understanding?

We have no records of the life and death of Jesus other than
the Gospels. Both from a religious and a psychological point of
view that record makes good sense. Change is always resisted, and
resisted most fiercely by the religious establishment. Bishop Gösta
Lindeskog's conclusion is essentially correct: Jesus found himself
in opposition to contemporary Judaism.[37] Once this is accepted,
the theory that the political factor was the exclusive cause of Jesus'
death falls to the ground. True enough, Messiahship carried political implications and in certain quarters Jesus' activities were
seen in this light. And the hierarchy did make use of a political
pretext to get rid of a dangerous individual; hence the difference

in the charges. Before the Jewish authorities the issue was religious; before Pilate it was political. The extent of Pharisaic involvement is not easy to assess. That the Pharisees were passive onlookers is contradicted by the fact that Jesus offended the sensibilities of the pious.[38] The contention that the trial, as described in the Gospels, is in contradiction to Jewish custom makes no allowance for human behaviour when religious sensibilities are offended. Furthermore, the laws quoted by rabbinic scholars in regard to capital punishment belong to a later age and may not have been in force at the time of Jesus.[39] Prof. Samuel Sandmel writes that on the question of the trial of Jesus Jewish apologists overstate their case: "so total has been the charge against us that we have been constrained to make a total denial."[40] The blame is not upon Jews but upon Christians who have put them in a position of defensiveness.

The whole of the New Testament rests upon a "theology of fulfilment." To abandon the basic presupposition that Israel's messianic hope is fulfilled in the person of Jesus means complete surrender of everything else. There is no Christianity without the theology of fulfilment. The Christology of the Church implies eschatological finality. It means that Jesus is the One who came and the One who is coming to complete the work of salvation. This was and remains a stumbling block to all those who prefer a relativistic philosophy of life. Both ancient and modern liberals feel uncomfortable with such a position, but this is exactly what Messiahship meant to Jews and Christians in New Testament times.[41] If the Gospel does not warrant a theology of fulfilment, the Gospel is not Good News. However, the claim to universalism must be on behalf of Jesus and not the Church. If the claim is made on his behalf, it must be made in his Spirit—in the Spirit of him who said: "I lay down my life . . . . No one takes it from me, but I lay it down of my own accord. I have power to lay it down, and I have power to take it again; this charge I have received from my Father" (John 10:17–18). Those who accuse the Jews of deicide have never read the Gospel as it ought to be read and have never met the Father who gave his Son for the salvation of the world.

Chapter **5**

The Way to Reconciliation

The healing process initiated by Vatican II will take a long time to show effect. Society always needs a scapegoat for its ills and the Jewish minority is very vulnerable in this regard. Deeply embedded prejudices are difficult to eradicate and the Jews are an easy target for those who have no scruples against exploiting anti-Jewish bias for selfish ends. The Church can do much to prevent such exploitation and to combat calumny. For this reason Vatican II with its "Declaration on the Jewish People" is of great importance. The first step is to acknowledge guilt and to repent of the evil.

The call to repentance has been sounded by both Roman and Protestant churches. Catholics have been more visibly and audibly active in the area of Jewish-Christian relationships than have Protestants. Yet in both churches sincere efforts are being made to repair the damaged relations and to prevent further injury. In this the late Pope John XXIII was a shining example. Friedrich Heer, a Viennese Catholic scholar, in his book *God's First Love,* cites Pope John's prayer "composed shortly before his death":

> We realize now that many, many centuries of blindness have dimmed our eyes, so that we no longer see the beauty of Thy Chosen People and no longer recognize in their faces the features of our firstborn brother. We realize that our brows are branded with the mark of Cain. Centuries long has Abel lain in blood and tears, because we had forgotten Thy love. Forgive us the curse which we unjustly laid on the name of the Jews. Forgive us that, with our curse, we crucified Thee a second time.

Heer in his dedication writes: "This book, by an Austrian Catholic, is dedicated to the Jews, Christian and non-Christian victims of the Austrian Catholic, Adolf Hitler."[1] A sense of guilt has found expression in much of the literature produced by Christians regarding the Jewish people. The Old Testament scholar of Göttingen, Prof. Walther Zimmerli, is most outspoken in his indictment of the German Church. The fact that it required the fearful explosion of Jew-hatred in the Third Reich to realize the implications of imputed guilt for the death of Jesus has stirred him to indignation. In his speeches to German audiences he insistently calls upon the people to repent of the past and he castigates "the godless impenitence of the Christian Church."[2] Other writers have expressed equal shock when confronted with the historic facts of Jewish suffering. Many of them are unsparing in their criticism and impatient with the slowness of reform.

Friedrich Heer pours scorn upon the Roman hierarchy, whom he accuses of reactionary hatred towards liberalism and democracy. He indicts the German bishops for loving the Vaterland more than God. He positively squirms at the thought that German Catholics celebrated the fall of Warsaw by ringing church bells and singing the Te Deum. He denies that the Cardinals Faulhaber and von Galen ever spoke out in defence of Jews.[3] But his main criticism is of Pius XII for handing German Catholicism over to the Third Reich. He calls Eugenio Pacelli (later Pius XII), who served as nuncio in Munich, "the German Cardinal." Heer agrees with Rolf Hochhuth that "an interdict and repeal of the unhappy Concordat" would have had considerable impact in restraining German maltreatment of Jews and other victims. He refuses, however, to put all the blame upon the Pope — he must not be made a scapegoat "for the fifteen hundred years of an erring Christian tradition."[4] Hochhuth in his play Der Stellvertreter (1963) indicts the Pope for his criminal behaviour in refusing to speak out openly in defence of the Jews, though he was well informed of what was happening in the extermination camps. On the other hand, the notorious Reinhard Heydrich, the Chief of the Security Police, accused the Pope of defending the Jews in his Christmas broadcast of 1942.[5]

The question of the Pope's silence remains a disputed issue. Anthony Rhodes, who deals with the behaviour of the Vatican during the Hitler regime, quotes Albert von Kessel, the German Privy Councillor at the Quirinal, to the effect that the Pope's open intervention would have accomplished nothing except to aggravate the situation. "We know," said von Kessel, "that a violent protest by the Pope against persecution of the Jews would have certainly put the Pope in great personal danger, and it would not have saved the life of a single Jew." Von Kessel likened Hitler's behaviour to that of a trapped beast which would react "to any provocation with extreme violence."[6] But fear for personal safety can hardly be used as a valid excuse for the Pope's hesitation to speak out forcefully on behalf of the persecuted. He was no mere onlooker in the fearful struggle. Heer cites an incident when the Pope was asked why he did not openly protest the liquidation of the Jews. His reply was: "Dear friend, do not forget that millions of Catholics are serving in the German armies. Am I to involve them in a conflict of conscience?"[7] It is obvious from this reply that the Pope still regarded Hitler's war of supreme importance in saving Europe from Communism. Heer suggests that the Church kept silent for fear of disturbing the Führer's struggle against Russia. This view is supported by the Roman Catholic historian Gordon C. Zahn.

Zahn accuses both the Catholic and Protestant churches in Germany of rabid nationalism. Like the Nazis, they stressed the typical Junker virtues of *Volk, Vaterland, Heimat, Heldentod* (nation, fatherland, homeland, a hero's death). In some cases opponents of the war were denied Holy Communion by army chaplains.[8] Zahn writes: "Faithful performance of duty was made a moral obligation."[9] On the Protestant side the situation was similar: "even the dissident Bekenntniskirche . . . was loyal to the nation's cause despite its record of heroic opposition to Hitler's regime."[10] Martin Niemöller, in many ways a great Christian, voluntarily offered to resume submarine duties while a prisoner in a concentration camp.[11]

According to Church teaching, war is justified only when there is no doubt that it is a "just war." Zahn raises the question: Was Hitler's war the kind of war the Church could approve of? Roman Catholics are prohibited from participating in an "unjust war." The German bishops and the Vatican knew that Hitler's war could not be justified; in spite of this there was complete acquiescence. The Vatican did not withdraw recognition of Hitler's regime, though it was obvious what course Germany was taking.[12] On the contrary, German bishops, especially the military bishops, not only supported the regime, but encouraged the war. Zahn singles out Bishop Franz Josef Rarkowski, of whom he says: "It would be difficult to over-emphasize the importance of Bishop Rarkowski's role in any analysis of Catholic support in Hitler's war."[13] Zahn stresses that Protestant and Catholic leaders of the Church were not against Nazi policy; what they objected to was Nazi ideology.[14] The Church encouraged "unconditional obedience" among the faithful. The oath of allegiance to Hitler was included in the Catholic Army Hymnal, published under the auspices of the military bishops: "I swear before God this sacred oath that I will render unconditional obedience to the Führer of the nation and Volk, Adolf Hitler, the Supreme Commander of the armed forces, and that, as a brave soldier, I will be ready at all times to stake my life in fulfillment of this oath."[15]

It is obvious that a Church so committed to the national cause was impotent to oppose the regime on matters of merely moral issues. On the face of it the Church was preaching high ideals: *Opferbereitschaft, Treue, Gehorsam, Pflicht, Ehre* (self-sacrifice, faithfulness, obedience, duty, honour), but in the setting of blind submission to authority these virtues became important tools for the military regime to utilize for evil ends. And it all happened with the connivance of the Church. Zahn describes this typical German attitude of good citizenship as the "bicycle principle"— bowing to those above, treading upon those below. He regards it as the basic structure of German society.[16]

Zahn is chiefly concerned with the Roman Catholic Church. Kurt Meier, Professor of Church History at Leipzig, draws a very similar, if not worse, picture of the Protestants. Even the *Bekenntniskirche* (the Confessional Church), the only part of the Protestant Church which was in opposition to Hitler, was chiefly concerned with its own membership. It objected to the so-called Aryan paragraph only because it affected members of the Church who were of Jewish origin. There was no outcry on behalf of the other Jewish citizens who were crippled by the race laws. There were an estimated three hundred thousand non-Aryans within the Church of whom only twenty-nine were ordained clergy. Most of the non-Aryan pastors had left the country prior to the outbreak of the war. The State Church accepted the racial laws as part of the new set-up. Wurm, Landesbischof of Württemberg, declared in 1942: "No one in the German Church questions the right of the State to promote the purity of the German nation by means of the race-laws" *(Rassengesetzgebung)*.[17]

On the Jewish presence in the Church, opinion was sharply divided. Those of the Confessional Church *(Bekenntniskirche)* opposed the racial laws as they affected baptized Jews; the nationalistic branch of the Church ("German Christians") accepted these laws with enthusiasm. But by 1943 the whole question of race was dropped even by the Confessional Church. There were, of course, always exceptions. Meier cites an address to Hitler by the Provisional Council of the Confessional Church which reads in part: "When Christians in the framework of National Socialism have anti-Semitism pressed upon them, making Jew-hatred an obligation, then there is in opposition to this the Christian commandment to love one's neighbour" (May, 1936).[18] Dr. Weissler, co-author of the address, paid with his life in a concentration camp for the impudence of daring to criticize. Another pastor, Julius von Jan, was punished for preaching repentance after the outrage of the *Kristall Nacht* in November, 1938. But these were isolated voices. Pastor von Jan later confessed: "We were all afraid to touch upon the most sensitive spot of the regime," namely, the race laws.[19] In fact, the State Church played into the hands of the regime with its declaration on April 4, 1939: "The Christian faith is the unbridgeable religious contradiction to Judaism." This was the kind of language the Nazis liked to hear and they made use of it.[20]

The ill-famed Eisenach Institute, established to serve the "German Christian" cause, concentrated upon the task of purifying the Church of Jewish accretions. Meier cites the following pronouncement by this body of theologians: "Because in the course of historical development degenerative Jewish influence made itself also active within Christianity, it has become the inevitable and decisive duty in today's Church-life to de-Judaize the Church and Christendom; such is the precondition for the future of Christianity" (May 9, 1939).

Prof. Hermann Diem's Easter letter to the laity (1943), calling for opposition to the State's persecution of the Jews, is a heartening incident at a time of gloom. In typical bureaucratic fashion the Church authorities rejected this letter for publication on the flimsy pretext that it lacked a signature.[21]

It would be wrong to convey the impression that the outrage committed against the Jews was accepted in dumb silence by everyone. There were incidents of protest but mainly from local congregations or individual members. The official body of the Church kept out of it. There was the incident when three members of one congregation put on the Jewish Star during a worship service in sympathy with their non-Aryan fellow-Christians. They were promptly denounced and arrested by the Gestapo. The pastor and other members of the congregation were punished for allowing non-Aryans to participate in an act of worship. Even offering comfort and encouragement to those destined for transportation was a punishable offence. To help a Jew under any circumstances was a crime in Nazi Germany.[22]

Meier cites a number of documents to show that many Christians were deeply troubled in their conscience by the behaviour of the official Church. Document 48, addressed to Landesbischof Meiser (Easter, 1943) and not signed for obvious reasons, reads in part: "As Christians we find the silence of the Church in Germany at the persecution of the Jews impossible to endure." This letter, apparently composed by members of a church in Munich, explains the reason for writing: "What prompts us is the simple commandment of love to neighbour."[23] Such stirrings of Christian conscience were, unfortunately, only isolated instances against a background of cowardly compromise and, in many cases, outright betrayal of Christ and the Gospel. However, Prof. P. C. Matheson's admonition must not be missed if critics are not to fall into the trap of smug superiority. He regards the failure of the Church in Germany as a distressing fact which constitutes a challenge to the rest of Christendom: "This is a subject with naught for any of our comforts. It raises gravest questions about the Christian faith and the Christian churches which we would simply evade by demanding or expecting of others, at safe distance of time, a readiness for martyrdom which we probably cannot identify in ourselves."[24] This is essentially true: it is easy to criticize. Nevertheless, it is painful to contemplate the many instances when the Church not only remained passive but seemed to support Hitler's racial policy, naively taking over some of the Nazi arguments. Thus a Church newspaper bluntly declared that the Jews were to be blamed for instigating the war and that the present "restrictions" imposed upon them were only too justified.[25]

In Western Europe outside Germany Christian opposition toward Hitler's racial policy was helpless in the face of German ruthlessness. When Utrecht's Archbishop protested the evacuation of Jews to the East, the Germans responded by evacuating Catholics of Jewish descent to concentration camps. Even the army found the behaviour of the SS intolerable, as can be seen from a letter by General Blaskowitz to Field Marshal von Brauchitsch. There was apparently no limit to Nazi cruelty both within the Reich and in occupied Europe. Their cynicism was such that at Maidanek extermination camp each child was given a sweet before entering the gas chamber.[26] Lord Russell describes the sequence of procedure with the Jews in Europe: "It was always the same story. Registration, segregation, humiliation, degradation, exploitation and extermination. These were the milestones on the road of suffering along which these unfortunate Jews made their last journey."[27] Christians were neither able nor equipped to beat such a devious foe at his own game. But the sense of guilt and shame remains.

The task of rethinking its attitude towards the Jewish people is an all-absorbing task for contemporary Christianity. For a Church which in the past regarded itself as infallible, it is humiliating to admit error. Friedrich Heer shows good insight into the matter of repentance when he writes: "There is no sweet truth. Truth in man's experience is bitter and can be acquired only through suffering."[28] As time moves on, the memory of the Holocaust grows fainter and there is the danger of minimizing, or even forgetting, the Christian part of the guilt in Jewish suffering. There are many who would skip over the ugly past in the name of peace and goodwill. Unfortunately, history has a habit of repeating itself, and what happened may happen again. There is constant need for vigilance.

The path to a better future begins at the point of repentance. Archbishop Coadjutor of Strasbourg, A. Alchinger, called upon the Vatican Council to confess openly the Church's erring ways regarding the Jewish people: "Now is the time," he said, "to admit the historic truth and to make public confession — even if the truth is bitter."[29] But truth, in essence, is never simply an academic listing of facts, but a challenge to face those facts and to change what can be changed. Michael Serafion, S.J., in a book dedicated to Pope Paul VI in proof of his devotion to the Church, writes: "No one who is aware of the basic facts of modern Europe can deny that the stakes and furnaces, the poisonous smoke and the stench in the extermination camps of National Socialist Germany are, if not exactly the logical result, nevertheless at least the drastic consequence of the attitude adopted by the average Christian towards Jews. Here Christendom stands close to the abyss of self-destruction."[30]

Such warnings from loyal members of the Church are not

issued merely in the interests of self-preservation, but as a matter of Christian conscience. We already noted that the Protestant record regarding the Jews is equally incriminating. Johan Snoek quotes Alfred Klausner: "In the course of research through all the Lutheran publications in the thirties and forties I have found no direct condemnation of the persecution of the Jews in Germany."[31] The indictment is not only against German Christianity but against the American churches as well. Snoek points out that three important Protestant denominations failed to raise their voices against the persecution: the Southern Baptist Convention, the Lutheran Church – Missouri Synod, the American Lutheran Church. Here we have the grave sin of omission on the part of the pious who did exactly what the Priest and the Levite did in the parable about the man who fell among robbers (Luke 10:29ff.). Yet it would be unjust to overlook the change that has taken place, especially since Vatican II.

The call to repentance has been sounded by many concerned Christians. Most particularly, theologians, both Protestant and Roman Catholic, have been active in this. Paul J. Kirsch compares the story of the Jewish people to the story of Jesus and relates both to Isaiah 53. He wants theologians to compare the Holocaust to the suffering of the Servant of the Lord, and in doing so Christians should be given the opportunity to repent of their part in the affliction of Israel. Of course, he realizes that not every Christian is guilty of anti-Semitism and that the Church is not the only source of anti-Semitism.[32] But this does not absolve the Church from her involvement in this particular sin.

Other writers are more outspoken, more insistent, and more critical. Their numbers are too many to specify by name. Those best known to the English-reading public for their extremely critical approach are James Parkes, A. Roy Eckardt, Rosemary Ruether, and Gregory Baum. But there are many other writers—English, French, Dutch, and German—who have made important contributions to the subject of Jewish-Christian relationships. Msgr. John M. Oesterreicher is in a category by himself. His contribution is conciliatory, honest and fair both to the Church and to Jewry. But even more effective than the literary effort is the collective voice of the Christian denominations which have denounced anti-Semitism as utterly in contradiction to the Christian faith. This is a new phenomenon and a break with a tradition of long-standing antipathy if not outright anti-Jewishness.

As far as theologians are concerned, two extraordinary and utterly diverse events have contributed to their renewed effort to understand Judaism and the Jewish people; namely, the Holocaust and the creation of the State of Israel. The first event raised the question of Jewish guilt and divine punishment for the Crucifixion; the second event attempted to answer the question of God's purpose and plan for historic Israel. We have already seen the importance Jews attach to the accusation of deicide. The question of Israel's existence as a free and independent State is of equal, if not greater, importance to the Jewish people. With regard to the almost insoluble problem of the displaced Arabs the churches have been reluctant to take sides for the obvious reason that justice for the one party means injustice for the other. Jews, naturally enough, have misinterpreted the Christian difficulty and have taken it as an indication of indifference to Jewish homelessness and suffering. But no responsible person can overlook the tragedy of either side. None other than James Parkes, a man who defended the Jewish cause for many years, wrote to the *London Times:* "Our positive contribution should be to say to *both* sides: 'you have not taken into sufficient account the rights of the other....'" The letter concludes: "We do not believe that either of you can secure any permanent gains or security from war, and we will do all in our power to help you both to make peace, and guarantee its protection."[33]

It was the Christian involvement in these two events which brought to the fore the age-old question regarding the Jews. Committees and study groups of Jews and Christians are at present active in most European countries and on the American continent. The World Council of Churches and its working committees on the Church and the Jewish people have made an important contribution towards a more Christian understanding of the Jewish plight.

The first to sound the call for repentance were the churches in Germany. The *Bruderrat* (fraternal council) of the Confessional Church released a statement on April 8, 1948, which acknowledged on behalf of the German people their guilt regarding the Jews: "We acknowledge with shame and sorrow how much we have failed and how guilty we have become in respect to Israel. We are now under the judgements of God ... so that in time of repentance we bow under God's mighty hand both as a Church and as a nation."[34]

The Synod of the Evangelical Church of Germany, meeting in West Berlin in April, 1950, declared in the name of the Church and the people that they were guilty of crimes of omission and commission against the Jewish people. The Synod warned Christians of God's judgement upon Germany and called for an act of repentance. It pressed for a total rejection of anti-Semitism in **every form and asked that Jewish Christians be made welcome in the spirit of brotherly love.**[35]

Outside Germany, the Provisional Committee of the World Council of Churches, which met in Geneva in February, 1946, acknowledged "with penitence" the failure of the churches to overcome anti-Jewish prejudice in the spirit of Christ. It called upon Christians everywhere to combat this evil and to stand by Jews suffering discrimination and persecution.[36] In Germany itself, as a requisite for Jewish-Christian understanding, churchmen were calling in no uncertain terms for repentance and reparation where possible. A leading voice was that of Dr. Otto Fricke, who in an address to the Evangelical Academy (October 24, 1949) described anti-Semitism as a system of inhumanity and a specific form of rebellion against God: "We have laden ourselves with terrible guilt," he said, "for what happened to all the Jews in our land and in the occupied countries of Europe." Fricke continued: "All this was committed in the name of the German people. We are a Christian nation and no one can lift the responsibility from us, not even God himself. 93% of our people are baptized in the name of the Triune God . . . . Anti-Semitism is of the spirit of inhumanity, of brutality and of hatred. Over against such sin of inhumanity stands the holy and living God."[37] Dr. Fricke explained to his audience that Christian maturity must be measured in terms of the Church's attitude towards Jews. The same subject was taken up by Adolf Freudenberg, who deplored the fact that the German Evangelical Church was so slow in uttering the word of repentance and declaring its collective guilt (*kein gemeinsames Wort der Busse*). Dr. Freudenberg described anti-Semitism as the ruination both of Jews and Germans and as a force still active in the land.[38]

Such were the voices which moved the German Church to rethink its attitude to the Jewish question and to do so on a national scale. The *Seelisberger Thesen* were adopted by Protestant and Roman Catholic theologians at a conference of the Hessian Society for Jewish-Christian Co-operation which met at Bad Schwalbach on May 8, 1950. This document begins with the admission that in

1933, in the midst of peace and without a shred of legal justification, Jewish citizens were suddenly submitted to a gradual process of destruction which ended in systematic mass-murder during World War II. The document acknowledges that the majority of Christians failed shamefully to show mercy to those under persecution. There is even at present, the document admits, a resurgence of anti-Semitic sentiment.

The theses formulated by the working committee of the conference stress the relatedness of the Old and New Testaments, the Jewishness of Jesus, the Church's constituency of Jews and Gentiles, the importance of love of neighbour, the unfairness of attributing Christ's suffering to Jewish guilt, the injustice of blaming the Jews for what is the means of salvation, God's unbroken faithfulness towards his people Israel, and the error of stressing Israel's rejection in Romans 11:15, whereas the whole emphasis is upon God's ultimate favour.[39]

Events in Germany during the Nazi regime inevitably affected Lutherans abroad. At first there was reluctance to protest, probably out of loyalty to the Mother Church. But as the crescendo of criticism rose immediately after the war both in Germany and elsewhere, a statement became inevitable. The Executive Committee of the Lutheran World Federation issued a statement in 1964 which testifies to an unresolved conflict between the traditional Lutheran theology of Grace versus Law and the biblical doctrine of Israel's election. We cannot reproduce all of the lengthy preamble (which leads up to the equally long "affirmations"), but in part it reads: "The relationship between Jews and Christians has been confused through the centuries by two wrong assumptions. The first assumption falsifies the Christian understanding by seeing the Jews of all times as identical with the Jewish group which in the first century rejected Jesus . . . . The second falsifies the Jewish understanding by seeing all Christians as in principle involved in the hate and persecution . . . by the official church and by nations claiming a Christian tradition." The Executive Committee declares itself unable to deal with Jewish misapprehensions, but for the Christian side it recommends an ongoing encounter with Jews and Judaism for a deepening of Jewish-Christian relations. It believes that such an attempt would result in "considerable revision" of theological orientation and of the teaching of Church history.

As to the "affirmations" of the 1964 statement, the Executive

Committee advocates Lutheran "solidarity with the Jewish people." The theological basis for such solidarity is the election and calling of Abraham's seed: "The Lutheran Churches, therefore, may not so appropriate the term 'the people of God' and 'Israel' to the church in such a way as to deny that they applied in the first instance to the Jewish people. They may not assert that the continuity of the church with the covenant people of Abraham puts in question the fact that present-day Judaism has its own continuity with Old Testament Israel."

These elaborate statements regarding the Church and Israel represent a compromise between the Lutheran theology of election through Grace and the election of Israel in terms of Old Testament Law. There is here a twofold continuity, the spiritual continuity on the basis of God's promise to Abraham, and the historic continuity on the basis of descent. The Lutheran declaration on Israel emphasizes that the Christian "solidarity with the Jewish people is to be affirmed not only despite the crucifixion of Jesus but because of it."

This document was presented to the Commission on World Mission of the Lutheran World Federation for approval at its annual meeting in Asmara (Ethiopia) in April, 1969, and was transmitted to the member churches for study and consideration.[40] An earlier document formulated in Germany by the Commission on World Mission in September, 1962, had already recommended dialogue between Christians and Jews on a personal basis. It concerned itself with the need to reexamine the Church's theological position regarding Israel, the Lutheran use of the Old Testament, the questions of the specific Lutheran emphasis of Gospel versus Law, faith versus works, etc. It recommended "an honest and penetrating examination of the attitude of Lutherans to Jews since the time of the Reformation," and stressed the importance of confronting the Lutheran churches with their responsibility towards the Jewish people. The document ended with a recommendation "to reevaluate the content and character of the Christian witness as it relates to Israel."[41]

A more recent consultation held under the auspices of the Lutheran World Federation in Oslo in August, 1975, concerned itself specifically with the question of Jewish missions. It affirmed the right and obligation of bearing witness to the faith, but at the same time acknowledged the "guilt and responsibility of Lutherans and other Christians" for fostering and allowing anti-Semitism. This document honestly acknowledges the characteristic bent of Lutheran theology towards anti-Jewishness: "We Lutherans must be aware of our particular forms of potential and actual anti-Semitism. An undiscriminating disparagement of the Law in our theology, preaching, instruction and piety, frequently has as its tragic result a caricaturing of the Jew as the epitome of hypocrisy and works-righteousness." The consultation therefore urged leading churchmen to take practical steps on regional and local levels to make effective the position papers produced by theologians. Above all, it called upon the Lutheran World Federation to perform the essential service of helping to deepen the sense of solidarity with the suffering Jews. To this end, the document proposed a number of steps which would result in a closer and more friendly relationship between Lutherans and Jews.[42]

In Germany the most effective means for reeducating Christians and bringing them closer to the Jewish people is the *Kirchentag* and its Committee for Service to the Jews. The full title is, *Deutscher Evangelischer Ausschuss für Dienst an Israel*. The *Kirchentag* has been a phenomenon in the life of German Christianity since the end of the war. The result of a lay movement founded in Hannover in 1949, it meets annually in the great centres of West Germany. It attracts large numbers of men and women who attend lectures, participate in discussions, worship, and dialogue with Roman Catholics and Jews. It is thus a fully ecumenical effort on a national scale. Some ultraconservatives have raised objections to the programme on the grounds that it provides an open forum for non-Christians to propagate their views. But these objectors are only a small minority whose protestations have proved ineffective.[43]

The efforts of leading scholars on both the Christian and the Jewish side have greatly contributed to the enlightenment of the German people. Such irksome questions as Jewish guilt for the Crucifixion of Jesus, Christian instruction in public schools about the Passion of Jesus, the problem of collective guilt, etc., have been openly discussed from every aspect.[44] There is also a Roman Catholic *Kirchentag* which engages in similar work.

The most authoritative voice within the Protestant communities is the World Council of Churches. This important representative body pronounced its condemnation of anti-Semitism at its First Assembly in Amsterdam in 1948. The text reads: "We call upon all the churches we represent to denounce anti-Semitism, no matter what its origin, as absolutely irreconcilable with the profession and practice of the Christian faith. Anti-Semitism is sin against God and man. Only as we give convincing evidence to our Jewish neighbours that we seek for them the common rights and dignities which God wills for his children, can we come to such a meeting with them as would make it possible to share with them the best which God has given us in Christ."

The Third Assembly of the World Council, which met at New Delhi in 1961, reiterated the statement of 1948 and renewed the plea to fight anti-Semitism. The resolution reads: "The Assembly renews this plea in view of the fact that situations continue to exist in which Jews are subject to discrimination and even persecution. The Assembly urges its member churches to do all in their power to resist every form of anti-Semitism. In Christian teaching the historic events which led to the Crucifixion should not be so presented as to fasten upon the Jewish people of today responsibilities which belong to our corporate humanity and not to one race or community. Jews were the first to accept Jesus and Jews are not the only ones who do not yet recognize him."

The last sentence of the resolution is the result of an amendment suggested by Bishop E. G. Gulin, a Lutheran from Finland. The reason for the amendment, the Bishop explained, was to make the resolution more irenic and to facilitate a more friendly approach to the Jewish people. Other speakers stressed the "irrevocable promises of God" to the Jews and the centuries of discrimination they have had to suffer. This was in response to one speaker who said that anti-Semitism was not the only social evil and that it affected only one people whereas there were other evils affecting a number of nations, such as racial discrimination and social injustice. The amendment passed by a vote of 194 to 130.[45]

Previously, the Second Assembly of the World Council of Churches at Evanston, Illinois (1954), had found itself deeply divided on political issues, chiefly about the State of Israel. "Christ the Hope of the World" was the overall theme of the Assembly. Arab Christians, especially, were opposed to the idea that Israel has a place in the Christian hope. The division resulted in a separate minority statement affirming Israel's special place in the Covenant and stressing that Jesus Christ is the Hope for the People of Promise just as he is for the rest of the world.[46]

The Committee on the Church and the Jewish People reported

in an official communication from Uppsala that "the New Delhi statement on anti-Semitism was followed up in a number of churches and church bodies."[47] Subsequently, the Southern Baptist Convention, meeting at Philadelphia in 1972, passed a resolution opposing "all forms of anti-Semitism" as contradictory to the Christian faith, and pledging itself to combatting this evil "in every honorable, Christian way."[48] Other Christian denominations, both in the United States and elsewhere, have passed similar resolutions.

The Greek and Eastern Orthodox Churches are more difficult to move. These communities are still deeply entrenched in traditional prejudice. Their liturgy, especially for Passion Week, bristles with anti-Jewish sentiment. Former Professor Athanase Negoitsa of Bucharest, now a priest in one of the city churches, deplores the rigidity and backwardness of his Church. He calls for a new spirit: "The time is overdue for us to change from a passive attitude to resolute action."[49] But the Eastern Churches move very slowly, if at all.

The greatest strides towards a new relationship with the Jewish people have been made by the Roman Catholics. Here there is a genuine effort noticeable on both the academic and parish level to live up to the spirit of Vatican II. For this there is a set of Guidelines issued by the Vatican concerning encounter with Jews and catechetical instruction. In Europe, but chiefly in the United States, many scholars and priests are engaged in building a bridge to the Jews. In this connection the efforts by the Institute of Judaeo-Christian Studies under the direction of Msgr. John M. Oesterreicher deserve special mention. The influence and concern of the Institute extend to liturgy, catechism, and religious textbooks. The Guidelines encourage the use of modern communication media such as the press, radio, cinema, and television, for the instruction of the faithful. Effective use of such means requires "the thorough formation of instructors and educators in training schools, seminaries and universities." In accordance with the spirit of Vatican II, the Guidelines call for continued dialogue with Jews so that both sides will understand each other in a better and deeper way. The Guidelines lay emphasis upon the continuity of the Christian faith with the Old Testament tradition and with Judaism. They suggest that "wherever possible, chairs of Jewish studies . . . be created and collaboration with Jewish scholars encouraged."

Pope Paul VI instituted a Commission for Religious Relations with Jews to function in connection with the Secretariat for Promoting Christian Unity (October 22, 1974). Such interrelation between organizations designed to promote, respectively, the objectives of Christian unity and Jewish-Christian relations is in itself a total departure from tradition and indicates a theological awareness of Covenantal continuity between historic Israel and the Christian Church.[50]

Chapter 6

Quest for a New Image of Jews and Judaism

If there is such a thing as good coming out of evil, we may say that the Holocaust opened Christian eyes to the remarkable persistence of Jewish life and tradition. The study of Jewish history and Jewish faith is increasingly becoming a Christian preoccupation on both the academic and social levels. There is an ever-growing literature on the subject, most of which is written with a new appreciation of Judaism and Jews and in a spirit of contrition for the ugly past.

Christian writers fall into two categories: those who espouse a missionary interest in converting the Jews, whether by direct or indirect influence; and those who regard conversion as an intolerable intrusion and the cause of all evil. Writers on both sides of the dividing line profess the Christian faith.

Karl Kupisch is a Christian scholar who sees the answer to Israel's problem in Jesus Christ. Jesus, he says, is the "storm centre" of the Jewish destiny. For Kupisch, Jewish survival is a sign of divine providence, as is the survival of the Christian Church. He believes that Jews and Christians belong together because both stand under God's election and determination. There can be no explanation for Jewish persistence in history other than the fact that God is still the Ruler of the world and he rules "in that he elects."[1] God's mysterious election of the Church of Jesus Christ extends to Jews and Gentiles; and though Israel is under judgement for rejecting the Messiah, God's faithfulness to his people has never ceased. For this reason Kupisch sees anti-Semitism as hostility to God's reign: "The Church of Jesus Christ must therefore say a determined No to every form of anti-Semitism." According to him "anti-Semitism" is a deceptive term; what it really stands for is *Judenhass* (Jew hatred) pure and simple. The result of *Judenhass* is that "in Europe we live upon the corpses of millions of murdered Jews." He rejects the excuse that anti-Semitism has a long history going back to pre-Christian times; it was the contribution of the Germans, he tells us, to provide for this evil a scientific, natural, historical justification. The result was a nihilistic philosophy which ended with the extermination camps of Auschwitz and Theresienstadt. For Kupisch the most distressing fact about anti-Semitism is that it prospered upon Christian soil. He quotes a Protestant theologian, Helmut Gollwitzer, who admits that the age-long Christian contempt of the Jews has generated a spirit of murder, though Christians ought to have known from the Sermon on the Mount that despising a brother leads to homicide.[2]

Unfortunately Kupisch is still caught in the medieval tradition that Israel's suffering is the result of divine wrath: "The rejection of the Messiah resulted in God's wrathful judgement [Zorngericht]."[3] But this is a view increasingly unpopular among Christian scholars, except for those who subscribe to an ultraconservative position. It is, however, still prevalent in schools and among the general public. Charlotte Klein, a Roman Catholic scholar, reports that at a German seminary she discovered a thoroughly negative view of Jews and Judaism in the essays the students wrote, though the students themselves were not prejudiced at all. She soon discovered that the caricature of Judaism was due to textbooks which the students took to be the official view of the Church. This raised for Dr. Klein the question: "Is the traditional interpretation of New Testament utterances of Judaism the only possible one?" Her conclusion is that it is not necessarily a betrayal of the New Testament to seek better and more accurate theological insight into the structure and significance of Judaism. Christians still have to discover, she says, that Judaism performs a positive role and is in no sense an anachronistic remnant of the past.[4]

Dr. Klein took the trouble to examine the literary output of some outstanding biblical scholars, both Catholic and Protestant, and soon discovered their writings are extremely negative with respect to Judaism. Such household names in the theological field as Eduard Lohse, Martin Noth, Rudolf Bultmann, Leonhard Goppelt, Ethelbert Stauffer, etc., have all made their own contribution to the prevailing prejudice among German readers. Occasionally, in her zeal, Dr. Klein overstates her case, and seems to be unnecessarily on the defensive where Judaism is concerned. But there can be no doubt that the older German Protestant theologians have made of Judaism a bugbear to frighten the faithful with the

Law, with legalism, with the Pharisees and the Scribes.[5]

On the Roman Catholic side the situation is no better, if not worse. Themes repeated in most theological textbooks include the annulment of the Covenant with Israel, the substitution of Christians for Jews, the punishment of the Jewish people for rejecting the Messiah, Judaism's lack of spiritual insight, etc. Dr. Klein takes to task Michael Schmaus, an outstanding Roman Catholic scholar, for supporting the view that Jewish suffering is the result of divine punishment. She writes: "This is a convenient way to explain the persecution of the Jews."[6] The remedy, to her mind, is for Christian scholars to start using original Jewish sources for a better appreciation of Judaism. She does not think a change of attitude is possible until scholars are better informed. Though Dr. Klein is given to oversimplification (for example, on the question whether there was a quarrel between Jesus and Judaism, which she denies), her concern is legitimate.

Like Charlotte Klein, many Protestant apologists for Judaism are condemnatory of Christian attitudes and actions. Prof. Franklin H. Littell of Temple University has no difficulty in seeing a "red thread" tying Justin Martyr and Chrysostom to Auschwitz and Treblinka. This Christian bent against Jews he sees as a greater evil than "vulgar anti-Jewish slurs in speech or discrimination in practice." The "false teaching" of the Church regarding the Jews opens wide the Christian "solidarity of guilt" and is the mark of "wholesale apostasy" from the faith. All this Littell ties to the Christian conviction that with the coming of Christ, Israel's mission came to an end. Here again there is a modicum of exaggeration, but on the main issue there can be no serious doubt. Auschwitz has raised the question of Christian credibility and has initiated a major crisis in theology. Prof. Littell insists that there is no way the Church can evade her responsibility for what happened in Europe during the war years. To categorize the Nazis as "neopagans" simply ignores the centuries of anti-Jewishness "which made murder of the Jews possible and logical." He charges that "Christendom was impregnated with hatred of the Jews" which prepared the way for the Nazi murderers.[7] The Church is therefore marked with the sign of Cain and needs radical purging. Prof. Littell quotes Karl Barth: "The question of the Jews is the question of Christ; anti-Semitism is the sin against the Holy Ghost."[8] The most pernicious form of anti-Semitism, Littell explains, is the one rooted in theology, for it is the fountainhead of all its other branches. Littell feels that not only Christianity but God himself is being questioned: the Holocaust has created a crisis of faith which is still unresolved. It is, as he calls it, the "unfinished business of the Christian churches, the running sore unattended by its leaders and weakening to its constitution." The waning influence of Christianity Littell attributes to the crisis of faith resulting from the Holocaust.[9]

While Prof. Littell belongs to the liberal branch of Protestantism, James Daane, Assistant Editor of *Christianity Today*, is a spokesman for conservatives. His book on anti-Semitism is orientated towards Scripture and attempts to elucidate this complex malady which so disrupts Jewish-Christian relationships. Daane deals with the question of Jewish responsibility for the death of Jesus and declares it irrelevant. In the light of the New Testament, the idea of guilt is misconceived. Nowhere, he declares, are the Jews condemned or rejected by God: "It is the Christ on the Cross, not the Jews, who is rejected and accursed by God." Responsibility for the Cross is a shared responsibility: "An anti-Semitism grounded in Jewish responsibility for the Cross disqualifies the Christian Church both for understanding and for preaching the gospel."[10] But unlike the liberal theologians such as Klein, Littell, and others, Daane is aware of an initial conflict between, on the one hand, Jesus, Paul, and the early Church, and, on the other, Judaism. This conflict, in the eyes of Jewish scholars, is regarded as the central source of all Christian anti-Semitism. This James Daane denies: "It would take nothing less than the denial of the Christian faith to remove everything that some Jewish people regard as anti-Semitic."[11] In Daane's view, Judaism as encountered in the New Testament was not only deficient spiritually but degenerate in character. Proof for this he sees in the rejection and Crucifixion of Jesus. The destruction of Jerusalem he understands as "an act of divine judgement." Like Kupisch, Daane sees the only solution for anti-Semitism as the Jews' acceptance of Jesus as their Messiah, for only thus can the "wall of partition" be abolished and unity between them and the Gentiles be established. Daane stresses the inherent Jewishness of the Gospel and the enduring character of Jewish election, but this can be understood only from beneath the Cross of Christ. Because Jews rejected the One on the Cross, they also misinterpreted their own election.

What one misses in Daane's exposition is a lack of confession and spirit of repentance for the sins of the Church. Herein he differs markedly from conservative Roman Catholic writers who also favour Israel's conversion but humbly acknowledge Christian misdeeds. In contrast to Daane, Alan Jenkins, a Congregational minister from Royal Oak, Michigan, speaks for Christians of every shade when he expresses shame and sorrow for all the misery Christianity has inflicted upon the Jews. To him the idea of deicide is preposterous and he deplores the fact that it is still taught in some church schools and preached from pulpits: *"This outrageous myth,"* he declares, *"was written on clouds of smoke which rose from the ovens of Buchenwald."* Jenkins feels equally strongly about the other Christian myth; namely, that the Jewish exile was a punishment for the Crucifixion of Jesus. This does not mean that all in Judaism was perfect. "It had its mechanical side, its superficial pieties, its bigotries, its worldliness"—but is this not true of all organized religion? "Is this not true of much of what passes for Christianity today?" Jenkins asks. Frederick C. Grant has said that at long last the Church has begun "to mumble a kind of confession." Alan Jenkins writes: "I apologize to the Jews for the mumbling!"[12]

As already indicated, the most outspoken critics of the Church's treatment of the Jews are Roman Catholics. Friedrich Heer quotes the scathing words of the theologian Heinrich Spaemann, who, in a broadcast over the S-W German Radio (March 8, 1965), said on the question of the Crucifixion: "As if we ourselves had no share in the Crucifixion of Jesus, as if similar things had not happened in our own lifetime—and in our own country and among our own people." Spaemann pointed out the curious inconsistency of remembering in the Church liturgy the Jewish children slaughtered by Herod at Bethlehem "while keeping silent . . . about the millions in Auschwitz and elsewhere."

Heinrich Spaemann challenged the Vatican to make an open confession of its dreadful guilt with respect to the Jewish people.[13] But is a confession of guilt enough? The more radical Roman Catholic writers are asking for a theological revolution which would not only rehabilitate Judaism as an equal partner in the Jewish-Christian dialogue, but also legitimate its status as a valid religion in its own right. The consequence of such a reorientation would be the complete abandonment of every vestige of missionary activity among Jews. Gregory Baum is an authoritative voice on the American continent for this radical position. As a matter of policy the Roman Church has officially abrogated every missionary attempt. Baum was driven to this position by "shattering reflection on the Jewish Holocaust" and the discovery of Christian involvement in the tragedy.[14] As Prof. Baum sees it, the Church had been justifying her attitude towards Jews in two ways: (1) it pretended that all Jews rejected Jesus and were rejected by Jesus; and (2) it concluded that all Jews were under a divine curse as a result. What the Church now has to do is rectify "these false and harmful expressions of Christian doctrine."[15] Baum sees Vatican II as only "the first step" in making up for past sins. The important thing now "is how soon the teaching of the Council enters our institutions and the hearts of our people . . . in giving visible expression to the spiritual bond that unites the Church and the Jews."[16]

That the two faiths, though different, do not contradict but rather supplement each other, is the theological stance of liberals. Foremost among them is Dr. Rosemary Ruether. She is not satisfied with a mere change of heart; what she wants is change of doctrine. According to her theology, the Christian claim to universalism is a "misappropriated idea of realized messianism" which inevitably leads to a position of inerrancy and absolutism. What is needed is to abandon Chalcedonian Christology and emphasize the humanity of Jesus instead of his divinity. Dr. Ruether wants a compromise between the Church and Judaism; she wants "to come to terms with this Jewish negation of the Christian faith," which is nothing less than coming to terms "with the Cross of human history which has not yet turned into a messianic victory." This raises the question: "In what sense is Jesus the Christ?" Rosemary Ruether has a ready answer: he is *not yet* the Christ, but is the paradigmatic archetype of man's aspiration "in reaching for the Kingdom." Because Jews already reach towards the Kingdom, there is no necessity for them to know about the story of Jesus; they already have other stories, "such as the story of Exodus."[17] Elsewhere Dr. Ruether explains that the Christian "affirmation of the Messianic Event in Jesus," just like the Exodus for the Jews, must not be understood as a "once-for-all" experience. Both are meant to be "open-ended" experiences pointing to the future. There can, therefore, be no competition between these two faiths: "the Jew and the Christian stand in parallel traditions, each having tasted grace, each looking for a fulfillment that is 'beyond.' " This new insight, says Dr. Ruether, requires "relativizing" our speech about the Messianic Event and the way we identify Jesus as the Christ.[18]

Such a radical break with Chalcedonian theology does not just reform Christianity; it abolishes it. Once the tension between Church and Synagogue is removed by turning Jesus into just another rabbi, the Church becomes a Gentile Synagogue and the Messianic Event is reduced to a myth. This is certainly not in keeping with the theology of Vatican II, which reaffirms that Jesus Christ is the *summus actus revelationis*—the ultimate act of revelation of God to mankind.[19]

Msgr. Oesterreicher characterizes Rosemary Ruether's position as left-hand theology, describing it as "a christology without Christ . . . faith turned into un-faith," which happens "when man takes the place of God."[20] This is not too far-fetched a description on the part of a perceptive critic. Dr. Ruether seems to have gone beyond the outer limits of the Church without knowing it, for she still regards herself as a Catholic theologian. On the Protestant side, some writers move within the proximity of Dr. Ruether's position. This, however, does not preclude their right to criticize the Church whenever there is justification for it. A leading voice of this group is Dr. James Parkes, a champion of the Jewish cause. However one may disagree with his position, he is a balanced and restrained writer, so typical of English scholars. This cannot be said about some of his followers in the United States.

Unlike Rosemary Ruether, Dr. Parkes admits that Christianity "cannot but be a missionary religion." Its mission is to all men, bond and free, male and female. The missionary approach characterized the Church from the very beginning: "a Church which has no mission is a dead Church."[21] At the International Conference of Christians and Jews in Toronto (1968), Dr. Parkes declared in his opening address: ". . . we are, and must always be a missionary religion." But for Parkes the term *mission* has acquired a different connotation. "Our mission," he continued, "is not to save as many sheep as we can bring within our own fold, but to serve the world and its Creator . . . ." "Mission" in his vocabulary is used not in the Christian but in the Jewish context, as he explains: "Here, I am entirely Jewish in my outlook. The ultimate purpose of life is the realization of the Messianic Age."

In a joking aside, Parkes told his audience that Karl Barth once accused him of being *ganz verjudet* (completely Judaized).[22] He has gladly accepted the label on the understanding that his being "bejewed" does not modify one single positive aspect of his

Christology.[23] We would therefore have reason to expect from Parkes both a positive attitude to the Jewish people and an orthodox affirmation of the Lordship of Jesus Christ. But this is not the case. There is no doubt about James Parkes's sympathy with Judaism, but his "positive Christology" leaves one doubting. Parkes deprecates the unfortunate Christocentricity of orthodoxy, which, in his view, leads to intolerance of non-Christians. Even more pronounced is his opposition to Jewish missions — Jews must not become Christians, and Christians must not become Jews.[24] His quarrel with orthodox Christianity is over the tenet that there is no salvation except in Christ. "It is surely time," he tells us, "that the Churches faced the fact that a christocentric gospel has not only led them into deplorable beliefs and activities, but has failed, of itself, to meet the whole human need."[25] In order to overcome Christocentricity, Parkes suggests a reformulation of the trinitarian doctrine in such a way as to free it of "the pathetic Divine bureaucracy" derived from the New Testament. The theological diagram which he provides in graphic form for solving the trinitarian problem is a geometrical exercise in ingenuity with no regard to Scripture. According to this diagram, Father, Son, and Holy Spirit is God and is not God.[26] At the same time, Dr. Parkes professes to make his stand on the Athanasian Creed, but chiefly, it would appear, for its negative phrasing: The Father is not . . . the Son is not . . . the Holy Spirit is not . . . . Revelation for Dr. Parkes is not tied to the Bible: Judaism, Christianity, and Humanism all have a share of it, each standing for a particular emphasis — righteousness, love, truth. These three virtues are not incompatible but neither are they interchangeable. It is for this reason that mission is out of place. The tension arising from the encounter of these three positions must not be resolved but maintained in the form of dialogue.[27]

Parkes's theology operates on the premise of a double Covenant: two religions, two chosen peoples with different tasks and missions. Judaism can in no way be a substitute for Christianity, nor Christianity for Judaism. Both are right and both must acknowledge the rightness of the other.[28]

We have dwelt on Dr. Parkes's theology because of his pervasive influence upon the churches, especially in Great Britain. His theology is not a compromise in the syncretistic sense. It is structured upon a deep dichotomy in the story of revelation: two ways, two rights, two Covenants, but only one God. The Pauline vision in Ephesians where in Christ the dividing wall of hostility is broken down, and Gentile and Jew are made one in him "that he might create in himself one new man in place of the two . . . in one body through the cross" (Eph. 2:11ff.), leaves Dr. Parkes totally unmoved; his theology is of a different kind. It works on the principle of "creative tension" and not upon the reconciliation wrought by Jesus Christ. What purpose such tension is meant to serve is difficult to say, and there is the added danger that it may become a source of renewed friction by reason of the frailty of human nature.[29]

If the theology of James Parkes is difficult to square with the Christian faith, that of his follower, A. Roy Eckardt, leaves one in a dazed state.[30] Eckardt has little to add to Parkesian ideology, except overemphasis and acerbity of language. He sadly lacks the restraint of his English mentor and shows even less consistency in his writings. Like Parkes, he professes Christianity as his faith and even makes some claims to orthodoxy. Also, like Parkes, he does not rule out Christian witness "in a manner that testifies to the uniqueness and integrity of the Christian faith." One would therefore expect that if "integrity" is preserved, mission to all those who are not Christians would be acceptable. But this is not the case, especially in relation to Jews. Eckardt denies that there is any justification whatsoever for preaching the Gospel to Jews. His reasons are that (1) "missions and anti-Semitism are inextricably associated" and (2) the believing Jew "does not need the Christian gospel as an answer."[31] The reason why the Jew can do without the Gospel is that there is no essential difference between Calvary and Sinai. Jewish and Christian teaching are identical, the only difference being in the mode of thinking. This has been the widely accepted Jewish argument since Franz Rosenzweig. Martin Buber put it succinctly in his dialogue with Karl Ludwig Schmidt at Stuttgart in January, 1933: "The Christian need not come to God through Judaism, nor the Jew through Christianity."

Eckardt takes up Parkes's idea that Judaism is essentially a social religion while Christianity is a personal religion. Therefore, both supply different needs and are legitimate in their own right. The Gospel is for the nations, the Torah for the Jews. The twofold Covenant, a notion inherited from Parkes, completely dominates Eckardt's thinking, and for an interesting reason. To accept a single Covenant would subordinate Israel to the Church. This must never happen because it is the Christian, the "younger brother," who is the subordinate. Eckardt regards it as "the height of presumptuousness" to imply that the elder brother "is not already a member of the household of salvation."[32]

However, Eckardt realizes that the superiority of the elder brother disturbs the balance of equality after which he is striving; in addition, he does not want to rule out the legitimacy of mission altogether. He thus finds himself with a curiously unbalanced system which fails to do justice to either side. After all that Eckardt has already said about the elder brother, the reader finds himself surprised by the sentence: "Membership in original Israel conveys no magical precedence or power." Dr. Eckardt may not realize it, but this is exactly what Paul said in different words (cf. Rom. 2:28f.; also Matt. 3:9). Eckardt sees Jews and Christians as being different but equal. The difference, according to Eckardt, is not in status but in precedence. In the "structure of the history of salvation" the Jew was before the Christian—this again is a thoroughly Pauline premise but the inference drawn therefrom is different. For Paul Israel's precedence entitles him to hear the Gospel first (Rom. 2:10); for Eckardt it makes the Gospel redundant.

The maze of Eckardt's reasoning becomes even more confusing when the reader suddenly comes upon the following sentence: "To put wholly aside Christian ministry to Israel is as wrong as to attempt to try to make Christians out of the Jewish people." What Eckardt means by "ministry" is difficult to fathom, unless perhaps he means the service the younger brother owes to the first-born. He chides the Dutch Reformed Church for still hanging on to the missionary commitment, and this in spite of accepting the principle of continuity between the Old and New Testaments and the desire for ecumenicity.[33] In the hands of Dr. Eckardt, Saul of Tarsus fares badly. Romans 9 to 11 is rejected out of hand as totally inapplicable to the present situation.[34]

It is not easy to follow the sequence of Eckardt's thought on any theological issue relating to the Jews. First we are told that one cannot set dialogue against witness: "There is no real dialogue without witness and no meaningful witness without dialogue." Then we are told that witness must aim at no results. For this he quotes approvingly J. C. Rylaarsdam's dictum: "If God's covenant with Israel is indeed an enduring one, all attempts to put it out of business by missions, however well intentioned, contradict God's purpose."[35] But almost in the same breath we are told that putting people into "once-for-all categories" is wrong and that Christians must not shut the door to any Jew who asks for admittance. To maintain that the Church is only for Gentiles is an idolatrous attitude and smacks of anti-Semitism. Eckardt assures the reader that he is totally against "possession" of privileges. Birth, he says, must not be a deciding factor in matters of faith. Yet missions must be rejected out of hand. The rejection of missions to Jews is for Eckardt a "confessional-theological affirmation." Jewish missions is without exaggeration Eckardt's *bête noire*. He regards it as an "attack upon the essence of Christian faith itself," because it puts in question God's election under the Covenant. Mission can be justified only among Gentiles — it has no place among Jews.[36]

The theological inconsistency one meets in Eckardt leaves the reader not only puzzled but sometimes breathless, yet there can be no doubt of his sincerity and righteous indignation at the fearful mistreatment of Jews by Christians.[37] Fortunately, for Eckardt, the glaring inconsistencies, especially on witness and mission, have now been rectified. As a result of criticism by the Jewish writer Levi A. Olan, both Parkes and Eckardt have now renounced categorically even the thought of missions to Jews. They now denounce the missionary effort in the strongest terms as a "travesty and even a blasphemy of seeking to make Christians out of Jews."[38]

Olan's complaint was that men like Parkes and Eckardt do not go far enough in pressing for a change in theological outlook. Eckardt agrees that a more radical reformation is necessary if Jewish-Christian relationships are to be based on sound foundations. This is not possible unless the Church abandons her secret hope that in the end Jews will come to acknowledge Jesus as their Lord and Saviour. Dialogue, Eckardt is convinced, can be fruitful only if this secret hope is rejected once and for all. He confesses that in his previous works he was still suffering "from a certain spiritual imperialism," but now he is a liberated man and as such desires to go beyond his position as expressed in *Elder and Younger Brothers*. In his own words: "I have long since rejected the Christian missionizing attitude towards Jews"; but now he intends to go even further. As a Christian he wants to "affirm unreservedly that the Jewish faith is true *for me*." But such a statement, Eckardt explains, only a Christian can make; a Jew cannot take a similar position and say that Christianity is a true faith for him.[39]

On two counts Eckardt and Rabbi Olan do not see eye to eye. Olan disagrees (1) that Jesus opened the Covenant to the Gentiles and (2) that there is any connection at all between Jews and Christians. This, of course, would leave Eckardt outside with the rest of Christendom. According to Olan, the Covenant is a Jewish affair and has nothing to do with Gentiles. "Christianity," he says, "is for Jews a wholly new and different religion, totally unrelated to the Covenant. Its Jewish origin is an accident of history." Eckardt finds such an extreme rejection difficult to swallow and accuses Olan of "Jewish Marcionism."[40]

On the question of the Covenant Eckardt has already modified his position. He no longer sees it as a mystery. Now he wants it secularized and humanized in the hope that this will make room for Gentiles. Eckardt's retreat is almost total. Even his reverence for Richard Niebuhr, his "great teacher," is unable to restrain his theological dissolution. He finds as too absolutist Niebuhr's claim that the unity of the human race can be achieved only in Jesus Christ.[41] By a process of theological inversion, Eckardt seems to have transferred the Incarnation from Jesus to the Jew. This is how he puts it: "The Jew becomes the Torah. The Jew is incarnation."[42] Because Christianity is so closely related to anti-Semitism, he is driven to doubt whether he can still remain a Christian without becoming guilty of anti-Semitism. To be a Christian implies bringing the world "into the Covenant through Jesus the Jew," which in turn means perpetuating anti-Semitism. Consequently, "the Christian gospel can no longer be preached." If it is a matter of choosing between truth and love, love is more important, for "blindness is a lesser evil than heartlessness."[43]

There is a disarming honesty about Roy Eckardt. He frankly admits that he is confused and that he has many more questions than he has answers.[44] He is also a man of humility and compassion. His last book ends on a note of repentance for the sins of others with an appeal to the "forgiving grace of God."

The reason for paying particular attention to Rosemary Ruether and Roy Eckardt is that both exemplify extreme revolt against embedded traditional views. Their radicalism has taken them to the very edge of the Christian faith. Other writers, though less outspoken, take an equally attenuating position with respect to the Messianic Event associated with the person of Jesus. It would appear that there is no way out of the dilemma: rejection of mission to Jews detracts from the uniqueness of Jesus. The corollary is a radical change in Christology: either Jesus is the Messiah in the traditional sense, in which case the Jews must be included; or he is a misunderstood and misinterpreted Jewish rabbi, in which case Jews do not need him for they have good rabbis of their own. The logic is simple enough. The question of missions to Jews is therefore more than a matter of sociological adjustment. In the context of the Christian affirmation regarding Jesus it touches upon the very foundation of the faith. That this is the case can be seen from another example of a clash between humanistic conviction and Christian loyalties.

Prof. Alan T. Davies of Toronto is a more disciplined scholar than Rosemary Ruether and Roy Eckardt. On the question of anti-Semitism he writes with eloquence and feeling. He is well read on the subject and understands the contemporary situation. But in the conflict between his theological sensibilities and his humanistic bent, the tension for him remains unresolved. As a result he finds himself in a contradictory situation by affirming "the once-for-all character of the Christological faith" on the one hand, and total rejection of missions to Jews on the other.[45] His disdain of mission leads him to say: "Any Christian who, in dialogue, is anxious to convert his Jewish counterpart only succeeds in exposing a persistent sickness in Christian piety that continues to plague Jewish-Christian relations."[46] In consequence Davies rejects any claim to the universal significance of Jesus as the Christ. For him every missionary endeavour is an expression of imperialism. Those who engage in it are absolutists who pretend to have a monopoly of the truth. Absolute theology, he tells us, assumes that God is to be found in Christianity and nowhere else. Davies understands mission as a "persistent sickness" which the Church must learn to overcome. Because "conversionism and anti-Judaism have been frequent bedfellows," there is no place for missionary work among Jews.[47] To proselytize Jews means to engage in anti-Semitism of one kind or another. Christians can approach Jews in dialogue, but only in dialogue which has no ulterior motives. It must be utterly neutral dialogue, though Davies realizes that there is a risk of conversion when people of different faiths meet, but this is an existential risk which is unavoidable. There must, however, be no conscious effort at exerting influence upon the opposite party. What they are to talk about, he does not say.

In Davies's exposition we meet the same contradiction we met in the case of Eckardt, though in more moderate language. Davies demands that there be no conscious seeking of converts, but this does not imply denial of the validity of conversion as such. His idea that religious dialogue can be neutral presupposes a state of innocence of both partners which by far transcends human experience. The man of faith is never a neutral person; he lives under loyalties and in obedience to his conscience before God. This applies to Jews, Christians, and everyone else.

If Rosenzweig muddled up men like Parkes and Eckardt, as Davies suggests, Davies himself has become a victim of Buberian dialectic. Either dialogue is conversation from a position of conviction or it is not dialogue in the accepted sense of the word.[48] In the philosophical tradition, Socratic dialogue has always meant talking with a purpose, and making a point no matter what the reaction of the opposite partner. When Socrates engaged in dialogue, it was to help the other person arrive at the truth, a truth which Socrates already knew and which resided in his interlocutor but had to be brought to the surface. If this reflects the absolutist attitude which Davies castigates, then we would ask: What is the alternative, except spineless latitudinarianism?

We will return to the subject of dialogue at a later stage. It is worth noting, however, that at least one Jewish writer realizes the indecency of the demand for the Church to abandon missionary endeavour altogether. Rabbi Henry Siegman suggests that such a demand is inadmissible even from a Jewish point of view. He says he can find no religious nor moral grounds on which to base such a demand.[49]

A major problem in Jewish-Christian relationships concerns the validity of the Old Testament. Anti-Semites frequently deprecate the Old Testament because they regard it as an essentially Jewish book. But even less prejudiced writers prefer the New Testament God of love to the Old Testament God of vengeance. This kind of misrepresentation was already made in the second century by the well-known heretic Marcion. Dislike of the Old Testament dominated the German Church chiefly because of Luther's fear of the Law. Schleiermacher, Hegel, Harnack, and a host of others felt truly embarrassed by the Christian association with Old Testament tradition. Propagandists used to poke fun at some Old Testament stories and there was considerable agitation among intellectuals to have the Old Testament removed from the school curriculum.[50]

This negative attitude to the Hebrew Bible was part of a deep-seated antipathy towards Judaism and Jews, under the pretext that the Jewish God is a God of vengeance. This is an injustice both to the Old Testament and to rabbinic Judaism. Psalm 130:3–4 well expresses the ethos of Old Testament piety: "If thou, O Lord, shouldst mark iniquities, Lord, who could stand? But there is forgiveness with thee, that thou mayest be feared." The teaching of the rabbis was similar: "Learn to receive suffering, and forgive those who insult you." They regarded an unforgiving person as utterly devoid of mercy. Not only the New Testament but also the rabbis prohibited requiting evil for evil. Mar Zutra, the fifth-century (?) exilarch, used to say when going to bed: "May everyone who has done me an injury be forgiven." It was in 1936, when the Nazis had already begun their persecution of Jews, that Rabbi Eisendrath exhorted his congregation: "Let Israel lead the way in forgiving all cruelties perpetrated by those who take his name in vain."

But can Israel forgive Auschwitz?

Rudolf Vrba, who at the age of seventeen found himself an inmate of Auschwitz, has told of his experience in the extermination camp and of his miraculous escape to reveal the facts to the world outside. When Vrba recounted his experiences at Auschwitz to the Papal Nuncio of Slovakia, the prelate shed tears. Anyone who reads the book *I Cannot Forgive* (1964) will easily understand why Dr. Vrba cannot forgive. Yet forgiveness is an inevitable necessity for human coexistence. The State of Israel had to come to terms with post-war Germany; and Germans in an effort at reparation spent billions of marks to try to make up for the untold suffering, though the lost lives are beyond monetary assessment. As in all human relations, the issue is whether a new start on better foundations is possible.

For such a start Christians must discover the truth about Jews and Judaism. To provide the conditions necessary for a new and more equitable Jewish-Christian relationship, churches must examine their age-old prejudices against Jews and their false theological assumptions. This implies not only a psychological reorientation on the part of men and women of goodwill. The whole corpus of Christian teaching regarding Jews must undergo a radical change. The negative image of the Jew must be replaced by a more factual image of a human being who like everyone else has his faults and his virtues.

It seems to this writer that the task of reconstruction has to begin with a better understanding of the New Testament Pharisees, for it is the picture of the Pharisee as a hopeless hypocrite that to a large extent moulded the Christian conception of the Jew. Jewish scholars are only too justified in their complaint that this distorted image of Pharisaism is reflected in Christian attitudes to Judaism and Jews. They vigourously reject the popular view that all Pharisees were hypocrites, a view which is reflected in the contemporary use of the word *Pharisee*.[51]

Most Christian scholars are now agreed that the Jewish complaint with respect to the traditional Christian perception of Matthew 23 is justified. The indictment of the Pharisees in this chapter is not applicable indiscriminately to the Pharisaic movement and to each Pharisee. Not only the Gospels, but also the Talmud is critical of some Pharisees, especially of those who make greater demands upon others than upon themselves. The Talmud notes seven classes of Pharisee of varying degrees of sincerity. It is only the "Pharisee of love" who is dear to God.[52] C. G. Montefiore sums up the issue regarding the depiction of the Scribes and Pharisees in the Gospels: "It is agreed that in A.D. 28 there were doubtless many black sheep among them, but it is also allowed that there were many white ones, as well as a large number of mixtures — grey sheep, not wholly white, but by no means completely black."[53] This is a fair assessment and holds true of human experience in every movement, political or religious. There was never a time when the same statement could not be made about Christians, yet it would be totally unjust to damn all Christians as hypocrites. The same rule must be extended to the Pharisees. Stamping all Pharisees as hypocrites is an injustice which has been the cause of much evil. A Christian scholar who represents a conservative position writes: "It is a tragedy that in Matthew the word 'Pharisee' has come to mean popularly a self-righteous, hypocritical prig. Unfortunately not even Christian scholarship was able over the centuries to rid itself of an unfair bias against the Pharisees."[54]

To the false and distorted image of the Pharisees must be added the libel that all Jews are guilty of the trial and Crucifixion of Jesus and that they are therefore under a curse. This has been, over the centuries, a second cause of prejudice against Jews and is still widely believed. This view is fortified by the obvious tension that existed between Jesus and the "Jews," especially as reflected in the Fourth Gospel. Reading the Gospels the unwary reader easily finds confirmation for his antipathy to Jews, especially when he is already biased against them by inherited tradition. This has prompted Jewish writers to describe the New Testament as the root of all anti-Semitism. Some have gone so far as to suggest expurgation of the offending passages if hostility towards Jews is to be allayed among Christians. However, Christians cannot be expected to tamper with the New Testament text. So scholars are in search of other methods, such as educating the Christian public to a better understanding of the history and background of the Gospels as these relate to the Jewish people. Such a task requires historical research and theological insight; above all there is need for a revision of textbooks, hymns, liturgy, and catechetical material which in the past contributed towards prejudice against Jews. But in the last resort, what is needed is a change of heart so that the Gospels are read in the spirit of Christ and in the fear of God. On this score James Parkes is only too right when he says: "It is the perpetual sneers, misrepresentations and contemptuous remarks of the theologians and even saintly preachers and otherwise admirable school textbooks which have separated Jews from the rest of humanity and made so appalling a crime as the holocaust possible." He blames the "perpetual denigration of Judaism" with its deadly effect upon the minds of the populace for giving rise to legal discrimination and popular persecution.[55]

Anti-Jewish prejudice is by no means dead; the past is still with us. Hilgard Heufken circulated a questionnaire among five hundred schoolchildren in Cologne. She received some revealing answers. The children spoke with respect of the Old Testament and the ancient Hebrews, but were negative about Jews. To the question, "Why did Hitler persecute Jews?" the most frequent answer was that they were guilty of the death of Jesus. Other schools produced similar results.[56] Children are given to simplistic answers but their thinking is moulded by tradition. Implied in their answers is a vengeful God who does not forgive even after these many years. The view is not peculiar to children; some outstanding scholars still hold on to it. Prof. Martin Kähler, an outstanding biblical theologian, when asked what he thought of contemporary Jews, answered: "The constant reappearance of anti-Semitism in history goes to prove that since the return from exile and the rejection of Jesus there evolved a specific type of Jew. Jewish dominance of international finance and the press will persuade even skeptics that dry [spröde] Judaism is not simply the result of restrictions imposed by Christian fanaticism."[57] Kähler explained that as a Bible-revering man *(Bibelverehrer)* he saw in the plight of the Jewish people a verification of the curse detailed in God's Word. It may come as a surprise that a man of Kähler's standing was so bound to tradition, but this is exactly why school-children half a century after Hitler's rise are still under the spell of this dreadful myth.

In order to get a feel for the background against which public opinion was shaped, we quote several other German Protestant divines on the eve of the First World War. Prof. Ludwig Lemme, of Heidelberg, an outstanding scholar and Privy Church-Council-lor *(Geheimer Kirchenrat)*, accused Israel of crucifying his Messiah even in his day by their strong hatred of Christianity. He declared Judaism an anachronism and hoped that Zionism would fail, for if successful it would only contribute to "anti-Christian obduracy."[58] And here is the view of Privy Councillor Oskar Pank of Leipzig: Since the Jews have nailed their Messiah to the Cross, they wander without king, sacrifice, altar, and Temple, scattered over all lands a foreign people among the nations, "a holy ruin, a senile figure that does not die" *(eine ergraute Gestalt die nicht stirbt).*[59]

This view of Judaism and Jews is not peculiar to German theologians. It was, and to a large extent is, the view held by many Christians. It was only after the Second World War, as a result of the Holocaust, that the traditional Christian image of the Jews began to be seriously questioned. The task of changing embedded opinion from a negative to a positive view falls to educators, pastors, and parents.

W. P. Eckert, who is concerned with the problem of what is taught in Catholic German schools about Jews and Judaism, sees signs of definite improvement, though much remains to be done. He quotes a number of works dealing with the question of Jewish-Christian relationships and providing guidelines for teachers and parents.[60] The process of change will take time and requires patience. The Vatican Guidelines, according to Claire Huchet Bishop, are "no more than a scratch of the surface." But even this is a beginning and will help towards reconciliation. She rightly attaches importance to the effect of textbooks and liturgy as a means of influencing the faithful. The concept of a "blood curse" resulting in the Diaspora as a sign of divine wrath, the concept of Judaism as legalistic and ossified, and of the Jews as an obdurate people, must disappear from Catholic teaching if there is to be a new beginning. Bishop goes even further: "Jewish-Christian reconciliation will be impossible as long as Christians are taught that the Church is the 'new people Israel,' and as such has supplanted Israel." She points to Romans 9:4 and 11:29, which totally contradict such a view. She sees no improvement unless the Church is willing to give up this theological stance and relate herself to Israel in a new and positive way. There can be no rapprochement until there is a complete theological reorientation. The alternative is "mutual misunderstanding and disappointment."[61]

Some Roman Catholic theologians in Germany and elsewhere have taken the Vatican Guidelines seriously and have endeavoured to introduce a new perspective into the teaching of the Church regarding the Jews. Gerhard Teske has shown that the Church calendar, the festivals, and the liturgy provide suitable occasion to relate the Christian faith to the Old Testament background and to stress the continuity between the Church and the Jewish people. He sees here vast opportunities for pastors and teachers to bring about a radical change of attitude in students without falsifying the faith. Theodor Filthaut regards the misconception that Israel's dispersal in the world is a just punishment for killing Jesus as a main obstacle — a "wall" which prevents ordinary Christians from seeing the Jews as God's people with a God-given purpose in the world.[62]

The United States Catholic Conference, to improve Jewish relations with the Church, has appealed to parishes to substitute alternative hymns for the Good Friday Improperia (or Reproaches)—two medieval hymns which, in representing Christ as berating those who are unfaithful to God, hint at the Jews without mentioning them. There is an effort being made at eliminating liturgical texts which may be construed as anti-Semitic. Sunday-school materials are under scrutiny in Roman Catholic and Protestant churches.[63]

The Venerable Carlyle Witton-Davies, Archdeacon of Oxford, warned the Christian public in Britain to beware of misinterpreting the Passion of Jesus during Lent so as to promote anti-Semitism inadvertently. He appealed to the document drawn up by the International Conference of Christians and Jews at Seelisberg, Switzerland, in 1947 (known as the *Seelisberger Thesen*) and specifically addressed to parents and teachers "to avoid promoting the superstitious notion that the Jewish people are reprobate, accursed, reserved for a destiny of suffering." There is also a plea to those engaged in the production of Christian literature "to ensure the correction of anything in Christian publications, especially of an educational character, which would conflict with the above principles" (i.e., as laid down at Seelisberg).[64] The Seelisberg document was used as a basis for the formulation of the so-called *Schwalbacher Thesen* accepted jointly by Roman Catholics and Protestants as guidelines for catechetical purposes.[65]

The importance of these and similar efforts cannot be exaggerated. Claire H. Bishop sees it as essential for the Church to "create a new Christian mentality in regard to Jews and Judaism." She stresses the immensity of the task of training parents, teachers, and clerics to think in a new way about historic Israel. This involves biblical, historical, and theological research at the university level, as well as changes in the areas of devotions, popular celebrations such as Passion plays, and communication media.[66]

An important contribution in the area of reeducation is being made by the German *Kirchentag*. The *Kirchentag* has been called the Diet of the German Churches.[67] A *Kirchentag* meeting in Berlin in 1961 put the Jewish people on the official agenda. The report issued after this meeting includes material dealing with the question of Jewish-Christian relations. The bibliography contains a section listing books suitable for teaching the young in the new spirit of ecumenicity. The title of the report on Israel is in itself a theological innovation: *Der Ungekündigte Bund (The Unannulled Covenant)*; that is, the Covenant with ancient Israel which is still valid. The *Kirchentag* issued a special appeal to pedagogues and parents to break the silence about the crimes committed against the Jewish people and to endeavour to learn together with the young the new insights that have come to light as a result of Jewish suffering.[68]

Elsewhere similar efforts are being made. The basic subject for discussion at a conference in Chicago (March, 1965) attended by Catholic, Protestant, and Jewish theologians was "Judaism and the Christian Seminary Curriculum." J. Bruce Long in his summary of the colloquy reports that it was agreed that "the most important prelude to any Jewish Christian dialogue is for Christians to grant to Judaism a degree of legitimacy, and thereby dispel the Jew's fear that the invitation to dialogue is nothing more than an invitation to conversion in dialogic garb." The term *legitimacy* means "recognition by the Christian that the presence of the Christian in covenant with God does not abrogate the covenant of Israel with

God."[69] As to practical suggestions, the conference recommended (1) that seminaries engage in the task of reexamining the traditional formulations of both Christianity and Judaism; and (2) that seminaries initiate programmes which result in better understanding of the social, economic, political, and religious conditions of Jews in America.[70]

In an extensive study on "Intergroup Problems in Protestant Curricula" Bernhard E. Olson of Union Theological Seminary discusses the latent bias against Jews among Protestant denominations in the United States. In the section entitled "Protestant Views of Judaism" Dr. Olson is led to the conclusion that "Conservative teachings (also) distort more than correct images of Jewish life and thought, judge Judaism as a false religion, and experience difficulty in discussing the continued existence of the Jewish people."[71] This statement, in all fairness, must be counterbalanced by what the author has to say of other sections of the Protestant denominations. He found that the fundamentalist Scripture Press to a large extent identifies with Jews and Judaism; it condemns anti-Semitism "and at times strongly defends the Jews against attack." He also found that in respect to social and cultural characteristics Jews appear in a positive light. But, on the other hand, ambiguity regarding Jews and Judaism is more prevalent among fundamentalist educators than among the liberals and neo-orthodox.[72] The picture that emerges is a blurred one; this is why Dr. Olson speaks of "ambiguity." One survey indicated, for example, that 48 percent of fundamentalist lessons in which Jews are mentioned make a positive impact; more than one-third of conservative lessons are also positive. The liberals and neo-orthodox show a much better percentage in this respect. He concludes that "even the most negatively disposed groups possess indigenous resources for presenting a positive portrait of the Jews."[73] What is required now is goodwill and understanding of the dangers when negative images of minority groups are presented. In regard to the Jews there is the additional danger that they may become reduced to "no more than a theological exegetical abstraction."[74]

In order to get a proper perspective on the Jews' relationship to the Church and to society, a thorough theological reorientation is required. This means correcting the image in the minds of many Christians from an attitude of contempt for the Jews to one of admiration for and understanding of their spiritual and social significance. Theologically speaking, we must learn to put new emphasis upon the continuity of Israel and the Church. Among some sections of the Protestant churches this has always been taken for granted, but for the Roman Catholic Church this means breaking new ground. Men like Gerhard Teske are leading the Church in a new direction by their emphasis upon the unbroken link between the Old and New Testaments. He writes: "Christ does not break with the past, which is also revelation, nor with the people from which He comes. The rejection of Christ by members of His chosen people is not a singular case, but can be traced all through Christian history."[75] The unity of Israel and the Church in the biblical context must be the basis of a theological reorientation regarding the Jewish people. As Karlheinz Sorger says, "Salvation history is one." In this respect Sorger finds the new German Catechism deficient in Old Testament emphasis, though it is an improvement upon the Roman Catechism of 1566 which pronounced: "Nothing of worth remained to the Jewish people, though the Lord had spared them . . . ."[76]

By including the Jews in the scheme of salvation the Church is facing a major revision in her theological understanding. The question which is being asked today is, How far is this new orientation supposed to go? The answer from the radical groups of the Church, both Catholic and Protestant, is that no limits must be imposed; everything is under scrutiny. This includes Christology and the trinitarian doctrine of God. Eva Fleischner regards it as the most promising element in the Christian encounter with Judaism that some theologians are prepared "to re-examine even the most fundamental Christian dogmas and to relativize doctrinal formulations, knowing that they can never contain adequately, once for all, divine revelation."[77] Not that Fleischner does not know the dividing line between Church and Synagogue. She knows only too well that between them stands the person of Jesus Christ, but in order to accommodate Judaism she is prepared to compromise for the sake of peace. Her argument is that in an age of "religious pluralism" the Church cannot insist that there is only one way to salvation. The present situation demands that we accept "the principle of dogmatic pluralism" as part of Christian doctrine. To the question, "Is religious pluralism part of the very stuff of salvation?" her answer is Yes, but with the following caveat: "This does not necessarily imply the negation of Christianity's mission, although it implies a different view of it."[78] By "different view" she means sharing religious insight ("treasures") with others and not bringing the "truth" to them as if they had none of their own.

This latitudinarianism which tends to obscure all demarcation lines and relativizes all positions opens pitfalls for a faith which is dogmatically structured. It is one thing to reexamine traditional prejudices in the light of biblical teaching, but quite another thing to tear up its foundations in the name of tolerance.

Such is the problem the Church faces in dealing with Jews and Judaism. This becomes especially evident in the effort at reeducating the youth with respect to Jews and Judaism: if there is no difference, why the separation? If there is a difference, what is it?

Helga Sorge, a trained educationalist, has endeavoured to cope with the problem of constructing "a new identity" of the Jewish people without denying the contradictions inherent in the situation when Church and Synagogue meet. The process is not an easy one and requires considerable pedagogical skill.[79]

Chapter 7

Who Is Jesus?

The question, "Who is Jesus?" dominates the story of the Gospels and the history of the Church. Jesus himself was directly asked this question by the crowd (John 8:25; 10:24), by the High Priest (Luke 22:67), and by Pontius Pilate (Mark 15:2). And many puzzled people asked, "Who is this man?" (Mark 4:41; 6:2f.; John 6:42; 7:15).

The answer to the question, "Who is Jesus?" depends largely upon the response and attitude of the questioner. This was so from the very beginning. For Peter, Jesus was the Messiah (Mark 8:29); for the High Priest he was a blasphemer (Mark 14:64). Claim to Messiahship constituted no offence; the offence lay in the kind of Messiah Jesus claimed to be. This was and still is the issue which divides Christians from Jews.

The original division was within the family: some Jews followed Jesus and some opposed him. The term *schisma* occurs three times in John's Gospel in the sense of dissension or division (7:43; 9:16; 10:19); later it came to designate the barrier between Jews who believed in Jesus' Messiahship and those who did not.[1] When the Church became almost entirely non-Jewish, the barrier grew into a flood of calumny and even hatred.

The Church, after a long-drawn-out dispute, clearly stated its position on Jesus as the Christ at the Councils of Nicea, Constantinople, and Chalcedon. These three landmarks constitute the Christian answer regarding Jesus of Nazareth. But it was never an answer acceptable to all Christians; this is so to this day. Those who take a unitarian position sympathize with Judaism; those who side with Paul and the Fourth Gospel find themselves at the opposite pole. The problem for the orthodox Christian is to remain faithful to his creed without disparaging Judaism. Unfortunately, opposition to Judaism frequently means dislike of Jews. This is the main contention of writers in the liberal camp. They say that Judaism and Jews are inseparable; if you dislike the one, you dislike the other; therefore, you must like both.

But underlying the liberal attitude towards Judaism is another issue which goes to the very heart of the Christian faith. Liberals are attracted to Judaism by reason of its rationality. The Christian faith lacks the logical consistency Judaism enjoys. On the purely rational level the faith of the Church seems to violate all the canons of logic and runs contrary to human experience. Christian theology functions with a peculiar kind of logic which can be expressed only in paradoxical terms: Jesus is a Man; Jesus is also the Second Person of the Trinity; God is One; God's Oneness is triune. This kind of language is offensive not only to Jews but to Christians of liberal mind. For Jews it is evidence that Christianity is mixed with paganism; for liberals it is evidence that traditional Christianity is based on a myth which lacks rationality. Because liberalism is at heart unitarian, there is a natural bond between liberal theology and Judaism; hence the strenuous effort to reduce the distance between them to a minimum. This can be done only at the expense of Christology.[2] Once Jesus is nothing more than the prophet of Nazareth, the teacher of the multitude, the preacher of lofty ethics, the master of parables, the friend of the deprived, the quarrel with Judaism is over and the parties are reconciled. On this basis the Church becomes the Gentile Synagogue living by the primordial Noachian laws.[3] Therefore, confrontation with Judaism raises fundamental questions for Christians and becomes the most important test of the Church's faith.

The question regarding Jesus is answered by Jews in a variety of ways. First, there is a totally negative attitude: Jesus is not and cannot be the Messiah, and for two reasons: he is a breaker of the Law and there are no visible signs of the Messianic Age. It is now unusual to meet violent reaction and bitter language on the part of Jewish orthodoxy but occasionally this does occur. An unrestrained attack upon Jesus and the New Testament was made by an English rabbi in an anonymous book entitled *The Disputation* (1972). According to the author, Jesus was mentally unbalanced and suffering from "delusions of grandeur." Jesus is characterized as having a "warped mentality" and as being an "arrogant neurotic." The picture drawn of the Nazarene is that of a crackpot and a madman. But Saul of Tarsus fares even worse, for the author accuses him of duplicity, cupidity, and a deliberate attempt to prostitute Judaism by mixing it up with paganism and idolatry. Paul was supposedly endowed with a "nimble and unscrupulous mind" and suffered from epilepsy and schizophrenia. As for the rest of the New Testament, the author of *The Disputation* is unable to find anything worthwhile. It consists of "deliberate falsehoods" intermixed with "rubbish." For the Church the anonymous rabbi can hardly find enough expletives to express his disgust. He calls it names like "pagan idiocy," "unadulterated rubbish," and plain "idolatry." In view of the complete bankruptcy of the Christian faith, there is only one hope for Christians, and that is to embrace Judaism. The Church "no longer has a belief or indeed a message . . . . Christianity and the other religions must cease, there can only be one religion."

The Disputation is an unusual book, written in a bitter spirit. Few Jews, even the most orthodox, would express themselves as negatively as does this anonymous writer. On the contrary, a sincere effort is being made to see Jesus, if not Christianity, in a more favourable light. Occasionally, even an orthodox Jew will try to evaluate the Christian faith positively, though he cannot understand it. Such an effort was made by Rabbi Hershel J. Matt in an article entitled "How Shall a Believing Jew View Christianity?"[4]

Rabbi Matt asks the question whether he, as a believing Jew, is under obligation to "impugn the full validity of Christianity—or is there another possible approach to the two faiths, whereby their respective claims to full validity can both be accommodated?" His answer is that an accommodation is possible though he fully realizes the dividing line between the two: "In one case, the *People* Israel [are] bearers of the Torah; in the other case, the *Person* of Christ [is the] one-man embodiment of Israel and the Torah." There are other differences such as the view of the Law, insistence on social justice rather than love, original sin, the question of atonement, etc. But there are also similarities such as faith in "mystery" and "miracle," in resurrection of the dead, in the coming of the Messiah, etc. Yet "no Jew can make basic Christian affirmations," such as "the Virgin Birth, the Incarnation, Resurrection, Christ as Saviour and the Trinity—and remain a Jew." But this does not mean total rejection. A believing Jew is not under obligation to deny the miracles performed by or "*in* Christ: surely the theoretical possibility that God could (if He so willed) cause conception to occur without the agency of a human male, or the dead to live again, is not a contradiction but an affirmation of

Jewish faith." Talmudic Judaism, Rabbi Matt reminds his readers, regards resurrection of the dead as an "article of faith." If Elijah and Elisha revived the dead, why not Jesus? But these claims are not empirically verifiable and are not within the realm of the personal, existential appropriation of the Jew—he does not know these affirmations within the experience of his faith. For this very reason he is not in a position to affirm or deny this "faith-knowledge of another." To do so would be "inappropriate, pointless, and even ridiculous." But there is an additional reason for a Jew to exercise caution; namely, the fact "that in the lives of countless men and women who profess Christ the power and presence of God appear to be evident."

In a sense, Rabbi Matt maintains, Christians and Jews share the same language concerning Christ, for after all "christ" means the anointed Messiah. For the Christian, the Messiah has come; the difficulty for the Jew is that evidence of the Messianic Age is lacking: "the end of war, poverty, suffering, sin, and death; the resurrection of the dead; the ingathering of scattered Israel to the Land of Israel and the rebuilding of the Holy Temple in Jerusalem; the final judgment, involving reward and punishment; the inauguration of the true community of mankind, where perfect justice and love and true fellowship are an enduring reality; in a word, the establishment of the Kingdom and Kingship of God upon earth." We have quoted this lengthy passage in order to show the kinship of vision and hope between a believing Christian and a believing Jew. Both the Synagogue and the Church are a body of believers who are waiting for ultimate redemption. Rabbi Matt suggests that we work and wait together "for the coming of the promised messiah." He warns that the waiting must not displace the working. The article ends with an expression of the hope "that he whose second coming is awaited by the Christian and he whose [first] coming is awaited by the Jew will be seen, when he comes, to have the same face . . . ."

Rabbi Matt's effort in the controversy regarding Jesus is unique. Jews usually, especially those of the liberal school, avoid theological affirmations. In considering Jesus, their emphasis is upon his Jewishness, and, latterly, his faithfulness to Judaism. Jewish scholars see in Paul a culprit who betrayed Judaism by introducing into the early Church pagan elements which ultimately resulted in trinitarian Christianity. Both sociologically and religiously their suspicion of the Church is very deep. This is, however, a suspicion shared by Jewry at large, as came to the surface in connection with the case of Brother Daniel.

A dedicated Zionist Jew by the name of Oswald Rufeisen, who saved many Jewish lives in Eastern Europe during the Second World War, survived the Holocaust by finding a hide-out in a monastery. He was converted to the Christian faith, became a Carmelite monk, taking the name Brother Daniel, and after the war emigrated to Israel. On the basis of the Law of Return promulgated in 1950 he requested citizenship. The authorities refused as in their eyes he was no longer a Jew. This in spite of the rabbinic rule that anyone born of a Jewish mother remains a Jew even though he becomes faithless. Brother Daniel appealed to the Supreme Court for a ruling on his case. The matter came before the Court in December, 1962, and the verdict was negative; except for one dissenting vote the Justices declared him ineligible for citizenship on account of his Christian faith. Moshe Silberg, the presiding Judge, explained that, though the Court was guided by secular and not religious law, the verdict in this case was founded on a religious consideration. He was quite aware of the contradiction, but that is part of Jewish life.[5]

There were voices of dissent both in Israel and abroad, but the majority were in favour of the verdict. Even so broad-minded a person as Rabbi Abraham Feinberg, a much respected leader of Liberal Judaism and a widely known champion of tolerance, was in favour of the verdict: "From the religious point of view, this Carmelite monk is no longer a Jew."[6] But Feinberg overlooked the fact that Brother Daniel was not before a religious court, but a secular one, and that by rabbinic law he was still a Jew, though a bad one. The oddity of the situation became even more apparent when, in a later case, an atheistic Jew was declared by a decision of the same Supreme Court in Jerusalem to be still a Jew before the law of the Land.[7]

The inconsistency is noted by Marc Galanter, a Jewish writer, who finds it difficult to accept that "a non-convert," even though "engaged in systematic and anti-Jewish activities, remains a Jew; a convert, however well disposed towards Jews and whatever contribution he may make to Jewish life, does not." Galanter is led to deduce from this strange contradiction that "*the* essential component of Jewishness" seems to be "antagonism to Christianity."[8] The *Jewish Chronicle* of London affirmed the position taken by the Supreme Court in Jerusalem: "Judge-made law is traditionally a reflection of the public mood; it was particularly and explicitly so in this case."[9] That the "public mood" is so pitched against the Jew who professes the Christian faith is the bitter legacy of the past. It is a past which is still very much with us in the present. The Jewish experience of Christians and Christianity is reflected in the attitude to Jesus. But at the same time Jews are fascinated and puzzled by the Man whom Christians call Saviour and Lord. Hence the persistent effort to explain him.

On the whole the Jewish study of Jesus has not progressed since Joseph Klausner's biography *Jesus of Nazareth* (English translation, 1925), though the background has been enlarged since the discovery of the Dead Sea Scrolls. In the first flush of enthusiasm both Jewish and Gentile writers jumped to the conclusion that Jesus was just another Essene preacher. Many Jews and not a few non-Jews still hold on to the idea that Jesus was a typical Essene trained in the school of Qumran. But this is only one of the positions taken by writers; other views are equally prominent — Jesus was a Pharisee, Jesus was a Zealot (a political rebel), an *am ha-aretz* (a man of the people), etc. For each of these views there are a literature and documentation, all depending on the presuppositions of the writer. As an example, we would cite the controversy between Hyam Maccoby of Leo Baeck College (London) and Jacob Neusner of Brown University. Maccoby's position is that "Jesus' teaching is in perfect accord with the teaching of Pharisaism; so much so that Jesus must be regarded as a Pharisee himself." There could be no possible reason for Jesus to attack Judaism; in fact he himself was a martyr for its cause. The Jewish populace was on his side, a fact which the Gospels falsify for propaganda purposes. The only collaborators in the trial of Jesus were the Herodians and the Sadducees, both representing a tiny minority in occupied Judea.[10] This position is rejected by Prof. Neusner, who takes more seriously the Gospels' "rich evidence of tension between Jesus and the Pharisees." Neusner asks: "Why should he call his fellow-Pharisees hypocrites?" According to Maccoby there were no points of difference between the Pharisees and Jesus on issues like breaking the Sabbath, forgiveness of sins, etc. Neusner asks: "If his Sabbath-breaking activities represented good Pharisaic law, then why should they be portrayed as obnoxious to Pharisees?"[11] The idea that Jesus was essentially a Pharisee, though different from them on some points of doctrine, has been held by Jewish scholars for some time.[12] But since the discovery of the Dead Sea Scrolls a new element has entered into the discussion regarding Jesus.

The Jewish-Christian writer, Christian D. Ginsburg (1831–1914), described as "the greatest biblical scholar of his day," occupied himself with the Essenes long before the discoveries of the Dead Sea Scrolls. His main sources were Philo, Pliny the Elder, Josephus, Solinus, Porphyry, Eusebius, and Epiphanius. His learned essay on the Essenes is remarkably accurate considering that he had to rely on secondary sources only. Ginsburg discovered a number of parallels between Essenism and Christianity which led him to the conclusion that "it will therefore hardly be doubted that our Saviour belonged to this holy brotherhood." For proof of the connection he falls back upon "the hidden years"—Jesus does not appear on the scene till the age of thirty —and upon the fact that Jesus found himself in opposition to the Scribes, Pharisees, and Sadducees, but never to the Essenes. However that may be, Ginsburg also knows about the great difference between the Master of Nazareth and the Essene mode of life: the Essenes were ascetics, he was not; they regarded themselves to be defiled by contact with those of a lower degree of holiness, he associated with sinners; they strove for personal spiritual happiness, he sacrificed himself for the salvation of others.[13]

Ginsburg regards Essenism as paving the way to Christianity and suggests that by reason of the similarity between their precepts and those of primitive Christians the Essenes embraced Christianity at an early date and ceased to be important after A.D. 40. Other writers are not as restrained. They place Jesus in the midst of the Essene community and overlook the differences as purely incidental. Unitarians have declared the Scrolls to be the source of all of Christianity except its supernatural doctrines, such as the preexistence of the Son of God, the Incarnation, the Resurrection, etc. Charles Francis Potter asserts that the Essenes were already Christians before Jesus was born.[14] Another non-Jewish writer, Johannes Lehmann, is convinced that since the discovery of the Dead Sea Scrolls a contradiction has appeared between the Jesus of history and the Christ whom the Church preaches.[15] Lehmann accuses Paul, the Church, and contemporary theologians of obfuscating the truth about the man Jesus, who was nothing more than a disciple of the Qumran sect. Perhaps the most persistent effort to turn Jesus into an Essene who modelled his career consciously on his predecessor, the Teacher of Righteousness, was made by Martin A. Larson. Though rejecting the fable of *The Passover Plot* (see p. 115), Larson questions that Jesus actually died on the cross: "Jesus may have taken certain drugs, well known among the medically expert Essenes . . . and recovered consciousness." He may in fact have thought himself to have died and been raised, though this was not the case. Larson suggests that Jesus had left the Essene Order "frustrated" but took their doctrine with him. The New Testament is essentially an Essene book. "Many of the early Christians were merely Essenes with a new name."[16]

Such association of Jesus with the Qumran sect is frequently taken for granted and presented as historic fact.[17] This, however, is not universally accepted by Jewish scholars. Solomon Zeitlin sees no connection between primitive Christianity and the Essene sect. For him Jesus is essentially a Pharisee and so were his disciples. The animosity between them as found in the Gospels is a later invention.[18] A. A. Kabak, who writes in Hebrew, and Shalom Ben-Chorin see in Jesus the forerunner of a typical Hasidic rabbi.[19] The latter has written extensively on the New Testament and on Christianity, but it is chiefly upon Jesus that his mind is centred. He confesses that he cannot eliminate Jesus from his life, "especially from my Jewish life." Like Martin Buber Ben-Chorin sees Jesus as a central figure in Jewish history. Jesus has stood, he says, at every bend of his road and kept on asking him, as he had asked his disciples at Caesarea Philippi, "Who am I?" The encounter between Ben-Chorin and Jesus of Nazareth is not an easy one. There is an argument between them: "I am sure that He will continue to wrestle with me as long as I have life, and that He will continue to meet me as, according to a legend, He met Peter on the Via Appia [near Rome], and as, according to the witness of the apostle Paul, He met him on the road to Damascus." This is no longer an academic but an existential challenge. But it is not a challenge to faith; it is rather a confrontation, in Leo Baeck's words, with the "witness of the Jewish history of faith."

Ben-Chorin confesses that since he left Christian Europe for Israel, Jesus has been even closer to him than ever before. Jesus puzzles him; he is drawn to Jesus, whose words cut like the sharp edge of a sword. But all the same the argument continues: "Painfully I have told Him all my life: You are not the Messiah, you are not the founder of the kingdom." Who, then, is Jesus? Ben-Chorin answers: Jesus in his person typifies the crucifixion and resurrection of the Jewish people: "Jesus, the Jew, the type of the Jew, is so close to me and can only be so close to us, as he can *never* be to the Christians of the nations, because 'He is ours.' "[20]

This emotional appropriation of Jesus while separating him from the Church's Christ is not unique among Jewish writers. The emphasis is entirely upon the Jewishness of Jesus. In this respect nothing has changed since Liberal Jewish attempts of pre–Second World War days.[21] In fact that emphasis is even more pronounced. Martin Buber's Jesus the "essential Jew" and the "Big Brother" has been taken up by a number of Jewish writers. They all delight in Julius Wellhausen's famous pronouncement that Jesus was not a Christian—he was a Jew.[22] A few Jewish scholars question the historicity of Jesus, but the majority "feel deeply that in Jesus of Nazareth a genuine, not imagined, figure of Jewish history and faith-history comes before us."[23]

Whereas Shalom Ben-Chorin, in spite of all his enthusiasm, simply repeats the views of Leo Baeck, Martin Buber, and many others, Prof. David Flüsser of Jerusalem has initiated a new, even revolutionary trend in the Jewish understanding of Jesus and Christianity. For Flüsser, contrary to prevailing Jewish views, "Christianity is not a pagan invention of the Hellenistic Christian communities." He supports this idea by appealing to the Book of Revelation, "where the main motifs of a fully developed Christology are already present." He believes that the concept of Jesus' Virgin Birth can be traced back to Jesus' view of himself as the beloved Son of his Father in heaven. The Virgin Birth is simply a mythological extension of Jesus' conviction regarding his relationship to God. In addition, Flüsser stresses that the Virgin Birth concept "was not foreign to the more mythologically-minded Jewish circles in antiquity." Prof. Flüsser points to a parallel view in Philo (*On Cherubim* 40–47).

Again, regarding the New Testament concept of the Messiah, Flüsser tells us that "the Christian conception of Christ did not originate in paganism, though it could be accepted without any difficulty by the pagan world." The origin for the Christian view of the Messiah is to be sought in Jewish apocalyptic circles and in Jewish mysticism. The same applies to the concept of Son of Man. This concept, Flüsser says, "is the highest, most godlike concept of the Saviour that ancient Judaism ever knew. He is the direct representative of God; he, so to speak, reflects the Glory of God."

All this we could not have known before the discovery of the Essene fragments. It would have been unimaginable even in an unorthodox Jewish writing to expect the title *God* as a description of the eschatological judge. But we now know that "the use of hypostatic terms was already extensive in the 2nd c. B.C. and it is not only typical of rabbinic Judaism, but is also to be found in Hellenistic Judaism."

Prof. Flüsser finds the reason for failure to see "the Jewish component of the Christian faith and ethics" in the inaccessibility of Jewish sources and in the difficulty of interpreting them correctly.[24] This, of course, would not apply to Jewish scholars, but prior to the Dead Sea discoveries all of them did in fact work on the principle that Judaism was a monolithic structure and that anything which was not contained in rabbinic ideology was of foreign provenance. If Flüsser is right in his reconstruction of first-century Judaism, then all the charges that paganism is the source of much of the New Testament, especially of Paul and the Fourth Gospel, fall to the ground. The implications for Jewish scholarship are tremendous and their effects will only gradually become apparent.

For Flüsser the mediating factor for Judaism and Christianity is the intertestamental period and not the Old Testament. Jesus belongs to the mainstream of Jewish religiosity and differs vitally from the Essene rigorists who reacted against "a new sensitivity of contemporary Judaism." This "new sensitivity" expressed itself in a sense of solidarity with mankind and emphasized the commandment of love over judgement and vengeance. Flüsser distinguishes the Semi-Essenes from the rigorists: the former worked out a mode of "peaceful coexistence" with the sinful world until the Day of Judgement. But even the teachings of the Semi-Essenes do not fit into the moral scheme of Jesus' teaching. His teaching "is unique and incomparable" and differs from contemporary Judaism: "According to the teaching of Jesus you have to love sinners, while according to Judaism you have not to hate the wicked . . . . In Judaism hatred is practically forbidden but love of the enemy is not prescribed."

In this connection Flüsser makes an interesting point which had escaped the present writer: the Old Testament concept of "righteousness" does not occur in the Gospels (except in Luke 1:75), while in Paul "righteousness and justification means mainly God's undeserved grace toward man."[25] This reveals something of Prof. Flüsser's perceptiveness in his reading of the Christian documents. The importance of Flüsser's work is perhaps best expressed by Ben-Chorin: "Flüsser is the first Jewish author to present the figure and teaching of Jesus for the general public without having the author's Jewishness especially stressed in the book." Flüsser writes using Christian idiom, but at the same time places Jesus in the midst of contemporary Judaism, but as a different kind of Jew.[26]

Other Jewish scholars have laboured hard but with less perception. Samuel Sandmel's *Jewish Understanding of the New Testament* (1957—now revised and republished by S.P.C.K.) simply repeats the established prejudices of ultraliberal scholarship which questions the historical reliability of much New Testament data. F. F. Bruce, a well-known New Testament scholar, accuses Sandmel of "excessive scepticism" in handling New Testament material.[27] Sandmel seems to be questioning most of the historical circumstances surrounding the Crucifixion of Jesus, and other details in the Gospels, so that nothing much is left to regard as authentic. He discounts the information about Paul contained in Acts. He separates Peter from Cephas, declaring them to be two different persons. He denies the Gospels tell us anything about Jesus himself, only about the faith in Jesus. Most Gospel incidents are invented for propaganda purposes. Jesus' Davidic descent is a mere "romance" invented by Jewish Christians. The story of Jesus' trial is "legendary and tendentious." Even the title *Rabbi* is inauthentic for it was not in use at the time of Jesus. Sandmel tries to soften the impact of his destructive criticism by telling his readers that the New Testament is sacred literature to Christians, who share a precious legacy with Jews. It is the literature of their Gentile neighbours who are fellow citizens and friends.[28]

In his later book *We Jews and Jesus* (1965), Sandmel confesses that his approach is partisan: "It is Jewish and not neutral." This work deals mainly with Christianity and Christians rather than with Jesus. As to the New Testament evidence about Jesus, the Gospels "present a contradiction": the portrayal of a believable background, but "questionable or even unbelievable incidents."[29] Sandmel is puzzled by the high credibility non-Jews ascribe to these documents. There is a curious naiveté about the learned professor: everything he approves of in the New Testament is Jewish and therefore authentic; the rest is to be discarded. The offensive part in the portrayal of Jesus, Sandmel finds in the authority with which he is endowed: forgiving sins, Lord of the Sabbath, etc. But in spite of the alleged inconsistencies and exaggerations, he regards Christianity as a form of Judaism. There were different varieties of Judaism at the time of Jesus, of which two have survived — rabbinism and Christianity.[30]

As for Jesus himself, we know almost nothing about him. The Gospels are not speaking about the man whom scholarship seeks, "but about the human career of a divine being." As to the teaching of Jesus, Sandmel is unable to find in it any "striking uniqueness." He agrees, however, "that he was a great and good man," though he did not exceed other great and good men "in the excellency of human virtues."[31] And Sandmel does issue the warning that the Jew "who does not know his own heritage" is unable to appraise Jesus.

It is apparently a mark of scholarship to be sceptical, critical, depreciative, and always concerned with the "teaching" instead of the teacher. But not all scholars fall under the spell of "objectivity." Geza Vermes, an expert on the Dead Sea Scrolls and Jewish studies, writes as a liberal Jew about Jesus and tries to see him in historical perspective. His view of Jesus is totally different from Sandmel's. Vermes writes: "No objective and enlightened student of the Gospels can help but be struck by the incomparable superiority of Jesus." Dr. Vermes allows that at least in one respect Jesus differed from the Prophets and his own contemporaries: "He actually took his stand among the pariahs of his world, those despised by the respectable. . . . Sinners were his table-companions and the ostracized tax collectors and prostitutes his friends." Vermes is impressed by the profundity of Jesus' insight and the grandeur of his character. This Man of Galilee, whom he describes as a miracle worker, healer, and exorcist, is at the same time the "unsurpassed master of the art of laying bare the inmost core of spiritual truth and of bringing every issue back to the essence of religion, the existential relationship of man and man, and man and God."[32] This is a different way of reading the Gospels by a sensitive and perceptive scholar. There seems to be more to Jesus of Nazareth than dry, critical scholarship is prepared to concede.

A voice of a different kind is that of Ferdynand Zweig, who spent five years in Israel as Visiting Professor in Sociology and Labour Relations at Tel Aviv University. He found the old religion as practised by the orthodox and imposed upon the State and the population by a small minority, "ritualistic, petrified and ossified, and deprived of its vivifying, life-enhancing and tender forces." At the same time the rest of the country "is atheistic, agnostic and religiously indifferent, disinterested or unconcerned." Prof. Zweig deplores the spiritual barrenness in a people with deep spiritual needs: "The Jew needs a creed for his very existence as much as anyone else needs air and water." It occurs to Zweig that help may come from the man Jesus, the stranger to Jewry. He asks: "Could it be that Jesus could give a new lease of life? Could a new, Israeli stage of Jewish religion, escape from the Ghetto wall made up of 613 bricks, and instead incorporate the personality and message of Jesus, the Jew from Nazareth, as a major prophet for Israel . . . of course excluding all Christianized stylization of Jesus Christ?"

Ferdynand Zweig is perfectly aware of the importance of his questions. "These are perhaps the most exciting, the most portentous questions, most pregnant with potentialities, affecting not only the people of Israel, but also those of the world at large."[33] The present writer is not aware of any other religiously minded Jew who has dared to propose a spiritual solution by turning to Jesus of Nazareth so openly and boldly. Jesus is frequently paid high compliments, as, for instance, by Rabbi Maurice Nathan Eisendrath and Rabbi Stephen S. Wise. But neither has ever come close to Zweig's position, except perhaps in Eisendrath's remark: "Who can compute what Jesus has meant to humanity; what he might yet mean for our sorely distracted and desperate day?"[34] Whether Jewry is to be understood within the term *humanity* is open to question.

Much ingenuity has been applied to explain Jesus in terms of his background and to interpret his quarrel with the Judaism of his day. It is sometimes conceded that there was a quarrel, not with Judaism as such, but with some of its representatives: Pharisees, Sadducees, etc. The French writer Robert Aron sees the rift as a result of the opposition between priestcraft on the one hand and rabbinism on the other. Jesus, like Korah of old, rebelled against the Temple cult and its entrenched priesthood. For Jesus, according to Aron, Temple worship was an anomaly; he dared to struggle against the establishment and died in doing so. There may be considerable truth in Aron's thesis, though the comparison with Korah is rather far-fetched.[35]

More exotic efforts are sensationalistic and devoid of scholarly value. The best known is Hugh Schonfield's *Passover Plot* (1965). The idea that Jesus arranged beforehand his own arrest and Crucifixion, that he was drugged and simulated death, and was then removed to safety, purports to be based on "evidence" derived from the Bible, the Dead Sea Scrolls, and other sources. The "Plot" is too fantastic to deserve discussion. The same applies to the effort by Robert Graves and Joshua Podro. Their book *Jesus in Rome* (1957) is based on the supposition that Jesus was taken off the cross and placed in the grave before he expired. He revived from his ordeal, met Paul on the road to Damascus, and made his way to Rome. The idea is not new; it goes back, according to Ben-Chorin, to an anonymous work of 1849 which purported to be a historical discourse by a contemporary of Jesus.[36] Prof. David Daube calls Graves's and Podro's effort "ingenious—but not history."[37] In an earlier work Graves and Podro had produced their own documentation for the theory. *The Nazarene Gospel* (1955) is a digest of the traditional Gospels reedited to suit their preconceived purpose. They explain: "Though our restoration of the Nazarene Gospel may not be correct in every detail, it is at least free from the historical objections to which the Canonical Gospels are exposed."

In spite of the prodigious effort made by Jews and Gentiles alike, the historical approach does not seem to answer the question, "Who is Jesus?" The answers offered by scholars are too many, too contradictory, and too confusing to satisfy an unprejudiced reader. There may be a more satisfying way of finding the answer, but this would lead out of the area of history into the area of faith. This road no Jew dare follow without compromising his "Jewishness."

Chapter **8**

What Is Judaism?

It is now an established rule among Jewish writers to stress that Jesus was utterly Jewish and that Christianity itself is the daughter, perhaps the illegitimate daughter, of Judaism. No one seriously disputes that Jesus was a Jew and that the Christian faith had its origin on Jewish soil. More recent studies have even stressed the Jewishness of the Fourth Gospel and of Paul himself—though many Jews are still in doubt about Paul. But the term *Judaism* itself is ambiguous. In Jewish usage "Judaism" means Pharisaic Judaism as evolved by the rabbis. Jewish writers only seldom distinguish the Judaism at the time of Jesus from rabbinism as it developed after A.D. 70. It is therefore of importance to note Jacob Neusner's admission that the kind of Judaism that survived after A.D. 70 "was different from the forms predominant before 70." What is noteworthy is his use of the plural *forms*. Since the discovery of the Dead Sea Scrolls it has become apparent that Judaism meant different things to different sects. After A.D. 70, Neusner tells us, the rabbis "turned the nation into a religious community," eschewing force in favour of faith. He describes the process as "Pharisaising or rabbinizing" the Jewish people. To our mind, the change was much more subtle and profound than political accommodation with Rome.[1] It was a shift from cultic worship to a scrupulous attention to the letter of the Law. "Torah," which originally meant a way of life in the Presence of God (as in Ps. 119), became a way of life by legal enactment.[2]

This is not to say that rabbinism was invented after A.D. 70. As a matter of fact, the Pharisees of Jesus' day were, in a sense, forerunners of the future spiritual leaders of the nation. "To be sure," writes Neusner, "not all laws before us portray with equal authenticity the life of pre-70 Pharisaism. But the theme of the laws, perhaps also the substance in detail, are precisely what they ought to have been according to our theory of sectarianism."[3] Yet Neusner does suggest that what the rabbis say about the Pharisees before A.D. 70 in all probability applies only to "post-70 rabbinical Judaism, [and is] not about pre-70 times."[4] The rabbis, according to Neusner, were a purely religious party, self-centred and partisan, their sole concern being "the proper observance of ritual and purity." He makes a distinction between the pre-Hillel Pharisees, who were politically minded, and the Pharisees as they appear in the Synoptic Gospels, concerned with tithing, purity laws, Sabbath observance, vows, etc.[5] Neusner sees the difference between the Pharisees and other Jews in that the former extended to the whole population outside the Sanctuary the laws of purity observed by the priests in Temple worship. It was the general consensus that "anyone who went to the Temple had to be ritually pure. But outside the Temple the laws of ritual purity were not observed, for it was not required that non cultic activities be conducted in a state of Levitical cleanness." The Pharisees thought otherwise: the whole of life and every activity were to be guided by the laws of purity, especially in respect to food. Approximately sixty-seven legal enactments were concerned with table-fellowship. Neusner deduces from this that, in accordance with Exodus 19:6 ("you shall be to me a kingdom of priests and a holy nation"), the Pharisees claimed priestly status for every Jew.[6]

A similar picture of the Pharisees is drawn by Asher Finkel. The key word in the Pharisaic school, he says, was "holiness," which for them meant obedience to the Priestly Code. "Holiness" in their understanding was identical with "separation" — "separation from the heathen and foreigners in order to preserve the identity of the Jewish people: separation or classification among its own members, segregating the priests and the strict observers of the Code from the nonobservers, the boorish and the common fold."[7] Finkel quotes Rabbi Pinhas ben Jair (third century): "Heedfulness leads to diligence, diligence to cleanliness, cleanliness to separation and separation to holiness" (*J. Shab.* 3c). The High Priest on the Day of Atonement, according to rabbinic tradition, had to go through a ritual of five baths and ten applications of water on hands and feet before performing his High-priestly functions.[8] Occasionally, the rabbis themselves were cynical about the elaboration of rules which were far-fetched and beyond reason. They spoke of rules which "hover in the air with nought to support them," and of "mountains hanging by a hair" — with special reference to the Temple ritual. But rules about what was clean and what unclean were regarded as based upon Scripture and as "the essentials of the Law."[9] Here are some examples of rabbinic casuistry provided by Finkel:

> Do you wash hands before or after pouring wine into a cup? Shammai: "First one washes hands and then fills the cup." Hillel took the opposite view.
> Shammai: fringes($\kappa\rho\dot{\alpha}\sigma\pi\epsilon\delta\alpha$)must be four fingers long. Hillel: three fingers is sufficient.
> Shammai: burnt offerings could not be brought on a holiday. Hillel said they could.
> Shammai: when grapes are pressed into a vat, their juice can make food susceptible to ritual impurity. Hillel opposed the view; to make him comply with Shammai's ruling, Shammai's disciples brought a sword into the house of learning — as a warning.[10]

Finkel has a problem as to where to place Jesus in the Pharisaic scheme. In the end he arrives at a compromise: Jesus ate with Pharisees, so he must have observed ritual cleanliness. Yet in the course of his ministry "he did deviate from the path of his contemporaries." According to Finkel, in controversial matters Jesus sided with the Pharisees; but in many ways Jesus followed the teaching and practice of the Essenes. To get out of the muddle Finkel arrives at the following conclusion: "Jesus showed tendencies both as a Pharisee and Essene teacher; a deviation from their ways emerged to clear the obstacles on the road to his personal mission."[11] Unfortunately for the Jewish scholar, the Gospels present us with quite a different picture and we have no other guide to go by.

John Bowker has posed a pertinent question: What *was* the offence of Jesus? If Jesus was a Pharisee, as some Jewish scholars make out, if he adhered to contemporary Judaism, why the controversy which ultimately led to his death? Bowker sees the answer to the puzzle in the fact that Jesus claimed on many occasions to have direct authority and power from God. In accordance with Maimonides's *Treatise on Rebels,* Bowker suggests that Jesus' offence was repudiation of Oral Law. But this does not solve Bowker's problem, because, as he admits, Jesus could not be treated as a rebellious elder on the basis of Deuteronomy 17:12. With disarming honesty, Bowker confesses that he has no answer.[12]

In a sense quite different from that made out by Jewish apologists, Jesus was a faithful Jew. For he came not to abolish but actually to *fulfil* the Law and the Prophets (Matt. 5:17). Thus his Judaism was of a different kind. David Noel Freedman is near the truth when he posits for the time of Jesus "a congeries of sects, each claiming to be orthodox, none actually normative."[13] Pharisaism was only one of these; there were rivals.

The present writer has argued that the prophetic tradition survived in the intertestamental period and came to life again under the inspiration and leadership of Jesus. It was essentially a messianic movement well prepared for by the messianic prophecies and the apocalyptic literature. Jesus consciously assumed the role of the Messiah and this is reflected in his attitude to the Law.[14] It is a fallacy to maintain that the Synagogue was the mother of the Church. If Solomon Zeitlin is right, there was in fact no Synagogue in the accepted sense at the time of Jesus.[15] It was only in the Diaspora that Jews had to organize a house of prayer. In Palestine, prayer was not confined to a special place; it was offered everywhere, according to Zeitlin. Rabbinic Judaism and the Christian Church share a common legacy, namely, the Old Testament. With this legacy goes a spiritual tradition in respect to morality and the messianic hope; otherwise the connections between Rabbinic Judaism and the Church are minimal. In fact, in several respects, primitive Christianity was closer to the Old Testament than was Pharisaism. This is especially evident in its reinterpretation of the cult which had begun with the Prophets (cf. the Letter to the Hebrews).[16]

R. Travers Herford overstated his case by presenting Judaism as an undivided and continuous entity. To say that Christianity broke away from the mother religion and began to move in a new orbit is a simplification of the case. Which was the mother religion? Was it the Temple cult? Was it pre-Destruction Pharisaism? The declaration against the *minim* (Jewish Christians) at Jabneh was not a "break" of a formerly uniform body, but an expulsion of a foreign element from the Synagogue.[17]

The "harsh words" about "Judaism" attributed to Jesus and Paul were real enough. These words were not aimed against the Jewish people, whose understanding and sympathy were sought, but against adversaries whose opposition was resented. In this regard Travers Herford is correct: "These words were flung out in the heat of the conflict, or written hastily to meet the need of the moment"—they were not meant to be a permanent declaration of truth.[18] It is incorrect to say, as Jewish scholars do, that the boundary of Judaism was crossed by Paul; all he did was to change from one form of Judaism to another—he left the Pharisaic party and attached himself to the disciples of Jesus. Jesus was not a Pharisaic Jew; he was a Prophetic Jew. He stood in the tradition of the Prophets of Israel who had little sympathy with the sacrificial cult and even less sympathy with a "commandment of men learned by rote" (Isa. 29:13; cf. Mark 7:1–13).

The saintly Leo Baeck characterized Christianity as a "romantic" religion whereas Judaism is a "classical" religion.[19] But the term *romantic* could also be applied to Isaiah with his messianic vision of a world in peace when the earth will be filled with the knowledge of the Lord as the waters cover the sea (Isa. 11). It may well be that Prof. Armaud Abecassis is right when he notes that it is one of the ironies of history and an odd paradox that the Torah was made into a religion. To his mind religion is frequently a hindrance and not an encouragement to keeping God's Law.[20] Of course, the same can be said about Christianity. Both the Torah and the Messianic Way are not religions in the traditional sense; they are ways of life. Seen from this perspective, there is no radical difference between them. Paul was not against the Torah; he was against the perverse idea that man in his own strength, by obedience to the minutiae of rabbinic Law, can ingratiate himself into God's favour. The problem of ceremonial or ritual Law the early Church solved in two ways: first, it declared that the Messiah had fulfilled it and thus brought it to an end (Rom. 10:4); second, by his sacrifice the Messiah had in his own person accomplished what the Law was unsuccessfully trying to do. This is the gist of the Letter to the Hebrews (cf. Heb. 8–10).

There is good reason why Jewish scholars concentrate upon Paul as the one who caused the schism in Jewry. The effort to explain him in a Jewish context has occupied Jewish writers for over a century. At first it was maintained that there was nothing Jewish about Paul; but since Joseph Klausner's feeble effort to appreciate the Apostle to the Gentiles, the attitude is gradually changing.[21] Shalom Ben-Chorin still works on the thesis, as did Klausner before him, that Saul of Tarsus was a typical representative of Hellenistic Judaism, which he describes as *synthetic-Judaism*. In the case of Jesus the opposite is true: "*He was arch-Jew, only-Jew who lived and taught in the midst of his people and its land.*"[22]

Far less grudging than Klausner, Samuel Sandmel pronounces

Paul a religious genius. He finds in him little evidence of "formal education or academic knowledge." Sandmel does not regard Paul as a "profound thinker," but as a man "of profound feeling, great emotional depth, more a lyric poet like Keats and Shelley than a philosopher like Thomas Aquinas."[23] Sandmel regards Paul as a typical Hellenistic Jew who had never been to Palestine before his conversion. Sandmel discards as mere myth the New Testament statement that Saul was a student in Jerusalem at the feet of Gamaliel (Acts 22:3). In this he differs from Klausner, who holds that there is inconclusive evidence that this was the case.[24] But in spite of Sandmel's historical scepticism, he makes a real and sincere effort to appreciate the Apostle. He allows that Paul was in every sense a Jew and that it was never his intention to abandon Judaism. In fact, Paul saw himself "as a true Jew," for at that time there was no such thing as Christianity. In Romans 2 (esp. vv. 28–29), Paul is not defining the true Christian, but the true Jew.[25]

The mistake in Prof. Sandmel's reasoning is hidden in his equation of Paul's concept of "Jew" with his own. Indeed, Paul knew himself to be a true Jew, but he questioned the view prevalent among his people that biology in itself is sufficient ground for a claim to Jewishness. In fact, the text denies it: "He is not a real Jew who is one outwardly, nor is true circumcision something external and physical. He is a Jew who is one inwardly, and real circumcision is a matter of the heart" (Rom. 2:28–29). This is not a statement dreamed up by Paul in order to destroy Judaism. Behind him is the authority of the Torah (Deut. 10:16; 30:6) and of the Prophets (Jer. 4:4; 9:26). All he did was to draw the ultimate inference from the Old Testament; namely, that the Law is not just a matter of the letter but of the Spirit, and that it must be written upon the heart rather than upon tablets (cf. Rom. 2:14–16; Jer. 31:33; II Cor. 3:3). It was on these grounds that Paul refused to make a distinction between Jew and non-Jew, declaring that those who belong to the Messiah have become Abraham's offspring according to promise. There is no difference between Jew and Greek (Rom. 10:12; Gal. 3:26–29), since both live by faith in the God of Israel.

After writing that "Paul never abandons particularism, for 'Israel' is still his particular concern," Prof. Sandmel adds that "Israel is no longer the Jewish people; instead Israel is now the 'Church.' " This is Sandmel's second mistake, for he sees the "Church" merely from a perspective of two thousand years of

Church history. Paul made no such distinction; for him the Israel of God was the body of believers enlarged by the presence of Gentiles in accordance with the messianic hope as expressed by the Prophets (Isa. 2:3; 66:18−23; Mic. 4:1−4).

It is astounding to see how little Jewish writers reckon with the Old Testament in their assessment of the New Testament. Paul's mind was dominated by the Hebrew Bible (or by the Septuagint), a fact completely overlooked by his critics. It is here that his utter Jewishness becomes evident, but he is essentially a messianic Jew and not a rabbinite. In many respects Sandmel's assessment of Paul's attitude is correct, especially in his chapter entitled "Paul the Jew" (*The Genius of Paul,* 1958). Where he goes astray is his limited, one-dimensional view of Jewishness as dictated by two thousand years of exile. If the learned rabbi had applied to his assessment of the New Testament his thesis that after A.D. 70 "the character of Palestinian Judaism changed almost completely" (that is, if he had kept in mind the distinction he sees between "biblical Judaism" and "rabbinic Judaism" as it evolved after A.D. 70), the results would have been different.

We do not think that Sandmel is doing justice to Paul by calling him a rebel. If he was a rebel, so were his Jewish cobelievers who declared a crucified man their Messiah. There is no trace of political, social, or religious rebellion in Paul's writing. On the contrary, he is a submissive man who is under the spell of a great vision which dominates his life.

Jewish writers have a problem with Paul. Since he does not seem to fit into any preconceived scheme, he is looked upon with suspicion. For Hyam Maccoby of the Leo Baeck Institute, Paul is anything but sincere; he detects in Paul "a touch of the charlatan." Maccoby resents Michael Grant's positive assessment of the Apostle (*Saint Paul,* 1976). He finds more credible a document newly discovered by Shlomo Pines (1966) which paints Paul in darkest colours: a man "consumed with ambition and envy," who used the name of Jesus only to establish his own authority.[26]

There is hardly a Jewish scholar who does not find fault with Saul of Tarsus. Hans-Joachim Schoeps's monograph on Paul is an exception in that he places the Apostle in a Jewish context and assesses him favourably. Schoeps denies that there is extreme Hellenization in Paul's make-up. He warns against the sort of approach adopted by Klausner and Sandmel, that is, the use of the Hellenistic interpretation as a clue to Paul's theology. On the contrary, Schoeps is able to explain the Pauline thought-pattern in rabbinic categories, though he is wary about Paul's "mysticism." Schoeps even finds parallels in Jewish messianic thought for the Pauline concept that "Christ is the end of the Law"—a very sore matter with Jews. Paul's greatest contribution is in his calling of the Gentiles—the mark of the messianic time. The Church consisting of Jews and Gentiles is the sign of the new era. The modern concept of two Covenants (Sinai and Golgotha) is a survival of Ebionite theology and anti-Pauline.

There is one passage in Schoeps's book which is frequently quoted and which well conveys the irenic attitude of its author: "The Church of Jesus Christ has not preserved the likeness [*Bildnis*] of its Lord and Saviour. If Jesus were to come back tomorrow, no Christian would be able to recognize his countenance. But it could happen, that he who is to come at the end of the days, whom the Synagogue and the Church expect, will bear the same face."[27] For Schoeps, the ultimate is not the Law, but the Covenant. For this reason Paul's critical assessment of the Law may fit well with the ancient Jewish concept of the fear of the Lord as a new realization of the Covenant. Accordingly, Schoeps sees here the possibility of "bringing home a heretic." This positive note on the part of a believing Jew is unique in the Jewish effort to assess Pauline theology.

Jacob J. Petuchowski, Professor of Rabbinics at Hebrew Union College (Cincinnati), had no difficulty in recognizing the originality of Schoeps's work. He writes: "Professor Schoeps has written a book on Paul which is different, and considerably more than a mere rehash of the conventional treatments by the historical school . . . . This book is a mine of information to Jewish and Christian readers about Paul's position in early Christianity, his doctrine of the Law and his concept of redemptive history."[28]

Paul's importance for our discussion lies in the question of his relationship to Jesus. If he invented his own messianism, entirely coloured by Hellenistic Judaism and devoid of Palestinian influence, then Jesus remains the Jew and Paul "the first Christian." But if Paul reflects a Jewish messianism indigenous to Judaism though different from Pharisaic ideology, then perhaps Jesus was the "first Christian" after all.

R. Y. Zwi Werblowsky, Professor of Jewish Religion at the Hebrew University (Jerusalem), tells us that "towards the end of the Second Commonwealth, Jewish messianic belief was a coat of many colours. The most divergent views co-existed side by side, ranging from expectation of a celestial Son of Man to that of a political liberator." Prof. Werblowsky adds an important point parenthetically; namely, that "universalistic messianic elements tended to recede from the consciousness of the majority of the nation." This is understandable considering the political situation in Palestine at the time.[29]

From the evidence we have, it would appear the the Judean Church was not as far from Jewish thought and expectations as some scholars make out. The Law was an important issue. Some Jewish Christians sought a compromise between rabbinism and messianic faith; others, like Paul, Barnabas, and the writer of the Fourth Gospel, saw in Jesus the fulfilment of the Law and the dawning of the New Age. To say, as Jacob Taubes does, that Christianity is utterly irrelevant to Jews, that it is not even a Jewish heresy, is overstating the case.[30] Jews and Christians are spiritual cousins though one would hesitate to say how many times removed. Erich Isaac makes the same mistake. In his view Christianity "as a religion [is] in its fundamental conception pagan."[31] To say this is to discount all the evidence of the apocalyptic literature of the intertestamental period and the evidence of the New Testament. There is no denying the gulf separating rabbinic Judaism from the Christian faith. In this respect Rabbi Louis Jacobs is both realistic and true to his convictions, which is more than can be said of liberal scholars on either side of the divide. He writes: "The doctrinal differences between Judaism and Christianity cannot be bridged, making it impossible for anyone to be a believing Jew and a devout Christian at one and the same time. The Christian doctrines of the Trinity, the Incarnation, the Virgin Birth and the Atonement have always been looked upon by Jews as running completely counter to the pure monotheism taught by Judaism. On this all Jews are agreed, even those who admire the personality of Jesus and the Christian ethic and who accept the idea that Christianity has an important role to play in God's world."[32] Thus the whole issue ultimately centres upon the question, "Who is Jesus?"

Rabbinic Judaism, which came into existence as a result of the exile after A.D. 70 and was originally meant to be an interim arrangement until the time of restoration, has become a fixed tradition. It exists by virtue of its negation of the Christian faith. Affirmation of Christianity would have meant dissolution of rabbinic

Judaism and with it the assimilation of the Jewish people into a greater community. Judaism was the bulwark which preserved Jewish existence as a separate and distinct people.[33] But this was achieved at the price of losing the prophetic vision of the unity of the human race under the God of Israel (cf. Isa. 2:2–4). The loss was on both sides, for the Church would have been immeasurably enriched by the presence of the Jewish people. The argument that this is as it ought to have been, since it provided for Jewish survival, is inconclusive. It can be argued either way. "Whatever proves itself in the course of history is of God," an argument already put forward by Gamaliel (Acts 5:38–39), would lead Jews to approve of Jesus; Prof. Werblowsky has shown the fallacy behind such a reading of history, though it is very prevalent in Jewish tradition.[34] Taubes rightly objects to "the argument from history," asking, "What can historical success prove for a religion like Christianity that claims to be not of this world and heralds the end of history?" On the other hand, failure in history would seem to indicate that it was not God's will that a particular people or religion should survive. In historical perspective it is not so much success as influence that counts. The influence of Jesus in shaping the history of the world is incalculable. Rabbi Maurice Eisendrath quotes a rabbinical colleague: "Jewish history was torn from its narrow setting in Palestine; through Christianity the Jew ceased to be a petty provincial strutting upon the narrow stage of Judea, but marched into the theatre of world significance and became a blessing to all humanity. If it had not been for Christianity, Judaism and the Jew might well have remained as insignificant as have been the followers of Zoroaster . . . ."[35]

This is not to deny the Jewish contribution to humanity apart from Jesus and the Christian faith, but in the realm of religion Jewish influence is negligible. Erich Isaac discusses the possibility of "Judaism for the Nations" now that Christianity is on the defensive: should Judaism pursue an active role, especially among the groups "which spontaneously have declared themselves to be Jewish"? He wants to know whether the proselytizing tradition within Judaism should be revived. He sees two obstacles in the way. First, "all men form one bond before God." In written Law there is no imposed obligation to propagate Judaism among the nations; to the contrary, the Law requires "the setting apart of Israel as a holy nation." But there is yet another obstacle: do Jews "believe in Judaism sufficiently to convert anyone else to it"?

It is obvious that Erich Isaac is no Paul in modern garb. He knows nothing about Paul's agonizing cry: "Necessity is laid upon me. Woe to me if I do not preach the gospel" (I Cor. 9:16). We are frequently told that Judaism is for Jews. Gentiles do not need it; all they need do is to live righteous lives in accordance with the rabbinic dictum: the righteous Gentile shall have a share in the world-to-come. How a Gentile should acquire righteousness is no direct concern of the Synagogue. Yet there is a deep yearning for the redemption of the world, and a personal Messiah, though liberal Judaism has exchanged him for the Messianic Age.

Arthur A. Cohen, in his introduction to Stephen S. Schwarzschild's essay on "The Personal Messiah," makes the following confession: "I believe in the coming of the Messiah, I believe in the resurrection of the flesh . . . . I have not the vaguest notion of precisely how God intends to accomplish these miraculous undertakings. [But] the extremity of history compels me either to affirm God as redeemer and justifier of his behaviour or to completely disown him. I must believe that the silence of God—for reasons I cannot fathom, but which I am obliged to honor in dismay—is not gratuitous." What follows is a magnificent expression of faith in the God of Israel on the part of a believing Jew.[36] It is this kind of faith that makes a Jew a Jew. In asking, "Who is Jesus?" we are asking, "Who is a Jew?"

Chapter 9

Who Is a Jew?

In the past there was no problem in identifying a Jew. He was known by his religious loyalty. Blood relationship, language, history, and culture were less important than commitment to the Torah. What the Torah meant to a committed Jew can be gauged from the Mishnaic tract *Pirkei avot*. Judaism centred upon study of the Torah and observance of the 613 precepts. Non-Jews could enter the Jewish community by conversion, circumcision, and baptism. History records at least one Turkish (or Finnish?) tribe accepting Judaism under King Bulan of the Lower Volga (eighth century). And from about the eighth to the tenth century the state religion of the Khazars was Judaism. There have been many Gentile conversions to Judaism both past and present. Some of these converts are outstanding men and women. They come from every nation and race under the sun. Abraham Kotsuji is a Japanese convert who adopted Judaism as a result of his love of the Bible and the Hebrew language.[1] Deborah Wigoder was an Irish Catholic who became an Israeli Jewess.[2] Aimé Pallière (d. 1949) was an unusual convert who practiced Judaism without abandoning Christianity; he remained a Catholic and was buried in the St. Michel Abbey.[3] It is estimated that there are about two thousand conversions to Judaism in the United States every year, chiefly for marital reasons. It is therefore incorrect to say that Judaism is an ethnic religion depending upon blood relationship.

Some Jewish leaders advocate active proselytism. Outstanding among them is David Max Eichhorn.[4] Eichhorn's thesis is "that Jews should militantly missionize among non-Jews." The basis for the missionary endeavour, as Eichhorn sees it, is that every Jew belongs to the divinely elected people and therefore has a God-given mission which he is obliged to realize: "the true nature of

Judaism is missionary."[5] This is exactly what Rabbi Moshe M. Maggal of Los Angeles is attempting to do on a large scale. Rabbi Maggal in his newsletter, "The Voice of Judaism," quotes the late Bishop James A. Pike's encouragement for this work of proselytism: "I am glad to see this work going on . . . . Every blessing."[6] The blessing of the bishop is of doubtful value to the rabbi, for he goes out of his way to belittle the Christian faith as irrational and superstitious. The rabbi's definition of a Jew is straightforward: "A Jew is a Jew because of his religion and not because of his race." For this reason everyone is welcome. "Neither race nor nationality excludes anyone from becoming a full-fledged Jew." The rabbi explains that by becoming a Jew one's race of origin remains unchanged: "he remains a member of the race he originally belonged to."[7] This is a view which would be contradicted by the orthodox.[8] To become a Jew always meant total incorporation into the community and becoming a new creature, so much so that one could marry his next-of-kin.

Albert I. Gordon makes a distinction between inner conversion and outer conversion. He distinguishes three categories of converts: (1) those who become proselytes *pro forma;* (2) those who are only marginal converts—Gentiles who are close to Judaism ("Judaeo-Christians"); and (3) the authentic converts *(gerei tzedek).* However, this concept of conversion is totally different from that of the New Testament. The sincerity of the convert is not the ultimate criterion; it is the legal act and not the motive that validates the conversion.[9]

There is a growing interest in proselytizing, especially in liberal circles. Rabbi Maurice Eisendrath, when President of the Union of American Hebrew Congregations, declared in a speech at San Francisco: "Our failure to launch an aggressive program of conversion reflects, I fear, an unbecoming distrust of the Gentile —an unpleasant provincial attitude towards our faith, as if it were an exclusive club into which one has to be born."[10] Conservative Jews are not far behind on the question of proselytizing. Asher Bar Zev suggests that the answer to a shrinking Jewish population in the United States is *"to attempt actively to convert non-Jews to Judaism."* He thinks this can be done tactfully enough so that other religions will not be offended. He foresees that a missionary approach will bring much strength to the cause of Jewish survival. Judaism, he stresses, has much to offer to "morally sensitive millions." Bahais, Baptists, Mormons, Catholics, all try to convert Jews; "why should not Jews do the same?"

Gilbert Kollin put the issue in a single sentence: "Conversion of Gentiles would be good for the Jews."[11] The liberal Union of American Hebrew Congregations made it a matter of policy: "We shall seek converts among the unaffiliated, both the unsynagogued and the unchurched."[12] It would appear therefore that there is a universalist element within Judaism which emphasizes religion rather than race. Yet religion is not the deciding factor for a person born of a Jewish mother. He is Jewish whether he is religious or not. He may be an atheist but he is still a Jew.

Robert Misrahi, Professor of Philosophy at the Sorbonne, in an address to the youth gathering of the B'nai B'rith in Luxemburg (May, 1972), called for disassociation between Judaism and Jewishness: "It is high time for Judaism to cease to be a religion." Nonreligious Judaism, according to Misrahi, is the new path for Judaism so that it can extricate itself from the *cul de sac* of religiosity and materialism. He rejects the conflict between orthodoxy and liberalism as a pseudo-conflict. For the modern Jew traditional thought-forms and simplistic reforms of those thought-forms are insufficient to meet the challenges of modern life. It is not enough to hang on to antiquated texts, no matter how reinterpreted. To meet the needs of modern Jews, a new kind of Judaism is required. To Misrahi "Judaism is not a religious doctrine but a social fact." He advocates total freedom for the individual to decide on the question of religion as a matter of private conscience. The rabbinate is not to exercise any authority whatsoever over Jews. Judaism must become free from external social forces and from the internal delusion of the religious consciousness which submits to a divine power as the supposed author of the Torah.[13]

It is obvious that Prof. Misrahi uses the term *Judentum* (Judaism) in a nonreligious sense: *Judentum* stands for the Jewish people as a historic entity irrespective of religious conviction. Prof. Misrahi's views on religion are not peculiar to himself. There is a large section of world Jewry (perhaps a majority) which is religiously indifferent but deeply involved nationally.

Jewish scholars give a wide variety of answers to the question, "Who is a Jew?" A symposium on the subject yielded an astonishing range of results which reflected the predilections of the participants.[14] Horace M. Kallen makes the astounding pronouncement that "no one is born a Jew." Jewishness is a decision made by an exercise of will: "except as [one] so decides and chooses, he is not inwardly a Jew." This is Pauline language and reveals something of the influence of the Christian ethos upon a Jewish philosopher. Eliezer Berkovits, on the other hand, who writes from a conservative position, defines being Jewish in messianic terms: "A Jew is a person through whom the messianic purpose of Jewish history may be led closer to its realization." This purpose is over and above political and national aspirations. "Without the messianic continuity," writes Rabbi Berkovits, "we have no morally justifiable claim to the land of our fathers." The task of a Jew, therefore, is to uphold the messianic vision, making it the basis of one's life-orientation. But the Jew's task also involves experiencing a oneness with the entire community of Israel. To be an Israeli does not necessarily mean being a Jew. Rabbi Levi A. Olan prefers a more synthetic definition which would include "religious faith, historic memory and a way of life." Such a definition would do justice to the long history of the Jewish people. To be a Jew means participation in the observances and rites for one's own enrichment and for the survival of the community at large. Abraham Menes, a Yiddish journalist, sees Jewishness as a matter of descent, whether of father or mother, preferably of both: "If one of the parents is a Jew, then the declaration 'I am a Jew,' should be quite sufficient."

To find a middle way which would satisfy different views, the Israeli Parliament decreed that a Jew is a person who was born of a Jewish mother and who has accepted no other faith. This, of course, does not cover the proselyte who becomes a Jew under the terms of rabbinic law. Prof. Kallen rightly speaks of Judaism in America in the plural. It implies a unity but no uniformity; it is rather "a free union of diverse associations of Jewish faiths and Jewish works" which constitutes American Jewry.[15] The same situation prevails elsewhere, especially in Israel. There is, however, a unifying principle once the emphasis is changed from Judaism to the Jewish people, that is, to the Covenant. In biblical terms the Covenant is not a "pact" between God and Israel, but God's gracious promise *to* Israel to be their God (Exod. 29:45). The Ten Commandments and the *Shema* (Deut. 6:4) are a declaration that God is the God of Israel and that there is no other God besides him (cf. Isa. 44:8). Hans-Joachim Schoeps has made a valid point which is frequently overlooked by Jewish writers; namely, that Israel's election is "an unconditional act of God's grace."[16] Schoeps juxtaposes not Church and Synagogue, but the Church and the people of Israel.[17] This corresponds perfectly both to the biblical pattern and to the Christian perspective of *Heilsgeschichte* (salvation history). In such a scheme Judaism is only incidental; what counts is the Jewish people under God's eternal promise. This was essentially the Pauline position: "The gifts and the call of God are irrevocable" (Rom. 11:29). The point is not Israel's merit, but God's faithfulness. On this issue Paul never wavers: "They are Israelites, and to them belong the sonship, the glory, the covenant,[18] the giving of the law, the worship, and the promises; to them belong the patriarchs, and of their race, according to the flesh, is the Christ" (Rom. 9:4–5).

It was the concept of the Covenant which determined Karl Barth's position regarding Israel's election. For him Israel is unique and unrepeatable: "No nation as such except Israel is the people of God." Rejecting every other "proof" of God's existence, Barth allowed only one: the survival of the Jewish people, which was to him the sign of God's utter faithfulness. To Barth the Church does not continue Israel's history. The "New" Covenant, though not different from the Old Covenant in substance, is yet different in "structure and economy." Israel remains within the Covenant despite the "suspension" *(Aufhebung)*. Barth refuses to understand "suspension" as "annulment" *(Ablösung):* the Church was never meant to replace Israel. Entry of the Gentiles into the Covenant was meant to augment the number of Jewish believers. The Jewishness of the Church Barth expresses in the following sentence: "The Church must live with the Synagogue, not, as fools say in their hearts, as with another religion or confession, but as with the root from which it stems." But he makes a radical distinction between *Judentum* (Jewish people) and the Synagogue.[19] The Synagogue he treats in harsh and unfriendly terms. He calls it "the phenomenon of unbelievers," a "spectre apparition," an "enemy of God, the Synagogue of death." These epithets resulted in Barth's being labelled an anti-Semite by Jews and some Gentiles. But this rests upon a misunderstanding of Barthian theology. Barth's reverence for the Jewish people is unmistakable and rests upon his belief in Israel's election. He even goes so far as to aver that only in the case of the Jews do nature and grace coincide, whereas for Gentiles grace has to overcome nature to make faith possible. For Barth the Jewish problem remains the Christ problem. The Incarnation means that God's Word became Jewish flesh. The blood of this people was in the veins of the Son of God. The key element here is not faith in the magic of biology, but faith in the God of history. In this respect Barth differs vitally from Franz Rosenzweig, who made biology the basis of Jewish election.[20] For Barth election has no basis other than God's unfathomable grace. For him Israel must be understood Christo-logically: Jesus in his election and rejection identifies himself with Israel. Barth regards anti-Semitism as a sign of Christian unbelief and a sin against the Holy Spirit.

In his theology regarding the Jews (Israel) Barth makes a con-sistent effort to deal with the subject of election in historical con-text and in Christological terms. His approach is original in that he incorporates historic Israel into the framework of the Church of God. The Jews, by divine decree, are God's people in a special sense.[21] The affirmation of Israel's continued election, however, is not peculiar to Barth. Together with the concept of Jewish rejec-tion there has always been the belief in Israel's ultimate restora-tion. In a sense, in the eyes of the Church, the Jews never ceased to be God's chosen people. Many of the harsh utterances which the Church fathers made in their writings *Adversus Judaeos* were their curious way of inviting the Jews back into the fold. Some of them were able to appreciate Jewish steadfastness and superiority over the heathen. Origen of Alexandria (c. 185–254) praises them for their morality: the lowest of the Jews, he says, knows and wor-ships the Supreme God. They have good reason to be proud of their spiritual tradition and are wise to keep aloof from the society of the impious. Jews, he says, are "possessed of a wisdom superior not only to that of the multitude, but also to those who have the appearance of philosophers."[22] Even Cyprian (d. 258), the Bishop of Carthage, who set out to show that the Jews "had departed from God and had lost God's favour," eventually issued an invita-tion for their return.[23] Augustine (354–430), the famous Bishop of Hippo, calls for a loving attitude towards the Jews: "Let us preach to the Jews, wherever we can, in a spirit of love, whether they welcome our words or spurn them. It is not for us to boast over them as branches broken off [cf. Rom. 11:17ff.]. Rather, let us consider by whose grace, and with what lovingkindness, and unto what kind of root it was that we were grafted." Augustine calls for humility and gentleness in dealing with Jews.[24] But these were exceptions. The literature *Adversus Judaeos* is replete with statements about Israel's rejection and punishment.[25]

The rediscovery of the Jewish people as the people of God came about as a result of the eighteenth-century revival. It had something to do with the reemphasis on covenantal theology in the Protestant Churches. The initial change had been made by John Calvin, who, on the grounds that man cannot evade the eternal counsels of God, refused to accept the notion that the Covenant with Israel had been abrogated. Though the Jews have no grounds "to plume themselves on the name of the Covenant," they are "the primary and native heirs of the gospel" and even their rejection does not leave them "utterly destitute of the heavenly blessing." God calls them holy because they were honoured with his sacred Covenant, while Gentile Christians are only "abortive children of Abraham, like a twig grafted into another stock, whereas Israel is the first-born in the family of God." Even their great contumacy cannot abolish their election: "We must consider, that in respect of the promise, the blessing of God still resides among them; and, as the apostle testifies, will never entirely depart from them, seeing that 'the gifts and calling of God are without repentance' (Rom. 11:29)."[26] "Israel," says Calvin, "was the Lord's favourite child, the others were aliens," and in the fulness of time the middle wall of partition will be broken down and Christians and Jews will be united as one people.[27]

The sixteenth-century Reformation universalized the reading of the Bible and made it accessible to the population; as a result the Old Testament greatly influenced both the language and thought-forms of the Protestant nations, chiefly Great Britain. The Bible became "the Englishman's book of books," as Hertzel Fishman puts it.[28] With the reading of the Bible there developed a millenarian theology in which the Jewish people were assigned an important role.

But it was chiefly as a result of the religious revival in Germany at the beginning of the eighteenth century that attention was fixed upon historic Israel. It was in Germany that the first organized missionary effort towards the Jews was initiated, no longer in the spirit of *adversus Judaeos,* but with respect for them as God's special people. A missionary tract directed towards the Jews by Johann Müller of Gotha, *Licht am Abend* ("Light at Eventide"), made a great impression and resulted in the formation of the Callenberg *Institutum Judaicum* in 1728. The tract was translated into many languages and was widely used.

Bishop Horne of Norwich wrote of the privileges the Church derived from the Jews and in an article entitled "The Case of the Jews" (1813) appealed to Christians to make preparation for "our elder brethren" to receive their Messiah.[29] Missionary societies were formed on the Continent of Europe and in England in the wake of the rediscovery of the Jews as the people of God and their ultimate restoration. In a way these pious Christians were the first Zionists in the modern sense in that they looked to an imminent return of the Jews to the land of their fathers. "Christian propaganda for the restoration of Israel" is included in Nahum Sokolow's detailed history of Zionism.[30] Long before Theodor Herzl's *Judenstaat,* Mrs. Finn, the wife of the British Consul in Jerusalem (1846–1863), noted in her *Reminiscences* that during a visit to Palestine Prince Alfred, the Queen's second son, while riding with his entourage, discussed with them "the prospects of the land and the Jews." Already in 1839 Mr. Finn's predecessor had been instructed by Lord Palmerston "to exert friendly protection on behalf of all Jews generally, whether British subjects or not." In 1849 the British Government accepted the care of all Russian Jews in Palestine. The Finns with other Christian friends went out of their way to find employment for Jews in Jerusalem: "We proposed to train men and boys on Abraham's Vineyard and afterwards to draft them into agricultural colonies." Mrs. Finn's father tried to raise money for the project but people in England found it hard to believe "that Jews would work or that the Holy Land was worth cultivating." Not so Mrs. Finn; she firmly believed "that this work will progress and that the Holy Land will again be peopled by its lawful owners, the Hebrew nation, and will again 'blossom as a rose.' "[31] William Hechler, an Anglican chaplain (d. 1931), was a loyal friend and advocate of Theodor Herzl and wholeheartedly identified with Herzl's vision of a restored Israel.[32]

Charles Orde Wingate, a captain with the British forces in Palestine, is described by the *Encyclopedia Judaica* (1971) as "a passionate supporter of the Jewish cause in Palestine." As a result of his dedication to the Zionist cause he was transferred to another position by the British Army in 1939. The story of the Jews in their struggle for statehood cannot be told without reference to this dedicated Christian. This is how one Jewish writer describes him: "Wingate was an extraordinary figure. A daring and imaginative soldier, he was a devout student of the Bible; it was through his religious conviction that Wingate became a passionate Zionist and volunteered for the job of training a Jewish defense force." Chaim Weizmann writes of him that he was idolized by the men who fought under him: "They were filled with admiration for his qualities of endurance, courage and originality."[33] It was Wingate who built up the Special Night Squads of the Haganah and laid the foundation of the Israeli Army. Not only is Wingate's achievement recognized in the pages of Jewish history, his name is perpetuated in a children's village on Mount Carmel, a College of Physical Education, and Wingate Square in Jerusalem. Wingate was killed in an air crash in the jungle of Burma in 1944; but his widow, Lorna, remained a faithful Zionist and was the leader of the Youth *Aliyah* (emigration agency) in Britain. Their contribution to the Zionist cause was entirely motivated by the religious conviction derived from the Bible that Israel is God's special people by reason of his promise.

Israel as God's special people is a long-held belief within evangelical Christendom. It stems back to the time when the Old Testament began to help mould the spiritual make-up of British culture. This can already be seen in the style of sermons preached in the mid-seventeenth century. The very language acquired an Old Testament texture: terms like *Zion, Jerusalem, Covenant,* and *Israel* were applied to the English Church and people.[34] "Building up Zion" was a favourite sermon topic. Richard Byfield in a sermon preached before the House of Commons on June 25, 1645, asked: "What is meant by Zion?" His answer was twofold: "It is the Metropolis of the Jews; therefore the whole Nation is called the Daughter of Zion." But this is not all; Zion also means the Christian Church "of Jews and Gentiles; and in general the Church of God." He went on to explain that "Christians of the Gentiles are called the Israel of God."

A sermon preached by William Sedgwicke on the occasion of a public fast (June 29, 1642) carried the title, "Zion's Deliverance, or Procuring Jerusalem's Restoration." It only incidentally referred to the Jews who, when converted, will perfect the Church's happiness. God "will . . . close up the breaches and raise up all the ruines and so establish them together, the praise of the earth." The "together" refers to the Church and Jews; but meanwhile the

Church is Israel and Zion: "Seek the good of Zion, this is the next to his glory, yea his glory is in Zion, therefore hath he put his name. This is the sure way to move him: all that you can say or do for his Church is acceptable to him." Sedgwicke ended his sermon with the words: "God will at last establish, and make Jerusalem a praise in the earth" — but he means the Church, and particularly the Protestant Church in England. Even when he quotes Zechariah 8:23 ("ten men from the nations of every tongue shall take hold of the robe of a Jew, saying, 'Let us go with you, for we have heard that God is with you' "), he has the Church, and not the Jews, in view. What is so remarkable is the naive identification of the Church with the story of the Hebrews and the occasional inclusion of the Jews in the scheme of ultimate redemption. It was this seventeenth-century brand of theology which laid the foundation for evangelical Zionism.

The tradition of Zionism in Puritan theology continues to affect the thinking of evangelical circles in Germany, Britain, Holland, and the United States. Christian Zionism is sustained by a preoccupation with prophecy, with special emphasis upon the role of the Jews and Christ's millennial reign.[35] An example of contemporary Christian Zionism is the Declaration of the Christian-Israel Friendship League, which met in seminar on August 25, 1978.

> We, an assembly of Christians of various denominations from seventeen states and Canada, met . . . to learn more about God's Ancient People Israel, do hereby make and publish the following resolutions:
>   1. We believe that Israel was, is, and always will be God's Chosen People.
>   2. We believe the Land of Israel was given to Jacob and his seed in perpetuity.
>   3. We believe it is the responsibility of every Christian to support Israel in prayer and in every other practical way possible.

The Declaration condemns Soviet "justice" for imprisoning Jews who desire to emigrate to Israel and quotes a number of Old Testament texts in support of its position.[36]

Christian affirmation of Israel's continued election is grounded in Pauline theology. The Apostle to the Gentiles, who fought for equality of status between Jew and Greek (cf. Rom. 10:12; Gal. 3:28; Eph. 2:14–22), held on at the same time to Israel's favoured status. On the surface this would seem a built-in inconsistency in Paul's thinking. But this is not the case, for, in Paul's view, Israel's position is not a matter of privilege but of calling. He asks: "What advantage has the Jew? Or what is the value of circumcision?" His answer is: "Much in every way" (Rom. 3:1–2). This is an astounding reply in view of Paul's insistence that God is no respecter of persons and that the Jew is not better off than the Gentile in relation to God (Rom. 3:9, 22, 27, 29; cf. Acts 10:34). The answer to the puzzle lies in Paul's absolute trust in God's promises, which cannot be annulled by human faithlessness (cf. Rom. 3:3).[37] He is and remains a God who changes not in his design and purpose. For this reason the distinction between Jew and Gentile persists even "in Christ," though before God they are equals.[38] The distinction is not theological but historical: Israel was first. Krister Stendahl quotes the authority of Johannes Munck that "Paul was positively related to Judaism even in his sharpest arguments in favour of the inclusion of the Gentiles into the People of God." But Stendahl overlooks the fact that then, as now, "Judaism" consisted of widely differing trends.[39] Pauline "Judaism," after his conversion, was prophetic Judaism with its magnificent vision of a united humanity under the God of Israel (cf. Isa. 19:23ff. and the many messianic texts in which the Gentiles are included). Pharisaic Judaism, with its strong emphasis upon separatism, was constitutionally unable to adjust to the messianic ideal: it expected a Jewish Messiah, exclusively for Jews.

It is odd that Prof. Stendahl would totally ignore the Prophets' influence upon Pauline thinking. To understand Paul is to understand early Hebrew Christianity, which was orientated not towards the Torah but towards the Prophets. The Law is only incidental to the New Testament. Herein lies its revolutionary character and its offence to Pharisaic Judaism. For Stendahl to say that, as a result of the Jewish No to the Gospel, Paul arrived at the conclusion that God had changed his plans and decided to include Gentiles in the Covenant, rests upon a total misunderstanding of the theological presupposition underlying early Christianity. Stendahl in fact admits that even without Paul there would have been a mission to Gentiles and that it actually began before Paul appeared on the scene.[40] Paul, like any first-century Jew, recognized that God does not change his plans. This is the gist of Paul's argument in Romans 9–11. It is obvious that behind Stendahl's stance is an effort to safeguard "the mystery of Israel's separate existence." This is a new element introduced from outside the New Testament perspective. Paul never thought in ethnic terms. He made no distinction between Jew and Gentile in respect to faith. In his theology there is no room for a privileged élite. In this regard E. P. Sanders's corrective is apropos: "Paul never intends to say that anyone can be saved apart from Jesus Christ."[41] This may sound intolerant to the modern mind, but Paul was no modern; he belonged to a different age.

Paul's attitude to Jews and Judaism is important in that it puts into perspective both ancient and modern Hebrew Christianity. He was and remained a Jew. What else could he be? His conversion was not a matter of changing his religion. Paul never departed from the God of Israel, the God of the Fathers, the God of the Covenant. But he ceased to be a Pharisee. The question of legalism was not at issue. Here again, Prof. Sanders is right — legalism became an issue at the time of the Reformation. What separated early Christianity from Pharisaic Judaism was that Torah obedience did not fit into the messianic scheme whereby righteousness before God comes through faith in Jesus Christ.[42] It is a mistake to single out Paul as if he were the only one to hold this view. There was Stephen, there was Barnabas, there was Philip, there were others who brought the Gospel to non-Jews. Paul's significance is that he left behind a corpus of letters in which he explains the meaning of being Jewish.

Who, in Paul's thinking, is a Jew? Paul distinguishes between outward and inward Jewishness (cf. Rom. 2:28–29). He denies that everyone who is descended from Israel is an Israelite: "Not all who are descended from Israel belong to Israel" (Rom. 9:6). This was so from the beginning: "through Isaac shall your descendants be named" (Gen. 21:12). Ishmael was a son of Abraham but only according to the flesh. Circumcision of the heart is more important than circumcision of the flesh. For this concept there was precedent both in the Torah and the Prophets (cf. Deut. 10:16; Jer. 4:4; 9:25–26). It would appear that, for Paul, Jewishness could not be taken for granted. To be a Jew is not a static condition; it is a calling and a responsibility. The dialectic of being and becoming appears here in all its force. In history privileges are meaningful only when they result in response to challenge: "What then? Are we Jews better off? No, not at all" (Rom. 3:9). God is not only the God of the Jews, but of the Gentiles also. "Since God is one . . . he will justify the circumcised on the ground of their faith and the uncircumcised because of their faith" (3:29–30).

Paul's position becomes clear when we allow full weight to the prophetic tradition that preceded him. Hence his confidence when he asks, "Do we then overthrow the law by this faith?" He answers, "By no means! On the contrary, we uphold the law" (3:31). Here "law" has a different ring from that of the Pharisaic tradition. This is "law" in the messianic context and seen with the eyes of the messianic hope. Hebrew Christianity has its origin in the prophetic vision of a new world and a united humanity. The Messiahship of Jesus was put to the test on this issue.

Chapter 10

Jews and Jewish Christians

Judaism is both universalist and particularist at the same time. Its universalism is of a peculiar kind: no Gentile need become a Jew; as long as he leads a righteous life he is acceptable to God. But Jewishness sets one apart from the rest of humanity. Being a Jew is not a choice but a tradition and strictly tied to ethnicity: "Judaism is not a universal religion," writes Rabbi Abraham Karp. He explains: "Rightly understood, it is a national religion. There would no be Judaism without Jews." Judaism stands for more than religion; it is "the sum of all ethnological characteristics which have their roots in the distinctively Jewish national spirit."[1]

This concern with Jewish survival as a separate group pervades Jewish society as its most important task. For this reason intermarriage with non-Jews is seen as a catastrophe. One Jewish writer, Monford Harris, has termed this preoccupation with Jewish existence "Jewishology." He sees it as a displacement of priorities: "God's oneness and uniqueness" does not occupy the Jewish mind, but "Jewry's oneness and uniqueness" is their main objective. Harris chides that this attitude prevails among Jews of every shade—the religious, the nonreligious, and antireligious; they all share the same concern. This is a sickness which requires a remedy so that Jewish uniqueness can be revitalized in the right direction. Harris sees the remedy in a return to *halakhah*—the code of Jewish religious law. This would change the focus from the "interim theology" of the present to an "honest biblically centred theology."[2]

Such a call to *halakhah* sounds pious enough but overlooks the central fact; namely, that there is a major crisis in Jewry in respect to rabbinic law. As one writer puts it: "The chasm between the *Shulhan Aruk* [the rabbinic code] and the people has within the last generation or two become fearfully wide."[3] How wide became ap-

parent in a symposium published by *Commentary* in April, 1961.
The editor asked thirty-one younger Jewish intellectuals in the
United States to state their personal views with respect to Judaism
and the Jewish people. The result was most revealing. Most of
them showed a negative or indifferent attitude towards the traditional faith. Prof. Malcolm L. Diamond of Princeton well summed
up the situation: "Since the Second World War [there] has been a
revival of formal religious affiliation rather than of religious faith.
Our age is not an age of return; it has more properly been characterized as an age of longing." Jason Epstein, publisher and editor,
confessed that he had visited the Synagogue three times in his
life—the last two occasions were a wedding and a funeral. About
his son he said: "He may become a Jew or anything else he
chooses." Irving Feldman, teacher and poet, confessed that Jewishness is being felt as a burden because it allows no private destiny but only the corporate destiny of the Jewish people. Nat
Hentoff, columnist and editor, wrote disdainfully of the present
state of Judaism in the United States, where the "absurd Conservative and Reform Temples" have made God the honorary chair-
man of the United Jewish Appeal (UJA); he deplored the "dis-
graceful self-involvement with their own 'status' in the community." He declared himself an atheist and hoped that his children
would "have no need for any 'religion,' Judaism included." John
Hollander, Professor of English at Yale, saw no value "in conventional affiliation with synagogue-stimulated culture" which would
bring him nearer to "tradition." Judith Jarvis, Professor of Philosophy, declared: "Being a Jew is not having a religion; it is like
having a nationality—Judaism is not international." Other contributors to the symposium made similar points; the emphasis was
always upon ethnicity, and not upon religion.

Perhaps Ned Polsky, another Jewish intellectual, well expressed
the mood and sentiment of the new generation of Jews not only in
the United States but the world over. He resented the imposition
of Jewish tradition, the Bar Mitzvah ritual, the idea of Jewish
chosenness, religion in general and God in particular. But he is
also anti-Zionist and even pro-Arab, holding Zionism to be a Jewish form of chauvinism. In this respect he speaks for only a small
minority. Barbara Probst Solomon, a novelist, who confessed to
"the memory of a noble religion" in which she no longer believed,
was puzzled by the formulation of the questions put to her by
Commentary: the concern was with upholding Jewish tradition in

the community, totally ignoring "the question of fidelity to a Jewish God." Religious observance is senseless unless it is inspired by belief in God. The most outspoken critic of the contemporary Jewish situation was the novelist Philip Roth. He was unable to detect any "complex of values or aspirations or beliefs" which could continue to bind one Jew to another, except for the negative bond of rejection of the myth of Jesus as the Christ. There is no positive bond which unites Jewry: "Our rejection, our abhorrence (finally), of the Christian fantasy leads us to proclaim to the world that we are still Jews—alone, however, what have we to proclaim to another? . . . Piety about 'tradition' does not satisfy."

The subject of tradition is the underlying theme, either by implication or direct reference, throughout the symposium. One is constantly reminded of "Fiddler on the Roof" and Topol's sonorous voice exclaiming, "Tradition! . . . Tradition!" But when a modern, Westernized Jew speaks of tradition, he does not mean rabbinic Judaism with its 613 precepts, or even biblical Judaism, except perhaps in the vaguest sense; he means folklore, Jewish custom and ethos. He experiences "separateness" as a primitive impulse, according to Prof. Allan Temko of Berkeley, in keeping with "the finest aspirations of the 20th century." Temko compares Judaism to a shell, or a "gorgeously wrought medieval armor" which has become obsolete. Temko looks for "a higher separateness — an unprecedented individualism liberated from historical mystique . . . ."

This symposium is an important document in that it reveals the antireligious attitude of the rising generation of intellectual Jews who exert decisive influence in the universities, literature, and the press. It is in the context of the spiritual vacuum within Jewry that contemporary Hebrew Christianity must be seen, especially the Jews for Jesus Movement.

The term *Hebrew Christian* is disputed both on the Jewish side and by some Christians. Jews categorically deny that one can remain a Jew when becoming a Christian: "Whoever accepts another faith thereby separates himself from the Jewish people. But he who does not adhere to the Jewish religion does not cease being a Jew." This definition of "Jew" is provided by Ephraim Shmueli, an Israeli historian. He distinguishes between "old" Judaism, which was based on a religious content, and the "new" Judaism, which "is grounded on the national will and on the awareness of the historic-cultural unity of the people."[4] The contradiction between the shift from religion to culture as the basic criterion of Judaism and the denial of the name *Jew* to one who has changed his religion does not seem to trouble Shmueli, nor the rest of Jewry, with some few exceptions.

Jewish Christians, in the United States especially, have abandoned the term *Hebrew Christian* for the term *Messianic Jew*. This creates an ambiguity which is misleading. There are many Jews who, in accordance with the Maimonidean Creed, wait for a personal Messiah and are therefore also "Messianic Jews," though they reject Jesus as the Messiah. The present writer has argued elsewhere that the term *Hebrew Christian* avoids this confusion. The Hebrew Christian has no quarrel with the people of his origin; his quarrel is with rabbinic Judaism. He could equally well call himself "Jewish Christian," as is customary in German *(Judenchrist)*, except that "Jewish" designates both ethnicity and religious affiliation. "Had the word 'Jew' no religious but only ethnic connotation, he [i.e., the Hebrew Christian] would have called himself a Jewish Christian, but by reason of his opposition to rabbinism . . . he calls himself a *Hebrew* Christian."[5]

There is also pressure on the part of some Christians to assimilate the Hebrew Christian to the extent of obliterating his origin. The Lutheran World Federation at its consultation in Denmark (May, 1964) raised the question of the position of Hebrew Christians in the Church: "Those who have received Jesus Christ in faith and baptism—even though they are descended from the people of the Old Covenant or belong to the heathen—, are all Christians and nothing else than Christians. With the designation of 'Jewish Christian' or something similar, is created a non-biblical division within the congregation." An official of the Lutheran World Federation explained to an officer of the International Hebrew Christian Alliance: "The Conference was of the opinion that the expression Jewish Christian *[Judenchrist]* or Hebrew Christian creates a dangerous religious tendency, by suggesting that difference of descent adds a certain quality to being a Christian. The conference was especially concerned with emphasizing the New Testament teaching, that in Christ there is 'no Jew nor Greek' and that racial and religious descent does not decide a person's Christianity. We would never speak of a Buddhist-Christian nor believe that his Buddhist origin affords him a special position or quality in Church or theology. The concept *Judenchrist* suggests that a Christian of Jewish descent continues to remain a Jew." It was this that gave rise to the objection to the appellation *Jewish* (or *Hebrew*) *Christian*. In this manner the Conference of the Lutheran World Federation expressed its concern regarding an issue which was initially raised by delegates from Germany who remembered the "German Christian" movement under Hitler with its emphasis upon blood and soil *(Blut und Boden)*. This is a legitimate issue which touches upon the homogeneity of the Christian community.

H. D. Leuner, a Hebrew Christian himself, has shown in his reply to the Lutheran objection to the term *Jewish* (or *Hebrew*) *Christian* that the comparisons are wrong and the theology is at fault. There is a difference between a Buddhist who becomes a Christian and thus disassociates himself from his pagan past, and a Jew who by accepting the Messiahship of Jesus only affirms his Jewish past. Leuner quoted a number of theologians, Germans and others, in support of his position.[6]

The Roman Catholic theologian Gregory Baum, another Christian of Jewish origin, writes: "The Jew is in the Church as in the house of his fathers; the Gentile is in the Church as an adopted son, and hence also in the house of those who by adoption have become his fathers. The baptized Jew is the elder brother of the baptized Gentile." Baum refers to Romans 11:24: the Jews are in the Church *secundum naturam,* according to their nature, while the Gentiles are joined to the Church *contra naturam,* against their nature.[7] The argument, of course, is valid only if "Church" is here understood in the context of the history of salvation to include God's relations with man before the birth of Jesus. "Church" in this context is not the result of a new religion but the uninterrupted acts of God which began with the call to Abraham and even before. "Church" is the community of believers under the Covenant which stretches from the day of Creation and will endure to the end of time. This view of "federal theology" makes Israel the representative of humanity at large: "The contention of classical federal theology is that God's covenant with Israel is only an aspect, though an important one, of the wider covenant involving mankind." Some of the Reformation theologians extended the Covenant to the whole of creation and to the whole stretch of history.[8] Such a view is inevitable if God is to be taken seriously as the One who is accountable for his acts.

In this context the term *"New" Covenant* acquires a meaning different from the connotation usually attached to it. The term has bedevilled Gentile theologians and led them to extraordinary conclusions. Marcion was only the first in a long line so to emphasize the newness of the Gospel as to detach it completely from its native roots. Cyril of Alexandria based his whole theology upon the newness in Christ in such a way as to declare everything which went before Christ as old and superseded.[9] In this Cyril followed a trend which began early in the Church and which ultimately led to the total rejection of the Old Testament by the "German Christians." Even within Roman Catholic orthodoxy, the Old Testament was an embarrassing presence as can be seen from the treatise by Bernhard Bartmann on the opposition between Judaism and Christianity. For Prof. Bartmann the Old Testament has nothing to offer to the Church; not even the Decalogue has binding force on a Christian. He explains that Jesus "knows himself as absolute [new] beginning."[10] The implications of such a position are theologically untenable for it plays havoc with divine sovereignty and disconnects past from present so that there is no continuity left, only discontinuity. The concept of discontinuity is based on the rejection of historic Israel. This is a view which Paul contradicts and which the Letter to the Hebrews never intended, though both use the adjective *new* in connection with Covenant.[11] But the Church fathers understood the newness as being total. Lactantius explains that because Jews resisted the wholesome precepts and departed from the divine Law God decreed that he would "change his Covenant [*testamentum*] and bestow the inheritance of eternal life upon foreign nations, and collect to himself a more faithful people out of those who were aliens by birth."[12] Elsewhere Lactantius cites Old Testament texts to prove "that the Jews were disinherited, because they rejected Christ, and that we, who are of the Gentiles, were adopted into their place."[13]

The rejection of historic Israel and the breach in the Covenant became a theological axiom in the Gentile Church. The emphasis upon absolute newness led to the idea of a "new Israel" and a new people of God with the result that there were two Israels—the *true* Israel, which is the Church, and the pseudo-Israel, which is the Synagogue. Jewish Christians therefore had no choice: to become a Christian believer meant to leave behind one's own people as the God-forsaken remnant of old Israel.[14] There was, however, a minority view which saw the Covenant in a different light. John Calvin was one of those who interpreted Jeremiah 31:31 differently:

"The new covenant is called new not because it is different from the first, for God does not contradict himself. . . . The first covenant was inviolable. . . . The meaning of 'new' does not refer to substance but to form." Johannes Cocceius (1603–1669), though placing emphasis upon the personal aspect of Covenant, yet refused to separate the saints of the Old Testament from those of the New Testament. They all belong to the same Church of God.[15]

In a limited sense Jewish messianism seemed to move towards universal inclusion of the Gentile world. Some rabbis saw messianic overtones in Zephaniah 3:9.[16] There were even views that the Messiah himself would be a Gentile proselyte.[17] Prof. S. H. Bergman has suggested a rational basis for an all-inclusive concept of Covenant: "The relationship to God is an essential part of the actuality of man as man." True humanism, therefore, would require an extension of the Covenant to include the human race. Messianic humanity is united humanity and there are already present nuclei working to this end.[18] But this latent universalism is kept in check by the deep conviction that Israel is a people apart. The ancient rabbis had a problem in respect to the God of Israel who is also the God of the nations. They asked: "Is he the Guardian of Israel only? Does he not guard all?" They answered: "He guards Israel only, but as a reward for guarding them, he guards all with them." C. G. Montefiore calls this "one of the oddest examples of the mixture of universalism and particularism."[19]

The tension between these two opposite trends derives from the knowledge that God is the Father of all mankind and in a particular sense is the God of Israel. For Judaism the problem remains unresolved. The universalism of the Prophets became obscured as a result of national catastrophe. Solomon Zeitlin correctly emphasizes that under prophetic influence the ethnic and racial Hebrew religion acquired universal characteristics: "The God of Israel became the universal God, and any one could join in worshipping Him."[20] But under postexilic conditions the attitude changed radically. There was total segregation from foreign influence to the extent that intermarriages were broken up and foreign women were sent away with their children (Ezra 10:18ff.). This trend towards separatism was accentuated by the Pharisaic party to exclude even Jews who were not strict in the observance of rabbinic precepts.

Paul made his stand on this issue. This indicates the change in his thinking since his Pharisaic days. The account in Acts 13 as to what happened at Antioch of Pisidia rings true and is attested to by Paul's writings. When the Synagogue, moved by jealousy, opposes the message that all who believe in Jesus, whom God had raised from the dead, are offered forgiveness of sins without distinction of race (Acts 13:38–39), Paul appeals to the Prophets, quoting Isaiah 49:6: "I will give you as a light to the nations, that my salvation may reach to the end of the earth." It was on the strength of the prophetic tradition that Paul and Barnabas turned to the Gentiles (v. 46). The universalism of the Bible is the most critical issue for Jewish survival. It is also a major issue for contemporary Hebrew Christianity. There can be no gainsaying the Jewish accusation that conversion opens the floodgates to assimilation. This is proved by the history of Jewish Christian families.

Assimilation with non-Jews occurs in a natural way by intermarriage. This is an inevitable process for two reasons. In the first place, the Christian faith abolishes the division of race. A believing Christian becomes a member of a family of equals no matter what his origin. There may be social discrimination but this can never be justified on religious grounds.[21] In the second place, a Jewish Christian has frequently no alternative to intermarriage by reason of the ostracism he or she suffers from the Jewish fold. The Jewish Christian circles are too small to provide marriage partners. But a more important principle is involved, namely, the unity of believers. If race is allowed to break the bond between believers, then messianic society does not exist. The Letter to the Ephesians deals with this issue in no uncertain terms: in Christ those who were once far off have been brought near by his breaking down of the dividing wall of hostility. The Messiah creates in himself "one new man in place of the two," thus making peace. The new Temple of which Jesus Christ is the chief cornerstone is a community where biological distinctions have been overcome by the blood of Christ (cf. Eph. 2:13ff.). This does not mean that every Jewish Christian is under obligation to intermarry: it means only that he or she is free to follow the prompting of the Holy Spirit in this matter.

The question of intermarriage is a deeply felt and widely discussed concern in the Jewish community. By reason of the revival of strong national sentiment not only among Jews but also among Jewish Christians, the subject agitates many Jewish believers. The most persistent voice against intermarriage was that of the late Dr.

Felix Propper of Vienna. Under his influence and guidance the Vienna branch of the Hebrew Christian Alliance addressed itself to Jewish Christians the world over to resist the temptation to assimilate.[22] The Vienna Declaration (March, 1955) was discussed at the International Hebrew Christian Alliance Conference in Chicago (1955) and rejected by a majority of the delegates. But it found support among European Hebrew Christians who had survived the war, chiefly from Holland.[23]

The issue of intermarriage goes beyond ethnic loyalties and touches upon important theological questions. But Dr. Propper in his tract *Sein oder Nichtsein* ("To Be or Not to Be") does not seem to be concerned with theology. His emphasis is entirely upon Jewish national survival.[24]

Christians who have decided that Israel's election came to an end with the coming of the Messiah, have no problem. But a problem exists for those who believe in the continuity of the Covenant and the importance of Israel's survival on the one hand, and the calling of the Gentiles on the other. We have already seen how James Parkes solved the problem by projecting two Covenants, one on Mount Sinai and the other on Golgotha. But such a solution contradicts the prophetic vision of a united humanity under the God of Israel and our Lord's High-priestly prayer for the unity of all God's people. Karl Barth solved the problem more ingeniously by making Israel as it were the counterpart or ectype of the Church; that is, that part of the Church which says No to Jesus Christ. In this way Jewish unbelief typifies the faithlessness of the Church in history.[25] But it seems to us that Barth's insistence upon the unconditional election of Israel bypasses the dialectic between being called and being chosen (Matt. 22:14) and the dominical principle of the Kingdom of God that the first will be last and the last first (Matt. 20:16; Mark 10:31; Luke 13:30). It is noteworthy that the Synoptic Gospels attach this latter logion to three *different* contexts. It is obviously a saying which played an important part in the message which Jesus preached. This is already indicated in John the Baptist's sermon that God is no respecter of person and can raise up children to Abraham from the stones of the desert (Matt. 3:9). He warns against the false confidence: "We have Abraham as our father." All this is in the spirit of the Prophets (cf. Jer. 7:4; Amos 3:2), who took a similar position. Barth, however, gets out of the difficulty by reducing the ultimate meaning of election to the response of the individual. In this respect he is on firm biblical ground: "The Christian concept of election is fundamentally individualistic." This does not mean lessening the importance of the community, but it means that in man's encounter with God it is not "humanity," or family, or clan, but the single human being who hears and responds: "Not all, but each individual is chosen." It is in and through them, the individuals, that God seeks, calls, and blesses the many, that is, the community at large.[26]

The dialectical tension between personal responsibility and group existence is a fact which pervades every community — Jewish, Christian, and secular. But in the biblical perspective it acquires particular importance in that the individual stands in the place of, acts on behalf of, decides for the majority. Here the democratic process is reversed: it is the voice of the individual in response to the Word of God which constitutes the "majority." This is demonstrated in the classical position of the Prophets. The prophet's lonely voice speaks against and on behalf of his people. In this respect the prophetic conscience differs fundamentally from the ordinary individual. Man usually hides behind majority existence to evade personal responsibility. He lives by proxy; taking pride in his people's past, he boasts of his ancestry and falls back upon the achievements of his race, or family, or clan. The claim to be a member of the Chosen Community substitutes for personal commitment and decision for God. This is a common human trait and is as prevalent among Christians as it is among Jews.

Seen in this perspective historic Israel is not a single entity: Israel consists of Israelites. Every Israelite is both a Jew and a human being. As a Jew he belongs to a special people; as an individual human being he is accountable to God before he is accountable to his people. When there is a clash of loyalties his choice indicates his priorities. In the case of the believing Jewish Christian his decision for Jesus the Messiah is an act of obedience to God. "We must obey God rather than men," was the answer of the early disciples to the Jewish authorities (cf. Acts 5:29). That the Jewish community makes no allowance for such a decision on the part of the individual indicates that its priorities have shifted from God to nationhood. The Jewish Christian finds himself in a prophetic role not by choice but from necessity. His act of obedience isolates him from the community and marks him as a rebel. His is a voice in the wilderness, experienced as a challenge and a threat by the community. The challenge consists in questioning the once-for-all decision against Jesus which is now hallowed by tradition; the threat consists in the breaking of ranks of a people for whom survival is the only and ultimate goal.[27]

The venture of faith requires the sacrifice of separate existence for a higher good, the unity of the human race in the Messiah, thus repeating the drama of death and resurrection. This is the principle of new life: unless the seed falls into the earth and dies, it remains alone, and produces no fruit (John 12:24). But no people is ready for such a sacrifice; this can be made only by the individual. Only in the life of the individual does election achieve its purpose in history. This Barth has seen with great clarity: "The isolated . . . those who in and with the message about Jesus hear and believe the promise of their own election, only they live as God's elect."[28] The others are called but not chosen.

The Greek poet Pindar (fifth century B.C.) is credited with the saying, "Labour to become what you are." Goethe repeated the dictum, *"Werde was du bist"* ("Become what you are"); or, "What you have inherited from your fathers, you must acquire in order to make it your own."[29] This principle is theologically sound. Election is never a possession, only a task, a calling, a privilege. It must not be taken for granted. Election implies sacrifice and responsibility. There are no short cuts to the Kingdom of God; without the Cross there is no Crown.[30] It is a futile complaint on the part of Martin Buber that he sees no evidence of a saved world, while standing by as an onlooker.[31] Only those who take up the Cross can know about salvation. This the Hebrew Christian knows from personal experience as he stands between his Christ-denying people and a Christ-betraying Church. To both he stands as a reminder that there can be no collective decision for God, only a personal one. This point is completely overlooked by David Berger and Michael Wyschogrod in their plea to would-be converts not to put faith in Jesus. Their main concern is the survival of the Jewish people, which they see threatened by intermarriage.[32]

An unusual example of an intensely personal response to Jesus is seen in the Israeli poet Pinchas Sadeh. In his quest for God Sadeh found himself irresistibly attracted to the person of Jesus—"the life story of the man who lived far off in time, but close to my heart." Sadeh's discovery is that man cannot redeem himself. His God-experience is intensely personal: "My voice was the voice of a single man facing a single God."[33]

In this respect, even so outstanding a Christian thinker as Helmut Gollwitzer fails to pay sufficient attention to the strictly personal character of the God-man relationship. Hence his vacillation between missionary commitment and cultural confinement: "Each must remain true to his tradition—Jews must remain Jews." Such talk in collective terms contradicts the prophetic stance and falsifies the facts of history: there is never a coincidence between personal faith and national religion. Jews will always remain Jews as long as the world remains the world, but the case of the individual is different. He may have to go outside the camp (Heb. 13:13) for the sake of conscience. Gollwitzer's identification of *Volk* with *Land* will be difficult to fit into Pauline theology. Rabbi Nathan Peter Levinson's strictures are not entirely without justification.[34]

Chapter 11

Conversion and Missions

Jews and Christians have inherited the same vocabulary from the Bible but they use it differently. This becomes evident in their respective understandings of the verb *convert*. For Jews conversion always means change of religion; it is thus an active and transitive transaction: you convert yourself or somebody converts you. Here is an example of how the term is used: "Children older than confirmation age should not be converted without their consent."[1] Implied is that the ritual of circumcision, or baptism, or both, are means of conversion. This is the way a non-Jew becomes a Jew. Consent and decision are, of course, important factors, but conversion is essentially a social act. The convert by joining the Synagogue joins a nation. Rabbi Sanford Seltzer explains that "the religious component of being Jewish" is subordinated to the ethnic and cultural features of Jewish life. This frequently bewilders and puzzles non-Jews who accept "conversion" for the sake of marriage. They ask: "How [can] a conversion, which essentially [is] a religious act, confer ethnic identity upon them?"[2] The answer is that Judaism serves the prime purpose of safeguarding Jewish continuity and marriage is a means towards this end. For this reason even "couples totally devoid of Jewish concerns," when married in accordance with rabbinic law and custom, are validly married. "Judaism," explains Rabbi Seltzer, "is committed to the preservation of the Jewish people and the transmission of a historic tradition to subsequent generations."[3] Samuel Cohon, discussing the question, "What makes a Jew?" explains that "Judaism is a national religion"; as long as a Jew has not joined another religion, though an unbeliever, he is still a Jew.[4] Theodore Bikel explains why he is a Jew: "For us the essence of Jewishness lies not in religion but in tradition; because I am to a great extent a product of that tradition, [I am a Jew]."[5]

For Christians, conversion has a totally different connotation. First, it has nothing to do with ethnicity; second, it is essentially a religious act, but not in the formal sense. This is only secondary. Rather, conversion indicates inward change. The verb *convert* is usually used in the passive sense: one undergoes conversion. It is a yielding under compulsion from above. Conversion *(metanoia)* indicates change of mind and heart brought about by the Holy Spirit. Paul, after his experience of conversion, ceased to be a Pharisee, but did not cease to be a Jew. This point is important for the distinction between Jewish and Christian conversion and bears directly upon the position of Jewish Christians.

Identification of Jewishness with rabbinism is a result of the Diaspora. Before and after A.D. 70 there were nonrabbinic Jews such as the Sadducees, the Qumran sect (Essenes?), the Jewish Christians, and probably others. Later the Karaites totally rejected rabbinism and the Talmud.[6] Karaites, explains Abraham S. Besicovitch, Professor of Mathematics at Cambridge and a Karaite himself, represent pure Judaism free from later accretions.[7] Seen in this light, Jewish Christianity was not a new religion; it was Judaism of a different kind.

It is not true that Jewish Christianity disappeared after the Fall of Jerusalem in A.D. 70, or after the Bar Kokhba debacle in 135. There is enough evidence to show that Jewish Christians persisted and even made considerable headway in winning fellow Jews to the messianic faith. Jacob Neusner has produced evidence of massive Jewish Christian influence in Edessa and Adiabene, in Nisibis and in Central Babylonia. There were churches of thoroughly Semitic origin in these districts, and they successfully resisted Hellenistic influence. He also notes that "Jews who converted to Christianity posed a problem to the late third century Babylonian rabbis." Prof. Neusner holds that the churches established by these Jewish Christians cannot be properly called Iranian, for they "were largely the creation of Semites, chiefly Jews along with other Aramaic-speaking peoples."[8]

Prof. Samson H. Levey found evidence enough to suggest that one of the leading second-century rabbis, Simeon Ben Zoma, was himself a believing Christian. Ben Zoma was a contemporary of Akiva, the most eminent spiritual leader at the time. According to tradition, Ben Zoma became demented as a result of his dabbling in mysticism. But Prof. Levey suggests that behind the suspicions of insanity lay "the best kept secret of the rabbinic tradition";

namely, that Ben Zoma was a Christian. Prof. Levey says that the rabbis "decided that it might be best to keep the matter as quiet as they could, so as not to lend strength to the aggressive evangelism of the early church and its zealous missionaries who were working among the Jewish people."[9] However, Prof. Levey fails to explain that these "missionaries" were no outsiders but believing Jews who were part and parcel of the Jewish community. The division was not as yet so complete as to separate Jew from Jew by reason of difference of religious conviction. Evidence for this is the fact that Ben Zoma himself was tolerated and treated as a teacher and sage in Israel. Levey expresses a measure of surprise that Ben Zoma remained in the community and was neither ostracized nor excommunicated, and that the rabbi still regarded himself as a Jew. The more so as, according to Levey, there is indication that Ben Zoma held orthodox Christian views in respect to "Jesus as God incarnate in human form," original sin, etc. If Prof. Levey is correct in his assumptions, at least some Hebrew Christian groups held a theology not much different from that of the Gentile Church.[10]

The tolerance displayed by the rabbis towards a colleague who differed in respect to theology may seem strange to us in view of the later animosity towards Jewish Christians, but it would seem that at an earlier age it was not yet a major crime to profess Jesus as Messiah and this in the Christian and not the Jewish sense. Jewish Christianity remained in close touch with the Jewish community for a long time and this in spite of the *birkat ha-minim,* the malediction on heretics.[11]

Walter Bauer has shown that Jewish Christians maintained connections with both the Church and the Jews.[12] This positive attitude towards the Jewish community has been a marked feature of Hebrew Christians in spite of the occasional traitor who went out of his way to malign his people. This is especially so in this present age, when Hebrew Christians are trying their utmost to identify with the Jewish community, though without success. The reason for this failure is primarily the memory of the past. Many Jews felt they had to accept baptism for reasons of expediency. Those Jews who were sincere believers and became Christians from conviction were declared outcasts and mourned as dead by their immediate families for breaking the ranks and joining the enemy. Some Jewish Christians engaged as professional missionaries among Jews, an activity which to the Jewish community is

the height of infamy. A missionary is called a "soul catcher." A
Jew who accepts Christian baptism becomes a *meshummad* (from
the Hebrew root "to destroy")—a person worthy of destruction.
To the Jewish mind, Christian baptism is the symbol of final separation from the community. The graphic description of the spiritual struggle between rabbi and priest for the soul of a young
Jewess in a Polish village the day before her baptism in Sholem
Asch's novel *Salvation* gives some indication of the Jewish sense of
loss. For the Jews "conversion" has acquired a pejorative and sinister quality, bringing disgrace to the rest of the family.

The Jewish feeling of execration found expression in the cor-
ruption of Jesus' name from Yeshua to Yeshu, which was intended to suggest in acronym form the cryptic sentence: "May his
name and memory be erased."[13] The custom of distorting the
names of converts in order to produce a pejorative effect was frequently practised. The death of a convert was not mourned by the
family, though legally a converted Jew was regarded as a Jew, al-
beit a sinner. But this was not an opinion universally accepted.[14]

Jews seldom believe that a conversion to Christianity is genuine.
Orthodox Jews today, like medieval Jewry especially, regard
Christianity as an idolatrous religion.[15] They find it difficult to believe that any honest Jew would decide to join a faith which denies
the unity of God. Only dishonest men, and for ulterior motives,
would accept baptism. That some Jews now accept the possibility
of genuine conversion is an indication of the change that is taking
place in the Jewish perception of the Christian faith. Thus Jacob
Katz admits the possibility of genuine conversion and allows that
some eminent Jews of high social and intellectual standing have
become Christian believers. The Jewish community mourn the
loss of these men, and he suggests that this is the reason why Jews
continue "in a state of permanent defence against Christianity."[16]
Rabbi Joel Sirkes (d. 1640) was particularly vehement towards
converts. He declared them all to be prompted by robbery, prom-
iscuity, and the desire for nonkosher food. Katz surmises that
"there must have been some cases of genuine conversion in this
period" (seventeenth century), but adds that "they were not a matter of much concern to Jewish society."[17] If that were the case,
why such vehemence on the part of Jewish leaders?

But most Jews do deny the possibility of genuine conversion.
To them every convert is "an unscrupulous hypocrite" who betrays his faith and his people. This defensive attitude developed

in an isolated and inward-looking society which could not afford the challenge of a rival faith. The result was spiritual barrenness because of the lack of stimulus from the outside. Jacob Katz says of medieval Judaism under ghetto conditions that it sank "into the lethargy of a mental attitude which accepted Jewish fundamental beliefs as uncontested truth."[18] Katz is unusual in his outspoken criticism of even liberal rabbis for their superficiality in dealing with the Christian faith. By reason of their closed-mindedness "they confined themselves to a more or less arbitrary interpretation of Christianity without proceeding to a critical examination of their own doctrines. They evaluated Christianity as a religion for Gentiles only, and did not for a moment conceive that it might face Jews with the temptation to become converted themselves."[19]

This cavalier attitude towards the Christian faith is a characteristic feature of Jewish scholars. Ignaz Maybaum recollects a remark by the neo-Kantian philosopher Hermann Cohen (1842–1918), who whispered to him: "Jesus Christ—a god! Never has anybody really believed this." Maybaum adds that he said it with a shudder.[20] This gives some indication of the built-in prejudice against Christian doctrine even in a man of great intellect.

That some Jews do accept Christian beliefs about Jesus remains to the Jewish community a perpetual puzzle. Even Katz, who admits the possibility of genuine conversion, has moments of doubt. In the case of Johann Augustus Wilhelm Neander, the great Church historian, he has his reservations: "I discovered," Katz writes, "that he became a real Christian, in the Protestant pietistic sense, only much later, as a result of some religious experience." And Katz says that the Christian faith of Julius Stahl, the spiritual leader of Prussian conservatism, developed "only gradually," implying that he was not a believer at the time of baptism. But this does not allow for growth and variation in the realm of faith. In one case, however, Katz accepts the possibility of genuine conversion. M. Drach, the son-in-law of the Grand Rabbi of the Consistoire de France, who himself was "a potential candidate for that position," suddenly declared himself a Christian believer. Katz is impressed with the story of his conversion but regards it as exceptional and rare. Drach became a Roman Catholic in Paris in 1823. Katz says of him: "Reading Drach's autobiography, one gains the impression that the Roman Catholic faith had overwhelmed him . . . ."[21]

Such admissions are rare on the part of Jewish writers. On the whole, Jewish Christians are regarded as charlatans. Rabbi Arthur Chiel writes cynically about Judah Monis (d. 1764), who taught Hebrew at Harvard for nearly forty years. Chiel questions the sincerity of Monis's conversion, pointing to the suspicion the clergy at the time had about his Christianity.[22] All this points to the fact that Jews have a problem with Jewish Christians. The only answer to the challenge they present is to question the sincerity of their faith. For the conversions which occur the Jews blame the missionaries. There is a rabbinic saying that "one must not steal the mind of a fellow man, not even of a Gentile." Jews accuse missionaries of having stolen the minds of Jewish converts to Christianity, most of them young, ignorant, or poor. They are convinced that underhanded methods entice Jewish men and women into the Church. Samuel Sandmel, alluding to the Constitution of the Madhya Pradesh State of India, which prohibits proselytizing by unfair methods, writes: "If you ask [whether] your missionaries to us employed means comparable to those here discounted, then the honest answer must be Yes. The responsible among you have disowned their methods; they needed disowning because they existed."[23]

These supposedly unfair means of winning Jews for Christ are understood to be bribery, taking advantage of poverty and ignorance, and the enticing of children and young people. The last-mentioned became a special issue in Israel, where some Jewish children attended Christian schools. The orthodox raised a furor of indignation and managed to win the sympathy of much of the population. They invented every possible calumny to scare Jewish parents and to embarrass the schools in question. In the London *Jewish Chronicle* a letter appeared under the heading, "Missionaries Are Our Misfortune." There was a concerted outcry in the Jewish press the world over. Rabbi Joseph B. Soloveitchik of Boston wrote: "In times past, when a Jew converted, he was simply lost to the non-Jewish community. But today . . . they convert a Jewish child and station him again among Jews, and he becomes a missionary. The effort of the Church is not to make non-Jews of Jews, but to revive the type of a Christian Jew, as the case of Brother Daniel illustrates."[24] The last remark is of special significance. The rabbi objects in either case: whether a Jew becomes a non-Jew, or remains a Jew, but becomes a Christian. He regards the Christian Jew who associates with Jews the greater danger to the community.

That Jewish children are being enticed to become "missionaries" is the invention of an overwrought mind. Dr. Raphael Yehuda Zwi Werblowsky, who teaches comparative religion at Jerusalem University, and who describes himself as "a strictly observant Jew," investigated the charges in respect to Jewish children. In each case he found no substance for the accusations. He even produced evidence to prove the falsity of these allegations; as a result, he himself was accused of being "a spokesman for the missionaries." He ascribes the agitation on the part of the ultraorthodox to a growing sense of powerlessness in imposing stricter rules of rabbinic observance upon the population.[25] A letter to the *Jewish Chronicle* from Abraham I. Carmel, a former Roman Catholic priest and now an orthodox Jew, reads in part: "Jews have always been tolerant to the point of weakness where religion is concerned. There are many non-Jews who regard this tolerance as a lack of conviction. In this case, the Jewish souls of our children are at stake, and I personally regard the Israeli attitude of treating this matter as a 'social problem' with contempt." What he asks for is intervention on the part of the State. Carmel's letter appeared in the spring of 1956. Some twenty years later the Israeli State did step in — and with a vengeance. Rabbi Yehuda Meir Abramowitz introduced into the Knesset a bill to make it an illegal act to give "bonuses" enticing Jews to change their religion. This bill became law on April 1, 1978. It provides five years imprisonment or a fine of fifty thousand pounds (Israeli) for the offence. The recipient of such "bonuses" is to be punished with three years imprisonment, or a fine of thirty thousand pounds.[26]

The law is so loosely formulated that it is open to much abuse and so restrictive as to put under suspicion any Jew dealing with Christians. The reaction of Christians both in Israel and abroad was instantaneous. The United Christian Council in Israel complained of "hasty passing" of the law during the Christmas season, and promised to fight for its annulment.[27] The European Lutheran Commission on the Church and the Jewish People sent a letter of protest to the Prime Minister, Menachem Begin, and copies to the Israeli President, to the Cabinet Ministers, and to the Director of the World Jewish Congress. The letter points out that the law in question contravenes the United Nations Declaration on Human Rights (articles 18 and 19), which Israel endorsed. The letter pleads: "For the sake of the welfare of Israel, we urge the earliest possible repeal of this law."[28] The head of the Roman

Catholic (Latin) Church in Israel, Bishop Hanna Kaldany, lodged a similar protest even prior to the passing of the law.[29] Other churches have made similar remonstrations. The impact was such that the Israeli authorities had to deny that the law was directed at any specific group and that there was any intention "to create difficulties for missionaries operating in Israel."[30] *De jure*, the law is on the statute book; *de facto*, it is at present in suspension as it cannot be applied without the direct permission of the Ministry of Justice. So far there has been no test case. If the law is applied literally, culpability would arise from offering a cup of tea to a Jewish friend.

Behind the antimissionary agitation is an effort to keep alive an old myth that missionaries succeed only by bribery and enticement. Circulating in the Jewish community are innumerable stories of innocent Jews who were seduced by missionaries offering money and other inducements. There are tales of forced baptisms in cellars, of branding arms with a cross so as to make return to Judaism impossible, and of various means of blackmail to retain the victims of missionary perversion. Such stories have acquired the status of folklore and are widely believed. The Yiddish writer, I. J. Singer, spins a tale of a mission in Warsaw where an attempt is made to entice a hungry young Jew by offering him food. The description of the interior of the mission and the chapel and of the method of indoctrination of similar victims is too fantastic to be believed even by the most gullible, yet the story has been translated and printed in a respectable Jewish periodical.[31] Singer describes the "naked Jesus" on the wall — a wooden statue of Jesus with a red beard — and other details which are totally out of keeping with the Warsaw mission, which was run by people completely committed to a Puritan tradition. It would appear that any distortion of fact is acceptable as long as it serves the purpose of alerting the unwary.[32]

Even the vaguest suspicion of crypto-Christianity is sufficient to arouse the ire of fanatics. Sholem Asch's trouble with the Jewish community was due to his positive presentation of Jesus and Paul in his novels. He placed Jesus and the messianic movement in Palestine in a thoroughly Jewish milieu and wrote about them with appreciation and reverence. After publication of *The Nazarene* (1939) and *Mary* (1949), the Yiddish daily *Forward* refused to accept any more of Asch's contributions, though he had been writing for the paper regularly; and the rest of the Jewish press followed its lead.

The Encyclopedia Judaica explains: "His critics claimed to discern the missionary element in all the writing of [a] dozen or so years . . . ."[33] Asch's most violent critic wrote a whole book to prove his crypto-Christianity. Chaim Lieberman, a columnist for *Forward,* accused Asch of "subservience to the Church" and of perverting "the unparalleled Jewish tragedy" for Christian propaganda. About Asch's literary effort, Lieberman writes: "There is no meaner, nor more callous piece of writing than this in all literature." According to Lieberman, Asch is neither Jew nor Christian but only a charlatan writing for personal gain: "You neither wear phylacteries, nor do you wear the cross; you have neither faith nor works. The whole thing to you is just an interesting and remunerative divertissement." Lieberman describes Asch as an "impostor" whose writing is nothing more than "childish prattle" —not an ordinary impostor but a "vicious" one. He characterizes Asch as "self-absorbed, self-important, shallow, vain, humourless and utterly godless, [daring] to invade the holy precincts of religion and dictate new precepts and statutes to Jewry." The vituperation of this scurrilous diatribe knows no bounds in name-calling. For Lieberman this seems to be a sacred task, as he explains, "to enlighten the Jewish public and so to undo at least some of the evil which he [Asch] had perpetrated against the Jewish community." Lieberman's outrage reached the ultimate in his reaction to Asch's suggestion in the *Chicago Daily News* that the birthday of Jesus ought to be celebrated as a Jewish holiday. Lieberman accuses Asch of having "thrust his people away for a mess of pottage and a handful of glory."[34]

Samuel Sandmel, who is equally critical of Asch's writings and regards them as "tedious," confesses: "Antagonistic as I am to Asch's work, when I read the merciless attacks on him by Chaim Lieberman . . . I ended up with deep sympathy for him."[35]

On this issue Jews know no tolerance. Stephen S. Wise, the most renowned Jewish leader at the time, "was compelled to resign his presidency of both the American Zionist Organization and the American Jewish Congress," writes Prof. Sandmel, for his friendly attitude to Jesus as a result of Joseph Klausner's work on the subject.[36] Anyone familiar with Klausner's book will know the limitations of his "positive" presentation of Jesus. But even this was enough to arouse criticism. In like manner Ahad Ha-Am (Asher Ginsberg) attacked C. G. Montefiore for admiring Jesus and for his mild attitude towards Christianity.[37]

Dr. Karl Stern's *Pillar of Fire* (1951), which tells the story of his conversion, prompted Bernard Heller to write a rejoinder under the title *Epistle to an Apostate* (1951). Chapter 8 bears the heading, "Pillar of Fire or Smouldering Stump?" Heller alludes to the mental imbalance of the eminent psychiatrist and suggests that he must have been suffering from schizophrenia. Heller's effort ends with Micah 4:5: "Let all peoples walk each one in the name of its God. But we will walk in the name of the Lord our God for ever and ever." It so happens that this is not the most liberal of texts the Old Testament can boast of.

By an odd twist of irony, the Epilogue of Heller's book, supposedly written by a non-Jew, betrays traces of having been written by a convert to Judaism. This writer admires Heller's self-control "while seeing the holiest possession [of the Jewish people] neatly dragged through the mire." Nothing that Dr. Stern says in *The Pillar of Fire* about Judaism deserves such an accusation. But in the cause of denouncing Hebrew Christians there are no limits to exaggeration.

Jews are puzzled by the attraction Jesus has for some of them. Why men of nobility like Henri Bergson should embrace the Christian faith as if Judaism is not good enough, they find difficult to understand.[38] Sholem Asch and Norman Cousins, both of high standing in the literary world, have never hidden their utmost respect and admiration for Jesus. Cousins maintains that "there is every reason for Judaism to lose its reluctance towards Jesus," whom he regards in his "towering spiritual presence" as a "projection of Judaism and not a repudiation of it." To the question, "Why is Jesus important to Jews?" Cousins answers, "The rediscovery of Jesus can help Jews in the most vital respect of all; he can help them to forgive their tormentors—including those who have done evil to them in Jesus' name."[39]

It is this spiritual quality of the Nazarene which Sholem Asch finds so fascinating: "Just as water fills up the hollowness of the oceans, so did he fill the empty world with the spirit of the one living God. No one before him and no one after him has bound our world with fetters of the law, of justice, and of love, and brought it to the feet of the one living Almighty God as effectively as did this personage who came to an Israelite house in Nazareth in Galilee—and this he did, not by the might of the sword, of fire and steel . . . but by the power of his mighty spirit and of his teachings."[40]

Sholem Asch, writing as a Jew, makes the following statement: "I consider my Christian brothers as the spiritual children of Abraham, Isaac, and Jacob, enlisted together with me to our birthright from God . . . ." Asch regards Christianity as the main factor in enhancing the significance of the Jewish people in the eyes of the world: "Without Christianity," he writes, "Jews would become a second tribe of Samaritans."[41]

The spiritual content of the Gospel makes a great appeal to Jewish youth brought up in the freedom of American democracy. Jewish leaders have probed the reasons why the younger generation is so susceptible to the Christian message. They usually blame self-alienation and ignorance of Judaism. Rabbi Moshe Adler admits, however, that "alienation from self is not the only cause of defection to Christianity, nor necessarily the cause of most defections . . . ." Making allowance for the "psychological dimension of the Jesus trip" among the young, he warns against the temptation "to write the whole thing off as some sort of mental aberration." To the contrary, he believes that some Jews become Christians "out of sincere, thought-out conviction," though this, of course, does not apply to all of them. At the same time he blames ignorance of Judaism, lack of Jewish education, and intermarriage. Rabbi Adler sees in intermarriage the greatest danger to Jewish survival. The blame for the success of the Jews for Jesus Movement he puts at the door of the missionaries. He accuses them of subversive methods such as "argumentative and manipulative techniques." At the same time he acknowledges that this turning to Jesus is a symptom and a warning "that Jewish life is ailing seriously."[42]

As a result of a more friendly attitude to Jews on the part of Gentiles and greater freedom within Jewish society, the Synagogue is faced with a new difficulty. The original appeal to Jewish loyalty and the deterrent of the possibility of Christian persecution do not carry the same weight as they did before. In the past becoming a Christian meant joining the enemy. But in contemporary Christianity, especially in the United States, there is little enmity left on religious grounds. In the Christian churches today there is a deliberate emphasis upon Jewish roots. The Jewish Christian believer is encouraged to remain loyal to his people and to be proud of his race. Jewish Christians themselves have for a long time fought against succumbing to the "Gentilizing error," as if renouncing their Jewishness were part of their Christian profession.

Even before the end of the last century Mark John Levy was a valiant fighter for the restoration of what he called Apostolic Hebrew Christianity. In London he founded the Christian Jews' Patriotic Alliance with the support of outstanding Jewish Christians. He wrote that the Episcopalian Church in 1916, and the Christian Church (Disciples) in 1917, as well as the Lutherans, Presbyterians, Methodists, and others had all "endorsed the scripturalness of our position." It is therefore not true that the churches insisted upon total absorption of the Jewish Christian. A poem Levy wrote in the late 1890s begins with the verse:

> Must Israel eat the flesh of swine
> Because, Lord Jesus, we are thine?
> Must we God's seal of faith forgo
> Because thy love the Gentiles know?

Levy's address to the Seventeenth Annual Conference of the Hebrew Christian Alliance of America (May 4–8, 1931), which was on the subject, "Hebrew Christianity and Jewish Nationalism," was received with enthusiasm by the delegates. They saw no conflict between their Christian profession and their Jewish loyalties. This is a prevailing attitude of Jewish Christians associated with the International Hebrew Christian Alliance. The Alliance completely identifies itself with the Jewish people in all their national aspirations. At the Eighth International Conference, held in Holland in 1950, the third year of the existence of the Israeli State, it was moved, seconded, and resolved to give thanks "to Almighty God for His goodness to His people in giving them once again an independent existence in the land of their fathers." The resolution declared "Hebrew Christian oneness with those who labour to build up Zion."[43] Expressions of loyalty and gratitude to God for the State of Israel dominated the Fourteenth International Hebrew Christian Conference, which was held in Jerusalem (October 4–7, 1975). The Conference declared itself "an integral part" of the Jewish people.[44]

David Shahar, an Israeli writer who is known as "a marvellous storyteller," describes an "apostate" by the name of Dr. Shoshan. This Jewish Christian has an attachment to his people, studies the Talmud, speaks Hebrew, and has arranged for his name to be written in Hebrew on his tombstone in a Christian cemetery. When asked to explain his close attachment to Jewish tradition, he replied that Jesus was a Jew who spoke Hebrew and who never departed from the Law. The gist of Shahar's tale is that syncretism does not work, for a person like Dr. Shoshan is a Jew to Christians and a Christian to Jews.[45] What Shahar does not realize is that the young Jews who decide for Jesus are not syncretists in his sense of the word. These men and women have a personal loyalty to Jesus Christ. Rabbi Harry Joshua Stern attributes the attraction to Christian mysticism. But this is not the whole answer, even for Rabbi Stern. He writes: "In all fairness it must be stated that some Jews came to Christianity out of conviction, especially in days when Christianity possessed no power."[46]

There is a growing recognition, especially in Israel, that *yehudi meshihiim* (Jewish Christians) are not necessarily estranged from their own people. The standard Hebrew dictionary, *Even Shushan*, describes Jewish Christians as "a sect of Jews that have declared themselves Jewish in their nationality and in their allegiance to the State of Israel, and Christian in their religion." The distinction between national custom and religious observance presents a delicate balance in contemporary Jewish society. Many irreligious Jews without any difficulty observe national custom as part of Jewish culture. Hebrew Christians try to do the same without compromising their religious convictions. At the First Hebrew Christian Conference of the United States (July 28–30, 1903), the issue was raised by three delegates. They condemned the "unscriptural attitude" of separating Christian Jews from their own people and pointed to the primitive Church, where there was no effort made to Judaize the Gentiles nor to Gentilize the Jewish followers of Christ: "We argue for absolute freedom and not for compulsion — freedom to exercise our liberty in Christ" even to the point of circumcising male children "and to observe any other of the rites and ceremonies of [our] fathers, not done away with by Christ and His Apostles or the primitive Church." They attached two conditions: (1) there must be no compulsion; (2) the decision must be left to each Hebrew Christian. The "rites and ceremonies" they had in view were not meant to be meritorious deeds to gain God's favour, but merely expressions of loyalty to their people.[47]

In Jewish circles the question is repeatedly raised: Why do Jewish men and women turn to Jesus, especially now that no social advantage accrues? What is the attraction? A Jewish Professor of Philosophy who was brought up in an orthodox home, who learned in childhood to dread the name of Jesus, and who knew nothing about Christianity until he became a mature adult, provides a clue. "With an entire ignorance of what constituted Christianity but possessing an ingrained aversion to it; an enemy of Jesus by accident of birth but without personal animosity," he met a Christian who totally changed his life. This Roman Catholic social worker was no missionary; he was not even a churchgoer, but he embodied the values which Jesus taught. It was in his presence that the Jewish man first learned "to mention the detested name without self-consciousness, and presently with wonder." This was the beginning. He received, as he says, from this Christian friend "the accolade of spiritual living based on the vital principle of an all-embracing love, a sentiment the doxologies I had chanted in my teens had never brought me. This man at one magic touch had crumbled my walls." Yet it was not the Christian friend who fascinated, but the figure behind him—Jesus. The Jewish philosopher explains: "I felt myself to be a Jew who was a Christian, a Christian who remained a Jew." Though he was never baptized and remained a stranger to Christian doctrine, he was in love with Jesus.[48]

Victor Gollancz (d. 1967), one of the best known and most highly respected publishers in Britain, is a similar case. Gollancz was a lover of Jesus without belonging to any church or adhering to Christian doctrine. The impact that Jesus made upon his life determined all his actions. These are his words: "Christ's teaching has made an impact as of the *utterly* true, Christ's personality has made an impact as of the *utterly* adorable, Christ's living and dying have made an impact as of the *utterly* good." But Gollancz never went beyond the humanity of Jesus—Jesus remained "within human possibilities."[49] Gollancz's dedication was to the Sermon on the Mount. But many Jews, quite logically, go beyond the "human possibilities" for it is not within the Jewish tradition to make idols of heroes. Jews are not allowed to "adore" a man by reason of his greatness and moral integrity.

Joseph Fletcher cites the case of a young Jewish Communist who was picked up in Paris by the Gestapo. Her crime, apart from being Jewish, was that she was guilty of organizing an underground escape route for fellow Jews. When she was about to be transported to an extermination camp, a nun, Mother Maria, stepped forward to take her place. The nun perished in a gas chamber at Belsen; the young woman survived the war and became a Christian.[50]

The Jews for Jesus Movement, in the United States and elsewhere, does not seem to be a movement towards Christianity in the traditional sense. It is rather a discovery of Jesus as the Messiah on the part of Jewish youth starved for spiritual values. Dr. Arthur W. Kac, in an informative study of this unusual phenomenon, explains that these young people have found in Jesus "what they have been vaguely searching for, the mystery of meaning in their lives." Now "they are eager to share their experience with others." For them Jesus has become real in that he has freed them from the power of evil. They find him able to break the power of drug addiction, to release them from the tyranny of sexual desires, and to heal minds corrupted by delving into the practices of black magic.[51] For this kind of need, Judaism apparently has no remedy. Its usual panacea is to go "back to tradition" and observance of the Law. It is only the love of Christ which both chastens and heals the human heart. In the school of Jesus love is learned and love is shared.

Here is the testimony of "a converted Jewess": "I did not 'believe' until I 'loved.' I fell in love with Christ, and tried to live with all my powers the Sermon on the Mount . . . ." This woman explains that before her encounter with Jesus she had no faith in God or man. But after her meeting with Jesus Christ she made the great discovery that it is not belief that makes a person Christlike but only love, the love of Jesus.[52]

Frederick J. Forell tells of an elderly Jewish widow who asked for baptism "because she sensed how much Jesus loved her."[53] This may sound sentimental and rather naive, but reveals the secret of the Gospel message.

John C. Trever asks the question: "Why did the Qumran community die, while Christianity lives?" He offers several answers: the Qumran sect was too eschatologically orientated and too narrow-minded to survive defeat; it was separatist and esoteric; it was ascetic; it was priest-centred; it was too rigid to adapt to changed circumstances.[54] These seem reasonable enough explanations but do not touch the heart of the matter. The real reason why Qumran perished and Christianity is alive is that there is no comparison between the Teacher of Righteousness and the Man on the Cross. Geza Vermes touches on the truth in attributing the drawing power of Jesus to his "genius" for laying bare "the inner core of spiritual truth" and for exposing "the essence of religion as an existential relationship between man and man, and between man and God."[55] But this still leaves out Jesus as a lover of man, presenting him only as a teacher. The secret of the Christian faith is not Christ's "genius" but his love. This is the underlying motif of much of the New Testament. Seen in this perspective, "conversion" has little to do with change of religion but has much to do with change of heart. What Jesus does for men and women, Jew or Gentile, is to give them new freedom to love God and to love each other.[56]

Chapter **12**

The Dialogue

For a long time dialogue and mission were taken to be synonyms. No one could conceive of mission without dialogue. In the New Testament *dialegomai* is used in the context of missions and means "to argue," "to reason," "to dispute," etc. The verb occurs several times in the Book of Acts in connection with Paul's witness to the Synagogue. Acts 17:17 may be translated: "[Paul] dialogued in the Synagogue with the Jews . . . ." And Acts 19:8: "Paul entered the Synagogue and for three months spoke boldly, dialoguing and pleading about the kingdom of God." The other verb in use is *sun-zēteō*, which means "to inquire," "to deliberate," "to debate with another person" (cf. German *Zwiesprache* — "talking with each other"). The Revised Standard Version wrongly translates Acts 9:29: "he spoke and disputed against the Hellenists." No wise missionary speaks *against* people; he speaks *with* people. The New English Bible translates correctly: "[Paul] spoke out boldly and openly in the name of the Lord, talking and debating *with* the Greek-speaking Jews" (so also Moffatt and the Luther Bible).

The "debate" with the Jewish people began early in the Church and actually goes back to pre-Christian times. In the name of God the prophet Isaiah invites his people to enter into a dialogue (Isa. 1:18)—*yakhah* means exactly this: "Come let us dialogue together, says the Lord." There are snippets of dialogue recorded in all the Gospels, but chiefly in John. The oldest extant extended dialogue between a Christian and a Jew has come down to us from the pen of Justin Martyr (c. 100–165). Adolf von Harnack's dubbing Justin's effort a "victor's monologue" fails to do justice to the Church father.[1] Justin's *Dialogue with Trypho the Jew* is a real dialogue between two disputants, though naturally enough it is Justin's

168

voice which dominates. Had Trypho written the account, he would have been the "victor." In such matters there can be no objectivity if the recorder of the dialogue is personally involved. For Justin the dialogue was not an academic exercise but a witness to his faith. Trypho took the opposite view, as was his right.

The concept of mission is built into the Christian message and into the structure of the Gospels. Some scholars, especially those of the Bultmannian school, question whether the missionary aspect goes back to Jesus himself.[2] They see in it a later development within the early Church. However, there can be no doubt that the missionary character of the Church appeared at the earliest possible time and began upon Jewish soil and among Jews before it shifted to the non-Jewish world.

From the very beginning, Christian mission was a dialogical effort involving the exegesis of messianic texts in the Old Testament: the Church "proved" from the Hebrew Bible that Jesus was the Messiah (cf. Acts 2:14ff.; 4:23ff.; 9:20; 17:2–4, 11). Preaching Jesus as Messiah involved constant reference to the Old Testament. The nonbelieving Jews attempted to refute that these Old Testament passages referred to Jesus.[3] Evidence of such controversy regarding Old Testament texts we find outside the New Testament in the *Dialogue with Trypho*. The idea that dialogue can be separated from mission and carried on in a spirit of neutrality would have appeared to Christians and Jews as a betrayal of the faith. Such an attitude of detachment is possible only in an age of syncretistic indifference which regards all truths as merely subjective and therefore equally valid. If dialogue between believers with differing views is taken seriously, it cannot take the form of a detached academic discussion. The results of an encounter in genuine dialogue may be varied: it may lead to a modification of views on both sides; it may lead to the persuasion of one party to the view of the other; it may end in an agreement to differ. But it can never be a matter of indifference. Stephen Neill writes: "If I take my partner in dialogue seriously, I cannot wish for him anything less than I wish for myself."[4] For him the aim of dialogue is decision.[5] When dialogue results in hostility, it has failed in its prime purpose.

The official disputations with Jews arranged by the Church in the Middle Ages with a view to persuading, were not dialogues in the accepted sense, for the Jewish party was hampered by fear of reprisals. Prof. Frank Talmage cites the thirteenth-century Rabbi

Solomon ben Moses' advice to fellow Jews to avoid entering disputes with Christians: "If the Jew be victorious, he will provoke wrath upon himself for belittling and refuting their faith. But if he is defeated and shamed and if on his account and through ignorance truth is silenced, his punishment is twofold." The rabbi therefore advises every Jew against disputation with the uneducated and with those of ill will, "for they will inform on him and on us . . . ."[6]

The modern concept of dialogue is a result of Martin Buber's influence. But already in the early twenties Ferdinand Ebner had laid the foundation for the psychological and philosophical implications of dialogical encounter. For Ebner, meeting another "Thou" constitutes a challenge to one's own existence as a thinking and feeling human being. The very presence of the other person means that one is faced with a question mark about oneself and must go through a process of reexamination. As a discussion of Ebner's views puts it: "The other person is not a 'thou,' who must believe me on my word, but an 'I' who is to test my theses by a totally impersonal mental process."[7] This kind of scrutiny calls for affirmation on the one hand and questioning on the other; that is, dialogue is speech and counterspeech. At the moment when the partners in dialogue agree to differ, the conversation has come to an end.[8] In the case of an encounter of two like-minded people, there is no dialogue at all, only an exchange of ideas. Genuine dialogue depends upon the full freedom of each partner to speak in accordance with conscience. Article 18 of the Universal Declaration of Human Rights adopted by the General Assembly of the United Nations (December 10, 1948) affirms every man's right to freedom of thought, conscience, and religion: "This freedom includes freedom to change his religion or belief in teaching, practice, worship and observance." The modern idea of dialogue is inextricably bound to the concept of freedom in democratic society. There can be no dialogue without freedom of expression.

Buber's perception of dialogue is not very different from that of Ebner. For Buber the very encounter of persons releases dynamic tension which calls for response. Only when one person responds to the other does he indicate his responsibility. In every dialogical encounter there is a creative potential in which one is the giver and the other the recipient. One is active and the other passive: "the attacking force and the defending force, the nature which investigates and the nature which supplies information, request begged and granted—and always both together, completing one another in mutual contribution."[9] Such turning to each other is a source of enrichment for both, according to Buber.

Buber's chief contribution to the meaning of dialogue is not in the area of methodology but in the perception of the human qualities involved. Dialogue is meant to be other than disputation in which each partner seeks to outwit his opponent. It demands attentive listening to the opposite point of view and honest response in full acknowledgement of one's own fallibility. These are its advantages, but dialogue also has its limitations. Respect for one's opponent may lead to the suppression of truth from a desire not to cause offence. Such a situation may arise in the teacher-pupil relationship. A teacher may refrain from impressing upon his pupil views which may cause offence to him or his parents. Plato tried to solve this problem on the philosophical assumption that all truth is innate and therefore latently present to the learner. All that the teacher is required to do is to act as "midwife" in order to facilitate the process of education.

The maieutic method rests entirely upon a philosophical assumption which cannot be substantiated from experience. Science depends upon facts arrived at by deduction or induction. Theology draws upon tradition and faith, both of which are acquired not by intuition but by the witness of believers. Faith cannot be "conveyed"; it can only be witnessed to. Witness means dialogue; dialogue means mission. Placed in the context of faith, dialogue as witness ends in proclamation. Ervin Nagy therefore rightly concludes that "*concretely conducted dialogue must have proclamation as its model,* and must preserve the structure of proclamation." But this does not exclude dialogue; the above statement is also reversible: ". . . it is necessary to stress *the nature of proclamation as dialogue.*"[10] Lawrence D. Folkemer takes a similar view, except that for him the two methods, though related, are yet separate: "Proclamation and dialogue are neither identical nor alternative and mutually exclusive acts." He formulated seven theses in an effort to relate proclamation to dialogue in terms of Christian witness. For him Christian proclamation is essentially witness.[11]

Jewish objections to the missionary effort have been loud and clear, though some Jews admit the necessity of missions for the Christian Church, which ultimately depends upon witness and not biological increase. But in making such an admission, they would exclude Jews from missionary outreach — it should be limited to Gentiles only. They look upon the missionary effort to Jews as a denial of Israel's special place in the story of revelation and therefore as an insult to Judaism. This touches upon the question of Jewish election, which is deeply ingrained in the psychological structure of every Jew. Even secularized Jews have a subconscious awareness of Israel's "chosenness."[12] This sense of election finds expression in the Hebrew liturgy and in much of the sermonizing in the Synagogue. Here is a typical paragraph from a sermon published in the *Jewish Chronicle* (London):

> The Living God enjoins that Israel shall live. Judaism is an indestructible element of the Great Design. The unfolding ages move inexorably to the fulfilment of history, towards the New Heaven and the New Earth, to the Kingdom of God in this world. This is the unchanging message of Judaism, and Israel is the messenger. Amid all the flux and eddies of history there is one constant: God is One, the Living God; and His prophet is one, the undying Jew.[13]

The missionary effort is regarded not only as a denial of Israel's election, but also as a deliberate attempt to disrupt Jewish life and ultimately to bring to an end Jewish separate existence. The sense of outrage which is engendered by missionary activity is reenforced by the experience of Auschwitz. Even Jews entirely estranged from the Synagogue regard "conversion to Christianity" as joining the camp of the persecutors—the *goyim* (Gentiles). Mordecai Gotfried of Tel Aviv, in a poem based on the Prayer of Thanksgiving for not being created a "heathen," writes that he has now turned away from the alluring voices which once charmed him, the voices of Goethe, Shakespeare, and Shelley: "I seek no more—how strange are now these books to me—praised be thou, O God, that thou hast not made me a Gentile."[14]

We have already seen that Jewish objections are not without foundation. Denial of Israel's continued election as a witness to the God of Israel persists in the Church, especially among theologians. Colin O'Grady takes Karl Barth to task for insisting on Jewish election even after the Christ event: "God has inaugurated a new covenant with man on the basis of faith in Jesus Christ and this supersedes and outmodes the old covenant." O'Grady requires the "rejectedness of Jews" to remind the believing Gentiles "of the absolute grace and mercy of their own election" in being grafted in to take Israel's place. This theology rests upon a radical break in the story of revelation: "The presence of the Jews re-

minds the Church of the transition from the old to the new covenant." All that is left to the Jews is conversion: they "must cease
being Israel by becoming more truly Israel"—and this can happen
only by accepting the Gospel.[15]

The negativity of such an approach, apart from its theological
misconception,[16] is both offensive and shortsighted. Reaction
comes not only from the Jewish side but from many Christian liberal theologians. Their protests have been strong enough to affect
the strategy of the historic churches to the point of abandoning
the missionary effort altogether. An important landmark in this
volte-face was Vatican II, one of whose documents reads in part:
"Since the spiritual patrimony common to Christians and Jews is
thus so great, this sacred Synod wishes to foster and recommend
that mutual understanding and respect which is the fruit above all
of biblical and theological studies and of brotherly dialogue." A
footnote explains that "reference to 'conversion' of the Jews was
removed . . . because to many Council Fathers it was not appropriate in a document striving to establish common goals and interests first."[17] Precedent for this omission was already set by Pope
John, who caused the removal of reference to "the conversion of
the Jews" in the Good Friday prayer. Dialogue is now to take the
place of "mission."

The change in Roman Catholic missionary circles was instantaneous: "No more proselytizing of Jews" became the motto. Fr.
John M. Oesterreicher writes: ". . . there is in the Church today
no drive, no organized effort to proselytize Jews, and none is con-
templated for tomorrow."[18] The most significant change of position took place in the circles associated with the Sisters of Sion, a
society expressly founded by two brothers, Alphonse and Theodore Ratisbonne, for the conversion of Jews. Fr. Oesterreicher
quotes "one of their unpublished position papers" to the effect
that the society "resolutely eliminated every attempt at proselytism
as contrary to the Church . . . ." The explanation which follows is
strangely confused. It reads: "Proselytism seeks to make conversion an end without taking into account God's mysterious con-
duct. He alone knows what is best for the soul."[19] Fr. Oesterreicher does not deny that the Church is under a missionary obligation, but as far as the Jews are concerned, its witness must take
the form of silence: "Even without preaching, she bears this testimony by her very presence, and so does the individual
Christian."

The right to "witness" is admitted at least by some liberal Jews.

The principle of witness (Christian or Jewish), according to Rabbi Henry Siegman, "need not be offensive to the religious sensibilities nor pose a barrier to Christian-Jewish relations." He recognizes, however, that the concept lends itself to abuse.[20] But Rabbi Siegman is an exception; the majority of Jewish leaders are against any form of Christian witness. Even so liberal-minded a person as Rabbi Abraham L. Feinberg reacted strongly to a Canadian Council of Churches report urging Protestant denominations to missionize Jews. He wrote to the Council that "this intensified program to convert Jews is tactless, unrealistic and misguided—however well-meaning and sincere. It widens the gap between church and synagogue and greatly disturbs a relationship which had become increasingly harmonious during these past years." He explains that he does not mean to deny the Church the right to propagate her faith "in African straw huts, Chinese bamboo houses and Eskimo igloos," but the case with Jews is different. To proselytize Jews is to weaken "a child's trust in the faith of his fathers," and therefore unfair: "Christianity is best for *others*—Judaism is *my* religion, the best I have ever known."[21] Another outstanding rabbi, a refugee from Nazi Germany, Dr. Ignaz Maybaum, takes exactly the same position: there are plenty of heathen to be brought into the Christian Church—but Israel belongs to a different order. "We say No to the Christian mission to Jews." The Jewish people has its own missionary destiny as the servant of God: "We Jews know that the choosing of Israel is irrevocable"—Jews need no conversion.[22] The traditionalists' reaction to missions is, of course, more violent, as can be seen from events in Israel and the law recently promulgated against missionaries.

But many Christian leaders are equally outspoken on the subject of missions to Jews. Reinhold Niebuhr made his position clear in a passage which has been widely quoted and much discussed. He regards the missionary attempts as not only futile but definitely wrong: "They are wrong because the two faiths despite differences are sufficiently alike for the Jew to find God more easily in terms of his own religious heritage than by subjecting himself to the hazards of guilt-feeling involved in a conversion to a faith, which, whatever its excellencies, must appear to him as a symbol of an oppressive majority culture."[23] Paul Tillich's attitude is equally critical of missions. He rejects active evangelism among Jews, but allows that if a Jew knocks at a church door, he should not be turned away. Tillich sees the function of Judaism as a corrective force in checking "tendencies in Christianity which drive toward paganism and idolatry." Therefore it must not be interfered with by missionary incursion.[24] Frederick C. Grant, formerly of Union Theological Seminary (New York), can see no reason why Jews should become Christians as the "additional matters" offered by the Christian faith will add little to their spiritual life.[25] Even Karl Barth, who carried on a running feud with the Synagogue, was averse to active missionizing, leaving Jewish conversion to the eschatological future.[26] Marcus Barth appears to be taking a similar position.[27] These are weighty names which carry considerable influence in theological circles and among Christians generally. The result is a turning away from active missionary enterprise in most of the historical churches. Mission among Jews is at present supported largely by conservative, fundamentalist groups and various Christian sects.

Decrying mission to Jews has become the fashion of the day. Some do so with considerable violence, others more gently. Among the gentle souls we would count Professor Robert T. Osborn of Duke University. He disagrees with the academics who reject mission to Jews for "vulgar" reasons, such as the demands of pluralistic society and relativistic attitudes. He also rejects the orthodox evangelical position because it fails to take account of the Jews as a special case. He has his own reasons why mission to Jews is inadmissible: the Jew by "definition" is a person who rejected the promise; the Gentile, on the other hand, again by "definition," is not a rejector of Jesus. To offer the Gospel to the Jew today means placing him in a situation of denying the decision of the past "when Judaism refused faith in Jesus." This to Osborn is an ungracious act. In case we misinterpret his thesis, let him speak for himself: ". . . the church cannot directly witness to the Jew the accepting grace of God in Christ without, paradoxically, rejecting the Jew and therefore Christ as the one who accepts the Jew. When the Christian witnesses directly to the Jew he requires the Jew to reject Christ or else to reject himself; in either case something unloving occurs to which Christ cannot be party."[28] According to Osborn, this does not apply to the Gentile, for the Gentile was never placed in the same historical situation.

Prof. Osborn's reasoning is more than unusual. Without wanting to be unkind it strikes one as deliberate quibbling in order both to be in favour with the Jews and to allow mission to Gentiles. For him there are three kinds of people: Jews, Christians, and Gentiles; and they all stand in a different relationship to God. This we deny: there is only one kind of people and they all stand in the same relationship to God; namely, as sinners in need of reconciliation and grace.

Prof. Osborn treats the term *Jew* as a collective noun—a theological abstraction which does not take into account the concrete existence of human persons. His "Jew" is different totally from every other member of the human race. Being a Jew is for him a historically determined *fait accompli* which is irreversible; what the fathers decided can never be undone. Such fatalism is contrary to both Jewish and Christian thought—there is no hint of *teshuvah* (turning, repentance) or *metanoia* (change of heart and mind) in Prof. Osborn's frame of reference. The apostolic mission to the Jews, according to Osborn, was "foundational" and unrepeatable; it was the "defining moment"; it was "once for all." Judaism became what it is by rejecting Jesus. It does not require much insight to notice that the professor is dealing with "Judaism" and not with living people. Failure of this type accounts for many of the misconceptions regarding the missionary work of the Church. Osborn is right in saying that "a Christian mission to the Jews is very vulnerable to the demon of anti-Semitism."[29] But there is danger in all human activities; there is danger in omission as well as in commission. The potential of anti-Semitism can never be a theological justification for the rejection of mission. Osborn's effort is not without merit, especially in his emphasis upon the gratuity of God's grace. He is wrong, however, in treating the "Jew" as an impersonal collective entity, overlooking the fact that the "Jew" is also a person before God, challenged to make decisions of his own. Osborn's conclusion, "If God wishes a Jew to become a Christian, it is for God to see to it," reminds one of the question uttered by Cain, "Am I my brother's keeper?"

What if God sent Prof. Osborn to tell the message of God's love in Christ to a person who happens to be a Jew? Would he do what Jonah did? Would he send the person he was to deal with to the rabbis instead? Here is a specific case: Naomi Bluestone is a medical doctor practicing in New York. She was brought up in an orthodox Jewish home, intensely Zionist. This is her confession: "Judaism offers nothing. For Judaism is fixated in a world of forty years ago. I am younger than that and my whole life has been passing by." She tells us that "Jewish religious education is incompatible with the needs of the adult individual." She is therefore not surprised that young people turn to other religions: "Judaism has been short-changing them." Dr. Bluestone herself does not believe in God any more, because she cried out for help "and got no answer." In her words, "Judaism needs an overhaul from bottom up. I offer myself as evidence. If I can defect . . . anyone can."[30] Supposing Prof. Osborn and Dr. Bluestone met face to face, what would he say to her?

"The conversion of Jews"—for and against—is widely discussed in Christian publications, but seldom in relation to definite human needs. The Fuller Theological Seminary Statement on Jewish-Christian Relations (1976) exhorts Christians to share the Gospel with the Jewish people. It also exhorts Jewish Christians to "retain their Jewish heritage, culture, religious practices and marriage customs within the context of a sound biblical theology expressing Old and New Testament truth." Christians of Jewish descent are to exercise their freedom in Christ and so enrich the life of the Church.[31] But W. S. LaSor, Professor of Old Testament at Fuller, is not too happy with this statement. He fears that "many Jews could see the entire statement as nothing else than a rephrased attempt to renew efforts at conversion of Jews." Why Jews should not be converted LaSor does not say. He lacks the theological dexterity of Robert Osborn and so entangles himself in contradiction: "The Bible nowhere speaks of converting Jews. However, the Bible does make clear, repeatedly and in many ways, that Jews, Gentiles—all men and women without exception—need to be converted."[32]

This kind of muddling the issue persists in many Church statements. "Double-talk" which confuses Christians and only adds to Jewish suspicions is evident. Here is a typical example: Prof. Herbert Schmid, President of the Swiss Jewish mission at Basle (founded 1830), writes: "The Gospel is destined for all people, but its acceptance is God's work and not the result of pseudo-missionary manipulations. . . ." Because "the term 'mission' can easily be misunderstood," it must be dropped. The organization is now renamed "The Foundation for Church and Judaism." Its task is not missionary in the old tradition but the fostering of "Jewish-Christian relations among Church people within an ecumenical context."[33] What Prof. Schmid is saying is that the original purpose of the society has totally changed and that its work is now "among Church people" on behalf of Jews. This means educating Christians concerning Jewish faith, tradition, and culture. Since the death of editor Robert Brunner (1971), *Judaica*, the society's quarterly journal, has taken on a different colour. The new editor, Roman Catholic scholar K. Hruby, has declared himself anti-missionary. Behind this change in perspective is an effort to reformulate the meaning of "mission" so as to detach it from Scripture and put it in the context of general ecumenicity.

In connection with this we might note that Prof. Tomaso Federici of the Pontifical University in Rome officially declared on behalf of his Church that it now rejects every form of proselytism even to the exclusion of preaching and witness. Instead it affirms "the permanence of Judaism in God's plan" and favours "dialogue with the Jewish people without mental reservations." Prof. Federici still uses the term *mission* several times over, but it is a kind of mission which excludes proselytism.[34] What all this amounts to is that one has to be born a Gentile to be a Christian, and that what is good (or good enough) for Gentiles, is not good (or good enough) for Jews.

The alternative to mission is dialogue. In every instance, Christian writers who deprecate mission are in favour of dialogue. The Jewish case is different. Orthodox Jews look upon dialogue with suspicion. The logic of their attitude to dialogue with Christians is straightforward. "The doctrinal differences between Judaism and Christianity cannot be bridged, making it impossible for anyone to be a believing Jew and a devout Christian at one and the same time," writes Rabbi Louis Jacobs. "On this all Jews are agreed, even those who admire the personality of Jesus and the Christian ethic and who accept the idea that Christianity has an important role to play in God's world." If this is the case, the rabbi quite consistently reasons, there is nothing to talk about except matters extraneous to faith. But this human beings do in any case irrespective of religious differences. Rabbi Jacobs therefore concludes that, in view of the wide divergence between the two faiths, "to speak of a dialogue or a common tradition is to blur distinctions which the adherents of both faiths consider of utmost significance and for which they have been prepared to offer life itself . . . . There are Jews who find such a dialogue distasteful and even harmful to faith."[35]

A. A. Cohen, a well-known writer, is in sympathy with Rabbi Jacobs: Jews and Christians "have nothing to say to one another, except in so far as they speak beyond and in spite of faith." Cohen seriously questions the whole idea of a so-called Judeo-Christian tradition; he declares it to be a myth. In spite of this, Cohen can see the positive side which accrues from dialogue in that it provides a forum for declaring one's faith.

There is an interesting tension built into the question of dialogue of which Cohen is well aware: as a believer he knows that "truth entails the telling of the truth and not simply the repetition of truth to ourselves (*sotto voce* and not overheard)." It requires "the telling of the truth aloud, to one another, over the chasm which separates us from each other and separates us from the completion in God to which we direct ourselves." But at the same time, he also knows of the "irresolvable opposition" which divides the two faiths and keeps them apart. "What the Church affirms the Synagogue must deny." What purpose, then, can dialogue serve?[36]

It seems to us that Cohen has come remarkably close to the biblical concept of mission: the proclamation of truth as we see it, irrespective of opposition on the part of the hearer. This kind of "missionizing" is called proclamation. Proclamation is not propaganda, for it is sustained by the faith that it is God and not man who does the "convincing."

For Jewish leaders, the question of dialogue remains unresolved. Those against it ask, "What is there to discuss, once we have agreed to differ?" Those for it say with Abraham Heschel, "No religion is an island." Rabbi Ignaz Maybaum explains: "In a Jewish-Christian co-operation the Jew gives Judaism, the Christian Christianity. What they give is a blessing. Jews and Christians are trustees of a blessing . . . . Jews and Christians prosper together or suffer together. The anti-Semite is not only anti-Jewish, he is anti-Christian; the anti-Semite hates and opposes messianic man, man with messianic hope." As Maybaum sees it, Christianity needs the immediacy of Judaism in order to break through the Christian myth to reach to God.[37]

This sense of mission as expressed by Rabbi Maybaum would not meet with favour from the orthodox. Rabbi Joseph B. Soloveitchik, Head of the Theological Seminary of Yeshiva University, is prepared to allow encounter between Christians and Jews as long as the meeting is not on a theological but a purely "mundane human level." Unlike A. A. Cohen, Rabbi Soloveitchik accepts the idea of a Judeo-Christian tradition, but with every emphasis upon Judaism, which "moulded the ethico-philosophical Christian world formula." What he means to say is that Judaism was the sole benefactor, receiving nothing in return. As for dialogue, "all of us speak the universal language of modern man," but in matters of faith there can only be opposition. To give way on matters of faith would result in "surrender of individuality and distinctiveness."[38] Those against dialogue see no connection, not even a historic one, between Judaism and Christianity, though it is frequently taken for granted by writers on both sides that Judaism is the mother of Christianity. Interestingly enough, neither Franz Rosenzweig nor Eugen Rosenstock-Huessy accepted the idea that there is a sharing of a common Judeo-Christian tradition.[39] To orthodox Jews, Christianity is a completely alien faith.

Jewish writers who favour dialogue with Christians usually belong to the liberal or reform Synagogue. At a Jewish-Christian symposium which met at St. Mary's College (Kansas) in February, 1965, there seemed to be no representation of Jewish orthodoxy. But even liberal Jews understand Christian-Jewish dialogue as mainly a social engagement and not a discussion of faith. Rabbi Marc H. Tanenbaum in his address to the symposium, "Design for the Future of Jewish-Christian Relations," cautiously skirted issues of faith in advocating discussions of "respective views," such as messianism, eschatology, and asceticism, adding a vague reference to "the theological basis of the relationship of Church and Synagogue to the social order, the temporal order—the theology of justice." These questions are worth discussing, but they are neutral questions which in no sense call for a declaration of faith.[40] Willingness to enter into dialogue with Christians is confined to the periphery of faith; it could not be otherwise.

In no sense does dialogue mean to Jews a rapprochement with Christian orthodoxy. Rabbi Morris Margulies made this perfectly plain at the symposium: "Judaism rejects most emphatically the Christian doctrine of the Trinity . . . . The conception of the Trinity is so foreign and alien to three thousand years of Jewish tradition that it simply cannot take hold at all. Sitting here as a Jew, I say to you emphatically that the doctrine of the Trinity impresses a Jew as preposterous."[41] This, of course, makes a dialogue of faith impossible, unless on the Christian side Christology is totally left out of the picture. To the liberal theologian, whose concern is chiefly social, the question regarding the Trinity has ceased to be an issue. He is fully aware that dialogue with Jews leads to an attenuated Christology and he prefers it that way. In this respect

William Hamilton's remark is to the point: "The reality and integrity of Jewish existence are what prevent the Christian from holding too rigid a Christological definition of God." Hamilton explains: " 'Apart from Christ I am an atheist,' is false; 'apart from Christ I am a Jew,' would be closer to the truth."[42] Some liberal writers give the impression that fascination with Judaism is the motivation behind their desire for dialogue with Jews. It is certainly noteworthy that the contributors to *The Myth of God Incarnate* (1977) fall back upon Judaism for their argument against the Chalcedonian definition. There can be no better tool for dismantling the Nicene Creed than Jewish monotheism.[43]

Jewish criticism of the trinitarian faith reached its height in Germany in the second half of the last century. There can be little doubt that it greatly contributed to the spread of anti-Semitism. Though approved by liberal theologians, it met with stiff resistance from clergy and laymen. Christians found it offensive to be told that theirs is a pagan faith and that the trinitarian creed is a survival of polytheism.[44] Jews have since learned moderation in their approach to Christianity but are greatly encouraged by the swing to unitarianism within the churches. The movement from mission to dialogue is an indication of the weakening of Christological conviction in favour of syncretistic accommodation. Liberals on both sides find common ground in ethical values, religious experience, and sociological concerns. For Jews dialogue provides a forum to present Jewish grievances; for Christians it offers an opportunity to make amends for the past. To the latter it is an outlet for conscience.

But this does not exhaust the encounter between Jews and Christians. Dialogue between individual believers on both sides has never ceased and is still taking place. These personal encounters have little to do with the official "dialogues" organized by Christian and Jewish groups which are seldom dialogues of faith. A true dialogue of faith is never a public affair, though with modern means of communication it can be publicized, as in the case of the dialogue between Pinchas Lapide and Hans Küng which was broadcast over the German South-West Radio (August 25, 1975). The requisite for such a meeting is that both partners speak from within the context of faith and listen to each other in humility of spirit. Rabbi Abraham Heschel has laid down the rule for such an encounter: "The first and most important *prerequisite of interfaith is faith.*" But he warns of the danger of substituting "interfaith" for faith.[45] Heschel approves of dialogue between Christians and Jews, for *"no religion is an island.* We are all involved with one another." Of all contemporary Jewish writers, Heschel seems to come closest to viewing the interfaith encounter as a personal experience "in terms of personal witness and example, sharing insights, confessing inadequacy." He does not shy away from meeting the other believer on the level of the experience of faith.[46] But like other Jewish writers he leaves no room for mission: "The mission to the Jews is a call to the individual Jew to betray the fellowship, the dignity, the sacred history of their people." On this he stands absolutely firm. There can be no change to something else: "Judaism has allies but no substitutes." The knot between Judaism and Jews is indissoluble: "An alternative to our existence as Jews is spiritual suicide, extinction."[47]

It appears that dialogue as understood by Jewish proponents violates the Buberian principle that the two partners meet each other without prejudice and preconceived ideas. This, of course, is asking the impossible from fallible human beings. On this score Buber's position is contradictory, for he admits the incapability of entering into the other person's frame of reference: "We are not capable of judging its meaning, because we do not know it from within as we know ourselves from within." This idea is frequently repeated by Jewish writers.[48]

By reason of the subjective nature of the dialogue, it would appear that there is a difficulty which cannot be surmounted. The moment either party takes up a neutral position it ceases to be a meeting between believers. Walter Jacob is aware of the difficulty and acknowledges that there is no point in meeting in an "aseptic atmosphere" as if it were a matter of an autopsy totally unrelated to living human beings. He acknowledges that there can be no neutrality ("emotion is necessary in dialogue") and that "one must have strong commitment; otherwise the enterprise loses its value." Therefore, to separate mission from dialogue is an artificial device. The pretence that neither party wants to influence the other rests on the false assumption that it is possible to suspend one's convictions while "dialogue" proceeds.

Non-Jewish advocates of dialogue seem to lack the scruples which trouble and disturb Jewish writers. They stand for dialogue at any price, maintaining that there is sufficient common ground for meaningful encounter. Though there is no justification for mission which is "anachronistic and humiliating to the Jews," there is every reason for dialogue. Reinhold Mayer is an interesting case: he writes as an associate of the *Institutum Judaicum*, founded by Prof. Callenberg of Halle in 1724 for the express purpose of training Christian scholars for missionary work among Jews. The Institute has now abandoned the missionary approach in favour of dialogue, on the assumption that these two methods are totally incompatible.[49]

Marcus Barth, whose own position regarding mission is sadly confused, was shocked to discover that spokesmen for Christianity at the Colloquium on Judaism and Christianity at Harvard in October, 1966, were unfaithful to their profession: "At times it looked as if Christians were ashamed not only of the dogmas of the Church but of Paul and John as well, and sought the pacification of the Jews at any price of the testimony of the better half of the New Testament." To his amazement "some Jews seemed to think more highly of Jesus than some Christians of Christ." Barth finds it difficult to see how there can be any serious dialogue at all unless Christians remain true to their faith in their encounter with Jews.[50] Manfred H. Vogel in his thoughtful analysis of the dialogical situation understands that encounter necessarily involves a tension between kinship and difference, and that the difference must be of "importance and significance." He writes: "Indeed, the more intimate the kinship is the more disturbing and significant does the difference become."[51] But if the difference be reduced to the minimum, what purpose is there in dialogue?

Genuine dialogue between Christians and Jews requires a position of faith on both sides. "Authentic dialogue," writes Vogel, "can mean only self-clarification, not the settling of an argument by winning the *Gegner* (opponent) to your side." But in our view, such limitation is both unnecessary and undesirable. It restricts discussion and creates a false self-consciousness. Why not allow both parties to speak freely, prayerfully and in faith? Such serious encounters of faith between individuals are a frequent occurrence. One well-known dialogue was carried on mainly by correspondence between cousins Franz Rosenzweig and Eugen Rosenstock-Huessy during the First World War. Another famous dialogue took place between the religious philosopher Martin Buber and the theologian Karl Ludwig Schmidt in 1933.[52]

More recently the French theologian (later Bishop) Jean Daniélou met in dialogical encounter with the jurist André Nathan Chouraqui (formerly an Algerian Jew, at the time of the dialogue an Israeli adviser to Ben-Gurion, and later assistant mayor of Jerusalem). Here there was no beating about the bush. Daniélou made it quite plain: "The fundamental dialogue is situated around the interpretation of the person of Jesus." This, according to Daniélou, is the essence of a dialogue between Christians and Jews; it concerns "the fulfilment of Israel's hope." What separates Jews and Christians, says the Roman Catholic scholar, is not a difference of mentality, culture, or even the conception of God; the issue is not just messianism, "or [even] that he [Jesus] was *the* Messiah." The scandal is Jesus himself! The scandal for Israel was, and remains to this day, Jesus' "declaration of his equality with Yahveh." Chouraqui's reply is typically tragic and Jewish at the same time: "Through the course of the centuries, the Jews have not encountered Christ, and what they knew of Christians was unfortunately not always the best." In this dialogue there was no doubt about Daniélou's position; the same cannot be said about Chouraqui. This well-known lawyer, though assured about his Jewishness, did not seem to be so certain about his faith. His main concern was Jewish survival.[53]

A more positive encounter between two believers was that of Pinchas Lapide and Hans Küng, broadcast over the German South-West Radio on August 25, 1975. The question they discussed touches upon the very essence of the difference between Church and Synagogue: "Is Jesus a Bond or a Barrier?" In the introduction it was explained that the discussion would concern "the Jew, Jesus of Nazareth, who stands between Jews and Christians." Both partners declared themselves "wholly committed" to their respective faiths. There was no intention on either side to be the victor.

Lapide complained that the Church has played false in respect to Jesus: "It has dejudaized him; it has hellenized him, and it has very effectively made him loathsome to us." Küng, on his part, observed that when Jews and Christians meet, they usually talk about generalities. In so doing they overlook the "real point of the controversy," namely, the person of Jesus: "Who is this Jesus of Nazareth?" The rest of the discussion centred upon Jesus, seen from the two sides—Lapide as a Jew, and Küng as a Christian. Lapide explained that as an orthodox Jew he cannot affirm, nor can he deny the self-abasement of God: the *Kenosis*, the Incarnation, the Resurrection. He refused to specify what God can and what he cannot do: "That would be absurd. *I don't know*." Lapide's last word: "Let us both study *with one another* and discover the earthly Jesus from below—as you say—and let us see where God will further guide us both."[54] There was a disarming honesty on the part of Lapide and a forthrightness on the part of Küng. Here faith met faith in a spirit of humility, neither scoring against the other, yet both open to hear what the other had to say.

Another example of dialogue in which the two partners speak freely and deal with matters of faith was the encounter between Jack Daniel Spiro, a reformed rabbi, and John Shelby Spong, an Episcopalian priest.[55] On this personal level, dialogue ceases to be apology or propaganda and becomes a testimony to faith. Publicly conducted dialogue is seldom free of ulterior motives. For Jews it frequently becomes a forum to justify the Arab-Israeli conflict;[56] for Christians it is used to make apology for past wrongs. Such expression of concerns has its justification and is undoubtedly useful, but cannot be described as a dialogue of faith or faiths. It is a purely social function.

Some Roman Catholic writers in their enthusiasm to amend old wrongs have gone far beyond the limits of their faith. A case in point is Eugene Fisher, for whom Jesus was a loyal Pharisee who never transgressed rabbinic Law. In his view the Matthean Gospel falsified the situation in its pandering to Gentile converts. Fisher feels comfortable with the idea of two Covenants and regards dialogue as a means to encourage Jews to be better Jews and Christians better Christians.[57]

Chapter 13

Persistent Issues

The intention of this final chapter is to rehearse what went before and so bring into focus the issues raised in this book. We also want to throw some light upon the Jewish predicament as seen from our particular point of view.

A perennial problem confronting man is his relationship to his neighbour. Human relationships are complex and depend upon many factors: political, economic, psychological, cultural, religious. It is simplistic to attribute a social malaise to one single cause. Man lives with man in tension. Animosity is the stuff of history. *Weltgeschichte ist Weltgericht* ("world history is world judgement"). Even within the unit of the family are rivalry and strain. Incompatibility has many facets and increases in proportion to proximity; the closer the kinship the greater the strain. In collective life the social forces press for homogeneity. Xenophobia is a built-in instinct in animal and man. The maturity of a nation can be measured by its attitude to strangers. There is an irrational fear towards those who are different, a fear we can easily rationalize since the faults of others are more conspicuous to us than our own.

Anti-Semitism

The term *anti-Semitism* is a misnomer: it does not apply to all Semites, only to Jews. Note also that it applies to all Jews without regard to individual fault or merit. Psychologists understand anti-Semitism as a reaction of the "in group" to the "out group." H. J. Eysenck characterizes the anti-Semite as a person afflicted by emotional instability who uses his prejudice for self-assurance.[1] Gordon Allport sees in the anti-Semite an "exclusionist personality" who likes his categories "fixed and clear." Such a person is possessed of a rigid mind, lives in a closed circle, is suspicious, provincial, and hostile.[2] Anti-Semites are by nature authoritarian and conservative. The otherness of the Jew is to them a threatening and disturbing factor.[3] They need a homogeneous society to feel comfortable. This means that Jews must either assimilate or leave. These alternatives were constant threats to Jewish existence in the Diaspora. Such is the price of minority existence. A third option for Jews has been an effort to dispel prejudice. This they have been attempting to do for centuries without much success, for anti-Semitism is not amenable to reason. Allport quotes Thomas Aquinas: "Prejudice is thinking ill of others without sufficient warrant."[4] The anti-Semite lives by primitive impulse, requiring no warrant for his sentiments. His stereotyped idea of the Jew is all-inclusive: all Jews are damned. Jewish apologetics as carried on by the Anti-Defamation League of the B'nai B'rith has met with an iron wall. The anti-Semite needs the Jew to compensate for his inner frustrations; the Jew has therapeutic value. Hitler used this latent need as a political tool.

Jewish survival depends upon separate existence. Life in the Diaspora was therefore always a problem. Anti-Jewish prejudice prevailed in pagan society as it did later in Christendom. In the larger centres of the Roman Empire, such as Alexandria, Antioch, Caesarea, and even in Rome, there were occasionally anti-Jewish riots.[5] The favoured position granted to Jews in the Empire only aggravated the situation, according to Emil Schürer, by encouraging Jewish segregation. The Gentiles regarded the Jews as a thorn in their flesh—a foreign, irritating body in society. Only in a community where being different is not an offence can Jews live unmolested. For this reason Jewish sympathies are always with liberalism and democracy, for only under such conditions can a minority survive.

If anti-Semitism is a misnomer, Christian anti-Semitism is a logical monstrosity. The Christian faith is too deeply rooted in Hebrew tradition to engage in Jew-hatred. Pope Pius XI, in a much quoted speech to the Belgian Catholic Radio Agency (September, 1938), pronounced anti-Semitism totally incompatible with the Christian faith. As Christians, he said, "spiritually we are Semites," for Abraham is our forefather. Jacques Maritain quotes the Roman Catholic author Léon Bloy (d. 1917) as saying that contempt for Jews is contempt for Jesus and the Virgin Mary, for the Apostles, and for God himself.[6] Bloy asks: "How then can we express the enormity of the outrage and the blasphemy involved in vilifying the Jewish race?" This is a difficult question to answer.

Some writers have attempted to explain away the apparent compatibility between Christianity and anti-Semitism in some people by arguing that anti-Semites are not good Christians (if they are Christians at all). The anti-Semite suspends reason when he claims to be a Christian and Jew-hater simultaneously. But those who argue in this way have not as yet come to grips with the ambiguity which adheres to the word *Christian*. As a matter of fact, Jews frequently call all non-Jews "Christians." Such use of the term is both illogical and unjust. Roy Eckardt, in his zeal, goes so far as to deny that the Nazis "were enemies of Christendom."[7] Indeed, the "teaching of contempt," to use Prof. Jules Isaac's phrase, has served many causes, but it must be remembered that the Nazis never made a claim to Christianity.

In the last analysis, anti-Semitism is a pathological phenomenon which is rooted in the human psyche and has to do with self-hatred. Those who advocate removal of offending passages in the New Testament which encourage contempt for Jews overlook the fact that these passages are being wrongly used as pretexts for a malady which goes much deeper and has its origin in what the Church calls original sin. There are enough Old Testament texts to supply the anti-Semite with all the ammunition he needs once the New Testament has been purged. The Hebrew Bible is far more "anti-Semitic" than anything to be found in the Fourth Gospel. Where there is a need to hate, reasons for hating can always be found. Expurgating the New Testament will make no difference. This is not to say that the Church is innocent. Her projected image of the Jew as a deicide under God's perpetual curse is nothing short of blasphemy. There can be no doubt that in countries like Poland, Rumania, Hungary, etc., the anti-Semitic spirit of hate and contempt was nourished and sustained by the clergy of the Church. The Church is guilty of a crime against the Jewish people and must repent in sackcloth and ashes.

The question arises: Which is to be blamed — human nature or the Christian faith? Many Jews and some non-Jews blame Christianity. But "Christianity" is an abstract noun devoid of concrete reality. It is a vague term which can be stretched in every direction. There are degrees of being a Christian. A better term would be "men and women who profess to believe in Jesus Christ." But many honour God with their lips though their hearts are far from him (Isa. 29:13; cf. Rom. 10:9). This indictment uttered against the people of God still stands. Such is the human condition: at heart man is a pagan and an idolater. Emmanuel Levinas, a foremost Jewish-French philosopher, blames the Church for her easy compromise with paganism. It does not pay, he says, to baptize the pagan gods and to incorporate pagan rites in order to gain cheap success. He thinks "that the unhappiness of Europe stems from the fact that the Church did not uproot enough."[8] He may not realize that idolatry is endemic to human nature and affects Jews as it does Gentiles.

The question we are faced with is unavoidable: What difference has the Christian faith made to human attitudes? Paul asked: "What advantage has the Jew?" (Rom. 3:1f.).[9] The same question must be posed in regard to the Christian. The same answer applies in both cases: "Much in every way." It is a great privilege to be brought up in a Christian home, to be taught the Christian faith, to be incorporated into the Christian Church, to be assured of God's "steadfast love" in Christ, and to be called to become a child of God. But in spite of all these privileges, the principle still holds that "many are called, but few are chosen" (Matt. 22:14). Unless there is a personal response these privileges are wasted. No one can become a Christian by proxy. In this regard Franz Rosenzweig was correct in his observation that Christianity begins anew with each individual.[10] This does not mean that the Christian believer bears no responsibility for the sins of the fathers; the law of heredity still obtains. But only by personal decision does he affirm his faith. According to Rosenzweig, the case of the Jew is different. His fulfilment is in his people. In their collective life the individual reaches his goal; and together the Jews have already arrived, while the Christian is always on the way.[11] Such a distinction between Christian and Jew we totally reject: man as an individual is always on the way; he is in the process of becoming human.

The attempts to explain anti-Semitism are many. Some Jewish writers see it as a hidden way of expressing resentment at the loss of the pagan gods. B. Halpern explains anti-Semitism as an "orphan" syndrome: "Monotheism, not Christianity, is the specific cause of anti-Semitism." By this he means that biblical faith was never assimilated by the Gentile Church. Underneath there is the atavistic longing for the pagan gods.[12] S. Levin endorses the theory: "Christianity is a religion of orphans. Contrary to Paul, and to all Christian claims to this way, Christians can never join the family of Israel on Pauline terms, but only by becoming part of Israel in the flesh, by converting to Judaism." In Levin's view, Christians, while refusing to become Jews and clinging to Paul's illusion, try to inherit and possess the God of Israel by destroying Israel, but their efforts are futile. "The Christian then remains an orphan and anti-Semitism must continue until he finds a father."[13]

Such elaborate metaphysics indicates the puzzlement the Jew experiences in his effort to explain the anti-Semitic sentiment. The fact is that there is no plausible explanation for anti-Semitism apart from the anti-Semite's need to find a scapegoat for his ills. Jew-baiting is only one aspect of group discrimination, though a persistent one. Wherever there is a minority there is discrimination. Sectarian animosities are the bane of religion. Racial animosities are the tragedy of mankind. Psychologist Kenneth B. Clark understands human civilizations as mere "objectivations of the inner turbulence of man." Power or status, he tells us, is the primitive driving force in all social systems.[14] It would seem that the more elaborate the civilization, the more intense the struggle for selfish ends. Gandhi was once asked his greatest grief. He replied: "The hardness of heart of the educated." When we remember that the leading lights in the Nazi hierarchy included men with doctoral degrees and university professors, we can appreciate Gandhi's point. Education is never a substitute for compassion, which is a rare human quality. This brings us back to our question: what difference has the Christian profession made to human behaviour?

"Christianity" as an abstract term is no substitute for actual living of the Christian faith. Like all abstractions the term *Christianity* belongs to what George Santayana called "verbal mythology" or the "hypostasis of words."[15] The addiction to regarding abstract concepts as existing entities is the peculiar legacy of Platonism. We must beware of generalizing. Stuart Chase has shown how easily words confuse and tyrannize! "The long agony of the people labelled 'Jews' is largely caused by semantic confusion. The abstraction 'Jew' is given an equipment of phantom characteristics . . . ." These characteristics bear no resemblance to the real person: "if you denounce him as a 'Jew' apart from his space-time characteristics, you perform a monstrous act. You are a victim of genuine hallucinations . . . for there is no concrete entity 'Jew' in the living world."[16] In life there are only individual Jews, each different from the other. The same principle applies to Christians. "Christianity" is a nonexistent abstraction. Kierkegaard insisted that the individual is the Christian category. He repeatedly denied that there is such a thing as "Christianity."[17]

The question we have posed ("What difference has the Christian faith made to human behaviour?") can be answered only in personal terms. It is individual men and women who respond to the challenge of the Gospel. To them Christ is the power of God and the wisdom of God (I Cor. 1:24), though this may seem foolishness to the nonbeliever (v. 23). There is a deposit of Christian values in the form of "culture" among the nations, but it is vague, and greatly attenuated, leaving plenty of room for anti-Semitism.

Such emphasis upon personal commitment, though rare, is not entirely foreign to Jewish thought. Rabbi Joseph Soloveitchik writes: "The great encounter between man and God is a wholly personal and private affair incomprehensible to the outsider— even to a brother of the same faith community."[18] On the whole, Jews are wont to place every emphasis upon collective decision but this is difficult to maintain under modern conditions in a pluralistic society. Today, Sol Roth admits, being a Jew loyal to Judaism is an "act of decision." One who makes this decision "has *chosen* Jewish life and that choice implies that he has removed himself from the other alternatives available in a pluralistic society."[19] All contingencies present an alternative. There can be no escape from personal decision. Both the Jew and the Christian must decide whether to accept the past as binding or to reject it. There is, however, a difference which must be mentioned. The Christian is not born a Christian; he becomes one. The case with the Jew is different: he is born a Jew. Traditionally, this has meant that Judaism is inherited as part of the equipment of being a Jew. This the Jewish Christian denies. For him Jewishness and Judaism are not synonymous. It would seem that under modern conditions Jews are making the same discovery: to live "Jewishly" is an act of will. There are, therefore, degrees of being Jewish, as there are degrees of being a Christian. A process of growth and development is implied. The Christian knows he is never completed; his task is to grow "to mature manhood, to the measure of the stature of the fullness of Christ" (Eph. 4:13). Some Christians remain dwarfs; they never mature.

This is no apology for anti-Semitism. It is, rather, a matter-of-fact statement about the human condition, whether we are Jewish or Christian.

Auschwitz and God

The enormity of Auschwitz is terrifying. It stands as a frightening reminder of man's unlimited capacity for evil. But in the perspective of history Auschwitz is not unique. What is unique is the sheer number of the victims and the reasons behind the Holocaust. Man without God acts in complete autonomy. When the Hitlerites decided that the Jews were superfluous, they declared them *Ungeziefer* (vermin) to be exterminated. The strong have always thus dealt with the weak. Tamerlane (Timur) the Mongol conqueror expected total submission from the vanquished. A city which dared to resist was reduced to ashes and its citizens were slaughtered. Their skulls were heaped tower-high as a warning to others. Tamerlane's motto consisted of two Persian words—*rasti rousti* ("might is right").[20] The Turks dealt with the Armenians no less cruelly. Some eighty thousand Armenians were massacred in 1894–1895. In June–July, 1915, the persecution was renewed in revenge for the declaration of war on Turkey by the Allies. "Men, women and children were robbed and murdered indiscriminately and the remainder were deported to the desert to fend for themselves."[21] There is no end to the tale of human cruelty. Man's capacity for evil seems to be unlimited.

Therefore, the formulation "God and Auschwitz" is too limited. The proper formulation is "God and Evil." The question, "If God is good, whence evil?" has tormented the believer more than the unbeliever. For the unbeliever there is no theological problem, only an existential one. Richard Rubenstein by abandoning faith has made peace with the universe; he is reconciled to the human lot in a world in which there is no place for man. But there is a problem for Elie Wiesel, as there is for every man who believes in a God who is both omnipotent and good. Hence the quarrel. No serious philosopher, from Plato to this very day, can avoid the fact of evil. For the God-believing person standing within the biblical tradition, the problem is insurmountable because the two principles of God's sovereignty and his goodness stand in contradiction. St. Augustine built his theology on these very principles—*omnis substantia a deo* ("all things are from God") and *omne bonum a deo* ("all good is from God"). But to keep these two sentences together he had to reduce evil to the status of *privatio boni* (an insufficiency of good). Such "depotentializing" of evil, to use a Jungian expression, overlooks its demonic qualities.[22]

Christian writers before Augustine and ever since have struggled with the problem of evil. The traditional method is to blame the devil by setting him up as a kind of anti-God. But this serves only to reduce divine omnipotence. The *Clementine Homilies,* which have much to say about the devil, in the end arrive at an agnostic conclusion: "It is not possible for us to have any thought or make any statement in regard to God." All we can do is to investigate what is his will as revealed to us by God himself so that when we are judged "we might be without excuse."[23] In other words, God's ways with man are beyond human comprehension. For the writer of the *Homilies,* God's otherness is such that human values do not apply: "God cannot be good or evil, just or unjust. Nor indeed can He have intelligence, or life, or any of the other attributes which can exist in man; for all these are peculiar to man [alone]." Yet God "alone is the cause of all good things." Elsewhere the writer explains that evil serves a purpose in that it is a tool for testing man's moral quality: "It is the judgement of God, that he who, as by combat, comes through all misfortune and is found blameless, is deemed worthy of eternal life."[24] What the writer of the *Homilies* seeks to prove is that the cause of evil is sin and not God. Suffering is a necessary by-product of sin.[25]

No theodicy is able to solve the mystery of evil; for evil is not only a moral malaise, it also has metaphysical dimensions. The difficulty about evil is its utter irrationality—by explaining it we explain it away. But for the Christian, God is not an onlooker who allows evil to play itself out. He becomes involved by submitting to it and taking his share in the suffering of man. This is the meaning of the Cross. The concept of a suffering God, though foreign to present-day Judaism, was not unknown to the prophet Isaiah. In the later part of the book, God is seen as the One who shares the affliction of his people (63:9). The rabbis quote this text for the very purpose of proving that "whenever Israel is enslaved, the Shekhinah is enslaved with them." (And not only in the case of the community, but even in the case of the individual, God shares in the affliction, for Psalm 91:15 says, "I will be with *him* [singular] in trouble.") Herbert Loewe remarks on Isaiah 63:9: "No verse from the Prophets is more frequently quoted by the Rabbis and more frequently made use of."[26] The rabbis present God as weeping for Israel because of the exile: "Like a father who says, 'My sons, my sons,' or like a hen who cries for her brood, so God declares, 'Look away from me, I will weep bitterly' (Is. 22:4)."[27] The "Servant Passages" in the Book of Isaiah present the Lord's Servant standing with and suffering on behalf of his people. This is especially evident in Isaiah 53.

Ulrich E. Simon is, therefore, on biblical grounds (both Old and New Testaments) when he writes about God's presence at Auschwitz, sharing the suffering and agony of his people. He calls God "The God of Auschwitz." Faith must take this view in order not to succumb to despair. Only in the light of Christ's Cross and Resurrection can we view Auschwitz without losing faith in God and man: "Without the God-Man Auschwitz would stand as a nightmare, the culmination of unreason and malice."[28] Connected with the question of Auschwitz is the question of forgiveness. To forgive what happened at Auschwitz is beyond human strength. Yet without forgiveness life is impossible. Auschwitz must be forgiven, though not forgotten. The word of forgiveness is a positive word; it heals and restores. It is the only possible No to the powers of darkness. Simon writes: "To say 'No' to Auschwitz is already to say 'Yes' to our ascent in faith, hope and love." Though the Christian has no theodicy for Auschwitz and is as puzzled and distressed by the presence of evil as is the Jew, his answer derives from faith in Christ, who suffers with and on behalf of tortured humanity.

On the Jewish side, so far, the only theodicy for Auschwitz was undertaken by Rabbi Eliezer Berkovits (*Faith After Auschwitz,* 1973).[29] This orthodox rabbi uses the classical sources of Judaism to interpret the Holocaust in the light of God's dealing with Israel. In no sense does he explain away the tragedy. At the same time he holds that the intelligent believer may both question God and believe in him. Rabbi Berkovits quotes a Hasidic saint who said: "For the faithful, there are no questions; for the non-believer there are no answers." The rabbi prefers "holy disbelief of the crematoria" to the facile faith of those who were not there: "If there is no answer, it is better to live without it than to find peace either in the sham of an insensitive faith or in the humbug of a disbelief that has eaten its fill."[30]

Therefore, the question, "Where was God?" remains, though both the believing Jew and the believing Christian agonize for an answer in the context of their respective faiths. The one clings to the God of the Covenant; the other looks to the Christ who died for our sins and rose for our justification (Rom. 4:25). Rabbi Berkovits is right: there must be no easy answer. The difficulty about God and evil cannot be resolved by logical argument. Prof. Elliot N. Dorff declares the problem intractable, and with good reason, because God's power and his goodness cannot be reconciled in human experience. The traditional view that God is both just and good is put under a question mark by Auschwitz. "Clarity about God's role in the Holocaust," writes Prof. Dorff, "demands that we sort out those two factors in what is meant by 'God.'" This does not mean that we should deny either of them. What Dorff suggests is separation of these two attributes for reasons of consistency. But in the context of faith he prefers to hold with the rabbis, thus accepting "inconsistency in order to encompass truth."[31]

In life there can be no consistency: this is the meaning of paradox. Paradox differs from antinomy in that it makes existential sense though in pure logic it is contradictory. We will have to apply the same principle to the question, "Where was the Church?" This is a question which concerns the Christians more than the Jews, for it raises a fundamental issue regarding the Church in history: is the Church to be found in the majority or is she represented by the saints only? In other words, is the Church continuously present in history, horizontally, or is her appearance in history a vertical phenomenon? Is she always Church, or does she become Church in moments of decision?

Rabbi Berkovits cites the case of Rabbi M. D. Weissmandel of Bratislava, who sought help from Archbishop Kametko on behalf of the Jewish community threatened with imminent expulsion.[32] He wanted the prelate to intercede with the President of Slovakia, Msgr. Tisso. Weissmandel happened to know the Archbishop personally. But he was not received; instead a note was sent with the following message: "This, being Sunday, is a holy day for us. Neither I nor Father Tisso occupy ourselves with profane matters on this day."

Tisso, though a priest, was a fervent anti-Semite. Kametko's response to the cry for help on behalf of people in dire need is a mockery of the Christian profession. Those who dub Pharisees as hypocrites will do well to ask to which class of people the Archbishop of Bratislava belonged. It is indeed difficult, if not impossible, to gainsay Uriel Tal's assertion that, although racial anti-

Semitism and traditional Christianity are ill-sorted bedfellows "starting from opposite poles and with no discernible principle of reconciliation, [they are] moved by a common impulse directed either to conversion or to the extermination of Jews." There is thus a connection between racial anti-Semitism and traditional Christianity in that both aim at what in effect amount to similar ends—though the motivations are vastly dissimilar.[33]

There can be no excuse for the inhuman behaviour of prelates who are supposed to represent the Church of Christ here upon earth. The story of the Priest and the Levite who passed by on the other side in order not to defile themselves with "profane matters" has been reenacted in history many times over. There is, however, the consolation that there is always a Good Samaritan among the faithful who acts on behalf of the Church. We would, therefore, have to admit that in her official capacity more often than not the Church has been invisible. But in the acts of mercy performed by individual Christians and Christian groups she has acquired visibility as the body of Christ. This has always been so and will remain so to the end of time. It would appear that the "Church" is not represented by the crowd of worshippers but by those few who are prepared to "share in the suffering of God in daily life."[34]

Who Was Jesus?

The question regarding Jesus is not peculiar to Jews. It is asked in every age and by many people. Not even Christians are exempt from asking the question. By the very nature of faith it must remain an open question until it is answered in a personal response of love towards Jesus as the Christ. For Jews the question is unavoidable for several reasons: (1) his Jewishness; (2) his worldwide influence; (3) the suffering they have endured at the hands of those who profess his name.

For centuries the Jewish answer was totally negative. Jesus was avoided and treated as a stranger. Jews could see nothing Jewish in him. It is only in recent times that "Jesus the Jew" is occupying Jewish scholars. Increasingly he is admired for his moral courage and his lofty teaching. There is evident pride in the fact that millions worship as their Saviour someone who happens to be a Jew. There is a repeated effort made to separate Jesus the Jew from the Christ of the Christian Church. Scholars frequently quote Julius Wellhausen's well-known remark: *"Jesus was not a Christian —he was a Jew."* Wellhausen continues: "He proclaimed no new faith, only taught the doing of God's will. The will of God for him as for the Jews was in the Law and in the holy Scriptures."[35] Increasingly, the Jewish quarrel is not with Jesus but with Christianity.

An outstanding example of Jewish preoccupation with Jesus is Shalom Ben-Chorin. In books and articles this Israeli scholar has returned to the subject of Jesus again and again. Here is a characteristic passage from one of his articles.[36] It begins on a strictly personal note:

> Now let me tell you something of my meeting with Jesus of Nazareth. Even if He is not all that many of you say He is, yet He is for me, for me as a Jew, a central figure, whom I cannot eliminate from my life, especially not from my Jewish life.
>
> Martin Buber's statement that he has since his youth accepted Christ as his Big Brother is well known. I would like to subscribe to this statement, but would also add that the older I get the closer have I come to the person of Jesus. He stood at every bend in the road, and again and again has put the question to me which He asked His disciples at Caesarea Philippi, "Who am I?"
>
> Again and again I had to argue with Him. I am sure that He will continue to wrestle with me as long as I have life, and that He will continue to meet me as, according to a legend, He met Peter on the Via Appia and as, according to the witness of the Apostle Paul, He met him on the road to Damascus.

This encounter with Jesus, Ben-Chorin explains, became closer after he left "Christian Europe" for Jewish Israel. The more he studied the New Testament, the more clearly he came to recognize its basic Jewish character: "And so the Book and the Jewish Man about whom it writes would not let me go." He found it impossible to banish the dialogue with his Big Brother out of his life: "Painfully I have told Him all my life: You are not the Messiah, you are not the founder of the kingdom." But Jesus, "the ever puzzling One, the gentle One, and the hard One, the forgiving and the hating One, the fanatical Jew and the whole-world-loving One, what did He say to me, and what does He say to the Jew who seeks to have an argument with Him?"

For an answer to this question Ben-Chorin goes not to the New Testament but to an apocryphal text which tells of Jesus meeting a man working on the Sabbath day. The Master asks: "Do you

know what you are doing? Woe to you if you do not know, but
blessed are you if you do know." Though Ben-Chorin misquotes
the text,[37] the point he makes is clear enough: it is not out of indifference that he is led to reject Jesus' final claim "but because of
sincere belief."[38]

What decides the issue whether Jesus is the Messiah or not is
the presence or absence of the signs of the Messianic Age. Martin
Buber, Ben-Chorin, H.-J. Schoeps, and other Jewish writers, deny
that Jesus initiated a new reign of God in history. The Kingdom
for which Christians and Jews pray is still invisible. Yet all these
writers, following Rosenzweig's lead, acknowledge the significance
of the Church as an act of God. In Ben-Chorin's words: "The
Church is 'from God.' *She is the school of the nations and Israel's temptation.*" The argument is from history: because the Church has endured through the ages and because God is Lord of history,
Christianity is God-willed, though only for Gentiles. This kind of
reasoning, already adumbrated by Gamaliel (Acts 5:33–39), is
widely held among Jewish writers today. It is, of course, a spu-
rious argument. Jacob Taubes rightly observes that such an argument "embodies a dangerous temptation to take what *is* for what
ought to be." He is therefore critical of those who make the argument from history a basis for accepting Christianity as
legitimate.[39]

For men like Shalom Ben-Chorin the alternative to a personal
Messiah is the Messianic Age, which will introduce God's Kingdom here upon earth. Salvation, in the Jewish view, Ben-Chorin
explains, is salvation from all evil in man, in humanity, and in nature. This has not yet taken place. Christians and Jews are still
praying, "Thy Kingdom come." Once Messiahship has been de-
mythologized and the Kingdom of God is understood as the reign
of justice, love, peace, knowledge of God, and harmony of the human heart, the difference between Christians and Jews will disappear, as both are looking towards messianic fulfilment.[40] In spite
of the discovery of the depth of human depravity, of which
Auschwitz is a stark reminder, the Jewish position has not
changed. At the centre of concern is still social organization and
not personal change. According to Taubes, the foundation of human life is the "sobriety of justice," and not the "romance" of love,
for which Christianity stands: "The 'yoke of the Law' is challenged
by the enthusiasm of love. But the 'justice of the Law' may, in the
end, be the only challenge to the arbitrariness of love."[41] The

question regarding Jesus is thus bypassed in two ways. (1) Insistence upon Jesus' Jewishness reduces him to historical proportions with no room for the transcendental character ascribed to him by the Church. (2) By declaring him a *chiffre* for the Kingdom of God Ben-Chorin has turned him into a symbol pointing away from himself to the moral values which he preaches. In either case he is not what the Church means by the Christ of God.

At the same time Jesus remains to many Jews both a puzzle and a temptation. A puzzle to explain and a temptation to resist. Walter Jacob writes that for Kaufmann Kohler (d. 1926), President of Hebrew Union College and a renowned scholar, Jesus was the "perfect Jew" worthy of admiration. Kohler "vacillated between admiration for Jesus and bitterness toward Christianity, which brought suffering to the Jewish people and much to mankind."[42]

Though it is not Christianity but Jesus that attracts and fascinates the Jewish scholars, yet they realize that the Christian faith and Jesus are so intertwined that they have become inseparable. "Who is Jesus?" therefore reflects upon "What is Christianity?" and vice versa. Two entities difficult to avoid and even more difficult to grasp.

Jews and Christians

Only gradually is Jewish scholarship coming to terms with the fact that Pharisaic Judaism at the time of Jesus was only one ingredient in the spectrum of Jewish faith. As a result of the discovery of the Dead Sea Scrolls, a totally new perspective of Jewish life in Palestine has opened up. Samuel Rosenblatt admits that the birth of Christianity must now be viewed in a new light. He surmises that the time of Jesus was "a period of intense spiritual ferment" and that sectarianism flourished at that time "as it had never done before or after."[43] Christian writers are equally forced to reassess the origins of primitive Christianity. David Noel Freedman is led to the conviction that primitive Jewish Christianity was "an authentic component of contemporary Judaism" though different from Pharisaic Judaism. Judaism at that time consisted of "a congeries of sects, each claiming to be orthodox, none actually normative."[44] This is a view which the present writer has held for some years.[45] The contemporary splintering of Judaism is not different from the situation that prevailed at the time of Jesus, except that all differing "sects" are now united in their rejection of

Christianity. They all are averse to the Christian doctrine of the Trinity and the place assigned to Jesus in the scheme of salvation. Moreover, the Church is seen as a danger to Jewish survival by reason of its universalism. Jewish writers argue that Judaism is also universalist—in two ways. It always keeps the door open for proselytes and it is generous to other religions by not insisting that one has to become Jewish in order to be saved. Rabbi Ben Zion Bokser explains the special kind of Jewish universalism in these words: "What is unique in Judaism and the core of its witness to other faiths is this concept of religious universality which acknowledges the legitimacy of diverse paths to God, whose ideal is a fellowship of faiths in which they offer each other mutual aid in the quest of God."[46] Rabbi Solomon B. Freehof writes: "We are the only universal religion that believes that other universal religions can co-exist with us."[47]

In this latitudinarian sense, Judaism is the prerogative of Jews but not essential to Gentiles. This is especially emphasized by liberal Jewish writers. Samuel S. Cohon writes: "Two different religions may exist simultaneously among two different peoples, each leading its adherents to human perfection or salvation, though in different ways, corresponding to the character of each religion." What they share as a common denominator is religion; the differences are only "secondary elements" derived from local and temporal variations in human society. Rabbi Cohon explains that religion, like the language of the heart, is inherent in all mankind, but it expresses itself in different "dialects and jargons as varied as the communities and nations of humanity." For this reason, Reform Judaism, we are told, does not ask the world to adopt Jewish faith and worship, which are the result of their own peculiar experience. What is essentially Jewish is already shared by all other faiths. Cohon, therefore, asks the question: "What makes a Jew?" His answer: "Judaism is a national religion"; as long as a Jew has not joined another religion, though an unbeliever, he is still a Jew.[48]

The same question is raised by Rabbi W. Günther Plaut of Toronto: "Why should a Jew persist in being a Jew—or should he?" His answer is somewhat different from that of Cohon: "Human history is the responsibility of the Jew, for it is ultimately he to whom the fate of man is entrusted. God and man wait for the perfection of the Jew." For Plaut the mystery of Jewish destiny is linked to God's revelation at Sinai. By "Sinai" he does not mean the revelation of words but of a Person. One of the consequences of Jewish faith was to bring forth not only Hillel but also Jesus. Plaut declares Christianity more than a historic accident; he sees it within the realm of the Jewish mission: *"If God willed Christianity, then surely it must be true and . . . part of the ongoing process of divine revelation."* Judaism is its mother, and the "deep pervasive hatred" on the part of the Church towards Judaism and its people is the hatred of a child for its mother. In history, Rabbi Plaut allows, Judaism and Christianity have both failed and succeeded. Christians are partners in the struggle for a "God-filled tomorrow." But Jews and Christians must go their own separate ways: "The election of Israel does not preclude the election of others . . . . God works in many ways." Plaut therefore looks at the "varied manifestations" of the Christian faith "with critical reverence."[49]

Rabbi Plaut is missionary-minded. The spiritual impoverishment in the world constitutes a challenge for Judaism to proselytize. He sees in the "constant stream of converts now being accepted, primarily by liberal rabbis," an indication of Judaism's potential.[50] But he does not extend the same privilege to Christians. They must not attempt to convert Jews, because the Jew needs no redemption in the Christian sense, nor does Jesus teach anything that is unknown to the Synagogue: "The ethics of Jesus are basically the ethics of Judaism."[51]

Jewish writers, however, do admit to a spiritual crisis within the Jewish fold. "The bulk of the Jewish community," writes Jacob Katz, has "become less fervently attached to Judaism, though without losing its reservations towards Christianity." He explains that in the past "Judaism has maintained itself as a minority by fierce resistance, compensating for deficiency in number by intensity of rejection." He suggests that unless the same method is applied today there is danger for Jewish survival. It is for this reason that Jews cannot afford to ally themselves with Christianity even in the fight against secularism.[52] Even more outspoken is Eugene B. Borowitz, who admits that "a large number of Jews are too secular to take Judaism or even Jewishness seriously yet have too much self-respect to surrender them entirely."[53]

Apart from the secularism which prevails in modern culture and deeply affects Jewish life, Auschwitz is still another reason for the spiritual crisis in Jewry. Jewish faith in all its forms was founded upon the perfectibility of man. But since Auschwitz, says Borowitz, "it is no longer possible to make the goodness of man the cornerstone of Jewish faith."[54] Borowitz errs, however, when he attributes the doctrine of man's nobility to the "liberal reconstruction" only; the rabbis of old and Judaism at large have always stood for the unfallen nature of man; hence their rejection of the doctrine of original sin.[55] The self-sufficiency of man, as conceived by Judaism, makes radical salvation unnecessary. The Gospel as the way of personal redemption has therefore no meaningful application to Jewish existence as God's special people. Franz Rosenzweig in a letter to his Jewish Christian cousin explains the metaphysical nature of Judaism in three articles of faith: (1) We have the truth; (2) We are at the goal; (3) God is already "our Father." He adds: To the Jew, that God is his Father is the first and most self-evident fact—he needs no third person "between me and my Father in Heaven." "The Jew can afford," says Rosenzweig, "his unmediated chosenness to God."[56]

This nondialectical approach to election as understood by the rabbis and propagated by Rosenzweig is the very foundation of Judaism. Karl Barth has done Jewry no service by so overemphasizing Israel's election as to lose the distinction between the individual Jew and the community as a whole. How the individual Jew participates in the covenantal promise to historic Israel is not solved by wholesale exemption from personal response. It is futile and naive to say the "world" is not visibly saved; therefore, Jesus is not the Messiah and we must wait for another. Eugene Borowitz is correct in his contention that the Covenant is no licence to passive existence: "That God is expected to act does not mean that man may do nothing but simply wait." He rightly understands the Covenant in dialectical terms. Though man's action is limited by reason of his natural limitations, this does not mean that it is devoid of significance: "Man's action is truly significant only when it takes place in accordance with God's will."[57] Christians believe that Jesus is deeply in the will of God, that his coming affects mankind, and that no one is excluded.

Franz Rosenzweig felt offended that his cousin Eugen Rosenstock-Huessy made claim to being Jewish. He declares such a claim "intolerable emotionally and intellectually." He writes: "For me you can be nothing else but a Christian; the emptiest Jew, cut off root and branch, and a Jew only in the legal sense, is still an object of concern to me as a Jew, but you are not.... I do not recognize this missionary-theological concept of 'Christian from Israel,' because it is positive and the Jew between the crucifixion and the Second Coming can only have a negative meaning in Christian theology."

Rosenstock-Huessy's claim to Jewishness was that he was born of Jewish parents. He became a Christian at the age of sixteen. But Rosenzweig is not prepared to make any allowances: Christianity is for pagans, not for Jews. Rosenstock-Huessy finds his cousin's attitude totally perverse; he calls it *superbia Judaica* (Jewish haughtiness). "For Judaism to stand upon its own inalienable right" and this in perpetuity, he finds naive and a relic of blind antiquity. It is exactly this kind of "boundless naive pride" exhibited by Jews that Christ came to redeem: "Christ redeems the individual from family and people through the new unity of all sinners, of all who are weary and heavy laden. That is Christianity, and its bond of equal need." To this Rosenzweig has only one reply: "The election of the Jews is something unique, because it is the election of 'one people,' and even today our peculiar pride or peculiar modesty . . . rejects an actual compromise with other peoples."[58]

It will be noticed that Eugen Rosenstock-Huessy speaks of individual Jews while Franz Rosenzweig operates with a collective noun—*Jews*. They thus speak at cross-purposes. Rosenstock-Huessy has no problem with the election of his people; his problem is the salvation of the individual. Here lies the difference between the Jewish and the Christian outlook. In Pauline terms, being born a Jew and becoming a Jew by the grace of God are two totally different concepts.

The Individual and the Nation

The coexistence of Christians and Jews is a historical fact. They meet and they speak to each other as they always have done. But their meeting and their speaking today have acquired a new quality of humanness since Vatican II. Whether we call it mission or dialogue is a matter of semantics. When one meets the other, they influence each other, they exchange views, they share experiences. On both sides, Christian and Jewish, there is a genuine effort at a more civilized and meaningful encounter. There are still prejudice and suspicion, but these are the marks of human limitation and will always be with us.

Civilized encounter means free exchange of views and values

not for the sake of compromise, but for mutual enrichment. Compromise would be fatal to both parties. The Christian is committed to witness. Witness can take a variety of forms. For Christians it is an essential expression of their faith. They owe it to others to reveal where they stand and what they believe. Under ideal conditions there ought to be no mission in the specialized sense, for the whole Church is meant to be a witnessing body to its faith by word and deed. This is what Karl Barth expects of the Church: to provoke the Jews to jealousy by truly living the Christian life. Such witness would be in accordance with Paul's missionary strategy (cf. Rom. 11:11). Barth writes, "The Church as a whole has made no convincing impression on Jews as a whole," though he admits that "it has seriously sought the conversion of individuals."[59] But is not Barth expecting too much of the "Church as a whole"? He knows of the fallibility of the Church and how easily the Gospel becomes "domesticated" *(Verbürgerlichung des Evangeliums).*[60] The Church in history never was and never will be the perfect Church, the bride of Christ, without spot or wrinkle (Eph. 5:27).

It is an unfortunate lapse on Barth's part to speak of conversion in collective terms, though he is right to treat "the relationship of the Christian community to the Jews, to the Synagogue, to Israel," as a special case, quite different from the missionary task to the Gentiles. He writes: "The Church must live with the Synagogue, not, as fools say in their hearts, as with another religion or confession, but as with the root from which it stems." But because his approach to the Jewish people is wholesale he remains sceptical about Jewish conversion. "Can there ever be a true conversion of the true Jews except as a highly extraordinary event?" he asks. Therefore, he can see no useful purpose served in continuing conversations. This does not mean "that the Christian community has no responsibility to discharge its ministry of witness to the Jews. Not at all!" But he does not seem to expect much from such a ministry once discharged. He asks: "If the Jew is to go back on the rejection of his Messiah and become a disciple, is there not needed a radical change . . .?" As in most cases, "Jew" in Barth's idiom refers to the Jewish community and not to the individual, and from the community he expects no "radical change."

Marcus Barth follows his father's example in speaking of Jewish conversion in collective terms and therefore leaving it to eschatology for a solution. This lapse into collectivism is parallelled by Leo Baeck's pronouncement: *Das jüdische Volk ist die Offenbarung* ("the

Jewish people is the revelation"). Marcus Barth is all for Christian witness, but, in his words, "what is called for is dialogue rather than mission."[61] His commentary on Ephesians ends with the insistence that Grace is God's chief attribute, and Grace to him means the divine decision "to unite Jews and Gentiles in Jesus Christ and to reveal his secret at the proper time," thus making peace.[62] But for some reason Marcus Barth prefers to postpone this decision to the end of time. Meanwhile Jewish men and women are left to await the End.

Mission and dialogue are two essentially different concepts of Christian witness. Dialogue is a group activity; mission is directed towards the individual. Dialogue implies postponement in time without urgency. Mission is prompted by a sense of urgency because time is limited in two ways—the End is already visible in Christ, the Lord is at hand; and man's own personal time is running out (cf. Rom. 13:11; I Cor. 7:29; Eph. 5:16). This sense of limited time "pervades St. Paul's life and underlies the whole New Testament. *Hic et nunc* is the keynote of Christian action."[63] A nation continues in time; a person has a short span of life. Christians who favour dialogue usually operate in collective terms; even when they say "Jew," they mean the nation. Christians concerned with individuals are dedicated to mission.

Hans Urs von Balthasar prefers the shift towards the community. We must learn to think, he tells us, not merely "of the individual Jew in Israel, but . . . in terms of a better understanding and convergence between the two separated halves of the people of God." This holistic approach is, of course, in line with the tradition of the Roman Catholic Church. Here whole nations become Christian en masse. But Balthasar is not quite consistent, for he stresses the importance of the remnant both in the Old Testament and in Pauline thought.[64] The concept of the remnant contradicts the holistic approach.

There is yet another angle which would support the concept of mission over against dialogue, namely, the prophetic tradition inherited from the Old Testament. The prophet is a *shaliah*—a messenger. He is sent to discharge his message whether the people hear or refuse to hear (Ezek. 2:5, 7). Rabbi Sholom A. Singer has noticed the antithetical nature between faith and law. Judaism, he tells us, has been struggling to incorporate prophecy into the legal system, so that "prophecy is now the hand-maiden of the law." But the effort has not been entirely successful. He writes: "It is my contention that Judaism was forced to opt for one of them, because of the ultimate irreconcilability between faith and law. Try as it did, it was unable to bring the two into a harmonious state of co-existence as equals within itself." As Rabbi Singer sees it, the Church made a shift towards faith, prophecy, and intuition: "Christianity represented a victory of intuition over institution, faith over works, evangelion over nomos, 'being' over 'becoming' " (not that Christianity escaped legalism; cf. the Canon Law—"and so the cycle repeats itself").[65] The Church, of course, has never managed to escape the legalistic trap, not even when it made "grace" the foundation of its theology. "The heart of man," says Bishop Stephen Neill, "appears to be incurably legalistic." He suggests that it is more difficult "to bring the legalist back into the realm of grace" than to bring a non-Christian into the Christian fold.[66]

There is a discernible nostalgic note in Rabbi Singer's statement: "We are doomed to live by the law of the Judaic spirit, and forever reach out for the preachment of Christian love." But he is wary of the overemphasis upon love: "faith alone without law endangers social stability, morality and human situations." Because both are the words of the living God they must not be separated. But the rabbi knows the effects the law has when deprived of "prophecy": "it aborts, stifles and eventually destroys."[67] The point we are trying to make is that "law" is a communal matter, love (and faith and prophecy) can be exercised only by individuals. Christian priorities are on the side of love, faith, prophecy. Jewish priorities are on the side of law, community, deeds. These different emphases need not necessarily divide; on the contrary, they could supplement and enrich both parties. But this is not the way human affairs are arranged. Behind these issues are historically developed structures which press for loyalty, and resist change. Communities do not change; they develop gradually over long stretches of time. Only individuals change, and, in the case of the Christian faith, the change is radical. That the individual Jew by reason of his Jewishness is exempt from change is to the Christian a cause for astonishment. He remembers his Master's surprise in conversation with Nicodemus: "Are you a teacher of Israel, and yet you do not understand this?" (John 3:10).

It is an unfortunate aberration to confuse Israel's election with the individual Jew's personal response to the living God. The role of a nation and the role of an individual are not identical. Though every individual is caught up in the destiny of his people, he has his own personal responsibility before God. He may be called to stand in judgement against his people for the sake of conscience, as the Prophets did. *Vox populi—vox dei* is a pagan principle. In the biblical perspective the voice of God is usually with the minority, the individual. Without the freedom of the individual to make a personal decision for God, man is denied his most sacred right. The whole question regarding Jewish Christians hangs on this issue.

The Christian Witness

Like Christianity Judaism does not speak with one voice. Rabbi Jacob B. Agus rightly says: "Modern Judaism contains a broad range of views." Some are negative regarding the Church, some are indifferent, some are positive. Rabbi Agus himself sees the Christian faith in a positive light. He is broad-minded enough to say: "It is incumbent upon Jewish scholars to reclaim the New Testament as an integral part of their domain of study and to develop the implications of the teaching that Christianity is an 'ecclesia for the sake of heaven,' employed by God as an instrument whereby humanity is being prepared for 'the kingdom of heaven,' *malchut shomayim.*"[68]

Even the question of the Trinity is being approached more carefully than was the case in the past. Rabbi Louis Jacobs, an orthodox Jew, naturally averse to the trinitarian doctrine, admits that Christians are not polytheists: "Christians deny most emphatically, with justice, that theirs is a belief in *Tritheism,* in three gods. Indeed, such a belief is considered to be grossly heretical by all Christians . . . . But from a Jewish point of view, the Christian belief is a breach of pure monotheism . . . . Particular objection has always been taken, from the Jewish side, to the Christian doctrine of the Incarnation."[69] Admission that Christians are not polytheists goes back to the Middle Ages, though the rabbis regard the doctrine of the Trinity as an unfortunate compromise. But there is at present a greater willingness to understand the Christian position.

The pioneer in the study of Christianity from a more positive angle was C. G. Montefiore. Rabbi Walter Jacob says that Montefiore was "the first Jew to view Christianity entirely sympathetically." In fact, Jacob feels that Montefiore showed excessive enthusiasm for the New Testament and that "Montefiore's Jesus" was for Jewish readers "not sufficiently human." Few contemporary scholars have shown the same breadth of vision and depth of spiritual insight as did Montefiore. He must be regarded as a pioneer in the area of Jewish-Christian dialogue. Though for Rabbi Jacob and others he went too far in his concessions to Christianity, still, as the rabbi says, Montefiore laid the foundations "for a broader-based understanding" between the two faiths.[70] Montefiore's legacy to Jewish writers is careful scholarship and an irenic spirit. Rabbi Jacob quotes a sentence from one of Montefiore's books: "If you are within, you cannot be impartial; if you are without, you cannot know."[71] This principle, of course, applies for both sides, though it is seldom taken into account. Once it is taken seriously, it can introduce a new note in the encounter between Christians and Jews.

The outstanding fact is that Jews and Christians are on speaking terms. Rabbi Henry Siegman explains that the objections raised by some Jewish leaders to dialogue "is fear of conversionary motives imputed to the Church." They look upon this new relationship opened by dialogue as "a tactical ploy to achieve the traditional ends"—which means conversion. Rabbi Siegman sees "a certain naiveté" in such a position, though he admits "that the Church still entertains the hope that this friendship will be more productive of converts to Christianity than were its earlier efforts." Rabbi Siegman concedes that the intention to convert another person is not morally or intellectually offensive, and that talking to each other does not constitute a danger to the Jew. Regarding Jewish fears he asks: "Are we not saying, then, that we are willing to talk only to those Christians who are less secure of their faith than we are of ours? . . . If we are to say that people may talk to one another only if each renounces in advance any effort to influence and convince the other, then meaningful communication among humans would come to an end. It is a patently absurd proposition, and no less so when applied to matters of faith."[72] Siegman criticizes Jewish orthodoxy as represented by Rabbi Eliezer Berkovits, which takes the view that "Judaism is fully sufficient" and that the Church has nothing to teach the Jew. This "reflects the same kind of triumphalism which Berkovits finds unattractive in the Church." Siegman interprets Jewish re-

luctance to meet Christians in dialogical encounter as fear of the
open society in which we live. For himself, Rabbi Siegman is prepared to meet Christians, no matter what their motives, "as long
as there exists no compulsion in the dialogue other than the compulsion of ideas."

Even the instinctive fear of assimilation is being reexamined in
a new light in view of contemporary conditions. It is not possible
to escape the assimilatory influence of a multicultural society.
Rabbi Ignaz Maybaum regards it a foolish thing "to turn 'assimilation' into an obscene word . . . . Assimilation can be a creative response," he writes, "to our gentile surrounding which prevents
Jewish life from stagnation."[73] This does not mean conversion,
but learning to adjust to ever changing conditions where interplay
of progress and conservatism is characteristic of European civilization. Maybaum says, "Where Jew and Gentile can live together,
history becomes human."

This exercise in humanity is the underlying rationale of the
Jewish-Christian encounter. It is a test for both faiths: neither can
afford to withdraw into itself, what Stephen Neill calls "introver-
sion." The Christian is committed to witness as the believing Jew is
committed to the Covenant; both are under the obedience of
God. There must be no easy compromise. In fact there must be
no compromise at all, no halfway gradations. The Jewish Christian is not half Christian and half Jew—he is totally Christian and
totally Jew. The non-Christian Jew must be totally a Jew, for only
thus can he speak from within his own context to his Christian
partner. The two Covenants, the two ways, the two equally valid
faiths, is a facile solution. Neill calls us to recognize the "warfare
of ideas" which is going on all the time. He says there must be no
truce—we are engaged in this warfare whether we like it or not.[74]
It is not good enough for Judaism to boast that it is not "the sole
custodian of the means of salvation."[75] Such latitudinarianism
lacks the mark of conviction. Frederick C. Grant is betraying a
trust by describing Christianity "as a revised and modified Judaism, not a rival, antagonistic religion."[76] Christianity is a fighting
faith. It is true to itself only when it engages in spiritual warfare.
But it must be a fair and gentle fight, especially in confrontation
with the Jewish people. Neill advises that "the mission to Israel
has to be carried out with utmost prudence and delicacy," especially in view of the Holocaust.[77]

Missionaries to Jews will be well advised to take the bishop's words to heart. There have been much imprudence and an appalling lack of delicacy. But preach we must. *He'emanti khi adabber* ("I believed, therefore, have I spoken," Ps. 116:10, KJV). But our speech must be cautious and in the fear of the Lord. The Christian is under obligation to be a witness to his faith, as is also the Jew (cf. Isa. 43:10, 12; 44:18; etc.). That our witness does not coincide is a human problem. This constitutes the basis for our conversation: Which is the more genuine witness to the God of Israel—the Torah or the Gospel, which includes the Torah but goes beyond it? A decision on the issue can never be made en masse. It is a matter of personal conscience. Regarding Jesus there can be no compromise and no mass decision. Whether Jew or Gentile, the challenge is the same. We quote James Parkes, for the special reason that he has consistently spoken against missions to Jews. These are his words: "I hold the Atonement wrought on Calvary to be of equal significance, whether they accept it or not, to all men"; and this he says in full knowledge that such a statement will prove repugnant to Jews.[78] This is the Christian claim. The response to such a claim can be made only by the individual. "Everywhere in life," says Kierkegaard, "there is a crossroad; each person stands one time at the beginning—at the crossroad—this is his perfection and not his merit . . . . But where he stands at the end . . . this is his choice and his responsibility."[79]

Epilogue

There is an obvious change in the air in respect to Jewish-Christian relationships. The change is noticeable in the way Christians speak and write about Jews and the way Jews reciprocate. On the Jewish side the changed attitude on the part of Christians has encouraged a more objective view of Jesus and of Christianity. Jewish scholarly research in New Testament studies and in early Church history has greatly contributed to a better understanding of the problems and issues involved. The traditional attitude of defensive apologetics is giving way, though only slowly, to open discussion and even self-criticism. The most startling development is the effort made by Jewish scholars to appreciate not only the "Jewishness of Jesus" but his immense significance for the nations of the world. Even Paul, who was always the victim of much prejudice, is increasingly looked upon in a new and appreciative light.

Unexpectedly, it is not Jews of the liberal school who are taking a more positive attitude towards the basic affirmations of the Christian faith, but the more orthodox. Thus, on the question of Jesus' Resurrection Pinchas Lapide and Hershel J. Matt, both observant Jews, refuse to deny the possibility of such an event. Lapide is quoted as saying, "I would not exclude such a resurrection as within the range of possibility."[1] Rabbi Matt is prepared to go even further. Though as a believing Jew he cannot affirm the doctrines of the Virgin Birth, the Incarnation, the Resurrection, the Saviourhood of Christ, and the Trinity, yet he does not feel free to deny them. Even the miracles "performed by Jesus *need* not be *denied* by a believing Jew." Both Lapide and Matt point to scriptural precedents on the question of the Resurrection. Matt quotes the Talmudic dictum: "He who says that the resurrection of the dead is not derived from the Torah has no share in the

211

world to come." Even on the hotly disputed question of the Trinity he takes a cautious position, neither affirmative nor negative. The "most" he is prepared to say is "that in the lives of countless men and women who profess Christ the power and presence of God appear to be evident." Rabbi Matt sees Christianity and Judaism as two vehicles of God's revelation; though separate, they are closely related. In his words: "The *People* of Israel [are] bearers of the Torah; in the other case, the *Person* of Christ [is a] one-man embodiment of Israel and the Torah." This is a remarkable admission for an orthodox Jew.[2]

The importance of Jesus for the Gentile world is now a widely accepted fact among Jewish leaders. Men like Franz Rosenzweig, Sholem Asch, Hans-Joachim Schoeps, David Flüsser, Pinchas Lapide, Hershel J. Matt, and a host of others concur in the view that Jesus is the true Messiah of the Gentiles. In Lapide's words: "Jesus is the Saviour of the Gentile Church." But he is not the Messiah of Israel, though, according to Prof. Schoeps, when the Jewish Messiah comes, it may yet be discovered that his face is that of Jesus of Nazareth. Lapide sees no contradiction in the distinction between Israel's Messiah and the Saviourhood of Jesus for the Gentiles: "I do accept the fact that he is the Saviour of the Gentile church. I do not think that his being the Saviour of the church and not the Messiah of Israel is necessarily a contradiction." This attitude goes back to some of the medieval rabbis who regarded Christianity and Islam as paving the way in preparation for the true Messiah whom Israel expects. Franz Rosenzweig had no difficulty in working out a Jewish eschatology in which the Church is assigned its proper place for the non-Jewish world.

This more positive and friendly assessment of the Christian faith is by no means universal. Pinchas Lapide has met with severe criticism for his admission that Jesus' Resurrection may rest upon fact, an admission which few Christian liberals would dare to make.

The position of Jewish Christians is more difficult. There were times when becoming a Christian for a Jew meant total assimilation. Jewish Christians were thus branded by the Jewish community as traitors. Today they are resented for their insistence upon their Jewishness. One Jewish writer, Theodore N. Lewis, calls it "unmitigated chutzpah" (arrogance) that these converted Jews claim to have become better Jews after having accepted Jesus as Messiah. Yet strange as it may seem to Jewish ears, there is much truth in the claim. Many of the young Jews in the Jews for Jesus Movement were estranged from Jewish tradition and even hostile to it. They recovered their Jewishness as a result of their conversion. Theodore Lewis is puzzled by this new phenomenon of a group of Jewish Christians proud of their Jewish heritage. He describes his encounter with a Jewish Christian woman, a leader in the movement: "What is hard to explain about this woman with inscriptions on her blouse proclaiming her faith in Jesus, and a button doing likewise, was that she was born in Jerusalem, raised in a kibbutz, served in the Israeli army, speaks Hebrew fluently, and that it wasn't until 1975 that she discovered Jesus in Pittsburgh .... As I talked to this charming woman in Hebrew I was intrigued by her apostasy, in which her young daughter shares, but not her husband who was present." Lewis admits that he was unable to conceal his "ridicule of her belief in Messiah Jesus," well aware that the lady in question resented his derision.[3] We may well ask, "Why the ridicule?" The answer is obvious: according to Jewish tradition there can be no connection between Jesus and his people (though Rabbi Lewis, a former leader of a Progressive Synagogue, could have been expected to be more open-minded).

It will require a complete reorientation on the part of Jewish intellectuals to adjust to the phenomenon of ordinary loyal Jews who believe that Jesus is the true Messiah. For this the burdensome legacy of the past will have to be shed and the ghetto mentality exchanged for a more tolerant attitude. Some believe that Israel is the place where this change will come about. Jesus will be regarded at least as sage and teacher, if not as Messiah, though at present there is little evidence of this.[4] That the traditional attitude is in a process of change is indicated in an article by Prof. David Flüsser on the new Jewish sensitivity towards Jesus.[5] This is bound to reflect upon the Jewish response to Jewish Christians. There are some indications that in this respect change is already taking place. Thus David Rausch of Ohio University is prepared to accept "believers in 'Messiah Yeshua'" as Jews belonging to a radical group deviating from the norm of Jewish practice. "We consider them Jews even though they certainly are far removed from our ideal."[6] There are others who take a similar view.

A more intractable problem is Gentile liberals for whom the Christian faith is a sociological phenomenon tied to a given culture. Because Jews represent a different sociological structure and a different culture they are not meant to be enticed to an alien faith. Frederick C. Grant expresses the opinion of a considerable group of Gentile scholars: "I wish we might give up all 'missions to Jews' and begin to understand one another; or the conversion of Christians to Judaism, though I would gladly see far more men and women converted to the imperishable heart of the Jewish faith, its utter trust in God, its utter devotion to his revealed will. It might even lead, eventually, to a revival of religious faith and a deepening of moral conviction, by which our world could be led out of its present chaos."[7]

This kind of sentiment corresponds well with the attitude of many Christians for whom their religion is a matter of tradition; it is a view most acceptable to Jews who regard Judaism as a national legacy. But such a stance is in direct contradiction to biblical and prophetic faith. As far as Jewish Christians are concerned, the view expressed by George Hedley of Hartford Seminary is more in line with their own thinking: "A Jew is anyone who considers himself Jewish. Beyond that, a Jew is anyone who shares Jewish attitudes and judgments whether or not he knows or admits their origin. And so all Christians are Jewish. Three major strands in Jewish tradition, resulting in three major values of human experience, have entered the standard pattern of our western, so-called 'Christian' world . . . . The prophets sounded the cry for social justice. The priests asserted the duties of humble reverence. The apocalyptists uttered the declarations of unconquerable faith and the vows of absolute loyalty."[8] Indeed, Jewish Christians think of their Gentile fellow-believers as in a real sense "Jewish" by reason of their relationship to Abraham through faith in Jesus (cf. Gal. 3:27–29). Gentile believers are now Abraham's offspring and therefore heirs according to promise.

There is, however, an in-built weakness in the Jewish Christian position when measured against the attitude of Paul in relation to Jews and Gentiles. The Jewish Christian emphasis upon Jewishness tends to make origin an additional ingredient in the drama of salvation. True enough, Paul did not advocate that Jews deny their Jewishness on becoming believers in Jesus the Christ. But neither did he regard Jewish origin as a favoured position vis-à-vis God. His theological rule was that in the Presence of God man has nothing to boast of whether he be Jew or Gentile (Rom. 3:27–31). There is, however, a hidden factor in the emphasis upon Jewishness which is of immense theological importance when rightly stressed. It points to the historic particularity of revelation in

God's dealing with mankind. This tie to a particular people has always been an offence to the advocates of free religion, and never more so than today. The new concept of ecumenicity which is meant to include all world religions is checked and hampered by the historic particularity of biblical faith. In this regard the Jewish Christian movement exercises a restraining influence upon the syncretistic tendencies in the contemporary Church. They are the living witnesses that "salvation is from the Jews" (John 4:22). They remind the Church by their very existence that faith in Christ and universal religion are totally incompatible. To believe in Jesus as Messiah means to submit to a particular historic context starting with Abraham and ending at Jerusalem when Jesus of Nazareth was hung upon a Cross for the sins of the world and was raised from the dead to the glory of God the Father.

That Jews are able to hear this message from Jewish lips in a Jewish idiom and in the context of Jewish life is a most remarkable sign of our times. In this respect the first-century situation repeats itself though the circumstances are different. Jesus still stands before his people both as an enigma and as a challenge. At the present moment the challenge is mainly moral but the religious aspect is not far behind.

The appearance of the Israeli State has created new and unforeseen problems. On the ethical question of Arab displacement many Jews are profoundly conscious of a conflict between political expediency and moral justice, of which Jews regard themselves as the historic guardians. The dilemma is formidable. Even those who have no doubts about the rightness of the Jewish cause feel uncomfortable about "denying national rights to another people while demanding recognition of [their] own national rights from that people." This sentence, phrased by Mordechai Nisan, reflects the position of Yehoshafat Harkabi, the former Chief of Military Intelligence in the Israeli defence forces. From a political point of view Harkabi's anguish is that of many other Jewish leaders, and stems from the two horns of the dilemma: there can be no yielding to the Arabs without endangering the safety of the State, but continued war is a physical impossibility. In Harkabi's own words: "Continuation of the conflict without settlement is a nightmare haunting many Israelis."[9] The impasse in which the young State finds itself is acutely felt and widely discussed among intellectuals in Israel today.[10] The distress is such that some leading thinkers and writers are advocating abandonment of Jewish separate existence and integration into the indigenous soil of Mediterranean culture. This is behind the so-called Canaanite philosophy.[11]

The problems confronting the Israeli State are compounded by the spiritual crisis of Judaism, which in its orthodox form has proved inadequate for the needs of the nation. The political stranglehold of the traditionalists is widely resented not only by the secularized but by many observant Jews themselves.[12] It is in this atmosphere of acute stress that an occasional voice is heard directing attention to the person of Jesus.[13]

Ferdynand Zweig spent five years as Visiting Professor of Sociology and Labour Relations at the Hebrew and Tel Aviv Universities. His book *The Sword and the Harp* is the result of personal observation by an open and highly educated mind. In respect to Jesus he says: "The figure of Jesus, the Jew from Nazareth, looms large on the Israeli horizon, although not much is said about him openly and most Jews cautiously refrain from mentioning his name in public."[14] The reason for the awareness of Jesus' presence is not merely historical (the biblical sites, the Christian tourists, the many churches). There is a spiritual need which Zweig believes Jesus could satisfy. His teaching and his injunction to love one's enemies Zweig regards as most relevant in the present spiritual climate of the nation. Prof. Zweig raises a question which few have ever dared to ask: "Were our forefathers right in rejecting Jesus?"[15] Once this fundamental question is raised the next one follows: "Why is it that more than half the world have accepted Jesus as God (Christians), or as a Prophet (Moslems), or as the Ideal Man (Humanists), while Jews of his own kith and kin have rejected him?"

"How to deal with Jesus" Zweig regards as one of the crucial problems for the Israeli Jew. This does not mean that he advocates Christianity and its doctrines as a possible solution for Jews. His concern is entirely with the person of Jesus, Jesus the man, Jesus the Jew "as presented by his Jewish disciples in the Synoptic Gospels." It is Jesus the teacher of love (even to one's enemies) whom Zweig regards as having "highly significant national-political implications" for Israeli Jewry today.

There is a point in Zweig's chapter on Jesus which exceeds his purely human approach to the Prophet of Nazareth. Zweig asks how Jesus "managed to conquer the whole world" by his spiritual power. How did this single Jew manage to attract the immense love and adoration of the world while his own people gave him only hatred and contempt? Zweig is puzzled by the fact that Jesus succeeded in accomplishing the task which the Bible has set for the people of Israel: he became "a light to the nations." In this the rest of Jewry has failed. Zweig asks: How is it that Jesus managed to shape and mould the world "while Jews played a losing game, rolling in the dust?"[16] Zweig is thus led to the central question: "Who is Jesus?"

To keep this question alive is the purpose of the present work. Believing men and women, both Jews and Gentiles, claim to know the answer. From the time of Simon Peter to the present day they know Jesus as "the Christ, the Son of the living God" (Matt. 16:16)—but to know this is a special grace. It is the grace of love which is able to see beyond the broken figure on the Cross the risen Christ stretching out pierced and loving hands to a suffering and desperate world.

NOTES TO THE INTRODUCTION

1. Cf. S. Zalman Abramov, *Perpetual Dilemma: Jewish Religion in the Jewish State* (1976).
2. Cf. *Zionism Reconsidered: The Rejection of Jewish Normalcy*, ed. Michael Selzer (1970).
3. Cf. Arthur A. Cohen, *The Natural and the Supernatural Jew* (1963).
4. Cf. *Unease in Zion*, ed. Ehud Ben Ezer (1974).
5. Cf. Roland B. Gittelsohn, "Jews for Jesus—Are They Real?" *Midstream*, May 1979.

NOTES TO CHAPTER 1

1. "Oswiecim," *Columbia Encyclopedia* (1950), p. 1459.
2. Cf. Gerald Reitlinger, *The Final Solution: The Attempt to Exterminate the Jews of Europe, 1939–1945* (1953), pp. 95ff.
3. At the Nüremberg Trials Goering argued that he had understood *Endlösung* to mean "total" rather than "final" solution, thus pretending that he had not realized what Hitler, Himmler, and Heydrich had in mind. Cf. Reitlinger, *Final Solution*, p. 83.
4. "Die Juden sind unser Unglück; Deutschland erwache, Juda verrecke."
5. Gustav Levinstein, "Zur Feier des 10-jährigen Bestehens des Central-Vereins deutscher Staatsbürger jüdischen Glaubens:

> Denn Deutsche sind wir, in dem Vaterlande,
> Ihm dienen wir mit unserem Herz und Blut,
> Mit ihm verknüpft sind aller Liebe Bande,
> Was einst uns lieb in unser Erde ruht
> In Deutschlands Munde leben Zions Lieder.
> Der Harfe Klang dieser seine Fluren weht,
> In seine ärmsten Hütten steigt hernieder—
> Der Trost des Weltalls—Israels Gebet.

6. Cf. H. D. Dietrich, *Die Schleuse* (1974). *Schleuse* (sluice) was the term used by the Gestapo to describe the process of deporting Jews and others to concentration camps. Even while imprisoned in Theresienstadt some Jews still hoped for a German victory (pp. 122f.).
7. Jacob R. Robinson, "Holocaust," *Encyclopedia Judaica* (1971), vol. 8, p. 856. Cf. Walter Laqueur, *The Terrible Secret: An Investigation into the Suppression of Information About Hitler's "Final Solution"* (1980); and also the review by Bernard Wasserstein, "Choosing to Know," *Times Literary Supplement*, 14 November 1980, p. 1288.
8. Henry Friedländer, *The German Church and the Holocaust* (1974), pp. 69ff.
9. Dietrich, *Die Schleuse*, p. 18.
10. Rudolf Vrba and Alan Bestic, *I Cannot Forgive* (1964), pp. 176ff. Dr. Vrba was one of the few who managed to escape from Auschwitz. Upon reaching his native land, he told the papal nuncio what was going on in the hell of Auschwitz. For the true story of a single family at Auschwitz, see Elie Wiesel, *Night* (1960).
11. See Nelly Sachs, *O the Chimneys*, a collection of German poems. Sachs, a German Jewess living in Sweden, was awarded the Nobel Prize for Literature in 1966 for *The Seeker and Other Poems* (English translation, 1970).

12. For statistics see Reitlinger, *Final Solution*, Appendix I, pp. 489ff., 501.

13. *Disputation and Dialogue: Readings in the Jewish-Christian Encounter*, ed. Frank E. Talmage (1975), p. 296.

14. Rabbi Eliezer Berkovits still prefers the traditional term *ḥurban* as against *shoa* (annihilation): "For the first time in our history the Exile itself is being destroyed" (*Tradition*, Fall 1974, p. 14).

15. *Disputation and Dialogue*, p. 298.

16. Robinson, "Holocaust," pp. 830ff.

17. Reitlinger, *Final Solution*, p. 452. For maps indicating the location of the main camps, see p. 451 and Robinson's article "Holocaust" in the *Encyclopedia Judaica*.

"Selections" refers to the periodic removal of inmates for gassing so as to make room for new arrivals. In concentration-camp language this was also referred to as *Sonderbehandlung* (special treatment) and "delousing."

18. Elie Wiesel, "Talking and Writing and Keeping Silent," in *The German Church Struggle and the Holocaust*, ed. Franklin H. Littell and Hubert G. Locke (1974), pp. 269ff. For a description of what was taking place at the gas ovens, see Joe Heydecker and Johannes Leeb, *The Nüremberg Trials* (English translation, 1962), pp. 312ff. See also Kurt Meier, *Kirche und Judentum* (1968), pp. 69ff., for Kurt Gerstein's macabre eyewitness account of the breaking down of a diesel engine which produced lethal fumes for gassing Jews packed together in a crowded cell. The "Gerstein Report" was presented at the Nüremberg Trials. Gerstein died under unexplained circumstances in the Military Prison of Paris on July 25, 1945.

19. Robinson, "Holocaust," p. 867.

20. For photographs see Robinson's article "Holocaust" in *Encyclopedia Judaica;* Lord Russell, *Scourge of the Swastika* (1954); *Guide to the Holocaust*, published jointly by Yad Washem in Jerusalem and Yivo Institute in New York (1973); Zosa Szajkowski, *An Illustrated Sourcebook on the Holocaust*, 2 vols. (1976).

For a survey of the literature see Henry Friedländer, "Publications on the Holocaust," in *The German Church Struggle and the Holocaust*, pp. 76ff.; Jacob Robinson and Yehuda Bauer, *Guide to Published Materials on the Holocaust*, 2 vols. (1970); *Anthology of Holocaust Literature*, ed. Jacob Glatstein et al. (1973); Irving Halperin, *Messengers from the Dead: Literature of the Holocaust* (1970); *Documents of Destruction: German Jewry, 1933–1945*, ed. Raul Hilberg (1971).

21. *Judaism*, Summer 1967, p. 272.

22. Robinson, "Holocaust."

23. Emmi Bonhoeffer, *Auschwitz Trials: Letters from an Eyewitness* (English translation, 1967), p. 18.

24. Gerd Korman, *Hunter and Hunted: Human History of the Holocaust* (1973), p. 11.

25. H. G. Adler, *Der verwaltete Mensch: Studien zur Deportation der Juden aus Deutschland* (1974), ch. XXI. Adler is also the author of *Theresienstadt 1941–1945* (1955).

26. Adler, *Der verwaltete Mensch*, p. 989.

27. Ibid., pp. 1026ff.

28. Ibid., pp. 868ff.

29. Ibid., p. 644. An edict of the *Reichsfinanzminister* (November 4, 1941) made provision for "ein Kartenblatt für jeden abgeschobenen Juden." A specimen faces p. 644.

30. Ibid., p. 786.

31. Ibid., p. 802.

32. Ibid., pp. 715–25.

33. Ibid., p. 565.

34. Dietrich, *Die Schleuse,* p. 92.

35. Adler, *Der verwaltete Mensch,* pp. 331, 349ff. "Bei den Juden wird kein Unterschied gemacht, ganz gleich in welchem Alter sie sind."

36. Ibid., p. 470.

37. "Die Endlösung der Judenfrage" was generally interpreted as resettlement of the Jews in the East.

38. The Italian authorities requested that Mrs. Jenni Cozzi, who had been deported to the concentration camp at Riga, be released as an Italian citizen. In spite of repeated attempts to free her the request was denied on the grounds that she would spread "horror tales" (Adler, *Der verwaltete Mensch,* pp. 267f.).

39. Ibid., p. 332.

40. Himmler spoke of the Jews as *Untermenschen.* It was the official policy to stamp the Jews as Germany's most deadly enemy. In the struggle with Jewry the Nazis allowed no compromise; there could be only the conqueror and the conquered (Adler, *Der verwaltete Mensch,* p. 60).

NOTES TO CHAPTER 2

1. Elie Wiesel, *Night* (1960), p. 71; cf. Gerd Korman, *Hunter and Hunted: Human History of the Holocaust* (1973), pp. 251ff.

2. Alexander Donat, *Out of the Whirlwind* (1964), pp. 57f.

3. Richard L. Rubenstein, *After Auschwitz* (1960), p. 70.

4. Quoted in Reuben Slonim, *Family Quarrel* (1977), p. 100.

5. Richard L. Rubenstein, "Some Perspectives on Religious Faith After Auschwitz," in *The German Church Struggle and the Holocaust,* ed. Franklin H. Littell and Hubert G. Locke (1974), pp. 261f. Rabbi Marc E. Samuels sees in Rubenstein's reaction to the Holocaust "compassionate and religious" sentiment: "One does not need to agree with Rabbi Rubenstein in his disbelief in God in order to understand his thoughtful reaction and the reasons for his disbelief" (*Judaism,* 1971, p. 457).

6. Richard L. Rubenstein, "Auschwitz and Covenant Theology," *Christian Century,* 21 May 1969, in reply to Leroy T. Howe, "Theology and the Death Camps," *Christian Century,* 19 February 1969.

7. Cf. Julian Huxley, *Religion Without Revelation* (1957).

8. For an agnostic description of faith (God as a reasonable proposition without absolute certainty), see Marc E. Samuels, "In Praise of Doubt," *Judaism,* Fall 1971, pp. 456ff.

9. Rubenstein, "Some Perspectives," pp. 261f.

10. Rubenstein, "Auschwitz and Covenant Theology."

11. Samuels, "In Praise of Doubt," p. 458.

12. That Wiesel refuses to yield to despair is not the view taken by Michael Berenbaum, *The Vision of the Void: Theological Reflections on the Works of Elie Wiesel* (1979). Berenbaum describes Wiesel as the "theologian of the void" (p. 163), but admits that there is an ambiguity in Wiesel's position: "He stands at the brink with respect to God; he loves Him and hates Him; he fears Him and yet tries to live

without Him . . . . Wiesel is torn by the ambivalence as he confronts the void" (the conclusion of the book). This ambivalence becomes especially evident in Wiesel's play "The Trial of God" (1979), which ends on an inconclusive note. The trial continues, even though both the prosecutor and defence attorney have shown themselves inadequate to continue with the case.

13. *Judaism*, Winter 1960, p. 89.

14. Cf. "Jewish Secularism in America—Permanence and Change," ed. Saul L. Goodman, *Judaism*, Fall 1960, pp. 324ff.

15. Elie Wiesel, "Talking and Writing and Keeping Silent," in *The German Church Struggle and the Holocaust*, ed. Franklin H. Littell and Hubert G. Locke (1974), p. 274.

16. Ibid., pp. 273f.

17. André Neher, *L'Exil de la Parole—Du Silence Biblique au Silence d'Auschwitz* (1970). On Elie Wiesel see Maurice Friedman, "Witness and Rebellion: The Unresolved Tension in the Works of Elie Wiesel," *Judaism*, Fall 1979, pp. 484ff. For an orthodox Jewish answer to the problem, see Michael Wyschogrod, "Auschwitz: Beginning of a New Era? Reflection on the Holocaust," *Tradition*, Fall 1977, p. 69.

18. *Commentary*, July 1961.

19. Cf. Slonim, *Family Quarrel*, p. 100.

20. Elie Wiesel, *One Generation After* (English translation, 1972), p. 10.

21. L. Rubinoff, in *Speaking of God Today: Jews and Lutherans in Conversation*, ed. Marc H. Tanenbaum and Paul D. Opsahl (1974), p. 141.

22. Rubenstein, "Some Perspectives," p. 264.

23. Franklin H. Littell, *The German Church Struggle and the Holocaust* (1974), p. 29.

24. Bertram Hessler, in *The Bridge*, ed. John M. Oesterreicher (1958), vol. III, p. 39.

25. Joe Heydecker and Johannes Leeb, *The Nüremberg Trials* (English translation, 1962), pp. 280, 314f.

26. Rubenstein, *After Auschwitz*, p. 99.

27. Gerald Reitlinger, *The Final Solution: The Attempt to Exterminate the Jews of Europe, 1939–1945* (1953), p. 38.

28. Emmanuel Ringelbaum, *Notes from the Warsaw Ghetto* (English translation, 1958). Cf. David Singer, "The Jewish Gangster," *Judaism*, Winter 1974. Singer makes the peculiar point that gangsterism in Israel is necessary for the normalization of Jewish life. It provides "a Jewish cathartic vehicle—for Jewish identity . . . . In a society in which crime is a way of life, the drive for Jewish 'normalization' . . . is [an] attempt to beat the *goyyim* at their own game" (p. 77).

29. Arno Plack, *Die Gesellschaft und das Böse* (1970), pp. 307ff.

30. *Judaism*, 1972, pp. 415ff.

31. For a full review see *Times Literary Supplement*, 11 March 1977, p. 269.

32. *Judaism*, Spring 1977, pp. 223f.

33. Ignaz Maybaum, *The Face of God After Auschwitz* (1965).

34. Emil L. Fackenheim, *God's Presence in History: Jewish Affirmations and Philosophical Reflections* (1970); idem, "The People of Israel Lives," in *Disputation and Dialogue: Readings in the Jewish-Christian Encounter*, ed. Frank E. Talmage (1975), pp. 296ff.

35. Eliezer Berkovits, *Faith After the Holocaust* (1973). For a review see *Judaism*, Winter 1974, pp. 119f.

36. Elliot N. Dorff, "God and the Holocaust," *Judaism*, Winter 1977, pp. 29f.

37. S. Levin, "A Battered People Syndrome," *Judaism*, 1977, pp. 119f.

38. Rubenstein, *After Auschwitz*, p. 87.

39. Ibid., pp. 89f.

40. Ibid., p. 125. This is an obvious allusion to Jean-Paul Sartre's play "No Exit."

41. Seymour Siegel, in *Speaking of God Today: Jews and Lutherans in Conversation*, ed. Marc H. Tanenbaum and Paul D. Opsahl (1974), p. 51.

42. Rubinoff, in *Speaking of God Today*, p. 135. For Fackenheim's 614th commandment, see Korman, *Hunter and Hunted*, p. 18: "The commandment consists of the determination to survive, to remember the Holocaust, not to despair of God and of His coming Kingdom, lest Hitler gain a posthumous victory."

43. Slonim, *Family Quarrel*, p. 101.

44. Uriel Tal, in *Speaking of God Today: Jews and Lutherans in Conversation*, ed. Marc H. Tanenbaum and Paul D. Opsahl (1974), p. 87.

45. Korman, *Hunter and Hunted*, p. 139.

46. Cf. the Kaddish prayers in the Hebrew liturgy.

47. For the translated text see *The Bridge*, ed. John M. Oesterreicher (1958), vol. III, pp. 327ff.

48. A traditional orthodox answer to the question of why God permits his people to suffer is suggested by Rabbi Elliot B. Gertel. It is "because of our sins: when God smites Israel or withdraws to enable others to do so, the people of the Covenant must seek some reason, some lesson, behind His refusal to spare the rod." Rabbi Gertel urges self-scrutiny but without self-denigration (*Tradition*, Fall 1976, pp. 79f.).

NOTES TO CHAPTER 3

1. H. D. Leuner, "Auschwitz as the Beginning of a New Era?" *Hebrew Christian Quarterly*, Autumn 1977.

2. Quoted by Eberhard Bethge, in *The German Church Struggle and the Holocaust*, ed. Franklin H. Littell and Hubert G. Locke (1974), p. 176.

3. Ibid., p. 167. For the Barmen Declarations see *Bekenntnissynode der Deutschen Evangelischen Kirche, Barmen, 1934: Vorträge und Entschliessungen* (1934).

4. Eberhard Bethge, *Dietrich Bonhoeffer, Theologe–Christ–Zeitgenosse* (1967), p. 685: "Nur wer für die Juden schreit, darf auch gregorianisch singen."

5. Gordon C. Zahn, in *The German Church Struggle and the Holocaust*, pp. 167f.

6. Bethge, *Dietrich Bonhoeffer*, p. 887.

7. Kurt R. Grossmann, *Die unbesungenen Helden: Menschen in Deutschlands dunklen Tagen* (1957). An English translation would greatly contribute to knowledge of conditions in Germany during the war.

8. Cf. Pinchas E. Lapide, *Three Popes and the Jews* (1967).

9. Cf. letters to the *Toronto Globe and Mail*, 21 and 25 May 1963; also Tullia Zevi, "Pope Pius and the Jews," *Canadian Jewish News*, 27 September 1963.

10. Cf. David Herstig, *Die Rettung* (1968); also *Times Literary Supplement*, 14 March 1968.

11. Carlo Falconi, *The Silence of Pius XII* (English translation, 1970). Anthony Rhodes, *The Vatican in the Age of the Dictators: 1922–1945* (1973), pp. 355ff., admits

that the Vatican made mistakes, but contends that on the whole the Church did everything possible to help. His book is an apologia for the Popes and the Church. For a careful discussion of Pope Pius XII's silence with respect to the Jews see Erich Beyreuther, "Pius XII und die Juden," *Judaica*, December 1970, pp. 204ff. For a review see *Judaism*, Fall 1971. The Roman Catholic position is told by Alexander Ramati, *While the Pope Kept Silent* (1978).

12. *The Bridge*, ed. John M. Oesterreicher (1958), vol. III, p. 377.

13. Cf. Ferdinand Leboucher, *The Incredible Mission of Father Benoit* (English translation, 1969).

14. Hugh Trevor-Roper, *The Rise of the Christian Empire* (1965), pp. 272f.

15. W. P. Eckert, *Judenhass* (1964), pp. 78f.

16. Philip Friedman, *Their Brothers' Keeper* (1957), pp. 152f.

17. Ibid., p. 146.

18. Ibid., p. 140.

19. Ibid., pp. 206f.

20. Ibid., pp. 184f.

21. *The Bridge*, vol. III, pp. 364ff.

22. *Times Literary Supplement*, 14 March 1968.

23. *The Bridge*, vol. III, p. 376.

24. *The Jewish Chronicle* (London), 4 September 1959, p. 19.

25. Ruth Gay, "Outwitting the Final Solution," *Horizon*, January 1977, pp. 431f.

26. Grossmann, *Die unbesungenen Helden*, pp. 29ff.

27. Ibid., p. 130.

28. Ignaz Maybaum, *Man and Catastrophe* (1941), p. 100.

29. Cf. *Baltimore Evening Sun*, 13 April 1979.

30. *Didascalia Apostolorum*, trans. R. Hugh Connolly (1929), pp. 184, 187.

31. *The Missal-Vesperal* (1932), pp. 943–47. For a critical discussion of the prayer see Kathryn Sullivan, "Pro Perfidis Judaeis," in *The Bridge*, ed. John M. Oesterreicher (1956), vol. II, pp. 212ff.

32. These prayers are quoted by John M. Oesterreicher, *The Bridge* (1970), vol. V, p. 25. See also the *Toronto Globe and Mail*, 28 March 1959. The press reported that "Pope John personally struck out the Latin words *perfidis* and *perfidia* which refer to the Jews."

33. Friedrich Heer, *God's First Love: Christians and Jews over Two Thousand Years* (English translation, 1970), pp. 334f.

34. Quoted by John M. Oesterreicher in an address on the subject of the brotherhood of Christians and Jews which he delivered to the congregation of Agudati Ahim in Taunton, Massachusetts (February 1964).

35. John M. Oesterreicher, in *Commentary on the Documents of Vatican II*, ed. J. Vorgrimler, vol. III, p. 6. See also David Panitz, in *The Bridge*, ed. John M. Oesterreicher (1970), vol. V, pp. 305ff.

36. Augustin Cardinal Bea, *The Church and the Jewish People* (1966), p. 64. The scathing criticism in an editorial of *Christian Century* (26 February 1964), taking the Council to task "for absolving the Jews of collective guilt" (as if Jews could be held guilty), is hardly justified.

37. *Documents of Vatican II* (English translation ed. Joseph Gallagher, 1966), pp. 25f., 34, 113, 663–67.

38. Bea, *The Church and the Jewish People*, p. 160.

39. Cf. *The Bridge*, vol. V, p. 269. On the question of deicide, see in the same

volume John M. Oesterreicher, "Deicide as a Theological Problem," pp. 190–204. He writes: "To my mind, the deepest case against the use of 'deicide' and 'deicides' is not the lack of scriptural and truly traditional basis but the fact that the two terms pervert the mystery of the Passion" (p. 203).

40. *Times Literary Supplement,* 22 July 1977, p. 901. The book being reviewed is Celia Heller, *On the Edge of Destruction: Polish Jews Between Two Wars* (1977).

41. Cf. Charles Y. Glock and Rodney Stark, *Christian Beliefs and Anti-Semitism* (1966).

42. Gertrude J. Selznick and Stephen Steinberg, *The Tenacity of Prejudice: Anti-Semitism in Contemporary America* (1969), pp. 110 and note, 111f.

43. Solomon Bernards, "Christian Faith and Anti-Semitism," *Concern,* 1 June 1967, p. 5.

44. Frank Talmage, "Christianity and the Jewish People," *Commentary,* February 1975, p. 57.

45. Hannah Arendt, *Origins of Totalitarianism* (1958), pp. 38, 169f.

46. Cf. Guenther Lewy, "The Jewish Question," in *The Catholic Church and Nazi Germany* (1964), p. 151 and note 18. Lewy acknowledges that many outstanding Roman Catholics in Germany attempted to combat anti-Semitism, but "a Church which justifies moderate anti-Semitism and merely objected to extreme and immoral acts was ill-prepared to provide an effective antidote to the Nazi gospel of hate."

47. Walter Sulzbach, *Die Zwei Wurzeln und Formen des Judenhasses* (1959), pp. 46, 48.

48. Ibid., p. 51.

49. Arnold J. Toynbee, *A Study of History* (1935), vol. III, p. 49. Toynbee compares Jews with Parsees and describes both as "fossilized fragments of Syriac civilization." Toynbee was answered by Maurice Samuel (*The Professor and the Fossil* [1956], p. 140), who accused the historian of "trivializing" Judaism by presenting it in terms of cultural and spiritual sterility.

50. Toynbee, *A Study of History* (1961), vol. XII, p. 478.

51. Marc H. Tanenbaum, "What Is a Jew?" in *The Star and the Cross: Essays on Jewish-Christian Relations,* ed. Katharine H. Hargrove (1966), pp. 18f. Tanenbaum himself is not entirely sure what constitutes a Jew—"by all conventional categories the Jew is an anomaly."

52. Eugene Fisher, "Typical Jewish Misunderstandings of Christianity," *Judaism,* Winter 1973, pp. 21ff.

53. Edward H. Flannery, *The Anguish of the Jews: Twenty-three Centuries of Anti-Semitism* (1965), p. 60.

54. *Die Juden und das Evangelium: Äusserungen hervorragender Christen der Gegenwart,* ed. G. M. Löwen (1913), p. 9.

55. Robert A. Graham, "The Right to Kill in the Third Reich," *Civilta Catholica,* quoted in *Toronto Globe and Mail,* 28 March 1975.

NOTES TO CHAPTER 4

1. Emil L. Fackenheim, "The People of Israel Lives," in *Disputation and Dialogue: Readings in the Jewish-Christian Encounter,* ed. Frank E. Talmage (1975), p. 300.

2. One of the favourite proof texts of the Church fathers was, "God hath

reigned from the tree." This supposed quotation from the Old Testament was regarded as a reference to Christ's Cross and Resurrection. It has been suggested
that the source was Psalm 96:10 (LXX, 95:10), but neither the Hebrew nor the
Greek warrants such a reading.

3. Commodianus, *Instructions* 38, 40.

4. Matthew 23:38f. is best translated when ἔρημος is treated as a gloss (cf.
R. V. G. Tasker, *The Greek New Testament* [1964]). The text would then read: ἰδοὺ
ἀφίεται ὑμῖν ὁ οἶκος ὑμῶν ("Behold your house is left to you empty [or
abandoned]"). Alan H. M'Neile suggests that the addition of ἔρημος is a reflection of Jeremiah 22:5 "and expresses a different thought, the destruction of the
city by the Romans" (*The Gospel According to St. Matthew* [1915], p. 342). The
Berkeley Version translates correctly: "See, your house is left forsaken to you . . .
you will no longer see Me at all until you say . . . ." Older commentators understood "house" to refer to the city and not the Temple; more recent scholars take
the opposite view (cf. *The Anchor Bible*).

5. On the subject of malediction, see Jakob Jocz, *The Jewish People and Jesus
Christ* (1954), pp. 56ff.

6. On the subject of legal discrimination, see Jocz, *Jewish People*, pp. 76ff.

7. Martin Luther, *Table Talk*, in *Luther's Works* (1967), vol. 54, p. 340.

8. Ibid., p. 239.

9. Nicolas Berdyaev, *Christianity and Anti-Semitism* (English translation, 1954),
pp. 16, 27. (The Russian text was published in 1938.)

10. Jules Isaac, *The Teaching of Contempt* (English translation, 1964); idem, *Has
Anti-Semitism Roots in Christianity?* (English translation, 1961).

11. Jules Isaac, *Jesus and Israel* (English translation, 1971), pp. 233f.

12. Berdyaev, *Christianity*, pp. 7f.

13. Isaac, *Jesus and Israel*, p. 116.

14. Dagobert D. Runes, *The Jew and the Cross* (1965), p. 88.

15. Blu Greenberg, "Report of a Jewish Teacher," *The Ecumenist*, September–
October 1974, pp. 84ff.

16. Krister Stendahl, in *Disputation and Dialogue: Readings in the Jewish-Christian
Encounter*, ed. Frank E. Talmage (1975), p. 334.

17. Ernest L. Abel, *The Roots of Anti-Semitism* (1975), p. 138; cf. Jakob Jocz,
"Christian Beliefs and Antisemitism," *The Church Herald*, 8 December 1967.

18. Cf. Berdyaev, *Christianity*, pp. 39f.

19. Augustin Cardinal Bea, *The Church and the Jewish People* (1966), pp. 87f.,
162.

20. Kurt Schubert, in *The Bridge*, ed. John M. Oesterreicher (1970), vol. V,
p. 150. Cf. also *Toronto Daily Star*, 22 April 1967.

21. On Pontius Pilatus see Josephus, *Wars of the Jews* II.11.2f.; also H. Adam,
History of the Jews (1887), pp. 20f. Pilate was deprived of his office as governor after
being accused before Vitellius, Prefect of Syria, of sanguinary massacres and wan-
ton disregard of Jewish sensibilities. He was sent to Rome for trial.

22. Solomon Zeitlin, *Who Crucified Jesus?* (1964).

23. Joseph Hager, *Bekhinot historiot (Historical Investigation)* (1952).

24. Haim H. Cohn, *The Trial and Death of Jesus* (English translation, 1971).

25. Ibid., pp. 157f.—"vanae voces populi non sunt audiendae."

26. Ibid., p. 151.

27. Ibid., pp. 147 (and note 17), 331.

28. Paul Winter, *The Trial of Jesus* (1961).

29. Zeitlin, *Who Crucified Jesus?*, pp. 165ff. Jewish writers have produced a large literature on the trial of Jesus. We list a small sampling of the material which has come our way: H. Golden, *The Case of the Nazarene Reopened* (1948); G. George Fox, *The Jews, Jesus and Christ* (1953); J. Z. Lauterbach, *Rabbinic Essays* (1951); "The Trial of Jesus," eight essays by various writers, *Judaism*, Winter 1971.

30. Jacques Cohen, *The Deicides: Analysis of the Life of Jesus* (English translation, 1872), pp. 272f., 280f.; cf. Ludwig Philippson, *Haben wirklich die Juden Jesum gekreuzigt?* (1876).

31. With the case of "Isorni v. de Nantes" as a background, a film of "The Jesus Trial" has been made; cf. *Toronto Globe and Mail*, 8 October 1974, p. 2; 18 September 1978, p. 5; 23 September 1978, p. 17. For a fair and friendly statement by a Roman Catholic scholar on the subject of Jewish involvement in the trial of Jesus, see Jeffrey G. Sobassan, "The Trial of Jesus," *Journal of Ecumenical Studies*, 1973, pp. 70ff.

32. In 1965 the Bishop of Troyes had suspended Abbé de Nantes from his priestly functions for his rabid anti-Semitism. In addition the Vatican repudiated all his writings in 1969 (cf. letter to the editor, *Toronto Globe and Mail*, 27 September 1978).

33. Richard L. Rubenstein, "Some Perspectives on Religious Faith After Auschwitz," in *The German Church Struggle and the Holocaust*, ed. Franklin H. Littell and Hubert G. Locke (1974), pp. 261f.

34. In Berdyaev, *Christianity*, p. 44.

35. Reinhold Niebuhr, *Leaves from the Notebook of a Tamed Cynic* (1957), pp. 122f.

36. Cf. *The Ecumenist*, July–August 1974. In this issue editor Gregory Baum gives a full report of the symposium.

37. Cf. David R. Catchpole, *The Trial of Jesus: A Study in the Gospels and Jewish Historiography from 1770 to the Present Day* (1971), p. 291.

38. Ibid., p. 269. It is noteworthy that Stephen, the first Christian martyr, was accused of preaching against the Temple and the Law: "We have heard him speak blasphemous words against Moses and God . . . . This man never ceases to speak words against this holy place and the law" (Acts 6:11, 13).

39. Ibid.

40. Samuel Sandmel, *We Jews and Jesus* (1965), p. ix.

41. Pagans were also offended by the claim to uniqueness. For example, Celsus, Porphyry, and Julian strongly objected to Christian absolutism (Leonhard Goppelt, *Christentum und Judentum im ersten und zweiten Jahrhundert* [1954], pp. 280f.).

NOTES TO CHAPTER 5

1. Friedrich Heer, *God's First Love: Christians and Jews over Two Thousand Years* (English translation, 1970).

2. Walther Zimmerli, *Israel und die Christen* (1964), pp. 29f.: "Es hat des grossen Grauens der modernen Judenvernichtung bedurft, die Kirche erschrecken zu lassen vor der gottlosen Unbussfertigkeit, in der sie von frühen Anfängen her über die Juden geredet hat."

3. Emil Fackenheim, "Jewish Faith and the Holocaust: A Fragment," *Commentary*, August 1968, pp. 30ff., is equally critical of Faulhaber and even of Bonhoeffer!

4. Heer, *God's First Love*, pp. 306ff., 313, 319f., 322, 327, etc. (Though writing as a Catholic, Heer does not appear to adhere to Christian orthodoxy.)

5. Cf. Anthony Rhodes, *The Vatican in the Age of the Dictators: 1922–1945* (1973), pp. 272f.

6. Ibid., p. 344 and note.

7. Heer, *God's First Love*, p. 323.

8. Gordon C. Zahn, *German Catholics and Hitler's War* (1962), pp. 14, 17n.

9. Ibid., p. 18.

10. Ibid., p. 57.

11. Dietrich Schmidt, *Pastor Niemöller* (English translation, 1959), pp. 120f.

12. Zahn, *German Catholics*, pp. 31, 76. Zahn's charge that the Vatican handed over the German Catholics to the State is borne out by Klaus Scholder, *Vorgeschichte und Zeit der Illusionen: 1918–1934*, vol. I in *Die Kirchen und das Dritte Reich* (1977). A similar charge could be lodged against the Protestants—they allowed all their Church youth organizations to be put under the sole jurisdiction of Baldur von Schirach. See the lengthy review of Scholder's work by Owen Chadwick, "Between God and the Führer," *Times Literary Supplement*, 20 October 1978, pp. 1205f.

13. Zahn, *German Catholics*, p. 144.

14. Ibid., pp. 142f.

15. Ibid., p. 15 and note.

16. Ibid., p. 20.

17. Kurt Meier, *Kirche und Judentum: Die Haltung der evangelischen Kirche zur Judenpolitik des Dritten Reiches* (1968), pp. 25ff. For Bishop Wurm, see pp. 33f., 40. The introduction of the racial laws created an outcry abroad, but not in Germany; cf. Lord Horder's letter to the *London Times* (31 March 1933) regarding the dismissal of all physicians of Jewish descent.

18. Meier, *Kirche und Judentum*, p. 30.

19. Ibid., p. 34.

20. Ibid., p. 33.

21. Ibid., p. 35.

22. Cf. H. D. Leuner, *When Compassion Was a Crime* (1966).

23. Meier, *Kirche und Judentum*, p. 124.

24. P. C. Matheson, "Christian Churches and the Jews in the Third Reich," *Judaica*, September 1971, pp. 145f., suggests several reasons for the failure of the Church in Germany: (1) the Gospel "had no cutting edge"—the Church was not morally but intellectually orientated; (2) the Church suffered from an exaggerated respect for authority and was politically naive; (3) the Church was hampered by "traditional structures" from exerting any weight in united action.

25. Meier, *Kirche und Judentum*, pp. 115f., document 41. For a more detailed account of Christianity in Germany during the Hitler regime as seen by the political police and the Gestapo, see *Berichte des SD und der Gestapo über Kirchen und Kirchenvolk in Deutschland, 1934–1944*, ed. Heinz Boberach (1971). The documents deal to a large extent with the racial laws and opposition to them.

26. Lord Russell, *The Trial of Adolf Eichmann* (1962), pp. 51f., 110ff.

27. Ibid., pp. 79, 123.

28. Heer, *God's First Love*, p. 223.

29. Quoted in Heer, *God's First Love*, p. 411.

30. Quoted in Heer, *God's First Love*, p. 392.

31. Johan Snoek, *The Grey Book* (1970). The quotation is from *American Lutheran*,

February 1965, p. 16. Snoek uses the word *Grey* in the title because the record of Christian reaction to Jewish persecution under Hitler is not entirely black nor white—but something in between. The subtitle reads: *A Collection of Protests Against Anti-Semitism and Persecution of Jews Under Hitler.*

32. Paul J. Kirsch, *We Christians and Jews* (1975), pp. 71, 77.

33. For the letter in full, see the Newsletter of the Committee on the Church and the Jewish People (World Council of Churches), 1973, no. 4, p. 9. Parkes received an award of $10,000 in 1973 for his contribution "to the world-wide struggle against anti-Semitism."

34. *Die Juden und wir Christen,* ed. Hans Kallenbach (1950), pp. 54ff. For a review of the Christian reaction to the Nazi persecution, see Hermann Greife, "Die nationalsozialistische Judenverfolgung als Herausforderung an Christentum und die Kirche," *Judaica,* March and June 1979.

35. *Die Juden und wir Christen,* pp. 57f.

36. *New York Times,* 24 February 1946.

37. *Die Juden und wir Christen,* pp. 41ff.

38. Ibid., pp. 50ff.

39. Ibid., pp. 61ff.

40. Newsletter of the Committee on the Church and the Jewish People (World Council of Churches), 1969, no. 2.

41. Newsletter of the Committee on the Church and the Jewish People (WCC), 1962, no. 4.

42. Newsletter of the Committee on the Church and the Jewish People (WCC), 1975, no. 4.

43. Cf. *Der Zeuge,* ed. H. D. Leuner, November 1967, pp. 22ff.

44. Cf. Helmut Weber, "Kirche und Judentum," *Der Zeuge,* July 1960, pp. 22f.

45. *The New Delhi Report* (WCC), 1961, pp. 148ff.

46. For a discussion of the Evanston Assembly from the Roman Catholic vantage point, see Edward H. Flannery, "Hope and Despair at Evanston," in *The Bridge,* ed. John M. Oesterreicher (1956), vol. II, pp. 271ff.

47. Newsletter of the Committee on the Church and the Jewish People (WCC), 1968, no. 4.

48. Newsletter of the Committee on the Church and the Jewish People (WCC), 1972, no. 3.

49. Newsletter of the Committee on the Church and the Jewish People (WCC), 1967, no. 1.

50. For the Vatican Guidelines for Catholic-Jewish relations, see *The Bridge,* ed. John M. Oesterreicher (1970), vol. V, pp. 257–62; *Encounter Today,* 1967, no. 3, pp. 79–82; Eugene Fisher, *Faith Without Prejudice* (1977), pp. 151–59.

NOTES TO CHAPTER 6

1. Karl Kupisch, *Das Volk der Geschichte: Randbemerkungen zur Geschichte der Judenfrage* (1960), pp. 186ff.

2. Ibid., pp. 158ff.

3. Ibid., pp. 199f.

4. Charlotte Klein, *Theologie und Anti-Judaismus: Abhandlungen zum christlich–jüdischen Dialog,* ed. Helmut Gollwitzer (1975), pp. 13f., 21.

5. Occasionally Dr. Klein goes beyond the allowable in apologetic. For example, she chides Joachim Jeremias for suggesting that the cleansing of the Temple by Jesus sealed his death (*Theologie*, pp. 93ff.); but how does she know that it did not?

6. Ibid., p. 106.

7. Franklin H. Littell, *The Crucifixion of the Jews* (1975), pp. 5, 25, 49.

8. Ibid., p. 65.

9. Ibid., p. 129.

10. James Daane, *The Anatomy of Anti-Semitism and Other Essays on Religion and Race* (1965), pp. 24f.; cf. idem, "The Anatomy of Anti-Semitism," *Christianity Today*, 13 March 1964, pp. 10ff.

11. Daane, *Anatomy*, p. 34.

12. Alan Jenkins, "I Apologize to the Jews for the Anti-Semitism of Christians," *The Churchman*, November 1967.

13. Friedrich Heer, *God's First Love: Christians and Jews over Two Thousand Years* (English translation, 1970), pp. 420f.

14. Gregory Baum, *The Ecumenist*, September–October 1971, p. 94.

15. Gregory Baum, *The Ecumenist*, February–March 1963, p. 36.

16. Gregory Baum, *The Ecumenist*, January–February 1966, p. 29.

17. Rosemary Ruether, "In What Sense Can We Say That Jesus Was 'The Christ'?" *The Ecumenist*, January–February 1972.

18. Rosemary Ruether, "Christian Anti-Semitism and the Dilemma of Zionism," *Christianity and Crisis*, 17 April 1972, pp. 91f. Dr. Ruether's position is elaborated in her book *Faith and Fratricide: The Theological Roots of Anti-Semitism* (1975). We quote one single passage: "The attribution of an absolute finality to the heightened expectations surrounding the life and death of Jesus must be regarded as a flawed way of appropriating the real meaning of eschatological encounter." A review in *Encounter Today* (1976, p. 164) says that the book "ruthlessly disposes of all the elements of our creed." Even so radical a writer as Alan T. Davies complains "that Rosemary Ruether dissolves Christianity into Judaism when she apparently denies any past historical fulfillment of the once-for-all character as far as the christological faith of the church is concerned" (*Anti-Semitism and the Christian Mind: The Crisis of Conscience After Auschwitz* [1969], p. 167n.).

19. Cf. Gregory Baum, "The Doctrine on Revelation at Vatican II," *The Ecumenist*, January–February 1966, p. 25.

20. John M. Oesterreicher, *Anatomy of Contempt* (1975); see also the review in *Encounter Today*, Summer–Autumn 1976, pp. 129f. (Jews quote Dr. Ruether as a Catholic theologian. In these days it is difficult to decide just what the limits of Catholicity are.)

21. James Parkes, *Prelude to Dialogue: Jewish-Christian Relationships* (1969), pp. 12, 30.

22. The epithet *verjudet* can be understood in a pejorative sense (e.g., as a racial slur) or in a theological sense (e.g., as compromising with the Gospel). It all depends on who says it and in what context.

23. James Parkes, *Jews, Christians, and the World of Tomorrow* (1969), pp. 16, 18f.

24. Parkes, *Prelude to Dialogue*, pp. 197, 209.

25. Ibid., p. 210.

26. Ibid., pp. 211f.

27. Ibid., p. 20.

28. On the subject of two Covenants, see Raphael H. Levine, *Two Paths to One*

God: Judaism and Christianity (1962). The author sums up his position: "Recognizing our basic oneness in unyielding faith . . . my path through Judaism is best for me." See also Paul Borchsenius, *Two Ways to God*, trans. Michael Heron (1968), esp. pp. 200ff.

29. James Parkes, *Foundations of Judaism and Christianity* (1960), p. 330.

30. Eckardt, who comes from a Methodist tradition, writes of Parkes: "We are blessed by an Anglican of the Anglicans"!

31. A. Roy Eckardt, *Elder and Younger Brothers: The Encounter of Christians and Jews* (1967), pp. 65, 144.

32. Ibid., pp. 152f.

33. Ibid., p. 74. Eckardt makes reference to the book *Israel en de Kirk* (German translation, 1961).

34. Ibid., pp. 66–70, and esp. 79.

35. Ibid., pp. 153, 157.

36. Ibid., pp. 156ff. Exclusion of Jews from the Church, Eckardt holds, would constitute "an affront to all Christians of Jewish origin." Yet when writing about Hebrew Christians, the author is not above a contemptuous tone.

37. Cf. Alice and Roy Eckardt, *Encounter with Israel: A Challenge to Conscience* (1970). For a review see *Judaism*, Winter 1971, pp. 120ff.

38. A. Roy Eckardt, *Your People and My People: The Meeting of Jews and Christians* (1974), p. 227. For Levi A. Olan's criticism see "The Jewish-Christian Dialogue: A Dissenting Opinion," *Religion in Life*, 1972, pp. 154ff. Eckardt's position that there should be no attempt to make Christians out of Jews is by no means an isolated instance. The present author has in his possession a letter from the General Secretary of a well-known religious publishing house in England in which a similar view is expressed, though in less forceful words. Be it noted that this gentleman's task is the shaping of Christian opinion in his country.

39. Eckardt, *Your People and My People*, p. 238.

40. Ibid., pp. 240f.

41. Ibid., pp. 242f.

42. Ibid., p. 244.

43. Ibid., p. 249.

44. Ibid., pp. 245f.

45. Davies, *Anti-Semitism and the Christian Mind*, pp. 168n., 186f.

46. Ibid., pp. 161f.

47. Ibid., p. 186.

48. Cf. Jakob Jocz, "The Jewish-Christian Dialogue," *Gordon Review*, Fall 1967.

49. Henry Siegman, in *Encounter Today*, Summer–Autumn 1976, p. 88.

50. Cf. *Das Judenchristen der Gegenwart*, ed. G. M. Löwen (1913), p. 19; *Das Judenchristentum in der religiösen Volkserziehung des deutschen Protestantismus von einem christlichen Theologen* (1893). The point the anonymous author of the latter work makes is that Christianity has its own independent existence and requires no "alien" support from the Old Testament.

51. According to the *Concise Oxford Dictionary*, a "Pharisee" is a "self-righteous person, formalist, hypocrite"; "Jew," as a verb, is a synonym for "to cheat."

52. Cf. *A Rabbinic Anthology*, ed. C. G. Montefiore and H. Loewe (1938), pp. 487f.

53. Ibid., p. 609. In *Jesus and the Pharisees* (1973), John Bowker writes: "The 'Pharisees' are attacked in rabbinic sources as vigorously as 'Pharisees' are attacked

in the Gospels, and often for the same reasons."

54. D. A. Hagner, "Pharisees," *Zondervan Pictorial Encyclopedia of the Bible* (1975), vol. IV, p. 750. An important contribution to our knowledge of the Pharisees' origin, doctrine, and life has been made by Jacob Neusner: *The Masters* (Part I of *The Rabbinic Traditions About the Pharisees Before 70 A.D.*, 1971) and *From Politics to Piety: The Emergence of Pharisaic Judaism* (1973). See also Bowker, *Jesus and the Pharisees.* Bowker properly asks: "What was the offence of Jesus, and why did anybody wish to take action against him?" The answer, according to Bowker, is that Jesus claimed to have direct authority from God (p. 42).

55. Parkes, *Jews, Christians, and the World,* p. 18. For a scholarly analysis of what are regarded as anti-Jewish passages in the New Testament, see *Antijudaismus im Neuen Testament?*, ed. W. P. Eckert, N. P. Levinson, and Martin Stöhr (1967), esp. E. Grässer, "Die Juden als Teufelssöhne in Johannes 8:37–47" (pp. 157–70). For an effort to make the Passion story less offensive, see John T. Townsend, "A Liturgical Interpretation of Our Lord's Passion," the first in a series of papers from the Israel Study Group of the National Conference of Christians and Jews (1977).

56. Cf. Willehad Paul Eckert, *Die Geistige Gestalt des heutigen Judentums* (1969), pp. 157f.

57. Martin Kähler, in *Die Judenchristen der Gegenwart,* p. 19. The German text reads: "Der in der Geschichte immer wieder auftauchende Antisemitismus belegt die Tatsache, dass der seit der Rückkehr aus dem Exil und der Verwerfung Jesu ausgebildete Typus ein fester ist. Und die Herrschaft der jüdischen Internationale auf dem Geldmarkt und der Presse könnte auch Skeptiker davon überzeugen, dass das spröde Judentum nicht bloss Ergebnis der Verfehlmung durch kirchlichen Fanatismus ist."

58. In *Die Judenchristen der Gegenwart,* p. 24.

59. Ibid., p. 31.

60. Among them are W. Trutwin, *Gesetz und Propheten: Lehrbuch zur Offenbarung über Geschichte des Alten Bundes für höhere Schulen* (1967); H. Heufken, *Die Judenfrage im Religionsunterricht* (1965–66); *Israel in Christian Religious Instruction,* ed. Theodor Filthaut (English translation, 1965).

61. Claire Huchet Bishop, *How Catholics Look at Jews* (1974), pp. 126f.

62. Cf. *Israel in Christian Religious Instruction.*

63. Ibid., p. 6. Cf. *Toronto Globe and Mail,* 30 March 1977. In his 1979 Lenten message, G. Emmet Carter, the Roman Catholic Archbishop of Toronto, called upon priests and laity to beware of anti-Semitism and to remember the link which connects the Church to the Jewish people. (For the text see *The Ecumenist,* May–June 1979, pp. 61f.)

64. Carlyle Witton-Davies, "Christians and Jews: How to Present the Story of Jesus' Trial and Death," *Church Times,* 15 March 1969, p. 9.

65. Cf. *Freiburger Rundbrief,* August 1950.

66. Bishop, *How Catholics Look at Jews,* pp. 113f.

67. Eva Fleischner, *Judaism in German Christian Theology Since 1945: Christianity and Israel Considered in Terms of Mission* (1975), p. 69.

68. *Der Ungekündigte Bund: Neue Begegnung von Juden und christlicher Gemeinde,* ed. Dietrich Goldschmidt and Hans-Joachim Kraus (1962), p. 123. Fleischner's *Judaism* provides an excellent survey of the post–World War II change in German Christian thought regarding the Jews.

69. *Judaism and the Christian Seminary Curriculum*, ed. J. Bruce Long (1966), p. 150. The definition of "legitimacy" was formulated by J. C. Rylaarsdam, one of the participants. Bias against Jews frequently occurs almost unconsciously. The English Jesuit Henry Davis in *Moral and Pastoral Theology* (1943) repeats a phrase from Thomas Aquinas (*Summa Theologica* 1.2, q. 102, a. 6, ad. 8) to the effect that Jews "were prone to cruelty"—therefore God forbade them to manhandle animals. Davis's textbook is widely used in Roman Catholic seminaries and has seen several editions. One wonders what effect such a statement has upon the minds of young seminarians.

70. *Judaism and the Christian Seminary Curriculum*, p. 154. Harvard University has been designated as the site of a major Center for Jewish Studies. The Center will include eight full professorships, twenty-four graduate fellowships, and a large library on Judaica.

71. Bernhard E. Olson, *Faith and Prejudice* (1963), p. 43.

72. Ibid., pp. 42f.

73. Ibid., p. 45.

74. Ibid., p. 286.

75. In *Israel in Christian Religious Instruction*, p. 47. On the subject of continuity John M. Oesterreicher has made a singular contribution. See especially his most recent monograph *Under the Vault of the Covenant* (the German title most aptly conveys the biblical image: *Unter dem Bogen des einen Bundes*) and also *The Israel of God* (1963).

76. In *Israel in Christian Religious Instruction*, p. 108.

77. Fleischner, *Judaism*, p. 135.

78. Ibid., p. 145. On pp. 115ff. Fleischner lists others who take a similar position.

79. Helmut Gollwitzer, Rolf Rendtorff, and Nathan P. Levinson, *Thema: Juden–Christen–Israel* (1978), pp. 113ff.

NOTES TO CHAPTER 7

1. Cf. Jakob Jocz, *The Jewish People and Jesus Christ* (1949), pp. 157ff., 181ff.

2. An extreme example of reductionist Christology is the symposium *The Myth of God Incarnate*, ed. John Hick (1977). It is noteworthy that Judaism looms large in this work and that the essayists usually refer to Judaism in connection with Christology. For a critique see *Christian Century*, 7 December 1977, pp. 1146f.

3. On the Noachian commandments, see Jocz, *Jewish People*, pp. 69, 318.

4. Hershel J. Matt, "How Shall a Believing Jew View Christianity?" *Judaism*, Fall 1975, pp. 391ff.

5. For a discussion of the verdict and its implications, see Jakob Jocz, "A Test of Tolerance," *Christianity Today*, 29 March 1963.

6. *Toronto Star*, 7 December 1962.

7. *Toronto Globe and Mail*, 24 January 1970.

8. Marc Galanter, "A Dissent on Brother Daniel," *Commentary*, July 1963, pp. 10ff.

9. *Jewish Chronicle*, 28 December 1962, p. 16.

10. *Times Literary Supplement*, 13 May 1977, p. 591.

11. *Times Literary Supplement*, 27 May 1977, p. 653. For Maccoby's reply see

Times Literary Supplement, 17 June 1977.

12. Cf. Jocz, *Jewish People,* p. 129. On points of difference between Jesus and the Pharisees see pp. 29f.

13. Christian D. Ginsburg, *The Essenes: Their History and Doctrines* (1956), pp. 24f. Ginsburg derives the name *Essene* from חסידים and places the community on the northwest shore of the Dead Sea (p. 26). Matthew Black, *The Scrolls and Christian Origins* (1961), p. 164, confirms that "the older explanation of the name Essene as a Greek equivalent of the Hebrew Hasidim" is now attested by the Dead Sea Scrolls.

14. Charles Francis Potter, *The Lost Years of Jesus Revealed* (1958), p. 129.

15. Johannes Lehmann, *The Jesus Report: The Rabbi Jesus Revealed by the Dead Sea Scrolls* (English translation, 1971), p. 149.

16. Martin A. Larson, *The Essene Heritage: The Teacher of the Scrolls and the Gospel of Christ* (1967), pp. 147ff., 154, 172, etc. Like Potter and Lehmann, Larson is chiefly sensational. There are a number of contradictions in his work apart from the guesswork in place of historical fact. Paul and the Fourth Gospel are described as representing "pristine Essene-Christian doctrine" with anti-Essene elements intermixed; apparently Larson can have it both ways (cf. p. 171n.). He finds in Essenism accretions from Zoroastrianism, the Greek mysteries, Pythagoreanism, and Buddhism—nothing is left out. But in this form Christianity was supposedly unacceptable to the pagan world (why?), so the Pauline literature and the Fourth Gospel had to be Hellenized (pp. xvi f.). Oscar Cullmann writes: "That Jesus was initiated into these secret doctrines (of the Essenes) as a member of the Essene community is pure and groundless speculation, for we have not the slightest hint on the subject, either in the N.T. or in Jewish writings" ("The Significance of Qumran Texts for Research in the Beginnings of Christianity," *Journal of Biblical Literature,* 1955, p. 213).

17. Cf. Max I. Dimont, *Jews, God and History* (1962), p. 89.

18. Solomon Zeitlin, specializing in the period of the Second Temple, has written extensively on the subject, chiefly in the *Jewish Quarterly Review.*

19. Cf. Shalom Ben-Chorin, in *Journal of Ecumenical Studies,* Summer 1974, p. 424.

20. Shalom Ben-Chorin, "Jewish Questing About Jesus Christ," *Hebrew Christian Quarterly,* Summer 1964, pp. 40ff.

21. Cf. Jocz, *Jewish People,* pp. 134ff.

22. For a survey of the literature on the subject see Shalom Ben-Chorin, "The Image of Jesus in Modern Judaism," *Journal of Ecumenical Studies,* Summer 1974, pp. 401ff.; idem, *Bruder Jesus* (1967).

23. Ben-Chorin, "Image of Jesus," p. 416; cf. Pinchas Sadeh, in *Unease in Zion,* ed. Ehud Ben Ezer (1974), pp. 246f.

24. David Flüsser, "Jesus in the Context of History," in *Crucible of Christianity,* ed. Arnold Toynbee (1969), pp. 225ff.

25. David Flüsser, "A New Sensitivity in Judaism and the Christian Message," *Harvard Theological Review,* 1968, pp. 107ff. Geza Vermes bears out Flüsser's assertion that the Dead Sea Scrolls do throw new light upon intertestamental and rabbinic Judaism ("The Impact of the Dead Sea Scrolls on the Study of the N.T.," *Journal of Jewish Studies,* Autumn 1976). But "the rabbinic literature, skilfully handled, is still the richest source for the interpretation of the original Gospel message and the most precious aid to the quest of the historic Jesus" ("New Sensitivity," p. 116).

26. Cf. David Flüsser, *Jesus* (English translation, 1969).

27. F. F. Bruce, in *Evangelical Quarterly*, October–December 1977, pp. 226f. It is difficult to understand why a Christian publishing house (S.P.C.K.—Society for the Promotion of Christian Knowledge) would issue a book contradictory to almost everything in which the Church believes.

28. Samuel Sandmel, *We Jews and Jesus* (1965), p. 123.

29. Ibid., p. 151; cf. *The First Christian Century in Judaism and Christianity* (1969), pp. 23ff.

30. Sandmel, *We Jews and Jesus*, p. 110.

31. Samuel Sandmel, *Jewish Understanding of the New Testament* (1957), p. 283.

32. Geza Vermes, *Jesus the Jew: A Historian's Reading of the Gospels* (1973), p. 224.

33. Ferdynand Zweig, *Israel: The Sword and the Harp* (1969), p. 229. The chapter entitled "The Figure of Jesus on the Israeli Horizon" (pp. 219ff.) is an effort to draw attention to the life-giving spiritual force contained in the Synoptic Gospels. While the Jews were in exile, they had to reject Jesus because the universalistic interpretation threatened Jewish survival. But in Israel today Jesus is an inevitable presence who can make an important contribution to the evolving Judaism of the Third Commonwealth. This is Zweig's position.

34. Maurice Nathan Eisendrath, *The Never Failing Stream* (1939), p. 357.

35. Robert Aron, *The Jewish Jesus* (English translation, 1971).

36. *An Important Historical Discourse on the Actual Manner of Jesus' Death According to an Old MS Found in Alexandria Written by a Contemporary of Jesus from the Holy Order of the Essenes, Translated from a Latin Copy of the Original* (the English title is by Ben-Chorin, *Journal of Ecumenical Studies*, Summer 1974). That Jesus did not die but only fainted was suggested by Werner Hegemann in *Christ Rescued* (1928; English translation, 1935).

37. David Daube, in *Jewish Chronicle*, 26 April 1957.

NOTES TO CHAPTER 8

1. Jacob Neusner, *From Politics to Piety: The Emergence of Pharisaic Judaism* (1973), p. 150.

2. Cf. Jakob Jocz, *The Jewish People and Jesus Christ* (1949), pp. 187ff.

3. Jacob Neusner, *The Rabbinic Traditions About the Pharisees Before A.D. 70* (1971), Part III, p. 290.

4. Ibid., p. 301.

5. Ibid., p. 305.

6. Neusner, *From Politics to Piety*, pp. 90, 121.

7. Asher Finkel, *The Pharisees and the Teacher of Nazareth* (1974), p. 43.

8. Ibid., p. 54.

9. Cf. Mishnah *Hagigah* 1:8 (Danby's translation).

10. Finkel, *The Pharisees*, pp. 141f.

11. Ibid., pp. 132–34.

12. John Bowker, *Jesus and the Pharisees* (1973), pp. 42, 46f., 51f. For Maimonides, see his *Code Book* 14 (Judges ch. 3).

13. David Noel Freedman, "An Essay on Jewish Christianity," *Journal of Ecumenical Studies*, Fall 1969, pp. 81ff.

14. Jakob Jocz, "Jesus and the Law," *Judaica*, August 1970, pp. 105ff.

15. Solomon Zeitlin, in *Jewish Quarterly Review*, January 1964, pp. 228ff.

16. Cf. Jakob Jocz, *The Spiritual History of Israel* (1961), pp. 81ff., 159ff.; idem, *A Theology of Election* (1958), pp. 31ff.

17. R. Travers Herford, "The Separation of Christianity from Judaism," in *Jewish Studies in Memory of Israel Abrahams* (1927), pp. 211ff.

18. Ibid., p. 220.

19. Ibid., p. 204.

20. Armaud Abecassis, "Gibt es eine jüdische Religion?" in *Religiöse Strömungen im Judentum heute* (1973).

21. Joseph Klausner, *From Jesus to Paul* (English translation, 1944), esp. "What Is Paul for the Jews?" pp. 600ff.

22. Shalom Ben-Chorin, "Jesus und Paulus in jüdischer Sicht," *Annual of the Swedish Theological Institute*, 1976, p. 19.

23. Samuel Sandmel, *The Genius of Paul* (1958), p. 7.

24. Klausner, *From Jesus to Paul*, pp. 309ff.

25. Ibid., pp. 43f. On the subject of Paul's alleged anti-Judaism, see Otto Michel, "Fragen zu I Thessalonicher 2, 14–16: Antijüdische Polemik von Paulus," in *Antijudaismus im Neuen Testament* (1967), pp. 50–59; also Marcus Barth, "Was Paul an Anti-Semite?" in *Israel and the Church* (1969), pp. 43–78.

26. Hyam Maccoby, in *Commentary*, December 1976; cf. Shlomo Pines, *The Jewish Christians in the First Century of Christianity According to a New Source* (1969) (in Hebrew).

27. Hans-Joachim Schoeps, *Paulus: Die Theologie des Apostels im Lichte der jüdischen Religionsgeschichte* (1959), p. 274.

28. Jacob J. Petuchowski, "Paul and Jewish Theology: A New View of the Christian Apostle," *Commentary*, September 1959, pp. 231ff. For a survey see Halvor Ronning, "Some Jewish Views of Paul," *Judaica*, June 1968, pp. 82ff. Ronning does not mention Schoeps's book. Richard L. Rubenstein mischievously suggests that "German-inspired" Jewish scholars, in order to avoid the issue of their own antinomianism, make of Paul a Hellenist and a Gnostic (cf. *Judaism*, Spring 1961, p. 190).

29. R. Y. Zwi Werblowsky, "Crises in Messianism," *Judaism*, Spring 1958, p. 111.

30. Jacob Taubes, "The Issue Between Judaism and Christianity," in *Arguments and Doctrines: A Reader of Jewish Thinking in the Aftermath of the Holocaust*, ed. Arthur A. Cohen (1970), pp. 402ff.

31. Erich Isaac, in *Arguments and Doctrines*, ed. Arthur A. Cohen, pp. 504ff.

32. Louis Jacobs, *What Does Judaism Say About . . .?* (1975), p. 85.

33. Cf. Jocz, *Jewish People*, pp. 302ff.

34. Werblowsky, "Crises in Messianism," pp. 112f.

35. Maurice Nathan Eisendrath, *The Never Failing Stream* (1939), p. 341.

36. *Arguments and Doctrines*, ed. Arthur A. Cohen, p. 519.

NOTES TO CHAPTER 9

1. Abraham Kotsuji, *From Tokyo to Jerusalem* (1964).

2. Deborah Wigoder, *Hope in My House* (1966); cf. A. I. Gordon, *The Nature of Conversion* (1967).

3. *Judaism*, 1970, p. 359.

4. Cf. David Max Eichhorn, *Conversion to Judaism* (1965); also *Judaism,* 1970, p. 355.

5. *Judaism,* 1970, p. 356; cf. *Judaism,* 1974, pp. 467ff. On the position of prose-lytes to Judaism see Ben Zion Wacholder, "Cases of Proselytizing in the Tosafist Responsa," *Jewish Quarterly Review,* April 1961, pp. 288ff. The Winter 1975 issue of *Judaism* relates the story of the conversion of an Italian group from San Nican-dro, a Finnish group, and a Japanese group. Note also the remark of Günther Plaut, *Your Neighbour the Jew* (1975), p. 75: "More Gentiles than ever before are turning to Jews and Judaism and making them their own."

6. Moshe M. Maggal, "The Voice of Judaism" (National Jewish Information Center for the Propagation of Judaism), September 1966.

7. *Chicago Tribune,* 7 January 1970.

8. Milton R. Konvitz, discussing personal freedom in relation to group con-sciousness, makes the following point with respect to the verdict on Brother Dan-iel: "It seems to say that it is impossible to separate completely Jewish ethnicity and Jewish religion." As far as the individual Jew is concerned, he "cannot claim absolute religious liberty or the separation of church and state" (*Judaism,* 1971, pp. 164f.).

9. Cf. Gilbert Kollin, "The Advisability of Seeking Converts," *Judaism,* Winter 1975, pp. 49ff.

10. Cf. *Christianity Today,* 7 January 1966, p. 47.

11. Cf. *Conservative Judaism,* Spring 1976, pp. 79ff.

12. *Judaism,* Winter 1975, p. 56.

13. Robert Misrahi, in *Religiöse Strömungen im Judentum heute* (1973), pp. 73ff.

14. "Who Is a Jew?—A Symposium," *Judaism,* Winter 1959, pp. 3–15.

15. Horace M. Kallen, "The Foundations of Jewish Spiritual and Cultural Unity," *Judaism,* 1957, pp. 110ff.

16. For Schoeps's views on election see Jakob Jocz, *A Theology of Election* (1958), pp. 64f.

17. Hans-Joachim Schoeps, *Jüdisch-christliches Religionsgespräch* (1949), p. 149 (this volume has since been revised, enlarged, and translated into English). We were gratified to find that Prof. Krister Stendahl makes a similar observation: the juxtaposition is not Judaism and Christianity, but the Church and the Jewish people (cf. *Paul Among Jews and Gentiles* [1976], p. 4; "Judaism and Christianity: Then and Now," in *New Theology,* ed. Martin E. Marty and Dean G. Peerman [1965], vol. II, pp. 153f.). Stendahl's conclusions, however, seem to be different from our own.

18. The RSV translates "covenant" in the plural, but we prefer the alternate reading ἡ διαθήκη; cf. *The Greek New Testament,* ed. United Bible Societies (1966). For the unity of the Covenant see Jakob Jocz, *The Covenant: A Theology of Human Destiny* (1968), pp. 238ff.

19. In German *Judentum* may mean "Judaism" or "Jewry" (i.e., "Jewish people"); hence the confusion.

20. Cf. Franz Rosenzweig, *Der Stern der Erlösung,* 3rd ed. (1954), pp. 49f.: "Wir allein vertrauen dem Blut" ("We alone put our trust in blood").

21. For a careful analysis of the Barthian position regarding Israel, see Fried-rich-Wilhelm Marquardt, *Die Entdeckung des Judentums für die christliche Theologie: Israel im Denken Barths* (1967). "Judentum" in this context means "Jewish people," not "Judaism."

22. Origen, *Contra Celsum* V.43.

23. Cyprian, Treatise XII: *Testimonies Against the Jews* I.23.

24. Augustine, *Tractatus Adversus Judaeos.*

25. Cf. A. Lukyn Williams, *Adversus Judaeos* (1935).

26. John Calvin, *Institutes of the Christian Religion* IV.xvi.14.

27. Ibid., II.xi.11.

28. Hertzel Fishman, *American Protestantism and the Jewish State* (1973), pp. 15f.

29. W. T. Gidney, *History of the London Society for Promoting Christianity Among the Jews* (1908), pp. 10f.

30. Nahum Sokolow, *History of Zionism* (1919), vol. I, pp. 163ff.

31. *Reminiscences of Mrs. Finn* (1929), pp. 196, 246ff., 249.

32. A short notice of William Hechler appears in Sokolow's *History of Zionism*, vol. I, p. 270. For a full account see Claude Duvernoy, *Le Prince et le Prophète* (1978).

33. Howard M. Sachar, *The Course of Modern Jewish History* (1958), pp. 389f. For a biography of Wingate see A. I. Hay, *There Was a Man of Genius* (1963).

34. Cf. Richard Byfield, "Zion's Answer to the Nation's Ambassadors" (1645); William Sedgwicke, "Zion's Deliverance and Her Friends' Duty: The Grounds of Expecting and Meanes of Procuring Jerusalem's Restoration" (1643); Stephen Marshall, "God's Master-piece: A Sermon Tending to Manifest God's Appearing in the Building Up of Sion" (1645); idem, "The Strong Helper, or The Interest and Power of Prayers of the Destitute, for the Building Up of Sion"; John Arrowsmith, "The Covenant—Avenging Sword Brandished" (1643). The works of John Bunyan are a classic example of the seventeenth-century English Puritans' use of Old Testament imagery and vocabulary.

35. Cf. F. S. Donn, *The Israel Way to Peace* (1957), p. 162. Loraine Boettner's statement that with the coming of the Messiah, "the special role assigned to the Jews has been fulfilled," is an exception (*The Millennium* [1958], p. 311).

36. *Jerusalem Post*, September 1978.

37. Cf. Jakob Jocz, "The 'Advantage' of the Jew," in *Jews and Christians: Preparation for Dialogue*, ed. George A. F. Knight (1965), pp. 78ff.

38. E. P. Sanders, "Paul's Attitude Toward the Jewish People," *Union Seminary Quarterly Review*, Spring–Summer 1978, p. 176.

39. Stendahl, "Judaism and Christianity," p. 161. Prof. Stendahl's mistake lies in using "Judaism" as a portmanteau concept which obliterates all the differences.

40. Stendahl's preference for the term *call* rather than *conversion* with respect to Paul's experience (*Paul Among Jews and Gentiles*, pp. 7ff.) overlooks the radical change in the Apostle's orientation and attitude.

41. Sanders, "Paul's Attitude," p. 183.

42. Ibid., p. 184.

NOTES TO CHAPTER 10

1. Abraham J. Karp, "The Father of American Reform Judaism" (a critical assessment of Rabbi I. M. Wise), *Judaism*, Fall 1958, p. 362.

2. Monford Harris, "Interim Theology," *Judaism*, Fall 1958, pp. 302ff.

3. Solomon B. Freehof (in a review of Boaz Cohen, *Law and Tradition in Judaism* [1959]), *Judaism*, Fall 1959, p. 379.

4. Ephraim Shmueli, "Dubnow's History Revisited," *Judaism*, Summer 1957, p. 214.

5. Jakob Jocz, "The Significance of the Hebrew Christian Position," *Hebrew Christian Quarterly*, April 1945, p. 11.

6. Cf. H. D. Leuner, "Ist die Bezeichnung 'Judenchrist' theologisch korrekt?" *Die Zeuge*, 1965, pp. 13ff.; cf. also *Lutherische Rundschau* (Stuttgart), July 1964; *Lutheran World* (Geneva), July 1964; *Lutherische Monatshefte*, March 1967.

7. Gregory Baum, *The Jews and the Gospel: A Re-examination of the New Testament* (1961), p. 244.

8. Cf. Jakob Jocz, *The Covenant: A Theology of Human Destiny* (1968), pp. 99ff. Augustine admitted that before there were Christians there was always a *populus Dei;* cf. Donald F. Winslaw, "The Maccabean Martyrs: Early Christian Attitudes," *Judaism*, Winter 1974, p. 82.

9. On Cyril of Alexandria and his predecessors, see Robert L. Wilken, *Judaism and the Early Christian Mind* (1971).

10. Bernhard Bartmann, *Der Gegensatz zwischen Judentum und Christentum* (1938), p. 74: *"Er weiss sich als absoluter Anfang."*

11. For a discussion of the subject see Jocz, *Covenant*, pp. 238ff.

12. Lactantius, *Divine Institutes* IV.11.

13. Lactantius, *Epitome of the Divine Institutes* 48 (cf. 49).

14. Cf. Jakob Jocz, *A Theology of Election* (1958), pp. 114–26; also the symposium *The New Covenant* (short essays by Hebrew Christians published by the International Hebrew Christian Alliance, 1966).

15. Cf. Johannes Cocceius, *Summa Doctrinae de Foedere et Testamento Dei* (1648).

16. Cf. H. Loewe, "The Ideas of Pharisaism," in *Judaism and Christianity* (1947), vol. II, p. 29.

17. Ibid., p. 40.

18. S. H. Bergman, "The Humanism of the Covenant," *Judaism*, Fall 1957, pp. 340ff.

19. *A Rabbinic Anthology*, ed. C. G. Montefiore and H. Loewe (1938), p. 557.

20. Solomon Zeitlin, "The Temple and Worship," *Jewish Quarterly Review*, 1961, p. 230.

21. Cf. the case of a young Jewish Christian who was rejected as escort for a debutante at Scarsdale (N.Y.) Golf Club (*Life*, 20 January 1961, p. 36; *Toronto Globe and Mail*, 13 January 1961).

22. Cf. Felix Propper, *Zum Leben Berufen—Die Judenchristliche Berufung* (n.d.).

23. Cf. *Der Judenchrist*, ed. Felix Propper, February 1956, pp. 3f.

24. Felix Propper, *Sein oder Nichtsein: Die Existenz des jüdischen Volkes* (n.d.).

25. Karl Barth, *Die Kirchliche Dogmatik* (1948), II/2, pp. 344f.

26. Cf. Jocz, *Theology of Election*, pp. 135ff., 141f.

27. For a fuller discussion of the subject of Israel as the People of the Covenant, see Jocz, *Theology of Election*, pp. 127–55.

28. Barth, *Kirchliche Dogmatik*, II/2, p. 352; see also what he says about "passing away" *(Vergehen, Vergänglichkeit)* as a condition for life (pp. 286f.).

29. "Was du ererbt von deinen Vätern hast Erwerb es, um es zu besitzen."

30. Cf. William Penn, *No Cross—No Crown* (1669).

31. Cf. Martin Buber, *Die Stunde und die Erkenntnis* (1936), p. 153; also Shalom Ben-Chorin, *Die Christus-Frage an den Juden* (1941), p. 24.

32. David Berger and Michael Wyschogrod, *Jews and Jewish Christianity* (1978), pp. 13, 61, 65. They concede, however, honesty of conviction on the part of Jewish Christians. This is a departure from traditional Jewish apologetics.

33. Pinchas Sadeh, *Life as a Parable* (1966), pp. 117–21, 138, 142, 180.

34. Helmut Gollwitzer, Rolf Rendtorff, and Nathan P. Levinson, *Thema: Juden–Christen–Israel* (1978), pp. 53, 56ff., 94ff.

NOTES TO CHAPTER 11

1. Sanford Seltzer, *Jews and Non-Jews Falling in Love* (1976), p. 35.

2. Ibid., p. 26.

3. Ibid., pp. 30f.

4. Samuel S. Cohon, *What We Jews Believe and A Guide to Jewish Practice* (1971), p. 70.

5. Theodore Bikel, in *Jewish Heritage*, Summer 1962, p. 41.

6. Cf. "Karaites," *Encyclopedia of Jewish Religion*, ed. R. Y. Zwi Werblowsky and G. Wigoder (1965): "The most striking difference between rabbinic Judaism and Karaism is the absence of 'rabbinic' custom."

7. Abraham S. Besicovitch, in *The Jewish Chronicle*, 24 February 1950. Karaites acknowledge the Pentateuch only and reject the Talmud.

8. Jacob Neusner, *Aphrahat and Judaism: The Jewish-Christian Argument in Fourth-century Iran* (1971).

9. Samson H. Levey, "The Best Kept Secret of Rabbinic Tradition," *Judaism*, 1972, pp. 462ff.

10. On the subject see Jakob Jocz, *The Jewish People and Jesus Christ* (1949), pp. 171ff. Shlomo Pines purports to have discovered a "new source" which throws light upon an early Hebrew Christian sect. Apparently the sect was opposed to the catholic church and to Paul. This document is described as embedded in a chapter of a Muslim anti-Christian polemic written in Arabic. Cf. *The Jewish Christians in the First Century of Christianity According to a New Source* (1969); also *Israel Academy of Sciences and Humanities*, vol. II, no. 13. For a discussion of the document see David Flüsser, "Die Christenheit nach dem Apostelkonzil," in *Antijudaismus im Neuen Testament?* (1967), pp. 66ff.

11. On *birkat ha-minim* see Jocz, *Jewish People*, pp. 51ff.

12. Cf. Walter Bauer, *Orthodoxy and Heresy in Earliest Christianity* (1971), pp. 259, 261, 267, 270f.; cf. also the Appendix by Georg Stecker, "On the Problem of Jewish Christianity," ibid., pp. 241ff.

13. Jacob Z. Lauterbach (*Rabbinic Essays* [1951], p. 482) admits that the shortening of Yeshua to Yeshu is an intentional mutilation, though he denies that it was originally meant to be so. It was only later that the name *Yeshu* was regarded as an abbreviation of a curse; cf. Jocz, *Jewish People*, pp. 59, 337 n.288. Pinchas E. Lapide explains that to call Jesus Yeshu "is both historically and philosophically correct and also corresponds to the contemporary usage in Israel for the name of Jesus" ("Jesus in Israeli School-books," *Journal of Ecumenical Studies*, Summer 1973, pp. 516f.). We notice, however, that the *Encyclopedia of Jewish Religion* avoids the name *Yeshu*—and for good reason.

14. Jacob Katz, *Exclusiveness and Tolerance: Studies in Jewish-Gentile Relations in Medieval and Modern Times* (1961), pp. 72ff.

15. Ibid., p. 162.

16. Ibid., p. 76.

17. Ibid., p. 149.

18. Ibid., pp. 136f.

19. Ibid., p. 168.

20. Ignaz Maybaum, *Trialogue Between Jew, Christian, and Muslim* (1973), pp. 155, 169.

21. Jacob Katz, "Judaism and Christianity Against the Background of Modern Secularism," *Judaism*, Summer 1968, pp. 299ff.

22. Arthur A. Chiel, "Judah Monis, The Harvard Convert," *Judaism*, Spring 1974, pp. 228ff.

23. Samuel Sandmel, *We Jews and You Christians: An Inquiry into Attitude* (1967), p. 99.

24. Quoted by Herbert Weiner, in "Christian Schools and Israeli Children," *Commentary*, July 1964, pp. 39ff.

25. Cf. *Jerusalem Post Weekly*, 4 July 1962, which contains Philip Gillon's interview with Zwi Werblowsky.

26. Penal Code Amendment Law No. 1313 of 23.11.1977 ("Enticement to Change of Religion"). In translation the text of the law reads:

> 1. GIVING OF "BONUSES" AS ENTICEMENT TO CHANGE OF RELIGION. He who gives, or promises to give money, an equivalent [of money], or another benefit in order to entice a person to change his religion, or in order to entice a person to bring about the change of another's religion, the sentence due to him is [that of] five years imprisonment, or a fine of 50,000 Israeli pounds.
>
> 2. RECEIVING OF "BONUSES" IN EXCHANGE FOR A CHANGE OF RELIGION. He who receives, or agrees to receive money, an equivalent [of money], or a benefit in exchange for a promise to change his religion, or to bring about the change of another's religion, the sentence due to him is [that of] three years imprisonment, or a fine of 30,000 Israeli pounds. [United Christian Council in Israel, Newsletter, 1978, no. 1]

27. *Jerusalem Post*, 31 January 1978, p. 12.

28. For the text see the Newsletter of the Committee on the Church and the Jewish People (World Council of Churches), April 1978, p. 7.

29. *Jerusalem Post*, 20 December 1977.

30. *The Canadian Churchman*, April 1978, pp. 6f.

31. I. J. Singer, "Converts," *Commentary*, December 1964, pp. 46ff.

32. Chaim Lieberman, who wrote a scurrilous book against Sholem Asch, reviewed the present author's monograph *The Jewish People and Jesus Christ* in the Yiddish daily *Forward* (26 January 1951) under the heading "Miserable and Lonely Souls." Each time he mentions the author's name he adds the epithet *meshummad* and goes out of his way to repeat it as frequently as possible. What he says of the book has no resemblance to fact. But Chaim Lieberman is not concerned with truth when it is a matter of maligning Jewish Christians.

33. "Asch, Sholem," in *Encyclopedia Judaica*.

34. Chaim Lieberman, *The Christianity of Sholem Asch: An Appraisal from the Jewish Viewpoint* (1953).

35. Samuel Sandmel, *We Jews and Jesus* (1965), p. 117 n.39.

36. Ibid., pp. 102f.

37. Ibid., p. 91.

38. Monford Harris tells how "the twentieth century meshummad Henri Bergson . . . stood as an old, frail man in line to register with his fellow Jews during the Nazi rule in France, despite the fact that the Nazis had granted him amnesty" (*Judaism*, Spring 1959, p. 111).

39. Norman Cousins, "The Jewishness of Jesus," *American Judaism*, vol. X, no. 1, 1960, p. 36.

40. Sholem Asch, *One Destiny: An Epistle to Christians* (1945), p. 5.

41. Ibid., p. 9.

42. Moshe Adler, "Alienation and Jewish Jesus-Freaks, *Judaism*, Summer 1974, pp. 287ff.

43. *Hebrew Christian Quarterly*, Autumn 1950, pp. 69, 72.

44. *Hebrew Christian Quarterly*, Winter 1975, p. 160.

45. David Shahar, *The Palace of Shattered Vessels: A Voyage to Ur of the Chaldees* (English translation, 1975); cf. *Jerusalem Quarterly*, Winter 1978, p. 43.

46. Harry Joshua Stern, *Entrusted with Spiritual Leadership* (1961), p. 62.

47. "Minutes of the First Hebrew Christian Conference of the United States" (July 28–30, 1903), pp. 43, 51.

48. "When the Wall Is Fallen," *Atlantic Monthly*, February 1945, pp. 91ff. (anonymous).

49. Victor Gollancz, *My Dear Timothy* (1952), p. 399; cf. idem, *More for Timothy* (1953), pp. 73, 77.

50. Joseph Fletcher, *Situation Ethics* (1966), p. 74. For a similar exchange—the case of a Jewess whose place was taken by Elizabeth Pilenko, a Russian emigré—see *The Bridge*, ed. John M. Oesterreicher (1958), vol. III, p. 268 n.337.

51. Arthur W. Kac, "Present-Day Jewish Attitude to the Messianic Movement of Jesus," *American Hebrew Christian;* see also "The Jesus Revolution," *Time*, 21 June 1971.

52. "Do We Believe? A Record of Great Correspondence in *The Daily Telegraph*, Oct.-Nov.-Dec. 1904," p. 129.

53. Frederick J. Forell, "Why Do Jews Become Christians?" *Hebrew Christian Quarterly*, Spring 1966, pp. 25ff.

54. John C. Trever, *The Untold Story of Qumran* (n.d.), pp. 161ff.

55. Geza Vermes, *The Dead Sea Scrolls in English* (1962), p. 14.

56. Cf. Hans Küng, *On Being a Christian* (English translation, 1976), pp. 256ff.

NOTES TO CHAPTER 12

1. Adolf von Harnack, *Texte und Untersuchungen* XXXIX (1913), p. 92 (*Judentum und Judenchristentum in Justins Dialog mit Trypho*).

2. Cf. Frank W. Beare, "The Mission of the Disciples and the Mission Charge: Matthew 10 and Parallels," *Journal of Biblical Literature*, vol. LXXXIX, part I (1970).

3. For the controversy with Christians on the meaning of texts, see Samuel E. Karff, "Aggadah—The Language of Jewish 'God-Talk,' " *Judaism*, Spring 1970, pp. 162f.

4. Stephen Neill, *Salvation Tomorrow: The Originality of Jesus Christ and the World's Religions* (1976), p. 38.

5. Ibid., p. 36.

6. Cited by Frank Talmage, in "Christianity and the Jewish People," *Commentary*, February 1975, p. 57.

7. Cf. *Theologische Rundschau*, vol. II (1959), pp. 113f.

8. Ferdinand Ebner, *Das Wort und die geistigen Realitäten* (1921); cf. also Jakob Jocz, "The Jewish-Christian Dialogue: A Theological Assessment," *Gordon Review*, Fall 1967, p. 190.

9. Martin Buber, *Between Man and Man* (1947), p. 97.

10. Ervin Valyi Nagy and Heinrich Ott, *Church as Dialogue* (English translation, 1969), p. 52; cf. also Jakob Jocz, "Mission as Propaganda or Mission as Proclamation?" *Hebrew Christian Quarterly*, Summer 1978, pp. 79ff.

11. Lawrence D. Folkemer, "Dialogue and Proclamation," *Journal of Ecumenical Studies*, Summer 1976, pp. 433, 436.

12. Cf. Jakob Jocz, *A Theology of Election* (1958), p. 39; also Arthur Herzberg, "The Secularity of Israel's Election," *Judaism*, Fall 1964.

13. *Jewish Chronicle*, 15 August 1958, p. 5.

14. Mordecai Gotfried, "The Blessing" (Yiddish), *Daily Hebrew Journal* (Toronto), 3 November 1958.

15. Colin O'Grady, *The Church in Catholic Theology: Dialogue with Karl Barth* (1969), pp. 48ff.; cf. Wolfgang Trilling, *Das Wahre Israel: Studien zur Theologie des Matthäus Evangeliums* (1958), p. 76.

16. For a theology of the unbroken Covenant, see Jakob Jocz, *The Covenant: A Theology of Human Destiny* (1968), pp. 268ff.

17. *Documents of Vatican II* (English translation ed. Joseph Gallagher, 1966), p. 665 and notes.

18. John M. Oesterreicher, *The Rediscovery of Judaism* (1971), p. 39.

19. Ibid., pp. 56f.

20. Henry Siegman, "Ten Years of Catholic-Jewish Relations: A Reassessment," *Encounter Today*, 1976, pp. 78ff.

21. A copy of Rabbi Feinberg's statement in reply to the Canadian Council of Churches (16 January 1957) is in the possession of the author.

22. Ignaz Maybaum, *Man and Catastrophe* (1941), pp. 155ff. Cf. *The Jewish Mission* (1949), p. 156: "With the Jew as God's Servant before it, Christianity must understand that here ends its mission to baptize all men. The Christian is a baptized heathen and as such no longer a heathen. But a baptized Jew uncannily contradicts both reason and faith."

23. Reinhold Niebuhr, *Pious and Secular America* (1958). A leading American rabbi remarked on Niebuhr's dictum: "If I were a Christian, I could not say what Niebuhr said" (in *Jews and Christians: Preparation for Dialogue*, ed. George A. F. Knight [1965], p. 172). For a Jewish-Christian's criticism of Niebuhr, see Victor Buksbazen, "Niebuhr and the Gospel for the Jews," *Christianity Today*, 8 December 1958.

24. Paul Tillich, "The Theology of Missions," *Christianity and Crisis*, 4 April 1955.

25. Cf. *Christianity Today*, 7 January 1966, p. 47; also Frederick C. Grant, *Ancient Judaism and the New Testament* (1959). Grant advocates giving up all missions to Jews; he would prefer to see "far more men and women converted to the imperishable heart of the Jewish faith."

26. Cf. Karl Barth, *Die Kirchliche Dogmatik* (1948), IV/3/2, pp. 877f. Barth's feud

with the Synagogue does not make him an anti-Semite. His attitude to the Jewish people is not affected by his view of Judaism: "In order to be chosen we must, for good or ill, either be Jews or else be heart and soul on the side of the Jews" (quoted in *The Death of Dialogue and Beyond*, ed. S. Seltzer and Max L. Stackhouse [1969], p. 67). Prof. Frank E. Talmage, *Disputation and Dialogue: Readings in the Jewish-Christian Encounter* (1975), p. 38, is totally wrong in accusing Barth of anti-Semitism. Talmage completely misunderstands and therefore misrepresents the Barthian position regarding Israel.

27. Marcus Barth, *The Broken Wall: A Study of Ephesians* (1959), pp. 133f.

28. Robert T. Osborn, "A Christian Mission to the Jews?" *Christian Century*, 28 November 1973, pp. 1168ff.

29. It seems to us that Osborn's insistence that the "Jew" is by definition a "Jesus-rejector" is equally vulnerable to the demon of anti-Semitism, perhaps even more so.

30. Naomi Bluestone, "Exodus from Eden: One Woman's Experience," *Judaism*, Winter 1974, pp. 96ff. For Pinchas Sadeh's views on Judaism see *Unease in Zion*, ed. Ehud Ben Ezer (1974), pp. 252ff.

31. For the text see *Missiology: An International Review*, October 1976; or Newsletter of the Committee on the Church and the Jewish People (World Council of Churches), March 1977, p. 9.

32. William Sanford LaSor, "The Conversion of Jews," *The Reformed Journal*, November 1976; also Newsletter of the Committee on the Church and the Jewish People (WCC), March 1977, pp. 10ff.

33. Cf. Newsletter of the Committee on the Church and the Jewish People (WCC), November 1978, p. 21.

34. Newsletter of the Committee on the Church and the Jewish People (WCC), June 1977; cf. "Die Mission und das Zeugnis der Kirche," *Judaica*, June 1977, p. 52. Not all Roman Catholics would go as far as Fr. Federici. Paul J. Kirsch does not exclude "witnessing," which he distinguishes from proselytizing. To Kirsch witnessing means "describing one's own beliefs and the experiences on which they rest." But he sees "no need to convert the Jews to Christianity; they are already with the Father" (*We Christians and Jews* [1975], pp. 95, 107).

35. Louis Jacobs, *What Does Judaism Say About . . . .?* (1975), pp. 85, 87.

36. A. A. Cohen, *The Myth of the Judeo-Christian Tradition* (1970), pp. 35, 170.

37. Ignaz Maybaum, *Jewish Experience* (1960), pp. 164, 167.

38. Joseph B. Soloveitchik, "Confrontation," *Tradition*, Spring–Summer 1964, pp. 22ff. See also, appended to the article, the February 1964 statement by the Rabbinical Council of America.

39. Cf. *Judaism Despite Christianity*, ed. Eugen Rosenstock-Huessy (1969), p. 22.

40. Cf. *Jewish-Christian Relations* (the proceedings of a symposium held at St. Mary's College, February 21–22, 1965), p. 110.

41. Ibid., p. 73.

42. William Hamilton, in *Towards a New Christianity*, ed. Thomas J. J. Altizer (1967), p. 278 n.18.

43. *The Myth of God Incarnate*, ed. John Hick (1977), pp. 98, 141ff., 178ff.; cf. Rosemary Ruether, *Faith and Fratricide: The Theological Roots of Anti-Semitism* (1975). It is Ruether's view that the Christian mythology regarding Jews is in need of a theological-Christological revision; cf. *The Ecumenist*, May–June 1975, pp. 60ff. Ruether has reached the acme in her Judaizing attempt when she advises Chris-

tians to accept "the oral Torah as an authentic alternative route by which the biblical past was appropriated and carried on." She advises Christians to learn the Talmud "side by side with the Church Fathers" ("Toward a New Covenantal Theology," in *Disputation and Dialogue*, pp. 325f.).

44. Cf. Uriel Tal, *Christians and Jews in Germany: Religion, Politics, and Ideology in the Second Reich, 1870–1914* (English translation, 1969), pp. 210ff.

45. Abraham Joshua Heschel, "No Religion Is an Island," in *Disputation and Dialogue*, p. 350.

46. Ibid., p. 348.

47. Ibid., p. 355.

48. Cf. Walter Jacob, *Christianity Through Jewish Eyes* (1974), pp. 95, 125, 173, etc.

49. Ibid., p. 6. Cf. Reinhold Mayer, *Judentum und Christentum* (1973), p. 162.

50. Cf. Marcus Barth, "Dialogue Is Not Enough," *Journal of Ecumenical Studies*, 1967, pp. 115–20.

51. Manfred H. Vogel, "The Problem of Dialogue Between Judaism and Christianity," *Journal of Ecumenical Studies*, Winter 1967.

52. Cf. Hans-Joachim Schoeps, *The Jewish-Christian Argument* (English translation, 1963).

53. *The Jews, Views and Counterviews: A Dialogue Between Jean Daniélou and André Chouraqui* (English translation, 1967).

54. Hans Küng and Pinchas Lapide, "Is Jesus a Bond or Barrier? A Jewish-Christian Dialogue," *Journal of Ecumenical Studies*, Summer 1977, pp. 467ff.

55. John S. Spong and Jack D. Spiro, *Dialogue: In Search of Jewish-Christian Understanding* (1975).

56. Cf. the editorial comments in *The Lamp* (Christian Unity Magazine), June 1969.

57. Eugene Fisher, *Faith Without Prejudice* (1977).

NOTES TO CHAPTER 13

1. H. J. Eysenck, *Uses and Abuses of Psychology* (1953), pp. 268, 272.

2. Gordon W. Allport, *Personality and Social Encounter* (1960), p. 213.

3. Eysenck, *Uses and Abuses*, p. 279.

4. Allport, *Personality*, p. 221.

5. Cf. Emil Schürer, *A History of the Jewish People in the Time of Jesus Christ* (English translation, 1961), II/2, pp. 273ff.; also Suetonius, *Lives of the Caesars*, "Claudius" 25.

6. Jacques Maritain, *Antisemitism* (1939), p. 27.

7. A. Roy Eckardt, *Elder and Younger Brothers: The Encounter of Christians and Jews* (1967), pp. 12f.

8. Emmanuel Levinas, *Difficile Liberté* (1963), p. 165; cf. Charles McCollester, "The Philosophy of Emmanuel Levinas," *Judaism*, 1970, pp. 344ff.

9. On the "advantage of the Jew," see Jakob Jocz, in *Jews and Christians: Preparation for Dialogue*, ed. George A. F. Knight (1965), pp. 78ff.

10. Franz Rosenzweig, *Der Stern der Erlösung* (1954), III/2, p. 127: "Der Christ ist ewiger Anfänger; das Vollenden ist nicht seine Sache"; also p. 147: "Denn in jedem Einzelnen, in jeder Seele beginnt es wieder von vorn."

11. Ibid., III/3, pp. 175f., 178.

12. B. Halpern, "From Prejudice to Genocide," *Commentary*, October 1964, p. 84.

13. S. Levin, "The Orphan Syndrome," *Judaism*, Winter 1973, p. 37.

14. Kenneth B. Clark, *Pathos of Power* (1974), pp. 165ff.

15. George Santayana, *Winds of Doctrine and Platonism and the Spiritual Life* (1957), p. 94.

16. Stuart Chase, *The Tyranny of Words* (1950), p. 230.

17. Cf. Sören Kierkegaard, *Einübung im Christentum*, trans. A. Bärthold (1894), pp. 246, 251f.

18. Joseph B. Soloveitchik, "Confrontation," *Tradition*, Spring–Summer 1964, p. 24.

19. Sol Roth, "The Doctrine of Separation," *Judaism*, Summer 1974, pp. 319ff.

20. Harold Lamb, *Tamerlane the Earth Shaker* (1928), p. 169.

21. "Armenia," *Encyclopaedia Britannica* (1942).

22. Cf. C. G. Jung, on *privatio boni*, in *Psychology and Religion* (1958).

23. *Clementine Homilies* XIX.10.

24. Ibid., XII.29.

25. Ibid., XIX.15–17.

26. *A Rabbinic Anthology*, ed. C. G. Montefiore and H. Loewe (1938), p. 63.

27. Ibid., pp. 95–96.

28. Ulrich E. Simon, *A Theology of Auschwitz* (1967). For a review see *Christianity Today*, 8 December 1967, p. 35. Robert E. Willis, a United Presbyterian (U.S.A.), is critical of Simon's book. He calls it unsatisfactory because it is an effort to accommodate the Holocaust "within the framework of Christian categories which themselves require rethinking" ("Christian Theology After Auschwitz," *Journal of Ecumenical Studies*, Fall 1975, pp. 471ff.). Willis accuses Simon of "a kind of Christian false consciousness" and "a persistent lack of sensitivity." This is an unfortunate misrepresentation as Dr. Simon has himself suffered exile, his father perished at Auschwitz, and his brother somewhere in the Soviet Union. For his autobiographical experience as a Christian, see *Sitting in Judgement: 1913-1963* (1978). Emil Fackenheim expressed the hope that one day a Christian writer would compose a legend about Christ's returning to Nazi-occupied Europe (*Christian Century*, 6 May 1970, p. 568). For people like Simon this is not legend but fact.

For the importance Simone Weil attaches to divine and human suffering, see Leslie A. Fiedler, "Simone Weil, Prophet out of Israel," in *Arguments and Doctrines: A Reader of Jewish Thinking in the Aftermath of the Holocaust*, ed. Arthur A. Cohen (1970), pp. 59ff.

29. For a review see *Judaism*, Winter 1974, p. 119.

30. Eliezer Berkovits, "Approaching the Holocaust," *Judaism*, Winter 1973, p. 20.

31. Elliot N. Dorff, "God and the Holocaust," *Judaism*, Winter 1977, pp. 27ff. Eugene B. Borowitz writes: "Any effort to explain the Holocaust would betray the event and our reactions to it . . . . Yet unbelief was equally impossible, because of the moral affirmation inherent in the very protest. We could not speak, but we could not not believe. We could only have a theology of non-non-belief." But this is not his last word. His last word is an affirmation of faith: "We know that God may try us, but He does not entirely abandon us" (*Judaism*, Spring 1968, p. 144).

32. Eliezer Berkovits, *Faith After the Holocaust* (1973).

33. Uriel Tal, *Christians and Jews in Germany: Religion, Politics, and Ideology in the Second Reich, 1870-1914* (1975), pp. 304f.

34. Dietrich Bonhoeffer, *Widerstand und Ergebung* (1966), p. 244: "Nicht der religiöse Akt macht den Christen, sondern das Teilnehmen am Leiden Gottes im weltlichen Leben."

35. Julius Wellhausen, *Einleitung in die drei ersten Evangelien* (1905), p. 113.

36. Translated from the German and printed in *Hebrew Christian Quarterly,* Summer 1964, pp. 40ff. Cf. "The Image of Jesus in Modern Judaism," *Journal of Ecumenical Studies,* Summer 1974, pp. 401ff. This important and lengthy article summarizes the Jewish effort to understand and assess Jesus of Nazareth.

37. Cf. Joachim Jeremias, *Unknown Sayings of Jesus* (1957), p. 49. For Luke 6:5 Codex D reads: "On the same day, seeing a man working on the Sabbath, he said to him, 'Man! If thou knowest what thou doest, thou art blessed. But if thou knowest not, thou art cursed and a transgressor of the Law.'"

38. Shalom Ben-Chorin, *Die Christus-Frage an den Juden* (1941), pp. 18f., 24ff.

39. Jacob Taubes, "Issues Between Judaism and Christianity," in *Arguments and Doctrines,* p. 406.

40. Shalom Ben-Chorin, "Der Messias," in *Jüdischer Glaube* (1975), pp. 277ff.

41. Taubes, "Issues," p. 418.

42. Walter Jacob, "An Assessment of Christianity," *Central Conference of American Rabbis,* Winter 1974, p. 52. The article deals more with Kohler than with Christianity.

43. Samuel Rosenblatt, "The Crucifixion of Jesus from the Standpoint of Pharisaic Law," *Journal of Biblical Literature,* 1956, pp. 315ff.

44. David Noel Freedman, "An Essay on Jewish Christianity," *Journal of Ecumenical Studies,* 1969, pp. 81ff.

45. Cf. Jakob Jocz, *A Theology of Election* (1958), pp. 31ff.

46. Ben Zion Bokser, "Religious Witness in Judaism," *Judaism,* Winter 1977, p. 65.

47. Solomon B. Freehof, in *Conversion to Judaism: A History and Analysis,* ed. David Max Eichhorn (1970), p. 162.

48. Samuel S. Cohon, *What We Jews Believe and A Guide to Jewish Practice* (1971), pp. 21, 63, 70.

49. W. Günther Plaut, *The Case for the Chosen People* (1965), pp. 28, 85, 91, 143, 144.

50. Ibid., p. 147.

51. W. Günther Plaut, *Your Neighbour the Jew* (1967), p. 82.

52. Jacob Katz, "Judaism and Christianity Against the Background of Modern Secularism," *Judaism,* Summer 1968, pp. 313–15.

53. Eugene B. Borowitz, "Hope Jewish and Secular," *Judaism,* Spring 1968, p. 134.

54. Ibid., p. 142.

55. Cf. Jakob Jocz, *The Jewish People and Jesus Christ* (1949), pp. 275ff.

56. *Judaism Despite Christianity,* ed. Eugen Rosenstock-Huessy (1969), p. 57.

57. Borowitz, "Hope Jewish," p. 136f.

58. *Judaism Despite Christianity,* pp. 99, 123, 131.

59. Karl Barth, *Die Kirchliche Dogmatik* (1948), IV/3/2, p. 878.

60. Ibid., II/1, pp. 156f.

61. Marcus Barth, in *Journal of Ecumenical Studies,* 1965, p. 383. Cf. Albert H.

Friedländer, *Leo Baeck: Leben und Lehre* (1973), p. 19.

62. Marcus Barth, *Ephesians,* vol. II (1974).

63. Jakob Jocz, " 'Foreign' Missions as a Theological Corrective," *International Review of Missions,* July 1946, p. 258; cf. "Confessing Christ Today" (statement of the World Council of Churches—Nairobi, 1975): "We need to recover the sense of urgency."

64. Hans Urs von Balthasar, *Martin Buber and Christianity: A Dialogue Between Israel and the Church* (English translation, 1961), p. 101.

65. Sholom A. Singer, "Faith and Law," *Judaism,* Winter 1973, p. 41.

66. Stephen Neill, *Salvation Tomorrow: The Originality of Jesus Christ and the World's Religions* (1973), p. 120.

67. Singer, "Faith and Law," p. 44.

68. Jacob B. Agus, "Judaism and the New Testament," *Journal of Ecumenical Studies,* Fall 1976, pp. 598, 603.

69. Louis Jacobs, *Principles of the Jewish Faith* (1964), p. 85.

70. Walter Jacob, "Claude G. Montefiore's Reappraisal of Christianity," *Judaism,* Autumn 1970, pp. 328ff.

71. C. G. Montefiore, *Some Elements of the Religious Teaching of Jesus According to the Synoptic Gospels* (1910), p. 5.

72. Henry Siegman, "Dialogue with Christians: A Jewish Dilemma," *Judaism,* Winter 1971, pp. 93ff.

73. Ignaz Maybaum, *Trialogue Between Jew, Christian, and Muslim* (1973), pp. 164f.

74. Neill, *Salvation Tomorrow,* p. 139.

75. Cf. Bokser, "Religious Witness in Judaism."

76. Foreword to Ben Zion Bokser, *Judaism and the Christian Predicament* (1967).

77. Neill, *Salvation Tomorrow,* p. 58.

78. James Parkes, *The Conflict of the Church and the Synagogue* (1961), pp. 200f.

79. Sören Kierkegaard, *Acht ausgewählte christliche Reden* (1901), pp. 17f.

NOTES TO THE EPILOGUE

1. *Time,* 7 May 1979, p. 72.

2. Hershel J. Matt, "How Shall a Believing Jew View Christianity?" in *Judaism,* Fall 1975, pp. 391–405.

3. Theodore N. Lewis, in *Midstream,* May 1979, p. 47.

4. Cf. Harry Austryn Wolfson, "How Jews Will Reclaim Jesus," *Jewish Institute Quarterly,* March 1925, p. 70.

5. David Flüsser, "A New Sensitivity in Judaism and the Christian Message," *Harvard Theological Review,* 1968, pp. 107ff.; cf. H. Cazelles, "Our Two Fidelities: A Catholic Point of View about Judaism," in *Cross Currents,* Fall 1964, pp. 441–50.

6. David Rausch, in *Midstream,* May 1979, p. 40.

7. Frederick C. Grant, *Ancient Judaism and the New Testament* (1959), p. 150.

8. George Hedley, *The Christian Heritage in America* (1947), p. 3.

9. Yehoshafat Harkabi, in *Midstream,* May 1979, p. 11.

10. Cf. *Unease in Zion,* ed. Ehud Ben Ezer (1974).

11. Cf. Yonatan Ratosh, "The New Hebrew Nation (The Canaanite Outlook)," in *Unease in Zion.*

12. Cf. Yeshayahu Leibowitz, "Jewish Identity and Israeli Silence," in *Unease in Zion*.

13. Cf. Ferdynand Zweig, "The Figure of Jesus on the Israeli Horizon," *The Sword and the Harp* (1969).

14. Ibid., p. 219.

15. Ibid., p. 221.

16. Ibid., p. 226.

Bibliography

Monographs

Abel, Ernest L. *The Roots of Anti-Semitism* (1975).

Abramov, S. Zalman. *Perpetual Dilemma: Jewish Religion in the Jewish State* (1976).

Adam, H. *History of the Jews* (1887).

Adler, H. G. *Der verwaltete Mensch: Studien zur Deportation der Juden aus Deutschland* (1974).

———. *Theresienstadt 1941–1945* (1955).

Allport, Gordon W. *Personality and Social Encounter* (1960).

Arendt, Hannah. *Origins of Totalitarianism* (1958).

Aron, Robert. *The Jewish Jesus* (English translation, 1971).

Arrowsmith, John. "The Covenant—Avenging Sword Brandished" (1643).

Asch, Sholem. *Mary* (1949).

———. *The Nazarene* (1939).

———. *One Destiny: An Epistle to Christians* (1945).

Augustine. *Tractatus Adversus Judaeos.*

Balthasar, Hans Urs von. *Martin Buber and Christianity: A Dialogue Between Israel and the Church* (English translation, 1961).

Barth, Karl. *Die Kirchliche Dogmatik* (1948).

Barth, Marcus. *The Broken Wall: A Study of Ephesians* (1959).

———. *Ephesians,* vol. II (1974).

Bartmann, Bernard. *Der Gegensatz zwischen Judentum und Christentum* (1938).

Bauer, Walter. *Orthodoxy and Heresy in Earliest Christianity* (1971).

Baum, Gregory. *The Jews and the Gospel: A re-examination of the New Testament* (1961).

Bea, Augustin. *The Church and the Jewish People* (1966).

Ben-Chorin, Shalom. *Die Christus-Frage an den Juden* (1941).

———. *Jüdischer Glaube* (1975).

Berdyaev, Nicolas. *Christianity and Anti-Semitism* (English translation, 1954).

Berenbaum, Michael. *The Vision of the Void: Theological Reflections on the Works of Elie Wiesel* (1979).

Berkovits, Eliezer. *Faith After the Holocaust* (1973).

Bethge, Eberhard. *Dietrich Bonhoeffer, Theologe–Christ–Zeitgenosse* (1967).

249

Bishop, Claire Huchet. *How Catholics Look at Jews* (1974).
Black, Matthew. *The Scrolls and Christian Origins* (1961).
Boettner, Loraine. *The Millennium* (1958).
Bonhoeffer, Emmi. *Auschwitz Trials: Letters from an Eyewitness* (English translation, 1967).
_____. *Widerstand und Ergebung* (1966).
Borchsenius, Paul. *Two Ways to God* (English translation, 1968).
Bowker, John. *Jesus and the Pharisees* (1973).
Buber, Martin. *Between Man and Man* (1947).
_____. *Die Stunde und die Erkenntnis* (1936).
Byfield, Richard. "Zion's Answer to the Nation's Ambassadors" (1645).

Calvin, John. *Institutes of the Christian Religion.*
Catchpole, David R. *The Trial of Jesus: A Study in the Gospels and Jewish Historiography from 1770 to the Present Day* (1971).
Chase, Stuart. *The Tyranny of Words* (1950).
Choraqui, André Nathan. "Dialogue Between Jean Daniélou and André Choraqui" (English translation, 1967).
Clark, Kenneth B. *Pathos of Power* (1974).
Cocceius, Johannes. *Summa Doctrinae de Foedere et Testamento Dei* (1648).
Cohen, A. A. *The Myth of the Judeo-Christian Tradition* (1970).
_____. *The Natural and the Supernatural Jew* (1963).
Cohen, Jack J. *Case for Religious Naturalism* (1958).
Cohen, Jacques. *The Deicides: Analysis of the Life of Jesus* (English translation, 1872).
Cohn, Haim H. *The Trial and Death of Jesus* (English translation, 1971).
Cohon, Samuel S. *What We Jews Believe and A Guide to Jewish Practice* (1971).
Commodianus. *Instructions for Christian Discipline Against the Gods of the Nations.*
Congar, Yves M.-J. *Dialogue Between Christians: Catholic Contributions to Ecumenism* (1966).
Cyprian. Treatise XII: *Testimonies Against the Jews.*

Daane, James. *The Anatomy of Anti-Semitism and Other Essays on Religion and Race* (1965).
Daniélou, Jean. "Dialogue Between Jean Daniélou and André Choraqui" (English translation, 1967).
Davies, Alan T. *Anti-Semitism and the Christian Mind: The Crisis of Conscience After Auschwitz* (1969).
Didascalia Apostolorum (English translation, 1929).
Dietrich, H. D. *Die Schleuse* (1974).
Dimont, Max I. *Jews, God and History* (1962).
Donat, Alexander. *Out of the Whirlwind* (1964).
Donn, F. S. *The Israel Way to Peace* (1957).
Duvernoy, Claude. *Le Prince et le Prophète* (1978).

Ebner, Ferdinand. *Das Wort und die geistigen Realitäten* (1921).

Eckardt, A. Roy. *Elder and Younger Brothers: The Encounter of Christians and Jews* (1967).

―――――. *Your People and My People: The Meeting of Jews and Christians* (1974).

―――――, and Alice Eckardt. *Encounter with Israel: A Challenge to Conscience* (1970).

Eckert, Willehad Paul. *Judenhass* (1964).

Eisendrath, Maurice Nathan. *The Never Failing Stream* (1939).

Eysenck, H. G. *Uses and Abuses of Psychology* (1953).

Fackenheim, Emil L. *God's Presence in History: Jewish Affirmations and Philosophical Reflections* (1970).

Falconi, Carlo. *The Silence of Pius XII* (English translation, 1970).

Filthaut, Theodor. *Israel in Christian Religious Instruction* (English translation, 1965).

Finkel, Asher. *The Pharisees and the Teacher of Nazareth* (1974).

Finn, Elizabeth Anne. *Reminiscences of Mrs. Finn* (1929).

Fisher, Eugene. *Faith Without Prejudice* (1977).

Fishman, Hertzel. *American Protestantism and the Jewish State* (1973).

Flannery, Edward H. *The Anguish of the Jews: Twenty-three Centuries of Anti-Semitism* (1965).

Fleischner, Eva. *Judaism in German Christian Theology Since 1945: Christianity and Israel Considered in Terms of Mission* (1975).

Fletcher, Joseph. *Situation Ethics* (1966).

Flüsser, David. *Jesus* (English translation, 1969).

Fox, G. George. *The Jews, Jesus and Christ* (1953).

Friedman, Philip. *Their Brothers' Keeper* (1957).

Gidney, W. T. *History of the London Society for Promoting Christianity Among the Jews* (1908).

Ginsburg, Christian D. *The Essenes: Their History and Doctrines* (1956).

Glock, Charles Y., and Rodney Stark. *Christian Beliefs and Anti-Semitism* (1966).

Golden, H. *The Case of the Nazarene Reopened* (1948).

Gollancz, Victor. *My Dear Timothy* (1952).

―――――. *More for Timothy* (1953).

Goppelt, Leonhard. *Christentum und Judentum im ersten und zweiten Jahrhundert* (1954).

Gordon, Albert I. *Jews of Suburbia* (1959).

―――――. *The Nature of Conversion* (1967).

Grant, Frederick C. *Ancient Judaism and the New Testament* (1959).

Graves, Robert, and Joshua Podro. *Jesus in Rome* (1957).

―――――. *The Nazarene Gospel* (1955).

Grossmann, Kurt R. *Die unbesungenen Helden: Menschen in Deutschlands dunklen Tagen* (1957).

Hager, Joseph. *Bekhinot historiot (Historical investigation)* (1952).

Halperin, Irving. *Messengers from the Dead: Literature of the Holocaust* (1970).

Harnack, Adolf von. *Texte und Untersuchungen* XXXIX (1913).
Hay, A. I. *There Was a Man of Genius* (1963).
Hedley, George. *The Christian Heritage in America* (1947).
Heer, Friedrich. *God's First Love: Christians and Jews over Two Thousand Years* (English translation, 1970).
Heller, Bernard. *Epistle to an Apostate* (1951).
Heller, Celia. *On the Edge of Destruction: Polish Jews Between Two Wars* (1977).
Herstig, David. *Die Rettung* (1968).
Heufken, Hilgard. *Die Judenfrage im Religionsunterricht* (1965–66).
Hochhuth, Rolf. *Der Stellvertreter* ("The Deputy") (1963).
Huxley, Julian. *Religion Without Revelation* (1957).

Isaac, Jules. *Jesus and Israel* (English translation, 1971).
_____. *The Teaching of Contempt: Christian Roots of Anti-Semitism* (English translation, 1964).
Isorni, Jacques. *Le vrai procès de Jésus* (1967).

Jacob, Walter. *Christianity Through Jewish Eyes* (1974).
Jacobs, Louis. *Principles of the Jewish Faith* (1964).
_____. *What Does Judaism Say About . . . ?* (1975).
Jeremias, Joachim. *Unknown Sayings of Jesus* (1957).
Jocz, Jakob. *The Covenant: A Theology of Human Destiny* (1968).
_____. *The Jewish People and Jesus Christ* (1949).
_____. *The Spiritual History of Israel* (1961).
_____. *A Theology of Election* (1958).
Josephus. *Wars of the Jews.*
Jung, C. G. *Psychology and Religion* (1958).

Kaplan, Mordecai M. *Judaism Without Supernaturalism* (1958).
Katz, Jacob. *Exclusiveness and Tolerance: Studies in Jewish-Gentile Relations in Medieval and Modern Times* (1961).
Kierkegaard, Sören. *Acht ausgewählte christliche Reden* (1901).
_____. *Einübung im Christentum* (1894).
Kirsch, Paul J. *We Christians and Jews* (1975).
Klausner, Joseph. *From Jesus to Paul* (English translation, 1944).
_____. *Jesus of Nazareth* (English translation, 1925).
Kotsuji, Abraham. *From Tokyo to Jerusalem* (1964).
Küng, Hans. *On Being a Christian* (English translation, 1976).
Kupisch, Karl. *Das Volk der Geschichte: Randbemerkungen zur Geschichte der Judenfrage* (1960).

Lactantius. *Divine Institutes.*
_____. *Epitome of the Divine Institutes.*
Lamb, Harold. *Tamerlane the Earth Shaker* (1928).
Lapide, Pinchas. *Ökumene aus Christen und Juden* (1972).
_____. *Three Popes and the Jews* (1967).
Laqueur, Walter. *The Terrible Secret: An Investigation into the Suppression of Information About Hitler's "Final Solution"* (1980).

Larson, Martin A. *The Essene Heritage: The Teacher of the Scrolls and the Gospel of Christ* (1967).

Lauterbach, Jacob Z. *Rabbinic Essays* (1951).

Leboucher, Ferdinand. *The Incredible Mission of Father Benoit* (English translation, 1969).

Lehmann, Johannes. *The Jesus Report: The Rabbi Jesus Revealed by the Dead Sea Scrolls* (English translation, 1971).

Leuner, H. D. *When Compassion Was a Crime* (1966).

Levinas, Emmanuel. *Difficile Liberté* (1963).

Levine, Raphael H. *Two Paths to One God: Judaism and Christianity* (1962).

Lewy, Guenther. *The Catholic Church and Nazi Germany* (1964).

Lieberman, Chaim. *The Christianity of Sholem Asch: An Appraisal from the Jewish Viewpoint* (1953).

Littell, Franklin H. *The Crucifixion of the Jews* (1975).

Long, J. Bruce. *Judaism and the Christian Seminary Curriculum* (1966).

Luther, Martin. *Table Talk.*

M'Neile, Alan H. *The Gospel According to St. Matthew* (1915).

Maritain, Jacques. *Antisemitism* (1939).

Marquardt, Friedrich-Wilhelm. *Die Entdeckung des Judentums für die christliche Theologie: Israel im Denken Barths* (1967).

Marshall, Stephen. "God's Master-piece: A Sermon Tending to Manifest God's Appearing in the Building Up of Sion" (1645).

Maybaum, Ignaz. *The Face of God After Auschwitz* (1965).

———. *Jewish Experience* (1960).

———. *The Jewish Mission* (1949).

———. *Man and Catastrophe* (1941).

———. *Trialogue Between Jew, Christian, and Muslim* (1973).

Mayer, Reinhold. *Judentum und Christentum* (1973).

Montefiore, C. G. *Some Elements of the Religious Teaching of Jesus According to the Synoptic Gospels* (1910).

Nagy, Ervin V., and Heinrich Ott. *Church as Dialogue* (English translation, 1969).

Neher, André. *L'Exil de la Parole: Du Silence Biblique au Silence d'Auschwitz* (1970).

Neill, Stephen. *Salvation Tomorrow: The Originality of Jesus Christ and the World's Religions* (1976).

Neusner, Jacob. *Aphrahat and Judaism: The Jewish-Christian Argument in Fourth-Century Iran* (1971).

———. *From Politics to Piety: The Emergence of Pharisaic Judaism* (1973).

———. *The Masters* (1971).

———. *Rabbinic Traditions About the Pharisees Before A.D. 70*, Part III (1971).

Niebuhr, Reinhold. *Leaves from the Notebook of a Tamed Cynic* (1957).

———. *Pious and Secular America* (1958).

Oesterreicher, John M. *Anatomy of Contempt* (1975).

———. *Ecumenism and the Jews* (1969).

_____. *The Israel of God: Old Testament Roots of the Church's Faith* (1963).

_____. *Der Papst und die Juden* (1962).

_____. *The Rediscovery of Judaism* (1971).

_____. *Under the Vault of the Covenant.*

Origen. *Contra Celsum.*

Parkes, James. *The Conflict of the Church and the Synagogue* (1961).

_____. *Foundations of Judaism and Christianity* (1960).

_____. *Jews, Christians and the World of Tomorrow* (1969).

_____. *Prelude to Dialogue: Jewish-Christian Relationships* (1969).

Penn, William. *No Cross—No Crown* (1669).

Philippson, Ludwig. *Haben wirklich die Juden Jesum gekreuzigt?* (1876).

Pines, Shlomo. *The Jewish Christians in the First Century of Christianity According to a New Source* (1969).

Plack, Arno. *Die Gesellschaft und das Böse* (1970).

Plaut, W. Günther. *The Case for the Chosen People* (1965).

_____. *Your Neighbour the Jew* (1975).

Potter, Charles Francis. *The Lost Years of Jesus Revealed* (1958).

Propper, Felix. *Sein oder Nichtsein: Die Existenz des jüdischen Volkes* (n.d.).

_____. *Zum Leben Berufen—Die Judenchristliche Berufung* (n.d.).

Ramati, Alexander. *While the Pope Kept Silent* (1978).

Reitlinger, Gerald. *The Final Solution: The Attempt to Exterminate the Jews of Europe, 1939–1945* (1953).

Rhodes, Anthony. *The Vatican in the Age of the Dictators: 1922–1945* (1973).

Ringelbaum, Emmanuel. *Notes from the Warsaw Ghetto* (English translation, 1958).

Rosenzweig, Franz. *Der Stern der Erlösung* (1954).

Rubenstein, Richard L. *After Auschwitz* (1960).

Ruether, Rosemary. *Faith and Fratricide: The Theological Roots of Anti-Semitism* (1975).

Runes, Dagobert D. *The Jew and the Cross* (1965).

Russell, Lord. *Scourge of the Swastika* (1954).

_____. *The Trial of Adolf Eichmann* (1962).

Sachar, Howard M. *The Course of Modern Jewish History* (1958).

Sachs, Nelly. *O the Chimneys: Selected Poems* (English translation, 1967).

_____. *The Seeker and Other Poems* (English translation, 1970).

Sadeh, Pinchas. *Life as a Parable* (1966).

Sandmel, Samuel. *The Genius of Paul* (1958).

_____. *Jewish Understanding of the New Testament* (1957).

_____. *We Jews and Jesus* (1965).

_____. *We Jews and You Christians: An Inquiry into Attitude* (1967).

Santayana, George. *Winds of Doctrine and Platonism and the Spiritual Life* (1957).

Schmidt, Dietrich. *Pastor Niemöller* (English translation, 1959).

Schoeps, Hans-Joachim. *The Jewish-Christian Argument* (English translation, 1963).

————. *Judisch-Christliches Religionsgespräch* (1949).
Schürer, Emil. *A History of the Jewish People in the Time of Jesus Christ* (English translation, 1961).
Sedgewicke, William. "Zion's Deliverance and Her Friends' Duty: The Grounds of Expecting and Meanes of Procuring Jerusalem's Restoration" (1643).
Seltzer, Sanford. *Jews and Non-Jews Falling in Love* (1976).
Selznick, Gertrude J., and Stephen Steinberg. *The Tenacity of Prejudice: Anti-Semitism in Contemporary America* (1969).
Shahar, David. *The Palace of Shattered Vessels: A Voyage to Ur of the Chaldees* (English translation, 1975).
Simon, Ulrich E. *Sitting in Judgement: 1913–1963* (1978).
————. *A Theology of Auschwitz* (1967).
Slonim, Reuben. *Family Quarrel* (1977).
Snoek, Johan. *The Grey Book* (1970).
Sokolow, Nahum. *History of Zionism* (1919).
Spong, John Shelby, and Jack Daniel Spiro. *Dialogue: In Search of Jewish-Christian Understanding* (1975).
Stendahl, Krister. *Paul Among Jews and Gentiles* (1976).
Stern, Harry Joshua. *Entrusted with Spiritual Leadership* (1961).
Stern, Karl. *Pillar of Fire* (1951).
Sulzbach, Walter. *Die Zwei Wurzeln und Formen des Judenhasses* (1959).
Szajkowski, Zosa. *An Illustrated Sourcebook on the Holocaust* (1976).

Tal, Uriel. *Christians and Jews in Germany: Religion, Politics and Ideology in the Second Reich, 1870–1914* (English translation, 1969).
Tasker, R. V. G. *The Greek New Testament* (1964).
Toynbee, Arnold J. *A Study of History*, vol. 3 (1935), vol. 12 (1961).
Trever, John C. *The Untold Story of Qumran* (n.d.).
Trevor-Roper, Hugh. *The Rise of the Christian Empire* (1965).
Trilling, Wolfgang. *Das Wahre Israel: Studien zur Theologie des Matthäus Evangeliums* (1958).
Trutwin, W. *Gesetz und Propheten: Lehrbuch zur Offenbarung über Geschichte des Alten Bundes für höhere Schulen* (1967).

Vermes, Geza. *The Dead Sea Scrolls in English* (1962).
————. *Jesus the Jew: A Historian's Reading of the Gospels* (1973).
Vrba, Rudolf, and Alan Bestic. *I Cannot Forgive* (1964).

Wellhausen, Julius. *Einleitung in die drei ersten Evangelien* (1905).
Wiesel, Elie. *Night* (1960).
————. *One Generation After* (English translation, 1972).
————. "The Trial of God" (1979).
Wigoder, Deborah. *Hope in My House* (1966).
Wilken, Robert L. *Judaism and the Early Christian Mind* (1971).
Williams, A. Lukyn. *Adversus Judaeos* (1935).
Winter, Paul. *The Trial of Jesus* (1961).
Wyschogrod, Michael, and David Berger. *Jews and Jewish Christianity* (1978).

Zahn, Gordon C. *German Catholics and Hitler's War* (1962).
Zimmerli, Walther. *Israel und die Christen* (1964).
Zweig, Ferdynand. *Israel: The Sword and the Harp* (1969).

Encyclopedias

Encyclopedia Britannica (1942).
Encyclopedia Judaica (1971).
The Encyclopedia of the Jewish Religion, ed. R. Y. Zwi Werblowsky and Geoffrey Wigoder (1966).
The Jewish Encyclopedia (1906).

Symposia

Anthology of Holocaust Literature, ed. Jacob Glatstein (1977).
Antijudaismus im Neuen Testament? ed. W. P. Eckert, N. P. Levinson, and Martin Stöhr (1967).
Arguments and Doctrines: A Reader of Jewish Thinking in the Aftermath of the Holocaust, ed. Arthur A. Cohen (1970).
Berichte des SD und der Gestapo über Kirchen und Kirchenvolk in Deutschland, 1934–1944, ed. Heinz Boberach (1971).
The Bridge, vols. I–V, ed. John M. Oesterreicher (1955–1970).
"The Church and the Jewish People"—Newsletters of the World Council of Churches.
The Crucible of Christianity, ed. Arnold Toynbee (1969).
Death of Dialogue and Beyond, ed. Sanford Seltzer and Max L. Stackhouse (1969).
Disputation and Dialogue: Readings in the Jewish-Christian Encounter, ed. Frank E. Talmage (1975).
Documents of Destruction: German Jewry, 1933–1945, ed. Raul Hilberg (1971).
German Church Struggle and the Holocaust, ed. Franklin H. Littell and Hubert G. Locke (1974).
Guide to Published Materials on the Holocaust, ed. Jacob Robinson and Yehuda Bauer, 2 vols. (1970).
Hunter and Hunted: Human History of the Holocaust, ed. Gerd Korman (1973).
Jews and Christians: Preparation for Dialogue, ed. George A. F. Knight (1965).
Judaism Despite Christianity, ed. Eugen Rosenstock-Huessy (1969).
Die Juden und das Evangelium: Ausserungen hervorragender Christen der Gegenwart, ed. G. M. Löwen (1913).
Die Juden und wir Christen, ed. Hans Kallenbach (1950).
Die Katholische Kirche und das Dritte Reich, ed. Albrecht Dieter (1976).
New Delhi Report—World Council of Churches (1961).

Nüremberg Trials, ed. Joe Heydecker and Johannes Leeb (English translation, 1962).

Religiöse Strömungen im Judentum heute (1973).

Speaking of God Today: Jews and Lutherans in Conversation, ed. Marc H. Tanenbaum and Paul D. Opsahl (1974).

The Star and the Cross: Essays on Jewish-Christian Relations, ed. Katharine H. Hargrave (1966).

Thema: Juden–Christen–Israel, ed. Helmut Gollwitzer, Rolf Rendtorff, and Nathan P. Levinson (1978).

Towards a New Christianity, ed. Thomas J. J. Altizer (1967).

Unease in Zion, ed. Ehud Ben Ezer (1974).

Der Ungekündigte Bund: Neue Begegnung von Juden und christlicher Gemeinde, ed. Dietrich Goldschmidt and Hans-Joachim Kraus (1962).

Zionism Reconsidered: The Rejection of Jewish Normalcy, ed. Michael Selzer (1970).

Journals and Miscellaneous Sources

American Judaism (Union of American Congregations)
Canadian Churchman (Anglican Church of Canada)
Canadian Jewish News
Christian Century
Christianity Today
Church Times (Church of England weekly)
Commentary (monthly published by the American Jewish Committee)
Commentary on the Documents of Vatican II, ed. J. Vorgrimler (1967)
Cross Currents
Documents of Vatican II, trans. Joseph Gallagher (1966)
Ecumenist
Freiburger Rundbrief
Harvard Theological Review
Hebrew Christian (International Hebrew Christian Alliance)
Horizon
International Review of Mission (London)
Jerusalem Post Weekly
Jewish Chronicle (weekly, London)
Jewish Heritage
Jewish Quarterly Review (new series)
Journal of Biblical Literature
Journal of Ecumenical Studies
Journal of Jewish Studies (Oxford Centre for Postgraduate Hebrew Studies)
Judaica (Beiträge zum Verständnis des jüdischen Schicksals in Vergangenheit und Gegenwart, Zurich)
Judaism: A Quarterly Journal of Jewish Life and Thought
Der Judenchrist, ed. Felix Propper
Religion in Life
Times Literary Supplement (London)

Toronto Globe and Mail
Tradition: A Journal of Orthodox Jewish Thought
Union Seminary Quarterly
Der Zeuge, ed. H. D. Leuner on behalf of the International Hebrew
   Christian Alliance

Index of Subjects

Absence of God, 30
Adiabene, 153
Adversus Judaeos, 132–33
Alexandria, 187
American churches, 70
l'Amitié-Chrétienne, 40
Am Yisrael ḥai, 35
Anti-Defamation League, 48, 187
Antioch, 147, 187
Anti-Semitism, 36, 41, 46–48, 50, 54–55, 59–61, 67, 70, 72–73, 75–77, 87, 89–92, 95–97, 132, 176, 181, 186–92, 195–96, 224 n.46, 231 n.63, 243 n.26, n.29
Apologia, 49, 58
Arabs, 215
Armenians, 192
Assimilation, 209, 212
Athanasian Creed, 86
Auschwitz, 7, 13–26, 93, 172, 192–96, 198, 201, 218 n.10, 245 n.28
Austria, 48

Baptism, 154–55, 242 n.22
Barmen Declarations (1934), 37, 222 n.3
Barnabas, 124, 138, 147
Bekenntniskirche. See Confessional Church
Belsen, 166
Belzec, 16
Birkat ha-minim (malediction on heretics), 154, 225 n.5, 239 n.11
Birkenau, 16–17, 26
"Bonuses," 158, 240 n.26
Brotherhood, 45
Buchenwald, 83
Bulan, King of the Lower Volga, 127

Bultmannian school, 169

Canaanite philosophy, 216
Chelmno, 16
Christian answer regarding Jesus, 102
Christian influence, 42, 50
Christian-Israel Friendship League, 136
Christianity, 45, 47–51, 56, 62, 67, 69, 82–83, 85–91, 96, 99–100, 103–04, 108–13, 116, 119–21, 124–25, 137–38, 143, 155–56, 162, 164–67, 175, 178–81, 188–91, 196–203, 206–10, 212, 230 n.50, 233 n.16
Christian Jews' Patriotic Alliance, 163
Christian witness, 171, 204–05, 207–10, 243 n.34
Christocentricity, 86
Christology, 60–62, 84–86, 91, 100, 103, 110, 132, 180–81, 232 n.2, 243 n.43
Church, 9, 11, 35–89, 108, 119, 121–25, 131–36, 143–46, 148, 154, 169, 172–73, 179–80, 184, 188–89, 195–96, 198–201, 204–08, 212, 215
Church fathers, 45, 54, 132, 145, 224 n.2
Church in Germany, 64–68, 227 nn.24–25
Clementine Homilies, 193, 245 nn.23–25
Codex D, 246 n.37
Colloquium on Judaism and Christianity (1966), 183
Commission for Religious Relations with Jews, 78
Commission on World Mission (Lutheran World Federation), 74
Committee on the Church and the Jewish People, 76–77

Communism, 65
Concentration camps in Poland, 16. *See also* Auschwitz; Treblinka
Confessional Church, 36, 65–67, 71
Continuity, 100, 232 n.75
Conversion, 152–67, 172–77, 204, 208–09, 213
Council of Chalcedon, 102
Council of Constantinople, 102
Council of Nicea, 102
Covenant, 24–25, 31–32, 52, 54, 59–60, 76, 81, 86–90, 98, 123, 130–31, 133, 137, 144–46, 173, 195, 202, 236 n.18, 242 n.16
Crucifixion, 57–62, 71, 74, 76, 82–83, 94, 112

Dachau, 39
Dead Sea Scrolls (Qumran literature), 9, 107–08, 115, 116, 199, 233 n.13, n.25
Decalogue, 145
"Declaration on the Jewish People," 45, 63
"Declaration on the Non-Christian Religions," 46
Deicide, 47, 55–60, 62, 71, 83, 188, 223 n.39
Denmark, 39
Deportations, 16–22
Despair, 30
Deutscher Evangelischer Ausschuss für Dienst an Israel, 75
Dialogue, 10–11, 74, 77, 83, 86, 88–89, 91–92, 98, 168–85, 203–05, 208
Diaspora, 9, 52, 96–97, 119, 153, 187
Didascalia Apostolorum, 44, 223 n.30
Discrimination, legal, 225 n.6
The Disputation, 103–04
"Document on the Old Testament" (Vatican II), 46
Dutch Reformed Church, 88

Eastern Churches, 77
Ecumenism, 61, 97–98, 100–01, 178
Edessa, 153
Eisenach Institute, 67
Election, 79, 89, 148–50, 172, 202, 236 n.16
Encyclopedia Judaica, 134, 160

Essene fragments, 111
Essenes, 107–09, 111, 153, 233 n.13, n.16
European Lutheran Commission on the Church and the Jewish People, 158
Euthanasia, 51
Evangelical Church of Germany, Synod of the, 72
Even Shushan, 164
Evil, 192–95

Faith, 23–25, 31–34, 52, 89, 91, 121, 126, 132, 138, 171, 180–85, 194, 196, 220 n.8, 245 n.31; crisis of, 28; and Law, 205–06
"Fiddler on the Roof," 142
Final Solution, 13, 22, 35
Finland, 39
Forgiveness, 194
Forward, 159
France, 48
Freiburger Rundbrief, 39, 231 n.65
Fuller Theological Seminary Statement on Jewish-Christian Relations, 177

Gamaliel, 198
Gangsterism, 221 n.28
Gas ovens, 16–17, 219 nn.17–18
Gentile converts to Judaism, 127
Gentiles, 79, 87, 89–90, 122–23, 126, 128–29, 131, 137, 145, 147–48, 156, 162, 172, 175–76, 187, 189, 198, 200, 204, 212, 213–14
"German Christian" movement, 144, 145
German Christian thought, 231 n.68
German-Jewish Alliance, 14
Germany, 36, 48, 65, 72, 93, 133, 136, 144, 181, 220 n.40, 224 n.46, 227 n.17, n.24, n.25
Gestapo, 21, 38–39, 41, 68, 165, 218 n.6, 227 n.25
God, 23–34, 76, 79, 93, 125, 130–38, 140, 142, 144, 146, 148–51, 155, 161, 163, 167, 176, 179, 191–96, 198, 202, 205–07, 214–15, 220 n.8, 222 n.48; quarrel with, 27–28, 32, 34, 52, 192; and evil, 32, 192–93

Godlessness, 8
Good and evil, 29–30
Gospels, 56–57, 61–62, 94–95, 107, 109, 111–13, 118, 169
Grace, 206
Great Britain, 86, 133, 136
Gross Wannsee Conference, 13
Guilt: of the German people, 71–72; of the Vatican, 83
Gypsies, 15

Halakhah, 140
Harvard University, 232 n.70
Hebrew Christian Alliance of America, 163
Hebrew Christianity, 137–39, 142, 147
Hebrew Christians. See Jewish Christians (minim)
Help for the persecuted, 37–43, 48, 59, 67–68
Herodians, 107
Hessian Society for Jewish-Christian Cooperation, 72
Holland, 39, 136, 148
Holocaust, 13, 15–16, 18, 23, 25, 29–33, 35, 43, 71, 79, 82, 84, 192, 220 n.5, 222 n.42, 245 n.28, n.31
Humanism, 86
Human relationships, 186
Hungary, 188

Incarnation, 132, 207
Institute of Judaeo-Christian Studies, 77
Institutum Judaicum, 134, 183
Intermarriage, 140, 146–47, 150, 162
International Conference of Christians and Jews, 85, 97
International Hebrew Christian Alliance, 143, 148, 163
Islam, 212
Israel, State of, 8–9, 33, 35, 52, 71, 76, 93, 158, 163, 215–16, 221 n.28; Parliament (Knesset), 9, 130, 158; Supreme Court, 106, 232 n.5
Israeli citizenship, 106
Israel's election, 45, 73–74, 82, 127, 131–36, 148, 172, 201–03, 206
Israel's rejection, 132–33, 145

Jabneh, 119
Jerusalem, destruction of, 82
Jesus Christ, 11, 43, 46, 53–54, 58–62, 70, 73, 76, 79, 81–82, 84–87, 90–91, 95, 100, 102–15, 119, 123–26, 132, 138–39, 142–43, 145, 147–48, 150, 155–56, 159–62, 164–67, 184, 191, 195–206, 208, 210–14, 216–17, 229 n.5, 233 n.12, 234 n.33, n.36, 246 n.36; as Essene, 107, 108, 118; the Jew, 9, 110, 114, 119–20, 196, 199, 211; as Messiah, 102–03, 144, 149, 154, 166, 169, 198, 212–13, 215; offence of, 118, 231 n.54; trial of, 58–59, 226 n.29, n.31
"Jew," 11, 104–05, 121, 127–39, 142, 149, 176, 187, 189–91, 202, 204–06, 208, 214, 224 n.51, 230 n.51, 236 n.8, 243 n.29, 244 n.9
Jewish-Christian dialogue. See Dialogue
Jewish Christianity, 153–54, 199
Jewish-Christian relationships, 7–8, 10, 43, 45–46, 50, 63, 70, 72–73, 78, 82, 89–98, 174, 177, 180, 209, 211
Jewish Christians (minim), 9–10, 12, 72, 112, 119, 124, 140–51, 153–54, 157, 161–64, 177, 191, 207, 212–15, 230 n.36, 238 n.21, n.32, 239 n.10, 240 n.32
Jewish-Christian symposium (St. Mary's College, Kansas), 180
Jewish Chronicle, 106, 157, 158, 172
Jewish conversion. See Conversion
Jewish election. See Israel's election
Jewish marriage, 152
Jewish missions. See Missions to Jews
Jewishness, 106, 127–39, 152–53, 163, 191, 212–14
Jewish orthodoxy, 129, 208
Jewish survival, 52, 140, 148, 150, 184, 187, 200–01, 234 n.33
Jewish view of Christianity, 104
Jews and the death of Jesus, 46, 52–53, 75, 82, 94–95, 97
Jews for Jesus Movement, 142, 162, 166, 213
John the Baptist, 148
Judaica, 178

Judaism, 9–10, 23–24, 28, 31–32, 43–45, 49–50, 55, 60–61, 67, 71, 73–74, 77, 79–107, 110–14, 116–26, 145–46, 152–53, 161–62, 166, 172, 174–83, 191, 193–94, 199–200, 205–09, 212, 214, 216, 224 n.49, 232 n.2, 234 n.33, 237 n.39, 243 n.26
"Judaism and the Christian Seminary Curriculum," 98
Judea, 53, 107
Judentum, 129, 131, 236 n.19, n.21

Kaddish prayers, 222 n.46
Karaites, 153, 239 nn.6–7
Khazars, 127
Kirchentag, 75, 98
Korah, 114
Kristall Nacht, 36, 67

Law of Return, 106
Laws of purity, 117
Legal discrimination, 225 n.6
Legalism, 138
Legitimacy, 98, 232 n.69
"Letter of Barnabas," 54
Liberalism, 103, 129, 187
Limburg trial, 51
Lublin-Majdanek, 16
Lutheran Church of Germany, 36
Lutheran World Federation, 73–75, 143–44

Madhya Pradesh State of India, Constitution of, 157
Maidanek, 69
Medieval Judaism, 156
Meshummad, 155, 240 n.32, 241 n.38
Messiah, 43, 50, 53–54, 79–82, 91, 96, 104–05, 110, 119–22, 126, 134, 137, 143, 146–50, 197–98, 212
Messiahship, 58, 61–62, 102, 139, 144, 198
Messianic: Age, 103, 105, 123, 126, 198; Event, 84–85, 90; faith, 153; hope, 43, 62, 119, 122, 139, 179; Jew, 143; man, 11; scheme, 138; society, 147; texts, 169

Messianism, Jewish, 120, 130, 146
Mission, 49, 83–92, 100, 137, 168–69, 171–79, 182, 203–05. See also Missions to Jews
Missionaries, 155, 157–59, 162, 210
Missions to Jews, 74, 86, 89, 91, 210, 214, 230 n.38, 242 n.25
Mława, Poland, 39
Myth of God Incarnate, 181

Nationalism, 65
Nazis, 13–15, 22, 30, 36, 67, 68, 81, 188, 190, 241 n.38
New Testament, 53, 56–57, 61–62, 80, 82, 86, 92–93, 95, 104, 109–12, 122, 124, 128, 137, 143, 146, 167, 168, 188, 194, 197, 205, 207–08, 231 n.55
Nihilism, 25, 28, 80
Nisibis, 153
Noachian laws, 103, 232 n.3
Nüremberg Laws, 14
Nüremberg Trials, 17, 30, 218 n.3, 219 n.18

Oath of allegiance to Hitler, 66
Old Testament, 92–93, 95, 97, 100, 111, 119, 121–22, 133, 135, 145–46, 169, 188, 194, 205, 225 n.2, 230 n.50
Oral Law, 118
Oswiecim, 13, 218 n.1. See also Auschwitz

Palestine, 119, 124, 134, 199
Paul the Apostle (Saul of Tarsus), 43, 54, 82, 88, 103, 105, 108–09, 111, 115, 116, 119–24, 126, 131, 136–39, 146–47, 153, 159, 168, 189–90, 197, 204–05, 211, 214, 233 n.16, 235 n.25, n.28, 237 n.40
Peasant War, 28
Peter (Simon), 102, 112, 197
Pharisees, 58, 62, 94, 107–08, 114, 116–20, 195, 230 n.51, 231 n.54, 233 n.12
Philip, 138
Pirkei avot, 127
Platonism, 190
Poland, 41, 188

Police, 19, 30, 38, 42, 227 n.25
Poniatowa, 16
Pontius Pilatus, 57–59, 62, 102, 225 n.21
Prayer for the Jews, 43–45, 173
Primitive Christianity, 108–09, 119, 199
Proselytism, 127–28, 157, 173–74, 178, 201, 236 n.5, 243 n.34

Qumran sect, 10, 108–09, 153, 166

Rabbinic Judaism, 9, 93, 116, 119, 122, 124–25, 137–38, 142–43, 153, 199, 233 n.25, 239 n.6
Race laws, 66–67, 227 n.17, n.25
Rackover, Yossel, 34
Reformation, 133, 138, 144
Reform Judaism, 200
Resurrection, 211–12
Roman Catholics, 27, 37, 40, 63–66, 77, 100, 243 n.34
Roman Empire, 187
Roman law, 58
Rumania, 188
Russia, 48, 65
Russian Jews, 134, 136

Sadducees, 107–08, 114, 153
Salvation, 48, 62, 86, 88, 100, 131, 144, 150, 198, 200, 203, 214–15
Sanhedrin, 57
Schisma, 102
Schism in Jewry, 120
Schutzstaffel (SS), 19, 68
Scribes, 108
Secretariat for Promoting Christian Unity, 78
Seelisberger Thesen, 72–73, 97–98
Septuagint (LXX), 122
Sermon on the Mount, 80, 165–66
Sisters of Sion, 173
Sobibor, 16
Son of God, 132
Son of Man, 110
Southern Baptist Convention, 77
Stephen, 138, 226 n.38
Stürmer, Der, 14
Suffering, 193, 222 n.48, 245 n.28

Swiss Jewish mission, 177–78
Switzerland, 40
Symposium of Christians and Jews (New York), 60–61
Synagogue, 10–11, 26, 44, 53, 85, 100–01, 105, 119, 123, 126, 131, 145, 152, 162, 168, 172, 175, 179–80, 184, 201, 204, 243 n.26
Synoptic Gospels, 117, 148, 216, 234 n.33

Talmud, 94, 153
Talmudic Judaism, 105
Tamerlane, 192
Technology, 29
Temple ritual, 117–18
Ten Commandments, 130
"Theology of fulfilment," 62
Theresienstadt, 14, 18, 21, 80, 218 n.6
Third Reich, 64
Torah, 116, 120–21, 127, 129, 137–38, 210, 212
Tradition, 141–42
Trawniki, 16
Treblinka, 16, 41, 81
Trinitarian doctrine, 86, 100, 105, 180–81, 200, 207, 212
Trypho the Jew, 43–44, 169
Turks, 192

Der Ungekündigte Bund (The Unannulled Covenant), 98
Ungeziefer (vermin), 48, 192
Union of American Hebrew Congregations, 129
Unitarians, 108
United Christian Council, 158
United Nations Declaration on Human Rights, 158, 170
United States, 47–48, 77, 85, 99, 127–28, 136, 141, 143, 162, 166
United States Catholic Conference, 97
Universalism, 62, 84, 140, 146–47, 200, 234 n.33
Untermenschen (subhumans), 22, 220 n.40

Vatican, 64–65, 83, 223 n.11, 226 n.32, 227 n.12; Guidelines for Jewish-

Christian Relations, 77, 96–97, 228 n.50

Vatican II, 8, 10, 36, 45–47, 61, 63, 69–70, 77, 84–85, 173, 203

Vichy Government, 40

Virgin Birth, 104, 110

Warsaw: ghetto, 30, 41; *Judenrat*, 30; fall of, 64

World Council of Churches (WCC), 71–72, 75–76

World Jewish Congress, 158

Xenophobia, 48, 186

Yeshua (Jesus), 155, 213, 239 n.13

Yiddish weekly (Buenos Aires), 33

Yom ha-shoah, 16

"Yossel Rackover Speaks with God," 34

Zionism, 9, 50, 96, 134, 136, 141

Zoroaster, 125

Index of Names

Abecassis, Armaud, 120, 235 n.20
Abel, Ernest L., 57, 225 n.17
Abramov, S. Zalman, 218 n.1 (Intro.)
Abramowitz, Yehuda Meir, 158
Adam, H., 225 n.21
Adler, H. G., 18–22, 219 nn.25–29, 220 nn.30–33, 35, 39–40
Adler, Moshe, 162, 241 n.42
Agus, Jacob B., 247 n.68
Ahad Ha-Am (Asher Ginsberg), 160
Akiva, 153
Alchinger, A., 69
Alfred, Prince, 134
Allport, Gordon W., 186, 187, 244 nn.2, 4
Altizer, Thomas J. J., 243 n.42
Ansbacher, Simon, 20–21
Arendt, Hannah, 48, 224 n.45
Aron, Robert, 114, 234 n.35
Arrowsmith, John, 237 n.34
Asch, Sholem, 155, 159–62, 212, 240 nn.32–33, 241 nn.40–41
Augustine, Bishop of Hippo, 132, 192–93, 237 n.24, 238 n.8

Baeck, Leo, 109, 110, 120, 204
Balthasar, Hans Urs von, 205, 247 n.64
Bar Kokhba, 54, 153
Barth, Karl, 36, 81, 85, 131–32, 148, 150, 172, 175, 202, 204, 238 n.25, n.28, 242 n.26, 246 nn.59–60
Barth, Marcus, 175, 183, 204–05, 235 n.25, 243 n.27, 244 n.50, 246 n.61, 247 n.62
Bartmann, Bernhard, 145, 238 n.10
Bar Zev, Asher, 128
Bauer, Walter, 154, 239 n.12

Bauer, Yehuda, 219 n.20
Baum, Gregory, 60–61, 70, 83–84, 144, 226 n.36, 229 nn.14–16, n.19, 238 n.7
Bea, Augustin Cardinal, 45, 47, 57, 233 n.36, n.38, 225 n.19
Beare, Frank W., 241 n.2
Beck, Dr., 21
Begin, Menachem, 158
Bel Geddes, Joan, 40, 41
Ben-Chorin, Shalom, 109–10, 112, 115, 120, 197–99, 233 nn.19–20, nn.22–23, 235 n.22, 238 n.31, 246 n.38, n.40
Ben-Gurion, David, 184
Ben Zoma, Simeon, 153–54
Berdyaev, Nicolas, 55, 57, 225 n.9, n.12, n.18, 226 n.34
Berenbaum, Michael, 220 n.12
Berger, David, 150, 238 n.32
Bergman, S. H., 146, 238 n.18
Bergson, Henri, 161, 241 n.38
Berkovits, Eliezer, 31, 32, 130, 194–95, 208, 219 n.14, 221 n.35, 245 n.30, n.32
Berlichingen, Götz von, 28
Bernards, Solomon, 48, 224 n.43
Berning, Bishop, 48
Besicovitch, Abraham S., 153, 239 n.7
Bestic, Alan, 218 n.10
Bethge, Eberhard, 222 nn.2–3, 6
Beyreuther, Erich, 223 n.11
Bezzel, Hermann von, 50
Bikel, Theodore, 152, 239 n.5
Bishop, Claire Huchet, 96–97, 98, 231 nn.61, 66
Black, Matthew, 233 n.13

265

Blaskowitz, General, 68
Bloy, Léon, 187
Bluestone, Naomi, 176–77, 243 n.30
Blumenfeld, Erwin, 30
Boberach, Heinz, 227 n.25
Boettner, Loraine, 237 n.35
Bokser, Ben Zion, 200, 246 n.46, 247 nn.75–76
Bonhoeffer, Dietrich, 36–37, 222 n.4, 226 n.3, 246 n.34
Bonhoeffer, Emmi, 219 n.23
Borchsenius, Paul, 230 n.28
Borowitz, Eugene B., 28, 201–02, 245 n.31, 246 n.57
Bowker, John, 118, 230 n.53, 231 n.54, 234 n.12
Brauchitsch, Field Marshal von, 68
Bruce, F. F., 112, 234 n.27
Brunner, Robert, 178
Buber, Martin, 87, 109, 110, 150, 170–71, 182, 183, 197, 198, 238 n.31, 242 n.9
Buksbazen, Victor, 242 n.23
Bultmann, Rudolf, 80
Bunel, Abbé, 40
Bunyan, John, 237 n.34
Byfield, Richard, 135, 237 n.34

Callenberg, J. H., 183
Calvin, John, 133, 145, 237 nn.26–27
Camus, Albert, 24
Carmel, Abraham I., 158
Carter, G. Emmet, 231 n.63
Catchpole, David R., 226 nn.37–39
Cazelles, H., 247 n.5
Celsus, 226 n.41
Chadwick, Owen, 227 n.12
Chaillet, Pierre, 40
Chase, Stuart, 190, 245 n.16
Chiel, Arthur A., 157, 240 n.22
Chomicz, Mrs., 41
Choms, Mrs., 41
Chouraqui, André Nathan, 183–84
Chrysostom, 81
Clark, Kenneth B., 190, 245 n.14
Cocceius, Johannes, 146, 238 n.15
Cohen, Arthur A., 9, 126, 178–79, 218 n.3 (Intro.), 235 n.30, n.36, 243 n.36, 245 n.28

Cohen, Boaz, 237 n.3
Cohen, Hermann, 156
Cohen, Jack J., 25, 32
Cohen, Jacques, 59, 226 n.30
Cohn, Haim H., 58, 225 nn.24–27
Cohon, Samuel S., 152, 200, 239 n.4, 246 n.48
Commodianus, 53, 225 n.3
Cousins, Norman, 161, 241 n.39
Cozzi, Jenni, 220 n.38
Cullman, Oscar, 233 n.16
Cyprian, Bishop of Carthage, 132, 237 n.23
Cyril of Alexandria, 145, 238 n.9

Daane, James, 82–83, 229 nn.10–11
Danby, H., 234 n.9
Daniel, Brother. See Rufeisen, Oswald
Daniélou, Jean, 183–84
Daube, David, 115, 234 n.37
Davidowicz, Lucy S., 47
Davies, Alan T., 91–92, 229 n.18, 230 nn.45–47
Davis, Henry, 232 n.69
Deveaux, 40
Diamond, Malcolm L., 141
Diem, Hermann, 67
Dietrich, H. D., 21, 218 n.6, n.9, 220 n.34
Dimont, Max I., 233 n.17
Donat, Alexander, 23–24, 220 n.2
Donn, F. S., 237 n.35
Dorff, Elliot N., 31, 195, 222 n.36, 245 n.31
Drach, M., 156
Dubnow, Simon, 9
Duvernoy, Claude, 237 n.32

Ebner, Ferdinand, 170, 242 n.8
Eckardt, Alice, 230 n.37
Eckardt, A. Roy, 87–92, 188, 230 nn.30–44, 244 n.7
Eckert, Willehad Paul, 96, 223 n.15, 231 nn.55–56
Eichhorn, David Max, 127, 236 n.4
Eichmann, Adolf, 16, 59
Einstein, Albert, 42
Eisendrath, Maurice Nathan, 93, 114, 125, 128, 234 n.34, 235 n.35

Epiphanius, 108
Epstein, Jason, 141
Eusebius, 108
Eysenck, H. J., 186, 244 n.1, n.3
Ezer, Ehud Ben, 218 n.4 (Intro.), 233 n.23, 243 n.30, 247 n.10

Fackenheim, Emil L., 16, 17, 31, 32, 52, 221 n.34, 222 n.42, 224 n.1, 226 n.3, 245 n.28
Falconi, Carlo, 38, 222 n.11
Faulhaber, Michael Cardinal, 39, 226 n.3
Federici, Tomaso, 178, 243 n.34
Feinberg, Abraham L., 106, 174, 242 n.21
Feldman, Irving, 141
Fiedler, Leslie A., 245 n.28
Filthaut, Theodor, 97, 231 n.60
Finkel, Asher, 117–18, 234 nn.7–8, 10–11
Finn, Elizabeth Anne, 134, 237 n.31
Fish, Harold, 30
Fisher, Eugene, 49, 185, 224 n.52, 228 n.50, 244 n.57
Fishman, Hertzel, 133, 237 n.28
Flannery, Edward H., 50, 55, 224 n.53, 228 n.46
Fleischner, Eva, 100, 231 nn.67–68, 232 nn.77–78
Fletcher, Joseph, 165, 241 n.50
Flüsser, David, 47, 110–12, 212, 213, 233 nn.24–25, 234 n.26, 239 n.10, 247 n.5
Focherini, Eduardo, 40
Folkemer, Lawrence D., 171, 242 n.11
Forell, Frederick J., 166, 241 n.53
Fox, G. George, 226 n.29
Frank, Hans, 30
Freedman, David Noel, 119, 199, 234 n.13, 246 n.44
Freehof, Solomon B., 200, 237 n.3, 246 n.47
Freudenberg, Adolf, 72
Fricke, Otto, 72
Friedländer, Albert H., 246 n.61
Friedländer, Henry, 15, 218 n.8, 219 n.20

Friedman, Maurice, 221 n.17
Friedman, Philip, 37, 39, 40, 223 nn.16–20

Galanter, Marc, 106, 232 n.8
Galen, Clemens August Cardinal von, 39, 64
Gallagher, Joseph, 223 n.37, 242 n.17
Gandhi, Mahatma, 190
Gay, Ruth, 223 n.25
Gerlier, Archbishop, 40
Gerstein, Kurt, 219 n.18
Gertel, Elliot B., 222 n.48
Gidney, W. T., 237 n.29
Gillon, Philip, 240 n.25
Ginsburg, Christian D., 108, 233 n.13
Gittelsohn, Roland B., 218 n.5 (Intro.)
Glatstein, Jacob, 219 n.20
Glock, Charles Y., 47–48, 224 n.41
Goering, Hermann, 218 n.3
Goethe, Johann Wolfgang von, 7, 8, 150, 172
Golden, H., 226 n.29
Goldschmidt, Dietrich, 231 n.68
Gollancz, Victor, 165, 241 n.49
Gollwitzer, Helmut, 80, 151, 228 n.4, 232 n.79, 239 n.34
Goodman, Saul L., 221 n.14
Goppelt, Leonhard, 80, 226 n.41
Gordon, Albert I., 27, 128, 235 n.2
Gotfried, Mordecai, 172, 242 n.14
Graebe, Hermann Friedrich, 17
Graham, Robert A., 51, 224 n.55
Grant, Frederick C., 83, 175, 209, 214, 242 n.25, 247 n.7
Grant, Michael, 122
Grässer, E., 231 n.55
Graves, Robert, 115
Greenberg, Blu, 56, 225 n.15
Greife, Hermann, 228 n.34
Grossmann, Kurt R., 37, 222 n.7, 223 nn.26–27
Grüber, Heinrich, 59
Gulin, E. G., 76

Hager, Joseph, 58, 225 n.23
Hagner, D. A., 231 n.54
Halperin, Irving, 219 n.20

Halpern, B., 189, 245 n.12
Hamilton, William, 181, 243 n.42
Hargrove, Katharine H., 224 n.51
Harkabi, Yehoshafat, 215, 247 n.9
Harnack, Adolf von, 92, 168, 241 n.1
Harris, Monford, 140, 237 n.2, 241 n.38
Hartl, Karl, 51
Hay, A. I., 237 n.33
Hechler, William, 134, 237 n.32
Hedley, George, 214, 247 n.8
Heer, Friedrich, 45, 63–65, 69, 83, 223 n.33, 226 n.1, 227 n.4, n.7, nn.28–30, 229 n.13
Hegel, Georg W. F., 92
Hegemann, Werner, 234 n.36
Heller, Bernard, 161
Heller, Celia, 224 n.40
Hentoff, Nat, 141
Herford, R. Travers, 119, 235 nn.17–19
Heron, Michael, 230 n.28
Herstig, David, 222 n.10
Herzberg, Arthur, 242 n.12
Herzl, Theodor, 134
Heschel, Abraham J., 179, 181–82, 244 nn.45–47
Hessler, Bertram, 29, 221 n.24
Heufken, Hilgard, 95, 231 n.60
Heydecker, Joe, 219 n.18, 221 n.25
Heydrich, Reinhard, 39, 64
Hick, John, 232 n.2, 243 n.43
Hilberg, Raul, 219 n.20
Hillel, 201
Himmler, Heinrich, 16, 18, 19, 30, 48, 218 n.3, 220 n.40
Hitler, Adolf, 7, 11, 13–14, 16, 19, 24, 31, 32, 35, 36, 38, 42, 43, 47, 48, 51, 59, 63, 65–66, 67, 68, 95–96, 144, 187, 218 n.3, 222 n.42, 228 n.31
Hochhuth, Rolf, 38, 64
Hoffmann, Charlotte, 42
Hollander, John, 141
Horder, Lord, 227 n.17
Horne, Bishop, 134
Howe, Leroy T., 220 n.6
Hruby, K., 178
Huxley, Julian, 25, 220 n.7

Ignatius, 53

Isaac, Erich, 124, 125–26, 235 n.31
Isaac, Jules, 55–56, 188, 225 nn.10–11, n.13
Isorni, Jacques, 59, 226 n.31

Jacob, Walter, 182, 199, 207–08, 244, nn.48–49, 246 n.42, 247 n.70
Jacobs, Louis, 124, 178, 207, 235 n.32, 243 n.35, 247 n.69
Jan, Julius von, 67
Jarvis, Judith, 141
Jenkins, Alan, 83, 229 n.12
Jeremias, Joachim, 229 n.5, 246 n.37
Jocz, Jakob, 225 nn.5–6, n.17, 230 n.48, 232 n.1, n.3, n.5, 233 n.12, n.21, 234 n.2, n.14, 235 n.16, n.33, 236 n.16, n.18, 237 n.37, 238 n.5, n.8, n.11, n.14, nn.26–27, 239 nn.10–11, n.13, 240 n.32, 242 n.8, n.10, n.12, 244 n.9, 246 n.45, 247 n.63
John XXIII, Pope, 44–45, 63, 173, 223 n.32
Josephus, 108, 225 n.21
Julian the Apostate, 226 n.41
Jung, C. G., 8, 245 n.22
Justin Martyr, 43, 53, 81, 168–69

Kabak, A. A., 109
Kac, Arthur W., 166, 241 n.51
Kähler, Martin, 95–96, 231 n.57
Kaldany, Hanna, 159
Kalinowski, 41
Kallen, Horace M., 130, 236 n.15
Kallenbach, Hans, 228 n.34
Kametko, Archbishop, 195
Kaplan, Mordecai M., 25
Karff, Samuel E., 241 n.3
Karp, Abraham J., 140, 237 n.1
Katz, Jacob, 155–56, 201, 239 nn.14–17, 240 nn.18–19, n.21, 246 n.52
Kaufman, Yehezkel, 9
Keats, John, 121
Kersten, Felix, 42
Kessel, Albert von, 64
Kielbasa, Maria, 41
Kierkegaard, Sören, 191, 210, 245 n.17, 247 n.79

Kirsch, Paul J., 70, 228 n.32, 243 n.34
Klausner, Alfred, 70
Klausner, Joseph, 107, 120–21, 122, 160, 235 n.21, nn.24–25
Klein, Charlotte, 80–81, 82, 228 n.4, 229 nn.5–6
Knight, George A. F., 237 n.37, 242 n.23, 244 n.9
Kohler, Kaufmann, 199, 246 n.42
Kohn, Hans, 9
Kolitz, Zvi, 34
Kollin, Gilbert, 129, 236 n.9
Konvitz, Milton R., 236 n.8
Korman, Gerd, 18, 33, 219 n.24, 220 n.1, 222 n.42, n.45
Kotsuji, Abraham, 127, 235 n.1
Kraus, Hans-Joachim, 231 n.68
Kristol, Irving, 28
Küng, Hans, 181, 184–85, 241 n.56, 244 n.54
Kupisch, Karl, 79–80, 82, 228 nn.1–3

Lactantius, 145, 238 nn.12–13
Lamb, Harold, 245 n.20
Lapide, Pinchas E., 38, 181, 184–85, 211, 212, 222 n.8, 239 n.13, 244 n.54
Laqueur, Walter, 218 n.7
Larson, Martin A., 109, 233 n.16
LaSor, William Sanford, 177, 243 n.32
Lauterbach, Jacob Z., 226 n.29, 239 n.13
Leboucher, Ferdinand, 223 n.13
Leeb, Johannes, 219 n.18, 221 n.25
Lehmann, Johannes, 108, 233 nn.15–16
Leibowitz, Yeshayahu, 248 n.12
Lemme, Ludwig, 50, 96
Leuner, H. D., 35, 144, 222 n.1, 227 n.22, 228 n.43, 238 n.6
Levey, Samson H., 153–54, 239 n.9
Levin, S., 31, 189, 222 n.37, 245 n.13
Levinas, Emmanuel, 189, 244 n.8
Levine, Raphael H., 229 n.28
Levinson, Nathan P., 151, 231 n.55, 232 n.79, 239 n.34
Levinstein, Gustav, 14, 218 n.5
Levy, Mark J., 163

Lewis, Theodore N., 212–13, 247 n.3
Lewy, Guenther, 224 n.46
Lichtenberg, Monsignor, 39
Lieberman, Chaim, 160, 240 n.32, n.34
Lindeskog, Gösta, 61
Littell, Franklin H., 29, 81–82, 219 n.18, 220 n.5, 221 n.15, n.23, 222 n.2, 226 n.33, 229 nn.7–9
Locke, Hubert G., 219 n.18, 220 n.5, 221 n.15, 222 n.2, 226 n.33
Loewe, Herbert, 193, 230 n.52, 238 nn.16–17, n.19, 245 nn.26–27
Lohse, Eduard, 80
Long, J. Bruce, 98, 232 n.69
Löwen, G. M., 224 n.54, 230 n.50
Luckner, Gertrud, 39
Luther, Martin, 54–55, 92, 225 nn.7–8

Maccoby, Hyam, 107, 122, 232 n.11, 235 n.26
McCollester, Charles, 244 n.8
M'Neile, Alan H., 225 n.4
Maggal, Moshe M., 128, 236 n.6
Maimonides, 118, 234 n.12
Malamud, Bernard, 26
Malicki, Mr. and Mrs., 41
Marcion, 92, 145
Margulies, Morris, 180
Maria, Mother, 165
Marie-Benoit, Père, 40
Maritain, Jacques, 187, 244 n.6
Marquardt, Friedrich-Wilhelm, 236 n.21
Marshall, Stephen, 237 n.34
Marty, Martin E., 236 n.17
Mar Zutra, 93
Matheson, P. C., 68, 227 n.24
Matt, Hershel J., 104–05, 211–12, 232 n.4, 247 n.2
Maybaum, Ignaz, 31, 42, 156, 174, 179, 209, 221 n.33, 223 n.28, 240 n.20, 242 n.22, 243 n.37, 247 n.73
Mayer, Josef, 51
Mayer, Reinhold, 183, 244 n.49
Meier, Kurt, 66, 67, 68, 219 n.18, 227 nn.17–21, n.23, n.25

Meiser, Landesbischof, 68
Melicki, Marian, 41
Mendelssohn, Moses, 23
Menes, Abraham, 130
Mezvinsky, Norton, 26
Michel, Otto, 235 n.25
Misrahi, Robert, 129, 236 n.13
Monis, Judah, 157
Montefiore, C. G., 94, 146, 160, 207–08, 230 nn.52–53, 238 n.19, 245 nn.26–27, 247 n.71
Moses, Solomon ben, 170
Müller, Johann, 133
Munck, Johannes, 137
Münster, Bishop of, 39

Nagy, Ervin V., 171, 242 n.10
Nantes, Georges de, 59, 226 nn.31–32
Neander, Johann A. W., 156
Negoitsa, Athanase, 77
Neher, André, 27–28, 221 n.17
Neill, Stephen, 169, 206, 209, 241 n.4, 242 n.5, 247 nn.66, 74, 77
Neusner, Jacob, 107, 116–17, 153, 231 n.54, 234 n.1, nn.3–6, 239 n.8
Niebuhr, Reinhold, 60, 174, 226 n.35, 242 n.23
Niebuhr, Richard, 90
Niemöller, Martin, 65
Nietzsche, Friedrich, 7
Nisan, Mordechai, 215
Noth, Martin, 80

Oesterreicher, John M., 45, 70, 77, 85, 173, 221 n.24, 222 n.47, 223 n.12, n.21, n.23, nn.31–32, nn.34–35, 224 n.39, 225 n.20, 228 n.46, n.50, 229 n.20, 232 n.75, 241 n.50, 242 nn.18–19
O'Grady, Colin, 172, 242 n.15
Olan, Levi A., 89–90, 130, 230 n.38
Olson, Bernhard E., 99, 232 nn.71–74
Opsahl, Paul D., 221 n.21, 222 n.41, n.44
Origen of Alexandria, 132, 237 n.22
Osborn, Robert T., 175–77, 243 nn.28–29
Ott, Heinrich, 242 n.10

Pallière, Aimé, 127
Palmerston, Lord, 134
Panitz, David, 223 n.35
Pank, Oskar, 96
Parkes, James, 70, 71, 85–87, 89, 92, 95, 148, 210, 228 n.33, 229 n.21, nn.23–27, 230 nn.29–30, 231 n.55, 247 n.78
Pascal, Blaise, 8
Paul VI, Pope, 69, 78
Pawlikowski, John, 60
Peerman, Dean G., 236 n.17
Penn, William, 238 n.30
Petuchowski, Jacob J., 123, 235 n.28
Philippson, Ludwig, 226 n.30
Philo, 108, 110
Pike, James A., 128
Pilenko, Elizabeth, 241 n.50
Pindar, 150
Pines, Shlomo, 122, 235 n.26, 239 n.10
Pinhas ben Jair, 117
Pius XI, Pope, 187
Pius XII, Pope, 38, 39, 64, 223 n.11
Plack, Arno, 221 n.29
Plato, 171, 192
Plaut, W. Günther, 200–01, 236 n.5, 246 nn.49–51
Pliny the Elder, 108
Podro, Joshua, 115
Polsky, Ned, 141
Porphyry, 108, 226 n.41
Potter, Charles Francis, 108, 233 n.14, n.16
Preysing, Count von, 39
Propper, Felix, 148, 238 nn.22–24

Ramati, Alexander, 223 n.11
Randt, Alice, 14–15
Rarkowski, Franz Josef, 65
Ratisbonne, Alphonse, 173
Ratisbonne, Theodore, 173
Ratosh, Yonatan, 247 n.11
Rausch, David, 213, 247 n.6
Reitlinger, Gerald, 16, 218 nn.2–3, 219 n.12, n.17, 221 n.27
Rendtorff, Rolf, 232 n.79, 239 n.34
Rhodes, Anthony, 64, 222 n.11, 227 nn.5–6

Riesmun, David, 9
Ringelbaum, Emmanuel, 30, 221 n.28
Robinson, Jacob R., 16, 218 n.7, 219
    nn.16–17, nn.19–20, n.22
Ronning, Halvor, 235 n.28
Rosenblatt, Samuel, 199, 246 n.43
Rosenstock-Huessy, Eugen, 180, 183,
    202–03, 243 n.39, 246 n.56
Rosenzweig, Franz, 87, 92, 132, 180,
    183, 189, 198, 202–03, 212, 236 n.20,
    244 n.10, 245 n.11
Roth, Philip, 9, 142
Roth, Sol, 191, 245 n.19
Rubenstein, Richard L., 24–25, 27,
    29–30, 32, 33, 52, 59–60, 192, 220
    n.3, nn.5–6, nn.9–10, 221 n.22, n.26,
    222 nn.38–40, 226 n.33, 235 n.28
Rubinoff, L., 29, 32, 33, 221 n.21, 222
    n.42
Ruether, Rosemary, 60, 61, 70, 84–85,
    90–91, 229 nn.17–18, n.20, 243 n.43
Rufeisen, Oswald (Brother Daniel), 106,
    157, 232 n.5, n.8, 236 n.8
Runes, Dagobert D., 56, 225 n.14
Russell, Lord, 69, 219 n.20, 227
    nn.26–27
Rylaarsdam, J. C., 88, 232 n.69

Sachar, Howard M., 237 n.33
Sachs, Nelly, 218 n.11
Sadeh, Pinchas, 150, 233 n.23, 239 n.33,
    243 n.30
Samuel, Maurice, 224 n.49
Samuels, Marc E., 25, 220 n.5, n.8, n.11
Sanders, E. P., 138, 237 n.38
Sandmel, Samuel, 62, 112–13, 120–22,
    157, 160, 226 n.40, 234 nn.28–31, 235
    n.23, 240 n.23, n.35, 241 nn.36–37
Santayana, George, 190, 245 n.15
Sartre, Jean-Paul, 28, 222 n.40
Schindler, Oskar, 41–42
Schirach, Baldur von, 227 n.12
Schleiermacher, Friedrich, 92
Schmaus, Michael, 81
Schmid, Herbert, 177
Schmidt, Dietrich, 227 n.11
Schmidt, Karl Ludwig, 87, 183

Schoeps, Hans-Joachim, 122–23,
    130–31, 198, 212, 235 nn.27–28,
    236 nn.16–17, 244 n.52
Scholder, Klaus, 227 n.12
Schonfield, Hugh—Passover Plot, 109,
    115
Schubert, Kurt, 57, 225 n.20
Schürer, Emil, 187, 244 n.5
Schwarzschild, Stephen S., 126
Sedgewicke, William, 135–36, 237 n.34
Seltzer, Sanford, 152, 239 nn.1–3, 243
    n.26
Selzer, Michael, 218 n.2 (Intro.)
Selznick, Gertrude J., 47, 224 n.42
Serafion, Michael, 69
Shahar, David, 163–64, 241 n.45
Shakespeare, William, 172
Shelley, Percy Bysshe, 121, 172
Sheptycky, Andreas, 41
Shmueli, Ephraim, 142–43, 237 n.4
Siegel, Seymour, 32, 222 n.41
Siegman, Henry, 92, 174, 208–09, 230
    n.49, 242 n.20, 247 n.72
Silberg, Moshe, 106
Simon, Ulrich E., 194, 245 n.28
Singer, David, 221 n.28
Singer, I. J., 159, 240 n.31
Singer, Sholom A., 205–06, 247 n.65,
    n.67
Sirkes, Joel, 155
Slonim, Reuben, 33, 220 n.4, 221 n.19,
    222 n.43
Snoek, Johan, 70, 227 n.31
Sobassan, Jeffrey G., 226 n.31
Socrates, 92
Sokolow, Nahum, 134, 237 n.30, n.32
Solinus, 108
Solomon, Barbara Probst, 141
Soloveitchik, Joseph B., 157, 179, 191,
    243 n.38, 245 n.18
Sorge, Helga, 101
Sorger, Karlheinz, 100
Spaemann, Heinrich, 83
Spears, Alan A., 57, 60
Spiro, Jack Daniel, 185, 244 n.55
Spong, John Shelby, 185, 244 n.55
Stackhouse, Max L., 243 n.26

Stahl, Julius, 156
Stankiewicz, Janina, 41
Stark, Rodney, 47–48, 224 n.41
Stauffer, Ethelbert, 80
Stecker, Georg, 239 n.12
Steinberg, Stephen, 47, 224 n.42
Steinmann, Monsignor, 48
Stendahl, Krister, 56–57, 137, 225 n.16, 236 n.17, 237 nn.39–40
Stern, Harry Joshua, 164, 241 n.46
Stern, Karl, 161
Sternfeld, 20
Stöhr, Martin, 231 n.55
Streicher, Julius, 14
Suetonius, 244 n.5
Sullivan, Kathryn, 223 n.31
Sulzbach, Walter, 48, 224 nn.47–48
Sussmann, Margarete, 28
Swinburne, Algeron Charles, 7
Szajkowski, Zosa, 219 n.20

Tal, Uriel, 33, 195, 222 n.44, 244 n.44, 246 n.33
Talmage, Frank E., 169, 219 n.13, 221 n.34, 224 n.44, n.1, 225 n.16, 242 n.6, 243 n.26
Tanenbaum, Marc H., 49, 180, 221 n.21, 222 n.41, n.44, 224 n.51
Tasker, R. V. G., 225 n.4
Taubes, Jacob, 124, 125, 198, 235 n.30, 246 n.39, n.41
Temko, Allan, 142
Tertullian, 53
Teske, Gerhard, 97, 100
Thomas Aquinas, 121, 187, 232 n.69
Tillich, Paul, 174, 242 n.24
Tisso, Monsignor, 195
Townsend, John T., 231 n.55
Toynbee, Arnold J., 49, 224 nn.49–50, 233 n.24
Trever, John C., 166, 241 n.54
Trevor-Roper, Hugh, 223 n.14
Trilling, Wolfgang, 242 n.15
Troyes, Bishop of, 226 n.32
Trutwin, W., 231 n.60

Utrecht, Archbishop of, 40, 68

Vermes, Geza, 113, 166, 233 n.25, 234 n.32, 241 n.55
Vitellius, 225 n.21
Vogel, Manfred H., 183, 244 n.51
Vorgrimler, J., 223 n.35
Vrba, Rudolf, 15, 93, 218 n.10

Wacholder, Ben Zion, 236 n.5
Wallenberg, Raoul, 42
Warshal, Bruce S., 31
Wasserstein, Bernard, 218 n.7
Weber, Helmut, 228 n.44
Weil, Simone, 245 n.28
Weinberg, Arthur von, 21
Weiner, Herbert, 240 n.24
Weissler, Dr., 67
Weissmandel, M. D., 195
Weizmann, Chaim, 135
Weizsäcker, von, 22
Welles, Edward R., 42
Wellhausen, Julius, 110, 197, 246 n.35
Werblowsky, R. Y. Z., 123–24, 125, 158, 235 n.29, n.34, 239 n.6, 240 n.25
Wiesel, Elie, 17, 23, 26–29, 192, 218 n.10, 219 n.18, 220 n.1, n.12, 221 n.15, n.17, n.20
Wigoder, Deborah, 127, 235 n.2
Wigoder, G., 239 n.6
Wilken, Robert L., 238 n.9
Williams, A. Lukyn, 237 n.25
Willis, Robert E., 245 n.28
Wine, Sherman, 25
Wingate, Charles Orde, 134–35, 237 n.33
Wingate, Lorna, 135
Winslaw, Donald F., 238 n.8
Winter, Paul, 58, 226 n.28
Wise, I. M., 237 n.1
Wise, Stephen S., 114, 160
Witton-Davies, Carlyle, 97, 231 n.64
Wolfson, Harry Austryn, 247 n.4
Wurm, Landesbischof, 66, 227 n.17
Wyschogrod, Michael, 150, 221 n.17, 238 n.32

Yerushalmi, Yosef, 61